"Petrus van Mastricht's remarkable *Theoretical-Practical Theology*, now being published in its first full English translation, is marked by a methodological program wherein each theological topic is treated in the fourfold order of exegetical foundation, dogmatical exposition, elenctical elucidation, and practical application. Here we discover one of the richest fruits of the Dutch *Nadere Reformatie* for the history of Reformed theology, combining scholastic rigor with earnest piety. Now in English, this work promises to open new avenues into an understanding of Continental Reformed thought, even as it offers theological wisdom for the contemporary church."

—J. Mark Beach, professor of doctrinal and ministerial studies,
Mid-America Reformed Seminary, Dyer, Indiana

"A new appreciation has grown in our time for the great post-Reformation theologians of the Reformed tradition, and Petrus van Mastricht was a towering giant among them. Jonathan Edwards thought he was better than Francis Turretin! Mastricht's magnum opus *Theoretical-Practical Theology*, however, is virtually unknown and unquoted today, accessible only to competent and determined Latinists. This translation does for Mastricht what Giger and Dennison did for Turretin—it provides a readable, critical, annotated English translation that puts Mastricht within easy reach of pastors, seminarians, and other students of theology. A sound and experiential divine, who (it may surprise you to learn) interacts with and criticizes Kabbalah and Islam as well as Descartes and Socinians, Mastricht is always concerned to show that true theology is practical and never merely notional. Truth is unto godliness."

—Ligon Duncan, chancellor and CEO, John E. Richards
Professor of Systematic and Historical Theology,
Reformed Theological Seminary

"The very title of this work, *Theoretical-Practical Theology*, indicates why, three centuries ago, Petrus van Mastricht's work appealed to Scottish ministers who studied under him or read his theology. Not least of these was his student James Hog, who would later famously republish *The Marrow of Modern Divinity*. In making van Mastricht's classic available in English for a new generation of students, pastors, and scholars, the Dutch Reformed Translation Society and Reformation Heritage Books are giving a great gift to the Christian church as a whole, and to students, pastors, and scholars in particular."

—Sinclair B. Ferguson, Chancellor's Professor of Systematic Theology,
Reformed Theological Seminary, and teaching fellow,
Ligonier Ministries

"Translating Petrus van Mastricht's *Theoretico-practica theologia* is a courageous endeavor that deserves respect. This large book, a unique synthesis of theoretical and practical aspects of theology, is an important specimen of seventeenth-century Reformed thought and piety. Complete editions have been available for a long time, but only in Latin (1682–1724) and in a Dutch translation (1749–1750). None of these texts are as informative as the present English translation; based on the Latin original, it keeps an eye on the eighteenth-century Dutch translation and provides ample background information."

—Aza Goudriaan, associate professor of historical theology,
Free University of Amsterdam

"It is reckoned by many that the Reformed faith came to its richest expression in the writings of the Dutch theologians of the seventeenth century. Among these the theoretical-practical theology of Petrus van Mastricht is a foremost production. Jonathan Edwards claimed that it 'was much better than any other book in the world, excepting the Bible, in my opinion.' Its English translation and publication is a notable achievement."

—Paul Helm, professor of the history and philosophy
of religion, emeritus, King's College, London

"With each translation of the formative Reformed theologians of the sixteenth and seventeenth centuries comes the possibility of our churches being renewed by forgotten treasures. This is one of those gold mines. So important is van Mastricht that even Descartes felt obliged to respond to his critiques and Jonathan Edwards drew deeply from the well of his *Theoretical-Practical Theology*. It is a distinct pleasure to recommend this remarkable gem."

—Michael Horton, J. Gresham Machen Professor of Systematic
Theology and Apologetics, Westminster Seminary California

"The release of this publication is one of the most important events in contemporary scholarship. Mastricht was the favorite theologian of Jonathan Edwards, the preeminent American religious mind. So Mastricht was not just one of the most significant Reformed thinkers; he also exercised inordinate influence on 'America's theologian.' All scholars and readers interested in Reformed theology and the inner workings of Edwards's mind will want to procure this series."

—Gerald McDermott, Anglican Professor of Divinity at
Beeson Divinity School and coauthor of
The Theology of Jonathan Edwards

"What if you could have a systematic theology that approached something like Turretin's precision and Brakel's devotion while, by design, helping men preach better? It would look like Mastricht. This has long been my favorite system of theology, and I have never been so eager to endorse and promote a book."
—Ryan M. McGraw, Morton H. Smith Professor of Systematic Theology, Greenville Presbyterian Theological Seminary

"Scholars and students alike should welcome this translation of Mastricht's *Theoretico-practica theologia*. Mastricht's work represents the full achievement of the Reformed orthodox theological program of developing an exegetical, doctrinal, elenctic or polemical, and practical approach to Christian doctrine. Whereas other theologies of the era, like Brakel's *Christian's Reasonable Service* or Turretin's *Institutes*, embody one or two of these emphases, Mastricht provides the full spectrum of Reformed orthodox thought and does so on a highly detailed and carefully defined level. The translation is a significant achievement."
—Richard A. Muller, senior fellow, Junius Institute for Digital Reformation Research; P. J. Zondervan Professor of Historical Theology, Emeritus, Calvin Theological Seminary

"Any serious student of Reformed theology needs to sit at the feet of Petrus van Mastricht. The challenge has been that to do so you needed to know Latin or Dutch. Thanks to the herculean efforts of the folks at the Dutch Reformed Translation Society and Reformation Heritage Books, English readers can now learn the art of 'living for God through Christ.'"
—Stephen J. Nichols, president of Reformation Bible College and chief academic officer of Ligonier Ministries

"Van Mastricht is one of the greatest of the Reformed Orthodox, exerting a profound influence on subsequent theologians, including Jonathan Edwards. His grasp of the tradition, his ability to interact with contemporary issues, and his careful articulation of orthodoxy exemplify the best of Protestant theology after the Reformation. Yet the lack of an English translation has meant that he has been known more by reputation than by content in the Anglophone world. Here at last is an English translation which will allow a whole new audience of pastors, theologians, and laypeople to draw once again on this profound theological source."
—Carl R. Trueman, professor of biblical and religious studies, Grove City College

"Mastricht's magnum opus is suited for the school (scholastic) in its definitions, divisions, brevity, and clarity; suited for wider instruction in its frequent recourse to catechetical interrogation and response; and especially suited for truth and godliness in its decidedly biblical-exegetical foundations and eminently spiritual applications. In his manual Mastricht holds together—and yet carefully distinguishes—what many before and after him are prone to separate. Developed when Reformed instruction for the ministry of the gospel was in full flower, the result is a deeply gratifying and wholistic account of Christian theology as 'the doctrine of living for God through Christ.'"

—Theodore G. Van Raalte, professor of ecclesiology and associate librarian at the Canadian Reformed Theological Seminary

Theoretical-Practical Theology

Volume 1: Prolegomena

PET. VAN MASTRICT,
PHILOSOPH. ET THEOL. DOCT. ET PROFESSOR,
in Academiis: Francofurt. ad Oderam, Duisburg. et Ultrajectinâ.

ΣΥΜΒΟΣ
Ὅταν ἀφεινῶς τότε. δεναλόν
ἔται.

Theoretical-Practical Theology

Volume 1: Prolegomena

by
Petrus van Mastricht

Translated by Todd M. Rester
Edited by Joel R. Beeke

REFORMATION HERITAGE BOOKS
Grand Rapids, Michigan

Theoretical-Practical Theology, Volume 1: Prolegomena
© 2018 by The Dutch Reformed Translation Society

Reformation Heritage Books
2965 Leonard St. NE
Grand Rapids, MI 49525
616-977-0889
orders@heritagebooks.org
www.heritagebooks.org

Printed in the United States of America
19 20 21 22 23 24/10 9 8 7 6 5 4 3 2

Library of Congress Cataloging-in-Publication Data

Names: Mastricht, Peter van, 1630–1706, author.
Title: Theoretical-practical theology / by Petrus van Mastricht ; translated by Todd M. Rester ; edited by Joel R. Beeke.
Other titles: Theologia theoretico-practica. English
Description: Grand Rapids, Michigan : Reformation Heritage Books, 2018–
Identifiers: LCCN 2018014361 (print) | LCCN 2018028430 (ebook) ISBN 9781601785602 (epub) | ISBN 9781601785596 (v. 1 : hardcover : alk. paper)
Subjects: LCSH: Reformed Church—Doctrines—Early works to 1800.
Classification: LCC BX9422.3 (ebook) | LCC BX9422.3 .M2813 2018 (print) | DDC 230/.42—dc23
LC record available at https://lccn.loc.gov/2018014361

For additional Reformed literature, request a free book list from Reformation Heritage Books at the above regular or e-mail address.

Contents

Part One
PROLEGOMENA AND FAITH

Book One: Prolegomena of Theoretical-Practical Theology

Third Theorem—*The Definition of Theology*

The Dogmatic Part

The Elenctic Part

The Practical Part

The Exegetical Part

Editor's Preface

On behalf of the Dutch Reformed Translation Society and Reformation Heritage Books, I am deeply grateful to be able to present you with the long-awaited introductory volume of Petrus van Mastricht's *Theoretical-Practical Theology*. The whole work is divided into three parts: Part 1, *Prolegomena and Faith*, makes up the large majority of the work, and is followed by a briefer Part 2, *Outline of Moral Theology*, and Part 3, *Sketch of Ascetic Theology: The Exercise of Piety*. This volume, *Prolegomena*, contains Part 1, Book 1 (1.1), and the rest of Mastricht's *Theology* will be published in six future volumes: 2. *Faith in the Triune God* (1.2); 3. *The Works of God and the Fall of Man* (1.3–4); 4. *Redemption in Christ* (1.5); 5. *The Application of Redemption and the Church* (1.6–7); 6. *The Covenant of Grace* (1.8); and 7. *Morality and Piety* (2.1–3, 3.1–4), with an estimated combined length of four thousand pages. God willing, these volumes will provide one of the most comprehensive methods of treating Christian doctrine in English in the history of Reformed theology.

Petrus van Mastricht (1630–1706) was a Dutch theologian who studied at Utrecht under Gisbertus Voetius (1589–1676), the leading scholar of the Dutch Further Reformation (*Nadere Reformatie*), and later became his successor. He pastored churches in the Netherlands and taught at the universities of Duisburg and Utrecht. Surprisingly, Mastricht's justly celebrated work on Christian doctrine, for which he became best known, has never been translated into English, with the exception of his section on regeneration.[1]

As a systematic theology or body of divinity, this classic—originally written in Latin and subsequently translated into Dutch and now being simultaneously translated into English and re-translated into Dutch—combines a rigorous, biblical, and scholastic treatment of doctrine with the pastoral aim of preparing the reader to live for God through Christ. Mastricht treats each theological

---

1. Petrus van Mastricht, *A Treatise on Regeneration* (New Haven, Conn.: Thomas and Samuel Green, 1769; repr., Pittsburgh: Soli Deo Gloria, 2002).

topic with a four-pronged approach: exegetical, dogmatic, elenctic, and practical. Educated Christians, theological students, pastors, and scholars will find that Mastricht's *magnum opus* provides a valuable model for moving from the text of Scripture to doctrinal formulation to experiential and practical application that will edify them.

This first volume provides an introduction to doing systematic theology. It serves as a kind of abbreviated presentation of what is now commonly called *prolegomena*—a Greek word that means "things said beforehand"—in this case, those necessary prerequisites that lay a good foundation for the study of Bible doctrine. Mastricht begins by addressing the nature of theology, showing its proper method, subject matter, and the definition of theology. He then discusses Scripture as the rule for doing theology, since it is the only infallible source and foundation for knowing God. Finally, Mastricht gives his rationale for the best distribution of theological topics.

This volume also includes Mastricht's homiletical aid, *The Best Method of Preaching*,[2] in which he succinctly shows how to use theology to preach more effectively to Christ's bride. Packing this little treatise with practical advice, he covers the basics of sermon preparation by considering sermon arrangement and sermon introductions, exegeting and explaining the text, preaching doctrinally, preaching to comfort believers, preaching against sin and for self-examination, exhorting unto good works, cautions in preaching, handling lengthy texts, and sermon delivery. Finally, this first volume also contains an informative and detailed translator's preface by Todd Rester and a helpful biographical preface by Adriaan Neele, who did his doctoral work on Mastricht.[3]

Ever since I read Jonathan Edwards's (1703–1758) frequently quoted statement a few decades ago that, "for divinity in general, doctrine, practice and controversy, or as an universal system of divinity, [Mastricht's *Theoretical-Practical Theology*] is much better than [Francis] Turretin or any other book in the world, excepting the Bible, in my opinion,"[4] I have longed for the day when

---

2. The editorial team has decided to include *The Best Method of Preaching* in this first volume before Mastricht's dogmatics, as Mastricht himself did in his original publication, to underscore that one of his primary reasons for writing his dogmatics was to provide assistance in preaching to ministers. In a later edition, Mastricht moved this valuable, succinct book to the end of his dogmatics without changing his emphasis on writing the whole to assist preachers. The translation provided here is slightly revised and improved from the original 2013 publication of this little book by Reformation Heritage Books.

3. Adriaan Cornelis Neele, *The Art of Living to God: A Study of Method and Piety in the Theoretico-practica theologia of Petrus van Mastricht (1630–1706)*, series 8, vol. 1 (Pretoria: University of Pretoria, 2005).

4. Jonathan Edwards to Joseph Bellamy, January 15, 1747.

this work would be translated into English. Since no one else was undertaking the task, I presented it to our Dutch Reformed Translation Society (DRTS), which, even though the major translation work would need to be from the original Latin edition, happily decided to commit itself to it due to its value and the fact that it does have a rich history in the first Dutch translation. Since I was appointed as chairman of the DRTS's Mastricht subcommittee to oversee and edit the work, it falls to me to thank those who have assisted in this task in a variety of ways.

First, I wish to thank my fellow Mastricht subcommittee members, John Bolt and Richard Muller, for their valuable assistance in helping me shepherd this project thus far so that the first volume could be published. Many thanks to the DRTS Board and especially its chairman, James DeJong, for supporting this project from the outset and patiently bearing with a variety of challenges in getting it off the ground. Thanks are also in order to Don Sinnema, who played a valuable role at various junctures in evaluating the translation.

Many thanks to Todd Rester for his diligent work in translating Mastricht from Latin into English, while also consulting the Dutch translation,[5] and for supplying the vast majority of helpful footnotes via his research in multiple archives and libraries. Thanks, too, to Michael Spangler for being our Latin editor, who carefully checked our primary translator's work and simultaneously assisted us in rendering Mastricht into more readable English without sacrificing accuracy.[6] Michael has helped immensely in making my work easier as an English editor.

We are also grateful to Reformation Heritage Books, and in particular Jay Collier, for helping us see this first volume (and hopefully six more to follow) through the printing process. A warm thanks also to Linda and Gary den Hollander for their expertise in typesetting and helping in the editing of this volume. Finally, thanks to all of you who have donated to this project financially, either explicitly by your earmarked gifts, or implicitly by becoming members of the DRTS. Many more such gifts are needed to see this work through to completion, so if you would like to support this endeavor, please forward your tax-deductible donation to the DRTS and receive our heartfelt thanks for partnering with us.[7]

---

5. Concurrent with this English translation, a new Dutch translation is being published in six volumes by Stichting Gereformeerd Erfgoed together with Gebr. Koster. The leader of this project is A. A. (Ton) Reukens (www. gereformeerderfgoed.nl/intekenen).

6. It should be noted that scriptural quotations in this set of books are translated directly from Mastricht's Latin.

7. Lifetime membership in the DRTS is available for a one-time tax-deductible gift of $100. Members support the society's continuing work, receive periodic newsletters, and may purchase

The many hours working on this project and editing this volume have been well worth the effort for all who have participated. With God's help, we anticipate publishing the future volumes of this important theological work on a regular basis. Please pray with us that God will use each volume for His glory and the welfare of the academy, the church, and every reader.

—Joel R. Beeke

society publications at the cost of production. Membership gifts may be sent to DRTS, P. O. Box 7083, Grand Rapids, Michigan 49510. For more information on the DRTS, see www. dutchreformed.org.

Abbreviations

ADB	*Allgemeine Deutsche Biographie*
ANF	*Ante-Nicene Fathers*
BBKL	*Biographisch-Bibliographisches Kirchenlexikon*
BWDN	*Biographisch Woordenboek der Nederlanden*
BWPGN	*Biographisch Woordenboek van Protestantsche Godgeleerden in Nederland*
LCL	*Loeb Classical Library*
NDB	*Neue Deutsche Biographie*
NNBW	*Nieuw Nederlandsch Biografisch Woordenboek*
TPT	van Mastricht, *Theoretico-Practica Theologia*
TRE	*Theologische Realenzyklopädie*

Translator's Preface

The *Theoretical-Practical Theology* is a composite work that incorporates content from the course of Petrus van Mastricht's academic career, including elements of his first efforts in publication, his work as a lecturing professor and presiding professor of disputations at three different institutions spanning from 1670 to 1698, other occasional works on Cartesian philosophy and, separately, on saving faith. While there is most certainly a homiletic interest and a pastoral concern for people's growth in Christian maturity, the intended audience of the 1698 edition is scholarly. This is evidenced by the marginalia that signpost the argument in the manner of a university disputation (*an sit? quid sit? qualis sit? objectiones, responsiones*). The tone of the work at times is variously analytic and discursive, other times his prose waxes elegant and fervent, and still other times it is a rapid-fire burst of lists: terms, works, references, figures, controversies, doctrinal consequences, and so forth. The overriding concern of the work is a high regard for God, preaching, Scripture, doctrinal orthodoxy, and personal godliness. Mastricht is a pastor writing to train pastors in an age when philosophical and scientific principles and commitments were radically shifting, Enlightenment thought was dawning and waxing, and the Dutch *Nadere Reformatie*, or Further Reformation (c. 1600–1750), was beginning to wane.

In the period of late Protestant scholasticism and confessional orthodoxy of the early modern period (approximately 1685–1725) just as a plethora of philosophical and scientific movements swept Europe wave after wave intellectually and institutionally, Mastricht coordinated three concerns in the early part of his work in a noteworthy way: "The best method of preaching," Scripture as the prolegomena of theology as a discipline, and saving faith in Jesus Christ, the very Son of God made flesh and the only Savior of sinners. First, it is noteworthy because other theological works of the period frequently would place exegesis and doctrinal theology into their own compendium, cases of conscience or practical theology into another manual, church history into another, and the art of preaching into still another. Mastricht sought to integrate these strands into one interwoven fabric while footnoting other more expansive treatments. Second, the study of Scripture, history, and polemics is a pastoral endeavor in the service of believing and living to God. Consider the placement of his treatment of preaching. Whether it was the first edition of the *Theoretico-practica theologia*, where his treatment of preaching occurs before the prolegomena proper for new seminarians, or the second edition translated here, where his treatment of preaching occurs as the last thing seminarians read, in either case Mastricht insisted that preaching and theology must be inextricably linked. Next, theology is living to God through Jesus Christ, and it is the burden of his work to demonstrate why and how Jesus Christ is the Savior of sinners and how Christians are to live personally before God in light of that fact. Fourth, Scripture is the foundational principle of the discipline of theology; reason is in its service, not the other way around. Fifth, and quite interestingly, Mastricht places saving faith between his prolegomena on Scripture and theology proper on God and the Trinity. In doing so, he indicates what is at stake for his seminarian and pastoral readers: the salvation of themselves and their hearers. These points taken together represent for him the basic path forward for a vibrant church, and the goal of his work is to convey these concerns to the next generations of pastors.

The academic discourse of theology necessarily involves the task of analyzing texts, describing concepts, establishing teachings or *doctrinae*, and sanctioning practices. At every point in the process there can be contested interpretations and practices within communities of believers. There are also histories to those contests that find their way into subsequent discussions. The result is that the tasks of exegesis and history, corporate memory, doctrinal development and doctrinal transmission, continuity and change, and community boundaries and identities are all bound up in the task of translation. The translator's task and challenge is to represent the thought of an author as clearly as possible, as well as the doctrines, developments, boundaries, and identities conveyed in the text. In the case of Mastricht's work here, the reader does not read very far without encountering boundary lines and markers between different communities. Mastricht consistently notes confessional boundaries between the Reformed, Lutherans, Roman Catholics, Anabaptists, and other sects old and new. Within confessional boundaries he will note disagreements and tensions between, for example, Jesuits and Dominicans, various stripes of Lutherans, and Anabaptists. Outside of the Christian religion, Mastricht occasionally engages in textual arguments with representatives of the rabbinic Jewish communities over the centuries as well as engaging with Islam. Such engagement is not unique to Mastricht in the early modern period, but it does demonstrate the breadth of learning that these old Protestant scholastics employed when encountering the intersections of history, theology, philosophy, and law, to name a few disciplines. It is also a characteristic mark of Protestant and Roman Catholic scholasticism throughout Europe in the early modern period to engage matters of contemporary concern with respect to religious and political establishments, community life, and how best to buttress Christian orthodoxy and the Christian State, or more vaguely *Respublica Christiana*, in some measure in the hearts and minds of every level of society.

In this period from the Reformation to approximately 1780, besides confessional boundaries there are also philosophical boundaries as well that frequently color questions of confessional orthodoxy, as these too impact conceptions of the civic realm and religious community. An ever-present and imminent concern that was looming over Mastricht's shoulder, so to speak, as he wrote, was the specter of what can be described as "Socinio-Cartesianism," that is, a broad concept of greater confidence in unregenerate human reason than reliance upon the Holy Scriptures and the work of the Holy Spirit through regeneration. In a previous age, this would simply be called pagan skepticism or cynicism. But in Mastricht's day, the philosophical pressure originates, in large part as he saw it, from methodological doubt and a high confidence in unregenerate human reason as the crucible and anvil upon which all truth was to be tested and forged anew. There was no topic of human endeavor or thought that would not be held up to scrutiny under the eye of autonomous reason. This seems to have formed the basis for his critique of Socinianism, certain Remonstrants, Descartes and his followers, and the progress of these influences in the Netherlands from the early seventeenth century onward. Mastricht, however, would hold that all truth, the human subject, and especially human reason must be tested and forged anew by God through the Scriptures. And so, the tension between the new philosophies and orthodox (i.e. Reformed) theology could not be more palpable. While Mastricht's work is concerned with doctrinal engagement, he was concerned with preservation and transmission of truth about God and salvation. Thus there is both an academic coolness in analysis merged with a fervent urgency.

One may wonder how such concerns impact the task of translation. On confessional matters, we see polemical terms utilized for groups with relatively fixed conceptual boundaries. For example, to broader, modern sensibilities it is generally a mark of Protestant chauvinism to refer to Roman Catholics as papists. And yet, this is one term that Mastricht frequently, if not in the majority of cases, deploys for Roman Catholics, especially for Roman Catholics after the Council of Trent who continued to argue for a global, papal power in the spiritual and political realms of the church and state. Mastricht took seriously a papacy that still claimed with Innocent III (1198–1216) that the pope has a *de jure* right to all temporal and spiritual power, and still attempted to influence international

politics and evangelization of the New World. This papacy was not in exile in
Vatican City but was an active European power. The papacy was deeply involved
in Spanish, French, Imperial, and Anglo-Irish politics in Europe as well as matters of evangelization and the spread of Roman Catholic colonial empires across
the globe. In some quarters of the Roman Catholic church in Mastricht's day,
at an academic level there were still hotly contested theological doctrines and
political policies for forced conversion. And so while today, broadly speaking,
Protestants typically view their Roman Catholic neighbors as ecumenical allies
in secular culture wars on matters of freedom of conscience, religious tolerance,
advocacy for all human life, religious education, and traditional historic formula-
tions of Christian marriage, the Protestant-Roman Catholic divide was always a
source of fear and suspicion in the seventeenth century.

At Mastricht's death in 1706, there was precious little religious tolerance
enshrined in law in Europe at all; quite the opposite. The ensuing panic of the
1672 *Rampjaar* (Disaster Year), in which the French crown swept through the
Netherlands and seized many major cities, rekindled fears of Roman Catholic
rule and persecution in the Netherlands. In France, the draconian policy of *les
dragonnades* (1681–1685), which quartered French dragoons with Protestant
households with implied permission to abuse the family until they converted
to Roman Catholicism or emigrated, initiated new waves of French Reformed
immigrants into the Netherlands and other Protestant lands. When King Louis
XIV's Edict of Fontainebleau (1685), also known more broadly as the Revoca-
tion of the 1598 Edict of Nantes, stripped Protestants of the right to practice
their religion legally, the waves became a flood of Huguenots out of France.
Prior to the Glorious Revolution in England (1688) and the prosecution of King
William III's wars in Ireland and Scotland (1689–1691), there was a deep fear
in the Dutch Republic and in England that King James II, a Roman Catholic,
would return the islands of Britain and Ireland to Roman Catholicism. On the
Protestant side, for example, King William III of England, a Dutch Reformed
Protestant on the English throne, approved the Toleration Act of 1689, which
only tolerated a slim segment of non-conformist Protestants who took the oaths
of allegiance and supremacy. Non-Roman Catholics did not gain the right to
openly practice their faith in France until the Edict of Versailles in 1787. Roman
Catholics did not gain the right to worship in Great Britain until the Roman
Catholic Relief Act of 1791.

I sincerely hope that readers will understand that a translator's task is to
convey an author's ideas and concepts, as well as attitudes, as clearly as possible,
which validates the use of pejoratives for historical purposes. Thus, where Mastricht utilizes the pejorative papist, for example, I have as well. The same could

be said for other pejorative terms in such a polemical age living under threat of religious wars. The converse can be said about Mastricht's positive use of terms referencing the Reformed as "the Orthodox," Reformed theology as "our theology," and, when referencing the objective doctrinal content of Reformed theology, this is "the faith" or "our faith."

Thus, I have endeavored to bring the reader into contact with Mastricht's thought as a point of academic and historic integrity. Profitable discussion and debate must follow from reading sources—even ones that are controversial at times. It is for theologians and defenders of the various denominations, sects, and religions to reflect on Mastricht's arguments and gauge their critical worth, contemporary utility, and polemical tone. Perhaps such reflection could further academic inquiry as well as stimulate constructive dialogue in our pluralist age where various denominations, sects, and religions are likely to inhabit the same intellectual, academic, and civic space more cheek by jowl than in Mastricht's day? It was Cicero who remarked that "to be ignorant of what happened before you were born is to be a child forever."[1] In this context of histories of doctrinal controversies, to be ignorant of historic doctrinal, exegetical, and practical differences in the present is one way to continue to argue like children.

With philosophical pejoratives, Mastricht was much more creative and seemed to view this realm as a much more active and current process of debate in his context. It is not simply that there are Cartesians (a static group-concept) or Socinians; Mastricht took these substantive nouns and developed a grammar for the process of decay he aimed to stem in the Reformed churches: Cartesians Cartesianize, Remonstrants Socinianize; there are even groups of people he labels Socinianizers (he coins a Greco-Latin neologism: Sociniζοντες; he does something similar for Cartesianizers) in the Reformed Church who are calling into question Scripture and theology proper on the basis of reason and methodological doubt. As far as I know, Mastricht did not speak of "Lutheranizing" Reformed or "papisticizing" Protestants, though he might signal that a particular theologian seems to have tendencies in a particular non-Reformed direction. In short, the polemics of confessionality are still alive and well in this work but the boundary lines are generally clear, which results in a static set of terms for other, more established confessional identities. But, the hotter sort of controversy for Mastricht was an active contest or a current disease process with respect to contested philosophical ideas and their influence on scriptural exegesis, doctrinal formulation, and practical matters of godliness and piety in Reformed synods

---

1. Marcus Tullius Cicero, *Orator*, 34.120; *nescire autem quid ante quam natus sis acciderit, id est semper esse puerum.*

and congregations. That is, as in the title of his anti-Cartesian work, the philosophical shifts impacting Reformed confessional orthodoxy (faith) and godliness
(life) in the late seventeenth century are a gangrene of innovations.[2]

I have attempted, and it is for others to judge whether I have succeeded,
to maintain the scholastic discourse with respect to terms and concepts, but I
have not sought to burden the reader with an archaic form of address or diction.
While it may seem desirable to keep long, extended sentences exactly as given
in Mastricht's Latin, in general it is not. The modern sensibility does not seem
to have the patience for layers of nested relative clauses and antecedents (and
English does not have the case system necessary to sustain the level of grammatical intricacy that the Latin original utilizes at times). Breaking complex Latin
sentences while maintaining the thread of his argument and the flow of his discourse in English has been both the goal and the ideal. I have also moved most of
the Greek and Hebrew terms and citations to the footnotes. On the relation of
this translation to the 1749–1753 Dutch translation of Mastricht's 1698–1699
Latin second edition, the authoritative text for this translation is the Latin second edition, but I have had an eye toward the Dutch as another helpful tool.
Where it seemed appropriate I have noted Dutch expansions and interpolations
on the Latin text as a resource for the scholar.

Scholastic theology of the Neo-Latin period is neither entirely Cicero nor
entirely Lombard, but has been influenced by both in various ways. The university of the late seventeenth century still uses scholastic discourse that would be
in many important ways similar to medieval university life: *lectio, disputationes,
repetitiones, orationes, collegia,* and so forth. But the humanist movements of the
previous two centuries also brought to bear more tools and techniques for textual analysis, etymological consideration, and historical and contextual research.
Mastricht, for example, evidences not only familiarity with the secondary literature surrounding certain questions of Rabbinic Judaism, but is also familiar with
various degrees of primary sources: texts, collations, anthologies, quote-books or
florilegia, and so forth. While Mastricht demonstrates a good level of classical
learning, it was not his chief concern to embroider plain doctrine with classical
filigree for display or pedantry. Mastricht did on occasion adopt a grand style of
rhetoric, but in the main, this is not so. Mastricht did use metaphors, similes, and
word plays on occasion as a way to stimulate a student's memory. He occasionally indulges in ironic humor in his polemical sections, but overall his work is a

---

2. Cf. Petrus van Mastricht, *Novitatum Cartesianarum Gangraena nobiliores plerasque
corporis theologici partes arrodens et exedens, seu Theologia Cartesiana detecta* (Amsterdam: Jansson-
Waesberg, 1677).

steady pace of analysis. When he disagreed with a fellow Reformed minister or professor who had published publicly, he exercised restraint and sought to specify where and to what extent he disagreed. Mastricht was also concerned with maintaining Reformed orthodoxy but he was willing to utilize other transconfessional sources with qualification and approval, if it seemed faithful to the text.

Part of the complexity of a text of this size is managing the vast array of languages Mastricht used and his extensive bibliography. Mastricht utilized a broad range of sources and evidences familiarity with many languages. Of course, Mastricht utilized the biblical languages of Greek, Hebrew, and Aramaic, and he did seem to work with other lesser known near-eastern and semitic languages. For example, there are instances where his exegesis compared Syriac, Ethiopic, and Beza's Latin and Greek texts from the Gospel of Matthew. For scholars of Hebrew, Mastricht generally used an unpointed text and was also quite comfortable in rabbinic literature or commenting on both the kabbalah and Christians who were enamored by mixing mystical Judaism into Christian exegesis. The result for the translation is that the Hebrew text and terms are exact reproductions of what the 1698–1699 text utilized. A similar practice is followed with respect to Mastricht's Greek. I have endeavored to direct the reader to relevant resources for further study of the biblical texts which he referenced or seemed to work from. Mastricht also read French, Dutch, German, and English. This is evidenced in that sometimes he will cite a work by a Latin title that never had a translation or version in Latin. Furthermore, he has been known to translate his Dutch, German, or French citations into Latin. Again, I have endeavored to find such non-Latin sources and in the majority of cases have been successful.

Along these lines, with respect to bibliographical notes and apparatus I have endeavored to supplement Mastricht's brief citations with full bibliographic references to material that may not be known to the English reader. While I have not been able to track down every edition that Mastricht cited, due to the blessings of digitized sources, finding lists like the Post-Reformation Digital Library (www.prdl.org), and a good deal of old-fashioned archival work in various research libraries, I have been able to locate the vast majority of his references in sixteenth- and seventeenth-century editions as well as nineteenth- and twentieth-century translations or critical editions. When I have seen these sources and the exact quote in question, I have footnoted as precisely as possible. If the work was only located but I was not able to see the citation, I have only footnoted the work without page numbers. For their ubiquity, presence in the public domain, and thus ease of access and availability online, I have referred the reader to Migne's *Patrologia Latina* and *Patrologia Graeca* as well as T. & T. Clark's series, the *Ante-Nicene Fathers* and the *Nicene and Post-Nicene Fathers*.

These libraries and institutions deserve a special note of gratitude for their assistance in my various research trips over the years. I wish I could list all the staff members who assisted, but space and time would not permit. These institutions deserve special mention: the staff of the Hekman Library special collections and the H. H. Meeter Center for Calvin Studies at Calvin College and Calvin Theological Seminary in Grand Rapids, Michigan, provided a tremendous amount of assistance; the staff of the special collections of the Barbour Library at Pittsburgh Theological Seminary; the splendid staff at the Leiden University library special collections in the Netherlands; the British Library in London in its efficiency and professionalism; and the Jonathan Edwards Center at Yale University. Dr. Adriaan Neele deserves special mention for the use of his private library.

Translation of this sort and magnitude is not for the faint of heart. It is a long, arduous, and solitary process that requires some degree of fellowship in order to endure. The most immediate and faithful source of encouragement has been my wife, Amy. Without her love and concern for me, this translation would not be here. I also had the privilege of the fellowship of the doctoral and graduate community at Calvin Theological Seminary in which peers and colleagues, dear friends, spurred me on in this work. Drew McGinnis, Jon Marko, Ted van Raalte, Jordan Ballor, Albert Gootjes, and David Sytsma each assisted this project in their friendship at various times. Michael Spangler was a welcome and greatly appreciated help as he read through the manuscript of volume one and advised me in the editing of this work. His assistance would not have been possible without the support of the Dutch Reformed Translation Society and the recommendation of its editorial committee. James DeJong, Joel Beeke, Richard Muller, and John Bolt have been faithful to advance this project and have over the years reaffirmed their support to me. This project would not have come to this stage without their personal leadership and encouragement. It is my hope that the translation of Mastricht's work advances understanding, appreciation, and discussion of the content, course, and goal of theology.

—Todd M. Rester

Petrus van Mastricht (1630–1706): Life and Work

Adriaan C. Neele

This introduction aims to do three things. First, it provides an overview of Peter van Mastricht's life: his early years, followed by the German and Dutch periods. Second, it provides a summary of his theological outlook, examining his theology in relation to preaching, and then looking at his distribution, method, and definition of theology. Finally, it considers Mastricht's reception, especially on the European continent, in Scotland, and in New England.

Early Years: 1630–1652

The city of Maastricht was captured in 1579 by the Spanish troops of the Roman Catholic king, Philip II, forcing many Protestants to leave the looted city. Among the refugees was the family of Cornelius Sc(h)oning (†1658), who took up residence in Cologne. Here, Cornelius took the family name "van Mastricht." Thomas van Mastricht (†1667), a son of Cornelius, married Jeanne le Planque (†1656), and their first son, Petrus van Mastricht, was born in November 1630 and baptized the following month as Pieter van Mastricht.[1] The event occurred in the Dutch Reformed refugee congregation in Cologne where both Peter's father and grandfather were elders. This congregation was internationally oriented, as attested by the minutes of the consistory's regular meetings with the German and French (Huguenot) members; ecclesiastical attestations of receiving and providing for members of Dutch refugee congregations in London;

---

1. For additional bibliographical information on Petrus van Mastricht: Petrus van Mastricht, *The Best Method of Preaching: The Use of Theoretical-Practical Theology*, trans. and intro. by Todd M. Rester (Grand Rapids: Reformation Heritage Books, 2013), 1–19; Adriaan C. Neele, *Petrus van Mastricht (1630–1706). Reformed Orthodoxy: Method and Piety* (Leiden: Brill, 2009), 27–61; A. E. van Tellingen, "Het leven en enige aspecten uit de theologie van Petrus van Mastricht (1630–1706)" (ThM thesis, University of Utrecht, 2003); W. J. van Asselt, "Petrus van Mastricht," *Biographisch Lexicon voor de geschiedenis van het Nederlands Protestantisme* (Kampen: Kok, 2001), 360. Henceforth, in other than technical bibliographical references, the forename "Peter" will be used in the text as an acceptable anglicized form of "Petrus." This biography of Mastricht is a revised and updated version of the one found in Adriaan C. Neele, *Petrus van Mastricht (1630–1706). Reformed Orthodoxy: Method and Piety* (Leiden: Brill, 2009), 27–61.

collections held for the Reformed refugee congregation in Strasburg; correspondence with Gisbertus Voetius (1589–1676); and the calling of Andreas Essenius (1618–1677) of Utrecht as their pastor, as well as the fact that members of the consistory and congregation traveled internationally and visited the *Messe Frankfurt* (Frankfurt Trade Fair) annually.[2] This congregation, with the nearby church at Mühlheim am Rhein, was pastored from 1639 to 1643 by Johannes Hoornbeeck (1617–1666)—the catechism teacher of Peter, his sister Magdalena, and their brothers, Johannes and Gerhardus.

Peter went to the famous *Schola Duisburgensis* (founded c. 1280) for a classical liberal arts education, where he met Theodor Undereyck (1635–1693), a fellow student and the later leader of one of the first Pietist conventicles. Following his studies in Duisburg, Mastricht arrived at Utrecht in 1647 to be treated for a handicapped foot but also to commence his study of theology at the Academy with Voetius, Carolus de Maets (1597–1651), and Hoornbeeck. The Academy of Utrecht was becoming the European summit of Reformed orthodoxy and Protestant scholasticism, the exponent of Voetius's overall vision that theology must be known and practiced (*Oratio inauguralis De pietate cum scientia conjugenda*, 1636). Students from the provinces of Utrecht, Zeeland, and Holland, as well as countries such as England, Hungary, Poland, and Scotland, received a thorough education. Both the "German"-born Mastricht and Utrecht's first female student, Anna Maria van Schurman (1607–1678),[3] who was a fellow member with Peter of the Cologne congregation, studied there. Didactic-dogmatic theology, which included the *Summa theologica* of Thomas Aquinas (1225–1274), the *Synopsis purioris theologiae* (1625), and the scholastic *disputationes* of Voetius's Saturday morning classes, along with exegesis of Scripture including attention to rabbinic interpretations, and both Voetius's and Hoornbeeck's emphasis on experiential and practical theology (*theologia practica*) would contribute to Mastricht's theological formation.[4] Three years into his studies, Mastricht defended the disputation, *De Esu sanguinis et suffocati ad act. XV*, for his catechism teacher.[5] A year later, when De Maets had passed away, the Academy called Samuel

---

2. Rudolf Löhr and Jan Pieter van Doorn, *Protokolle der Niederländisch-Reformierten Gemeinde in Köln von 1651–1803* (Köln: Rheinland Verlag Düsseldorf, 1971), vols. 1 and 2.

3. Pieta van Beek, *The First Female University Student: Anna Maria van Schurman* (Utrecht: Igitur, 2010), 15.

4. Joel R. Beeke, "Gisbertus Voetius: Toward a Reformed Marriage of Knowledge and Piety" in *Protestant Scholasticism: Essays in Reassessment*, eds. Carl R. Trueman and R. Scott Clark (Carlisle, Cumbria, England: Paternoster Press, 1999), 227–43.

5. Johannes Hoornbeeck, *De Esu Sanguinis et Suffocati ad Act. XV*, resp. Van Maestricht (Utrecht: Henrici Versteeg, 1650).

Rutherford (1600–1661) of St. Andrews University, Scotland, who declined, recommending Essenius instead. That same year, Mastricht studied at the University of Leiden and traveled briefly to England "for studies in language and practical or Christian ethics."[6] In 1652, Mastricht finished his studies of divinity at Utrecht and returned to Cologne, bringing his attestation of church membership to the consistory on August 5.

The German Period: 1652–1677

Cologne and Xanten (1652–1662)

Upon returning to Cologne in 1652, Mastricht was called by the congregation of Xanten as *vicarus* or assistant pastor—a call he accepted in early 1653, although he kept his ecclesiastical membership at the congregation of Cologne.[7] Not much is known of his work in Xanten. The congregation was served by the influential minister at the Brandenburg Court, Johann Kunsius, from 1646 to 1652 and belonged, along with other Reformed churches of the Lower Rhine such as Duisburg, to the predominantly Cocceian classis of Cleve.[8] The ministers of these churches were primarily trained at universities in the Low Country, particularly at Leiden University, having Johannes Cocceius (1603–1669), among others, as professor. For Voetius's student from Cologne, however, this was apparently not discordant, for he asserted later in life that the Cocceian-Voetian contention was greater than necessary.[9] In the meantime, Mastricht kept in contact with his home congregation in Cologne by attending, for example, the baptism of a child of his sister Magdalena and her husband, Daniel Behaeghel, in 1658.[10] Moreover, the consistory of Cologne recommended the congregation of Mühlheim am Rhein in August of 1655 to call Mastricht as a candidate of

---

6. This grand tour may have included Heidelberg. Cf. Henricus Pontanus, *Laudatio Funebris in excessum doctissmi et clarissimi senis, Petri van Mastrigt* (Utrecht: Guilielmi van de Water, 1706),****. (Here and in notes 76 and 152, asterisks are the form of pagination.)

7. Löhr and van Doorn, *Protokolle*, 2:419, implies a membership from 1652 to 1671.

8. Cf. Jonathan I. Israel, *The Dutch Republic: Its Rise, Greatness, and Fall, 1477–1806* (Oxford: Oxford University Press, 1998), 665.

9. Petrus van Mastricht, *Theoretico-practica theologia qua, per singula capita theologica, pars exegetica, elenchtica et practica, perpetua successione conjugantur; accedunt historia ecclesiastica, plena quidem, sed compendiosa, idea theologiae moralis, hypotyposis theologiae asceticae etc. proin opus quasi novum* (Utrecht: Thomae Appels, 1699), 1074: "Hinc, comprimis post decessum Celeb.Coccei A 1658 [1669, AN] ex contentionibus major concitata est animorum συρραξις quam res exigebat." (Thus, especially after the death of the famous Cocceius in 1669, because of contentions, a greater conflict of minds was stirred up than the matter required). All references to Mastricht's *Theoretico-practica theologia* are from the 1699 edition unless otherwise noted.

10. This baptism was administered by Petrus Montanus, who was called on November 14, 1653, with the particular approval of the French members. Cf. Löhr and van Doorn, *Protokolle*, 1:35, 37.

sacred theology with many good gifts and piety of life (*"sacrosanctæ theologiæ candidatus van seer goede gaven en stichtelijke van leven sijnde"*)[11]—a call he did not accept. The reason may have been the care of his mother, who passed away the following January, as well as his working on *Vindiciae veritatis et authoritatis sacrae scripturae... adversus dissertationes Chr. Wittichii*, Mastricht's first work of philosophy.[12] The motivation for this publication was the *Disputatio* of Christopher Wittich (1625–1687), preacher at the Reformed church of Duisburg and professor of theology at the newly founded University of Duisburg.[13] Wittich appreciated Descartes's philosophical thought[14] and argued specifically that the scriptural passages Voetians referred to as incompatible with Cartesianism should not be construed literally—a point Mastricht strongly opposed.[15] Mastricht's anti-Cartesian conviction was an early response in the context of his time and his point of disagreement occasioned a less favorable reception of Cartesianism at the synod of Duisburg—an area that belonged politically, along with the university, to the Elector of Brandenburg, Frederick Wilhelm (1620–1688).

Glückstadt (1662–1667)

The city of Glückstadt (Schleswig-Holstein) was approximately 250 miles north of Xanten and located between the lower Elbe River and the North Sea. The city was strategic for the Brandenburg constituency, serving as an international business center and, with Copenhagen, as a Danish royal city.[16] With a significant Dutch trading presence cooperating with Portuguese-Dutch Jews, Remonstrants, Contra-Remonstrants, and Mennonites, the city was known for being ecumenical and tolerant, so that the Reformed, Remonstrants, and Mennonites could operate an elementary school together and share a church building.[17] The Reformed church of Glückstadt, in the Hamburg Classis,[18] called Mastricht

---

11. Ibid., 1:58 (minutes 39.1). August 5, 1655.

12. Petrus van Mastricht, *Vindiciae veritatis et authoritatis sacrae scripturae in rebus Philosophicis adversus dissertationes D. Christophori Wittichii* (Utrecht, 1655). (A Vindication of the Truth and Authority of Holy Scripture, in Things Philosophical, against the Dissertations of Christopher Wittich.)

13. Günter von Roden, *Die Universität Duisburg* (Duisburg: Walter Braun Verlag, 1968), 240. B. Glasius, *Godgeleerd Nederland, Biographisch Woordenboek van Nederlandsche Godgeleerden* ('s-Hertogenbosch: Gebr. Muller, 1853), 2:471. Jonathan I. Israel, *Radical Enlightenment, Philosophy and the Making of Modernity 1650–1750* (Oxford: Oxford University Press, 2001), 25, 26.

14. Christoph Wittich, *Dispvtatio Theologica de Stylo Scriptvrae Quem adhibet cum de rebus naturalibus sermonem instituit* (Tevtopoli: Ravins, 1655).

15. Mastricht, *Vindiciae veritatis et autoritatis sacrae scripturae*, cap. VI.

16. Karl Rasmussen, *Glückstadt im Wandel der Zeiten* (Glückstadt: Augustin, 1966), 2:193.

17. Rasmussen, *Glückstadt im Wandel der Zeiten*, 2:169–71.

18. Cf. Pontanus, *Laudatio Funebris*, 10.

in 1661 or early 1662 as full-time pastor. The church building had been a gift of the Danish king Christian IV (†1648), and services in it were attended in the summer months by the queen of Denmark, Charlotte Amalie, during Mastricht's pastorate. In this international and ecumenical environment, Mastricht published, in 1666, the *Theologiæ didactico-elenchtico-practicæ prodromus*, his first work of theology, and a forerunner of the *Theoretico-practica theologia* (*TPT*).[19] The title of the *Prodromus* (Precursor or Forerunner) indicates, furthermore, a threefold work concerning *De creatione hominis*, *De humilitate et superbia erga Deum*, and *De conversatione cum Deo*—respectively, the creation of man, humility and pride with respect to God, and walking with God. It was Mastricht's first work listed in the *Index librorum prohibitorum* (*Index of Forbidden Books*).[20] A closer look at the *Prodromus* reveals that the pastor of Glückstadt begins each chapter with the exegesis of a biblical text in the original language, from which he infers doctrinal, elenctic, and practical considerations—Mastricht's trademark for all subsequent theological publications.

In the fall of that year, Mastricht returned to Cologne when his father passed away—a visit, moreover, that became an extended break from his pastorate and a point of contention between Glückstadt's pastor and parish. Correspondence from that time shows that the congregation complained about Mastricht's progressive stand regarding the traditional church order, while Mastricht criticized the congregation concerning his inadequate remuneration and the dilapidated parsonage or manse, reminding them that he was forced to spend the winter of 1664–1665 in the Dutch United Provinces. Furthermore, Mastricht asserted, he lacked time for academic work—a desire reflected in his writing of the *Prodromus* for the "Nazarites" (cf. Num. 6), the students of divinity. The work, written upon the advice of Voetius and Hoornbeeck,[21] is dedicated to his father and to the consistory of the Reformed church at Hamburg[22]—the latter was instrumental in resolving the strained relationship between Mastricht and the "happy

---

19. Petrus van Mastricht, *Theologiæ didactico-elenchtico-practicæ prodromus tribus speciminibus* (Amsterdam: Johannem van Someren, 1666). Hereafter called *Prodromus*.

20. *Index librorum prohibitorum* (Matriti: Emmanuel Fernandez, 1747), 903.

21. Petrus van Mastricht, *Theoretico-practica theologia: qua, per capita theologica, pars dogmatica, elenchtica et practica, perpetua sumbibasei conjugantur; praecedunt in usum operis, paraleipomena, seu sceleton de optima concionandi methodo* (Amsterdam: Henrici et Viduae Theodori Boom, 1682), præfatio, "Sisto tandem theologiæ Theoretico-practicæ, diu promissæ Tomum-primum…consilio Celebb. Theologorum Voetii & Hoornbeekii, ejus prodiret Prodromus)." (At last I present the first volumes of my long-promised "Theoretical-practical Theology," …at the counsel of the most famous theologians Voetius and Hoornbeeck.)

22. Members of the consistory included Daniel Sachsio and Andre de la Fontaine as ministers, as well as elders and deacons. Cf. Mastricht, *Prodromus*, title page.

city" (Tychopolis), the Glückstadt congregation. When the prolific writer, Simon Oomius (1630–1706), formerly Mastricht's classmate in Utrecht and minister in Kampen, read the *Prodromus*, he wanted the author to complete this work of "practical theology."[23] Upon return to Glückstadt, Mastricht received a call by the Royal House of Denmark to serve the church at Copenhagen—a call he declined in favor of a university appointment.

Frankfurt an der Oder (1667–1670)

With the change from Lutheranism to Reformed orthodoxy in 1613 by the House of Brandenburg, the University of Frankfurt an der Oder became known as the "easternmost bastion of Calvinism" and a "second Heidelberg."[24] In 1667, Elector Fredrick Wilhelm offered Mastricht a professorate in Hebrew and practical theology at the university.[25] Following the Thirty Years' War (1618–1648), the city was undergoing reconstruction with respect to the university, civic life, and the church. During this time, the ruler of Brandenburg forged a union of the Lutheran and Reformed churches. The newly formed church was comprised of local people as well as English and Huguenot refugees—an influx of people who also imported, respectively, English Puritan piety and Ramism. With university students from the area and from Poland, Lithuania, Hungary, Bohemia, and Northwest Germany,[26] the church and university enjoyed a reputation for being irenic and unionistic.[27] The university intended not only to educate new Reformed leaders but also to help stem the tide of Lutheran criticism.[28] The elector of Brandenburg instructed the university, also known as the *Toleranz-*

---

23. Simon Oomius, *Disseratie van de Onderwijsingen in de Practycke der Godgeleerdheid* (Bolsward: Samuel van Haringhouk, 1672), 388, "Petrus van Mastricht, die in de jaere 1665 heeft uytgegeven zijn *Theologiae Didactico-Elenchtico-Practicae Prodromus*, in drie preuven, van de Scheppinge des menschen, van de Ootmoedigheydt en Hoogmoedigheydt nevens Godt, en van de Wandel met God; welcken arbeydt ick van herten wensche volmaekct te sien." (Petrus van Mastricht, who has published his "Prodromus of Didactical-elenctical-practical Theology in 1665," in three parts, Of the creation of men, of humility and pride with respect to God, and of walking with God; which labors I wish wholeheartedly to see completed.)

24. Nischan, *Prince, People, and Confession*, 129; Mühlpfordt, "Die Oder-Universität," 19.

25. Mastricht is listed in the university register as "Petrus von Mastricht, Coloniensis Ubius." Mr. Ralf-Ruediger Targiel, Stadtarchiv Frankfurt an der Oder is acknowledged.

26. Gawthrop, *Pietism and the Making of Eighteenth-Century Prussia*, 45. Jonathan Israel notes that the elector of Brandenburg had a tolerant outlook in theological and intellectual matters. Pointing out his ecumenical approach to the Lutheran and Calvinist confessional blocs in Brandenburg, Israel asserts that the elector was inclined toward the Cartesian-Cocceians rather than Voetian Calvinist orthodoxy. See Israel, *Radical Enlightenment*, 30.

27. O. Feyl, "Die Viandrina und das östliche Europa," in *Die Oder-Universität Frankfurt*, 109, 116, "*irenisch-unionistisch.*"

28. Nischan, *Prince, People, and Confession*, 129.

universität, to appoint only irenic professors who were "moderate and not quarrelsome...prominent, learned people."[29]

In this pro-Calvinist but confessionally hybrid state of Brandenburg, Mastricht succeeded the Old Testament scholar and Hebrew expert, Gregor Frankius (†1651).[30] With full academic ceremony—from which he abstained the rest of his life[31]—he accepted, at the age of thirty-six, his professorate in Hebrew and practical theology. His inaugural address was on the necessity of *praxis* and theory for the theologian and for theology, a theme that was familiar to him already during his study at Utrecht.[32] In his address, Mastricht argues for the importance of the *praxis* of the theologian and of theology directed to the glory of God—an importance that ought to show itself in the teaching of the faculty of theology, in the lives of the divinity students and the ministers, and in the church as a sacrosanct community.[33] The newly installed professor reminded the elector and his audience, "Let us advance the combining of practice with theory"; the *theoretica* and *practica* of the *vivendi Deo*.[34] Mastricht served on the faculty of theology with Johann Christoph Bec(k)mann (1641–1717), who was sympathetic to the theology of William Ames (1596–1643).[35] The Hebrew faculty comprised a leading European center in Hebraic studies,[36] having a renowned press for oriental and Hebrew language publications, including the Babylonian Talmud,[37] which contributed to Mastricht's standing as a Christian Hebraist.

Moreover, during his period at Frankfurt an der Oder, Mastricht probably published the *Methodus Concionandi*, a preaching method for ministerial students—Mastricht's first work of homiletics.[38] In it, Mastricht stresses

---

29. Gerd Heinrich, "Frankfurt an der Oder" in *Theologische Realenzyklopädie (TRE)*, ed. Gerhard Muller (Berlin: de Gruyter, 1977, 1988), 339.

30. Heinrich, "Frankfurt an der Oder," 338.

31. Pontanus, *Laudatio Funebris*, 11, "quas phaleras fortean usque ad suprema fata spievisset, si salvo ordine et legibus Academicis illis potuisset abstinere" (these trappings he would perhaps have spurned, even to death, if good order and the laws of the academy had allowed him to abstain from them).

32. Petrus von Mastricht, *Perpetua praxeos cum Theoria in Theologicis pariter et Theologis Συμβιβασις, oratione inaugurali lectionibus HebræoTheologicis præmissa...accedit...programma invitatorium* (Francofurti ad Viadrum: Friderici Eichorne, 1668).

33. Mastricht, *Perpetua praxeos cum Theoria in Theologicis*, [10–12].

34. Mastricht, *Perpetua praxeos cum Theoria in Theologicis*, [14–15].

35. Feyl, "Die Viandrina und das östliche Europa," 121.

36. G. Mühlpfordt, "Die Oder-Universität 1506–1811," 71.

37. Heinrich, "Frankfurt an der Oder," 340.

38. Petrus van Mastricht, *Methodus Concionandi* (Francofurti ad Viadrum: M. Hübner, [c. 1669]). This undated publication is for the following reason assigned to the late 1660's: (1) the letter type is half-seventeenth century, (2) the text is similar but different in layout to Mastricht's 1681 disputation *De optima concionandi methodo paraleipomena: in usum theologiae*

the need for a fourfold approach to the composition and preaching of a sermon—exegesis, doctrine, elenctic, and practice. This method of preaching was illustrated with the biblical text of Colossians 3:1, capturing his later definition of theology: theology is the doctrine of living to God, through Christ (*theologia est doctrina vivendi Deo, per Christum*). In 1669, Mastricht was promoted as *Theologiæ et Philosophiæ doctor* at the University of Duisburg after a public defense of the disputation *De natura theologiæ* and an oration *De nomine et omine doctoris theologi*.[39] The former expounded the doctrinal and practical dimensions (*theoretico-practica*) of the nature of theology, while the latter elaborated the theme of his 1668 inaugural address: the essence and endeavor of the theologian. With the doctorate in hand, Mastricht was called to the Brandenburg University of Duisburg in 1670.[40]

Duisburg (1670–1677)

The elector of Brandenburg founded the University of Duisburg in 1655 for the expansion of Reformed teaching, for the training of jurists for Brandenburg's cities, and for its geographic position between the Jesuit schools of Emmerich and Düsseldorf.[41]

Mastricht inaugurated his professorate with an address on the obligation of the academic oath (*De religione jurisjurandi academici*), a subject that he most likely chose due to the influence of his younger brother, Gerhardus van Mastricht (1639–1721). Gerhardus was born in 1639 at Cologne. In 1665, he obtained his doctorate in jurisprudence in Basel,[42] but became professor of history and Greek

---

theoretico-practicae (Utrecht: Meinardi a Dreunen, 1681), and (3) Mastricht's reference in the disputation that he used the method in his seventeen years of preaching, thus from 1652–1669, is absent in the *Methodus Concionandi*. Cf. Mastricht, *Theoretico-practica theologia*, 1225: "Optimam igitur appellabam…utpote quam, per septendecim annos…expertus essem commodissimam."

39. H. Kaajan, "Mastricht (Petrus van)," in *Christelijke Encyclopaedie voor het Nederlansche volk*, ed. F. W. Grosheide and G. P. van Itterzon, 2nd revised edition (Kampen: Kok, 1959), 4:252.

40. The universities of Duisburg, Frankfurt an der Oder, and Halle belonged to the elector of Brandenburg.

41. Roden, *Die Universität Duisburg*, 61. See also for the Duisburg University, W. Ring, *Geschichte der Universität* (Duisburg: Stadtarchiv, 1920); Joseph Milz, *Die Universität Duisburg 1655–1818* (Duisburg: Buschmann, 1980); Gernot Born and Frank Kopatschek, *Die Alte Universität Duisburg 1655–1818* (Duisburg: Mercator Verlag, 1992). These four authoritative books on the history of the Duisburg University do discuss Mastricht, unlike most books on the history of the Utrecht University. See for example, J. A. Cramer, *De Theologische Faculteit te Utrecht in de 18e en het begin der 19e Eeuw* (Utrecht: Broekhof, 1936) and Aart De Groot and Otto J. De Jong, eds., *Vier eeuwen Theologie in Utrecht* (Zoetermeer: Meinema, 2001).

42. Gerhardus van Mastricht, *Disputatio Iuridica Inauguralis de Adulteriis, Dispvtatio Ivridica Inavgvralis de Advlteriis* (Basel: Decker, 1665). See also Johann F. G. Goeters, "Der reformierte Pietismus in Bremen und am Niederrhein im 18. Jahrhundert" in *Der Pietismus im achtzehnten*

at Duisburg's university in 1669 and its rector in 1670—the year his brother, Peter, was appointed. The latter served from 1670 to 1677 on the faculties of both theology and philosophy, as well as teaching Hebrew and oriental languages.

Mastricht's work proceeded in the context of university, church, theology, and philosophy at Duisburg. He served on the faculty of theology with Christoph F. Crell (1626–1700),[43] the son of Wolfgang Crell of Frankfurt an der Oder University, and with Johann H. Hugenpoth (1634–1675), who succeeded the Cocceian Martinus Hundius (1624–1666).[44] The faculty favored biblical exegesis over dogmatic theology,[45] while Hugenpoth continued Hundius's advocacy of the Cocceian covenant theology, and Crell was against any form of ecclesiastical separatism. He opposed the influence both of Jean de Labadie (1610–1674) and of Mastricht's former Duisburg schoolmate, Undereyck, who served a congregation at Mühlheim am Ruhr (1667–1671) and promoted conventicles.[46] In fact, the churches of the entire Lower Rhine area leaned toward the practice of godliness (*praxis der Gottseligkeit*).[47] Mastricht's position toward the Labadists, however, was far less combative than Crell's. When, in 1671, the Labadist movement made inroads in the Reformed congregations of the Lower Rhine area, Pierre Yvon (1646–1707), the emerging leader of the "separating Reformed

---

Jahrhundert, ed. M. Brecht, K. Depperman (Göttingen: Vandenhoeck & Ruprecht, 1995), 2:249. In Bremen he attended the St. Stephani church, whose pastor, Friedrich Adolf Lampe (1709–1720), had served the congregations of Weeze (classis Cleve, 1703–1706) and Duisburg (1706–1709). At Bremen, Gerhardus functioned on a regular basis as diplomat for the city council. Moreover, in 1719 he compiled a catalogue of his massive book collection, *Catalogus Bibliothecæ Gerh. V. Mastricht* (Bremen: Herman Braueri, 1719). Gerhardus's *Historia Juris Ecclesiastici* (Halle: Christopher A. Zeitleri, 1705), which is dedicated to the elector of Brandenburg, is considered his most important work in the field of ecclesiastical jurisprudence. Since 1718 this work has been listed in the pontifical *Index Librorum Prohibitorum*. Gerard and his wife Magdalena had four children, Anna, Magdalena, Gerhardus Jr., and Petrus (1682–1711). Cf. C. Owens Peare, *William Penn: A Biography* (Philadelphia: J. B. Lippincott Co., 1957). Cf. Petrus van Mastricht, the Younger, *Brüderliche Ehren-Pflicht auff die eheliche Verknüpfung des Herrn J. L. Meinertzhagen mit der Jungfrauen Saren Magdalenen von Mastricht.... am 23 Mai/2 Junnij 1693* (Bremen, 1693). (Brotherly duty of honor of the lawful wedding of Mr. J. L. Meinertzhagen with the young lady Sarah Magdalena von Mastricht…on May 23 / June 2, 1693).

43. Christoph F. Crell succeeded the Cartesian Johannus Clauberg (1622–1669).

44. Martinus Hundius was brother-in-law of Johannes Cocceius and served the theological faculty from 1655 to 1666. Cf. Heiner Faulenbach, "Johannes Coccejus," in *Orthodoxie und Pietismus*, ed. Martin Greschat (Stuttgart: W. Kohlhammer, 1982), 168. See also Roden, *Die Universität Duisburg*, 242.

45. H. Schneppen, *Niederländische Universitäten und deutsches Geistesleben von der Gründung der Universität Leiden bis ins späte 18. Jahrhundert* (Münster, 1960), 88.

46. Wallmann, *Der Pietismus*, 26; Schneppen, *Niederländische Universitäten*, 90, 91.

47. H. Heppe, *Geschichte des Pietismus und der Mystik in der Reformirten Kirche* (Leiden: Brill, 1879), 483, 485.

Pietists,"[48] met with Voetius at Utrecht, with the House of Brandenburg at Duisburg, with Undereyck at Mühlheim am Ruhr, and also with Mastricht at Cologne. With Mastricht, Yvon discussed Christian doctrines and his view of the kingdom of God.[49] In addition, the question of church and separation was probably discussed, as Mastricht included an extensive preface, entitled *De membris ecclesiæ visibilis* (The Members of the Visible Church), in his work, published later that year, on the doctrine of faith, *De fide salvifica syntagma theoretico-practicum* (Concerning Saving Faith in Theory and Practice)—the second work of Mastricht's listed on the *Index librorum prohibitorum*.[50] Despite his disagreement with the Labadists, Mastricht discussed the central question—church or separation?—in an irenic way,[51] contrasting the objective character of Reformed doctrine with the subjectivism and separatism of this movement. The exposition of the doctrine of saving faith followed Mastricht's division of biblical exegesis, doctrinal formulation, elenctical consideration, and practical application. In 1673, Mastricht became the rector of the university, while, in the meantime, his publications

48. Andreas Plagge, "YVON, Pierre," *Bautz Biographisch-Bibliographischen Kirchenlexikons*, Band XXII (2003).

49. Saxby, *The Quest for the New Jerusalem*, 175. Cf. H. Faulenbach, "Die Anfänge der Pietismus bei den Reformierten in Deutschland," in *Pietismus und Neuzeit: ein Jahrbuch zur Geschichte des neueren Protestantismus* (Göttingen: Vandenhoeck & Ruprecht, 1979), 4:222; Max Goebel, *Geschichte des Christlichen Lebens in der Rheinisch-westphaelischen evangelischen Kirche* (Koblenz: Bädeker, 1849), 232: "in Köln besprach er [Yvon] sich mit dem dortiger niederländischen Prediger Peter von Mastricht…über die wichtigsten Wahrheiten des Christenthums und Reiches Gottes." (In Cologne he [Yvon] spoke with the Dortiger Dutch preacher Petrus van Mastricht…about the important truths of Christendom and the kingdom of God).

50. Petrus van Mastricht, *De fide salvifica syntagma theoretico-practicum: in quo fidei salvificae tum natura, tum praxis universa, luculenter exponitur; cum praef. de membris Ecclesiae visibilis seu admittendis, seu rejiciendis, oborienti scismati moderno applicanda* (Duisburg: Franc. Sas, 1671). See *Index librorum prohibitorum* (Matriti: Emmanuel Fernandez, 1747), 903.

51. The *Allgemeine Deutsche Biographie* (*ADB*) (München: Leipzig, 1912), 20:580, asserts that Mastricht's book is one of the best works addressing the question of church or separation. "In höchst irenischem Tone behandelt er in demselben die Gründe der damals unter den sogenannten Labadisten entstandenen seperatistischen Bewegung am Niederrhein. Dem Subjectivismis derselben setzt er in geschicktester Weise den Objectivismus der reformierten Kirche in Lehre und Verfassung entgegen, wodurch er jenem Seperatismus vielen Abbruch tat." (In a highly irenic tone he deals with the reasons of the time among the so-called Labadists, a separatist movement in the Lower Rhine, contrasting the objective character of the Reformed doctrine to the subjectivism and separatism of the movement.) Cf. Ring, *Geschichte der Universität Duisburg*, 136. Roden's citation calls for "ironische" instead of "irenischem," and notes, "Gegen Seperatismus und Labadismus nahm er [van Mastricht] Stellung. Er zeigte sich in seinen Schriften als entschiedener und starrer Vertreter des alten System." Cf. Roden, *Die Universität Duisburg*, 165. See also W. Goeters, *Die Vorbereitung des Pietismus* (Leipzig: J. C. Hinrichs'sche Buchhandlung, 1911), 282n2: "Ganz milde ist auch das Urteil des Peter van Mastricht, in seiner Schrift *De fide salvifica*…."

had reached the Netherlands. Although the theological faculty at Franeker nominated him for professor, Herman Witsius (1636–1708) was chosen instead.[52]

In contrast to Mastricht's irenic position toward the Labadists was his fierce opposition to Cartesianism. His attentiveness to Cartesianism commenced at the University of Duisburg with Johannes Clauberg (1622–1665) and Wittich,[53] but increased in the 1670s. For Mastricht, there was sufficient reason to address this new philosophy at the provincial synod of Cleve[54] and to publish the *Novitatum Cartesianarum gangraena, seu theologia Cartesiana detecta* (Gangrene of the Cartesian Novelties, or Cartesian theology uncovered)[55]—his magnum opus of philosophy. With the ideas of Descartes in hand, Wittich attempted to reconcile theology and philosophy. Mastricht, however, asserted that the *primum Cartesianismi fundamentum*, Descartes's principle of "universal doubt," was catastrophic for Reformed theology, undermining the place of philosophy as a handmaiden to theology, and in particular *theoretico-practica* theology, as he argued in the dedication to King William III of Holland and England and the preface of the work.[56] If reason and philosophy become the source of absolute certainty instead of Scripture, Mastricht argued, an author of such writings was *"atheus quidem sed Cartesianus"* (an atheist, certainly, but a Cartesian).

The *Gangraena* became the most influential of all late seventeenth-century academic assaults on Cartesianism.[57] In this context of the academy and church, theology and philosophy, Mastricht continued his work at Duisburg, contributing to a *festschrift* of Hugenpoth[58] and holding disputations regarding *De casu*

---

52. J. van Genderen, *Herman Witsius, bijdrage tot de kennis der Gereformeerde theologie* ('s-Gravenhage: Guido de Bres, 1953), 50. Mastricht is incorrectly listed as "professeur à Franeker" in Charles van Hulthem, *Catalogue raisonné de la précieuse collection de dessins et d'estampes, au nombre de pres` de 30,000, formant le cabinet de M. Ch. van Hulthem* (Paris: A. van der Meersch [1846], 243.

53. According to Feyl, Johannes Clauberg was the first German Cartesian. Cf. Feyl, "Die Viandrina und das östliche Europa," 123. See also, Roden, *Die Universität Duisburg*; H. Schneppen, *Niederländische Universitäten*, 77, 78, 90; Israel, *Radical Enlightenment*, 30, 31, 35. Israel notes that contrary to Frankfurt an der Oder, Cartesianism became dominant at Duisburg as early as 1651.

54. Wolfgang Petri, *Die Reformierten Klevischen Synoden im 17. Jahrhundert*, vol. 3: 1673–1700 (Rheinlag-Verlag: Cologne, 1981), 54.

55. Petrus van Mastricht, *Novitatum Cartesianarum Gangraena, Nobiliores plerasque Corporis Theologici Partes arrodens et exedens, Seu Theologia Cartesiana detecta* (Amsterdam: Jansson, 1677). This work was reprinted in 1678 and 1716. Cf. idem, *Theologia Cartesiana detecta, seu gangraena Cartesiana: nobiliores plerasque corporis theologici partes arrodens et exedens* (Deventer: Daniel Schutten, 1716).

56. Mastricht, *Novitatum Cartesianarum Gangraena*, dedicatio, praefatio.

57. Israel, *Radical Enlightenment*, 215.

58. Petrus van Mastricht, *Vita viatoris quasi transitus, omnia finem*, in Johann Hermann Hugenpoth, *Lachrymae Academiae Duisburgensis* (Duisburg: Franconis Sas, 1676).

conscientiae (Concerning the Case of Conscience) and the doctrine of God.[59] The theological disputations, such as *De existentia et cognitione dei* (Concerning the Existence and Knowledge of God), also adhered to the fourfold division: exegesis, doctrine, elenctics, and practice.[60]

Despite Mastricht's appointment as the preacher of the university, his convening of weekly services for the students, and major publications in theology and philosophy, the year 1677 became another turning point in Mastricht's life. On the one hand, the Synod of Duisburg of the Reformed church desired more oversight of the theology professors at the university, but this fell under the jurisdiction of the House of Brandenburg.[61] On the other hand, Mastricht's preaching became a point of contention when the Synod of June 1677 complained about a Pentecost sermon held at the famous St. Salvador Church. The professor and university preacher thereby defied the rule of the synod that a professor was not permitted to preach in regular church services. In addition, he also deviated in the sermon on John 16:8–11, unconventionally noting that the prince of this world is Christ.[62] Mastricht refused to discuss the matter with the delegates of the synod, asserting that he was accountable to the elector and not to the ecclesiastical authorities. The whole issue became moot, however, when Mastricht accepted a call later that month from his alma mater to succeed none other than Voetius.[63]

---

59. Petrus van Mastricht, *Diatribe Theologica…De Casu Conscientiae: An Viduus Uxoris Novercam, Salva Conscientia, Ducere posit?: An saltem non sit dispensabile, tale Matrimonium? Immo &, si partibus de eo convenerit, per Magistratum dispensandum?* Pars 1 et 2, Johannes Adolphus Eylerdt (Duisburg: Franconis Sas, 1676); idem, *Theologiae Theoretico-Practicae Disputatio Quinta, De Existentia Et Cognitione Dei,* Wilhelmus Mercamp (Duisburg: Franconis Sas, 1677).

60. The discussion of a topic on the doctrine of God by Mastricht was not unique in his time. His colleague at Duisburg, Johann Hermann Hugenpoth, wrote *Dissertatio Theologica Continens Aliquot Positiones De Actione Dei Circa Indurationem Cordis Human,* resp. Joannes Theodor Helmius (Duisburg: Franconis Sas, 1670). His later colleague, Frans Burman at Utrecht held a disputation on the divine omnipresence in the spring of 1676.

61. Goebel, *Geschichte des Christlichen,* 111: "[I]n 1677 ließ die general Synod den sonst sehr recht gläubigen, und berühmten Prof. Petrus van Mastricht, wegen seiner 'fremden und ärgerlichen Auslegung von Joh. 16, 8–11,' wonach Christus selber 'der gerichete Fürst der Welt' sein sollte, zur Rede stellen; Mastricht empfing die Depurtirten aber gar nicht als solche, 'weil die Synod ihm nichts verzuschreiben haben.'"

62. Petri, *Die Reformierten Klevischen,* 55. (In 1677, the general synod weighed in on the otherwise very faithful and famous professor Petrus van Mastricht, because of his "strange and malicious exposition of John 16:8–11," where "Christ was presented as the Prince of the World." Mastricht did not receive the deputies, because, "the synod could not write him anything.")

63. Ring, *Geschichte der Universität Duisburg,* 137. Mastricht, *Theoretico-practica theologia,* 1059: "Gisbertus Voetius…cui ego successi in professione." Mastricht held the same position in Duisburg that Voetius held in Utrecht, namely, professor of theology and Hebrew.

The Dutch Period: 1677–1706

Utrecht (1677–1682)

The first generation of the teachers of Utrecht's academy had passed away—Mastricht's teacher, Voetius, in November 1676—and, prompted by Essenius's death in May 1677, the faculty recommended "professor Maestricht of Duisburg" to the city council (*vroedschap*). Mastricht accepted the offer of one thousand guilders per annum in June, and was furnished by the States General (*Staten Generaal*) with a passport to travel with his furniture and books to Utrecht. On September 7, Mastricht delivered an inaugural oration, *De academicae ultrajectinae voto symbolico: sol justitae illustra nos* (Concerning the Motto of the Utrecht Academy: Sun of Righteousness Shine upon Us),[64] and, as Utrecht's only professor at the time, served as professor of practical theology.[65]

Immediately upon arrival, Mastricht continued the work on the doctrine of God that he had begun at Duisburg. His student, Theodorus Groen, defended the disputation *De omnisufficientia Dei*,[66] and Baldiunus Drywegen and Jacobus de Clyver, both from Zeeland, defended the disputation *De essentia, nominibus et attributis Dei in genere* (On the essence, names, and attributes of God in general), a theme that Mastricht worked on until the spring of 1678.[67] That same year, the faculty was expanded with the appointment of Melchior Leydecker (1642–1721), and the consistory of the Reformed church at Utrecht added Mastricht to its number as an elder approved to preach.[68] In the years following, Mastricht held various disputations on the assurance of salvation, the nature of theology, and

---

64. Kernkamp, *Acta et Decrata Senatus* (Utrecht: Kemink, 1938–40) 2:31, "Clarriss. Vir D. Petrus van Mastricht, theol. Profess. in Curiam civitatis vocatus atque inde per amplisse viros consulares Booth et Nellesteyn primum in conclave academicum ac porro in cathedram deductus, orationen inauguralem recitavit 'de sole justitiae.' Hinc iterum in conclave ac deinceps a Collegis professoribus donum reductus et salutationibus ac gratulationibis singulorum exceptus est honorifice." The "*sol justitae illustra nos*" in the title of Mastricht's inaugural adress refers to the logo of the Univeristy of Utrecht. Cf. Roelof van den Broek, *Hy leeret ende beschuttet: over het wapen en de zinspreuk van de Universiteit Utrecht* (Diesrede Utrecht, 1995).

65. Pontanus, *Laudatio Funebris*, 20, "Unicus est inter Reformatos Doctores, quos novi qui nomine et titulo Professoris Theologiæ Practicæ est insignitus."

66. Petrus van Mastricht, *De omnisufficientia Dei*, pars prior Theologiæ theoretico-practicæ disputatio sexta Theodorus Groen (Utrecht: Meinardi à Dreunen, 1677).

67. Petrus van Mastricht, *Theologiae theoretico-practicae disputatio septima de essentia, nominibus et atrributis Dei in genere*, Pars 2, Balduinus Drywegen (Utrecht: Meinardi a Dreunen, 1677); idem, *Theologiae theoretico-practicae disputatio septima de essentia, nominibus et attributis Dei in genere*, Pars 3, Jacobus de Clyver (Utrecht: Meinardi a Dreunen, 1677); idem, *Theologiae theoretico-practicae disputatio septima de essentia, nominibus et attributis Dei in genere*, Pars 4, Isaacus Ravensbergius (Utrecht: Meinardi a Dreunen, 1678).

68. Mastricht, *Theoretico-practica theologia*, 1225, "auditores palam profiterentur, se tantundem saltem utilitatis, percipere ex istis repetitionibus, ac ex ipsis concionibus."

Roman Catholic teachings[69]—some that were attended by (foreign) students from other schools as well as ministers. Illustrative is the defense by the Scotsman, James Hog, of a disputation about the assurance of salvation on March 20, 1680,[70] in the presence of other Scottish students studying at Leiden, Thomas Hog, Jacob Kirton, Donald Cargill, and John Dickson as well as the ministers Jacobus Borstius (1612–1680) of Rotterdam and Jacobus Koelman (1632–1695).[71] While Mastricht continued his teaching in systematic theology, moral theology, and church history,[72] Herman Witsius of the University of Franeker succeeded Franz Burman (†November 12, 1679) in 1680. Meanwhile, Mastricht continued his anti-Cartesianism, opposing Petrus Allinga (†1692) in a pamphlet pseudonymously published as Cephas Scheunenus (Petrus Schoning)—his former family name.[73]

In addition to his academic work, Mastricht served in various administrative capacities at the university from 1681 onward, including as *rector magnificus*. A

---

69. Petrus van Mastricht, *Disputationum practicarum prima de certitudine salutis ejusque natura*, Johannes Kamerling (Utrecht: Meinardi a Dreunen, 1678); idem, *Disputationum practicarum tertia de certitudine salutis, eique opposita praesumptione seu securitate carnali*, pars prima, David de Volder (Utrecht: Meinardi a Dreunen, 1679); idem, *Disputationum practicarum tertia, de certitudine salutis, eique opposita praesumptione seu securitate carnali*, pars secunda, Jacobus Hoog (Utrecht: Meinardi a Dreunen, 1680). Petrus van Mastricht, *Theologiae theoretico-practicae, sub prelo sudantis, specimen de natura theologiae primum*, Petrus Dix (Utrecht: Meinardi a Dreunen, 1680); idem, *Theologiae theoretico-practicae specimen, de natura theologiae secundum*, Hugo Fittz (Utrecht : Meinardi a Dreunen, 1680); idem, *Theologiae theoretico-practicae specimen de natura theologiae tertium*, Johannes Best (Utrecht: Meinardi a Dreunen, 1680); idem, *Theologiae theoretico-practicae specimen de natura theologiae quartum*, Johannes Kelfkens (Utrecht: Meinardi a Dreunen, 1680). The defense of Fittz and Best was also attended by Guiljelmus Saldenus (1617–1694). Petrus van Mastricht, *Ad illust. episcopi Condomensis expositionem doctrinae, quam vocat, Catholicae*, diatribe prima de consilio auctoris, Rutgerus van Bemmel (Utrecht: Meinardi a Dreunen, 1680); idem, *Ad illust. episcopi Condomensis expositionem doctrinae quam vocat Catholicae*, diatribe tertia *de adoratione creaturarum*, Petrus Westwoude (Utrecht: Meinardi a Dreunen, 1680); idem, *Ad illustr. episcopi Condomensis expositionem doctrinae quam vocat Catholicae*, diatribe quinta *de invocatione sanctorum*, Petrus Lastdrager (Utrecht: Meinardi a Dreunen, 1680); idem, *Ad illustr. episcopi Condomensis expositionem doctrinae quam vocat Catholicae*, diatribe septima *de cultu imaginum et reliquiarum*, Johannes Rodenborgh (Utrecht: Meinardi a Dreunen, 1680).

70. Petrus van Mastricht, *Disputationum practicarum tertia, de certitudine salutis, eique opposita praesumptione seu securitate carnali*, pars secunda, Jacobus Hoog (Utrecht: Meinardi a Dreunen, 1680). James Hog is listed in the student records of the Utrecht Academy as Jacobus Hoog.

71. Mastricht, *Disputationum practicarum tertia, de certitudine salutis, eique opposita praesumptione seu securitate carnali*, title page.

72. Genderen notes that each of the professors, Mastricht, Leydekker, and Witsius, understood the whole of theology as their field of work. Cf. Genderen, *Herman Witsius*, 79.

73. Cephas Scheunenus, *Cartesianismi Gangræna insanabilis. Duodecim erotematum illustrium decadibus, frustra curata per P. Allingham, pastorem...enneade erotematum vulgarium, demonstrata a C. Scheuneno* (Utrecht: Meinardi à Dreunen, 1680).

day after his installation as rector, he welcomed Prince Ludwig of Brandenburg on behalf of the city of Utrecht.[74] The Brandenburg connection, cemented at Frankfurt an der Oder and Duisburg, continued. More importantly, however, was the publication of the first four books of the *TPT* (1682)—a work that had begun at Glückstadt and continued with several disputations held at Duisburg and Utrecht. The work was introduced with a disputation on homiletics, *De optima concionandi methodo paraleipomena*,[75] a slightly modified version of the *Methodus concionandi*. Mastricht argued that the *TPT* was to be used in the preparation of preaching.[76] Well-timed or not, Mastricht's work of theology was dedicated to Prince Ludwig's father, Frederick Wilhelm. In the year of his rectorate, he held disputations on the covenant of grace,[77] dealt with ecclesiastical matters regarding the value of the *colloquia* and *testimonia* of the students at the Utrecht academy,[78] and conferred a doctorate *honoris causa* on Franciscus Ridderus (1620–1683) and Guiljelmus Saldenus (1627–1694).[79]

1683–1687

The years 1683–1687 opened another window for the international world of Utrecht's university. The Hebraist Johannes van Leusden (1624–1699) published a definitive edition of the *Synopsis criticorum* by the Englishman and Scripture commentator, Matthew Poole (1622–1679)—a work commended by Mastricht in *De optima concionandi methodo*—while Van Leusden's correspondence with Increase Mather (1639–1723) concerning the Native American language as a form of Hebrew resulted in a gift from Harvard College to the Utrecht academy of the *Biblia Americana* by John Eliot (c. 1604–1690), the missionary to the Native Americans.[80] Furthermore, New England's theology was not unknown at

---

74. Kernkamp, *Acta et Decreta Senatus*, 3:65.

75. Petrus van Mastricht, *De optima concionandi methodo paraleipomena: in usum theologiae theretico-practicae*, Henricus Wagardus (Utrecht: Meinardi a Dreunen, 1681).

76. Petrus van Mastricht, *Theoretico-practica theologia: qua, per capita theologica, pars dogmatica, elenchtica et practica, perpetua sumbibasei conjugantur; praecedunt in usum operis, paraleipomena, seu sceleton de optima concionandi methodo* (Amsterdam: Henrici et Viduae Theodori Boom, 1682), ***.

77. Petrus van Mastricht, *De Foedere Gratiæ*, pars prima, ex theologiæ theoretico-practicæ libro quinto caput primum Hemmo Hovius (Utrecht: M. à Dreunen, 1682); idem, *De mediatore foederis gratiæ*, pars tertia, ex theologiæ theoretico-practicæ libro quinto, caput secundum, Theodorus van Breen (Utrecht: M. à Dreunen, 1682).

78. Kernkamp, *Acta et Decreta Senatus*, 2:69.

79. Kernkamp, *Acta et Decreta Senatus*, 2:70: "Convocato Senatui…proposuit Rector… D. Francisco Riddero…D. Guilielmo Saldeno…."

80. *Bibliothecam celeberrimae apud Utrajectionos Acedemiae hac sacrorum Bibliorum versione Indica donat Crescentius Matherus, Collegii Harvardini apud Cantabrigienses in Nova Anglia Praeses pro tempore*. Eliot's translation of the Bible resulted in the publication of the Mamusse

Utrecht, as Mastricht wrote an approbation of Thomas Shepard's (1605–1649) *De Gezonde Geloovige* (*The Sound Believer*) in 1685.[81] The writing of approbations by Mastricht with the faculty at Utrecht was not uncommon, as is noted, for example, in 1684 for Saldenus's *Otia theologica* (Theological Leisure).

Students from abroad traveled to Utrecht and heard Mastricht there, such as the later pietistic court preacher Conrad Bröske (1660–1713) in 1685, and in 1686, Colonel John Erskine, the grandfather of John Erskine D.D., Jonathan Edwards's primary correspondent in Scotland. Colonel Erskine studied law at the Utrecht Academy in 1686–1687, but also attended theology lectures by Mastricht and visited him several times with fellow Scottish students. He notes, for example, in his diary on June 7, 1686, "I was a while with Professor van Mastricht: he was very kind and I do take him to have true religion."[82]

Finally, Mastricht continued his disputations on spiritual desertions,[83] a theme he had explored since at least 1680 as a continuation of the thought of *De geestelijke verlating* (*Spiritual Desertion*)[84] of his teachers—and worked on his magnum opus of theology. The second volume was published in 1687, dedicated this time to the Electorate of Hesse.

Wunneetupanatamwe Up-Biblum God, aka: Algonquian Bible. As such it is mentioned in the minutes of the meeting at the Faculty at Utrecht as the "Biblia Americana."

81. Thomas Shepard, *De Gezonde Geloovige* (Amsterdam: Joannes Boekholt, 1686). Other works of New England ministers that were translated into Dutch, for example, are Thomas Hooker, *De ware zielsvernedering en heilzame wanhoop*, trans. J. Koelman (Amsterdam: J. Wasteliers, 1678); Thomas Hooker, *De arme twijfelende Christen, genadert tot Christus*, trans. Jacobus Koelman (Amsterdam: J. Wasteliers, undated), and Solomon Stoddard, *Een leidsman tot Christus* (Leiden: Buurman & De Kler, [c. 1680]).

82. W. Macleod, ed., *Journal of the Hon. John Erskine of Carnock* (Edinburgh: University Press for the Scottish Historical Society, 1893), 192; cf. 184 (April 6, 1686): "I was seeing Professor Van Mastricht, with Mr. Melvel and Pardiven. He gave a large testimony of the church of Scotland, particularly on church discipline, affirming it to be the purest that has been since the apostles' days"; see also 219 (January 4, 1687): "I was seeing Professor Van Mastricht who was most civil and kind to me, and useful company."

83. Petrus van Mastricht, *Disputationum practicarum de desertione spirituali*, prima, eruditorum crisi subjicit Henricus Nahuys (Ultrajecti: ex officina Meinardi a Dreunen, 1680); idem, *Disputationum practicarum de desertione spirituali*, secunda, eruditorum crisi subjicit Daniel Bongart (Utrecht: Meinardi à Dreunen, 1680); idem, *Disputationum practicarum de desertione spirituali*, tertia, publice tueri conabitur Daniel le Roy (Utrecht: Meinardi à Dreunen, 1683); idem, *Disputationum practicarum de desertione spirituali*, quarta, publice tueri conabitur Samuel Kaposi (Utrecht: Meinardi à Dreunen, 1683).

84. Gisbertus Voetius and Johannes Hoornbeeck, *Spiritual Desertion*, trans. John Vriend and Henry Boonstra, ed. M. Eugene Osterhaven (Grand Rapids: Reformation Heritage Books, 2012).

1688–1699

Following the publication of volume two of the *TPT* (1687), Mastricht's disputations focused on the doctrines of transubstantiation, the unforgiveable sin, the Son as Sponsor for those who belonged to him in the eternal pact, election, and the obedience of faith.[85] The latter was foundational, according to the German Lutheran theologian Johann Friedrich Mayer (1650–1712), for Mastricht's moral theology.[86] In the midst of his academic teaching, writing, and ecclesiastical consulting, Mastricht moved in 1689 to a house on the Oudegracht—within walking distance from the Dom church and the university. His brother Gerhardus moved the same year to the Hanseatic city of Bremen to become legal advisor and diplomatic representative of the city council (*syndikus*). There he most likely attended the conventicles that were organized by Peter van Mastricht's former classmate, Undereyck. When the latter published his major work, *Der närrische atheist* (1689), it received commendations from the Cocceians on the faculties of Duisburg and Marburg, and from Johannes van der Waeyen (1639–1701) at Franeker University. The work was translated into Dutch, requiring an approbation by "those who know High German language." It was Peter van Mastricht who wrote a preface in *De dwaase atheist, ontdekt en van sijn dwaasheyd overtuygd* (1690; The Foolish Atheist Discovered and Persuaded of His Foolishness) written by Theodorus Undereyck, the Bremen pastor and important catechist of Cocceius's federal theology.[87]

Mastricht's expertise in Cartesian philosophy was called upon by the Amsterdam classis of the Reformed Church in connection with the minister and philosopher-theologian Balthasar Bekker (1634–1698), who questioned

---

85. Petrus van Mastricht, *Diatribe Theologica, De Peccato simpliciter irremissibili*, resp. Mauritius Seelig (Utrecht: F. Halma, 1688); idem, *De transubstantiatione*, resp. Joannes Wilhelmus Walschardt (Utrecht: Francisci Halma, 1688); idem, *Diatribe theologica, De aeterna Christi sponsione*, resp. Arnoldus de Blankendael (Utrecht: Francisci Halma, 1690); idem, *Diatribes Theologica, De Usuris*, pars prior, resp. Jacobus Schuarz (Utrecht: Francisci Halma, 1690); idem, *Diatribes Theologica, De Usuris*, pars posterior, resp. Jacobus Schuarz (Utrecht: Francisci Halma, 1690); idem, *Disputatio theologica, De Electione ad salutem*, resp. Joannes von Ham (Utrecht: Francisci Halma 1691); idem, *Disputatio theologica, De obedientia fidei*, par. 1, 2, J. Witzonius (Utrecht: Francisci Halma, 1691); idem, *Disputatio theologica, De obedientia fidei*, par. 3, J. A. Breen (Utrecht: Francisci Halma, 1691).

86. Aegidi Strauchi, Johann Friedrich Mayer, *Theologia Moralis* (Leipzig: Joh. W. Fickweillerum, 1708), 335, "Anno 1691 scribere coepit *Theologiam Moralem* cujus summam in dissertatione *de Obedientia Fidei….*"

87. Theodorus Undereyck, *Der Närrische Atheist/ Entdeckt und seiner Thorheit überzeuget/ In Zwey Theilen In dem Ersten/ Als ein solcher/ der da wissentlich willens und vorsetzlich/ ihme selbst und anderen/ die Gedancken/ welche sie von Gott haben/ nehmen wil. In dem Zweyten/ Als ein solcher/ der da unwissend und ungemerckt/ auch unter dem Schein des wahren Christenthums/ ohne GOtt in der Welt lebet* (Bremen: Herman Brauer 1689); Theodorus Ondereyk, *De dwaase atheist: ontdekt en van sijn dwaasheyd overtuygd en nu om sijn voortreffelijkheyd*, trans. Jodocus Fridericus Rappardus (Amsterdam: Jan Groenwoud, 1702).

the existence of Satan, spirits, magic, and witchcraft in *De Betoverde Weereld* (1691) (The World Bewitched),[88] with Cartesian philosophical observations and scriptural objections. Mastricht supplied the Amsterdam classis with his *Contra Beckerum* (1692), in which he asserted that Bekker was placing philosophy above Scripture and that theology was being surrendered to the axiom "philosophy is the infallible interpreter of Scripture."[89] Shortly after that, Bekker was deposed from the ministry.

Those who visited Mastricht, such as students from Scotland or travelers from Germany, were honored to have him write on occasion in their *album ami-corum*, in which Mastricht, for example, quoted from a sermon of Bernard's on the Song of Solomon:

> There are those who seek knowledge for the sole purpose of knowing:
> and that is shameful curiosity.

> There are those who seek knowledge in order to sell their knowledge:
> and that is shameful profit.

> And there are those who seek knowledge in order to be known:
> and that is shameful vanity.

> But there are also those who seek knowledge in order to edify:
> and that is charity.

> And there are those who seek knowledge in order to be edified:
> and that is prudence.[90]

---

88. Baltasar Bekker, *Naakte uitbeeldinge van alle de vier boeken der Betoverde weereld, verton-ende het oogmerk van den schryver tot wechneeminge van vooroordeelen en een kort begryp des ganschen werx* (Amsterdam: Daniel van den Dalen, 1693). Bekker argued in four volumes his Cartesian philosophical and scriptural objections to ideas such as magic, Satan, spirits, and witchcraft. The book was immediately translated into English, German, and French.

89. Petrus van Mastricht, *Ad virum clariss. Balthasarem Bekkerum epanorthosis gratulato-ria occasione articulorum*, quos venerandae Classi Amstelodamensi exhibuit, die 22 Janu. 1692 (Utrecht: Anthonium Schouten, 1692), 25, "qui Religionem Reformatam profitentur, cum *Philoso-phiam infallibilem Scripturarum interpretem* proclamarent."

90. Handschriftenabteilung der Zentralbibliothek Zürich, MSS Hans Konrad Ott-Usteri, "Bernh[ard] in Cant[icum] Homil[iam], xxxvi:

> Sunt qui scire volunt eo fine tantum ut sciant:
> et turpis curiositas est.
> sunt qui scire volunt, ut scientiam suam vendant:
> et turpis quaestus est.
> et sunt qui scire volunt ut sciantur ipsi:
> et turpis vanitas est.
> Sed sunt quoque, qui scire volunt ut aedificent:
> et Charitas est.
> et sunt qui scire volunt ut aedificentur:
> et prudentia est.

In the years that followed, Mastricht's number of disputations decreased significantly, with the exception of his work on Isaiah 53. The main reason for this was his continuing labor on the *Theologia Moralis* and *Theologia Ascetica*, which accompanied the final edition of the *TPT*, published in 1698.[91] This major milestone was a revised edition of the volumes published from 1682 to 1687, which includes the supplements on moral and ascetic theology.[92] This time, the publication was not dedicated to the House of Brandenburg but to the city council of Utrecht, the *Ed. Achtbare Heeren Borgermeesteren en Vroedschap deser Stad* (Honorable Mayors and Council of This City),[93] with an epigram of his brother, Gerhardus, praising the conjoining of the *scientia praxi*. Mastricht's magnum opus of theology, which he had begun thirty years earlier in Glückstadt, was finished—Simon Oomius's wish of 1672 was fulfilled,[94] and the work was immediately reprinted in 1699. The *TPT* is notably lacking in autobiographical material, with few references to earlier works, such as the *Prodromus* and *De fide salvifica*, the exception being the *Novitatum Cartesianarum gangraena*.

1700–1706

The early years of the eighteenth century brought changes to the faculty of Utrecht, known for its Reformed orthodoxy. Mastricht's colleague, Herman Witsius, had left for the University of Leiden and was succeeded by the German

---

91. Petrus van Mastricht, *Theoretico-practica theologia: qua, per singula capita theologica, pars exegetica, elenchtica et practica, perpetua successione conjugantur; accedunt historia ecclesiastica, plena quidem, sed compendiosa, idea theologiae moralis, hypotyposis theologiae asceticae etc. proin opus quasi novum* (Utrecht: Gerardum Muntendam, 1698); idem, *Theoretico-practica theologia: qua, per singula capita theologica, pars exegetica, elenchtica et practica, perpetua successione conjugantur; accedunt historia ecclesiastica, plena quidem, sed compendiosa, idea theologiae moralis, hypotyposis theologiae asceticae etc. proin opus quasi novum* (Utrecht: Thomae Appels, 1699). The edition of 1698 is now a rare printing; the 1698 and 1699 editions are identical, including the repeated pagination of 325–424. Cf. Mastricht, *Theoretico-practica theologia, præfatio,* "In *moralibus* pariter & *Asceticis,* explicatior esse debuissem."

92. Books I–IV and V–VIII were published respectively in 1682 and 1687. Mastricht, *Theoretico-practica theologia: qua, per capita theologica, pars dogmatica, elenchtica et practica, perpetua sumbibasei conjugantur; praecedunt in usum operis, paraleipomena, seu sceleton de optima concionandi methodo* (Amsterdam: Henrici et Viduae Theodori Boom, 1682, 1687). The chapters *De Foedere Gratiæ* and *De Mediatore Foederis gratiæ* were modified between 1682 and 1698.

93. Kernkamp refers to the *vroedschap* minutes of March 7, 1698. Kernkamp, *Acta et Decreta Senatus,* 2:160: "De vroedschap heeft de Heer Petrus Mastricht, SS Theol. Professor, vereerd met de somme van drie honderd vijftien gulden voor de dedicatie van zijn boek, geïntituleerd: Theologia Theoretico-practica."

94. Cf. footnote 23 above. Oomius's own magnum opus, however, *Institutiones Theologiæ Practicæ,* remained unfinished. Cf. Gregory Schuringa, "Embracing Leer and Leven: The Theology of Simon Oomius in the Context of Nadere Reformatie Orthodoxy" (PhD diss., Calvin Theological Seminary, 2003), 13.

Reformer, Henricus Pontanus (1652–1714). Mastricht was limited to teaching from home, due to physical weakness, but continued to hold public lectures on Monday and Tuesday afternoons.[95] The controversial appointment of a Cartesian professor of theology, Herman A. Röell (1653–1718),[96] led the city council to request Mastricht to live in "peace and friendship," for they knew of his anti-Cartesian views and did not want open conflict to prevail.

After a prolific life of teaching, writing, and preaching, Mastricht died on February 9, 1706, due to a wound on his crippled foot caused by a fall from a kitchen step.[97] The funeral oration was given by Henricus Pontanus and was attended by Mastricht's fellow professors and ministers and the Utrecht magistrate. His brother Gerhardus, with his son Petrus—who studied at the University of Frankfurt an der Oder—were also present.[98] Pontanus described the deceased professor as weak in health, while serving the academy and church with all his strength, underscoring Mastricht's maxim taken from 2 Corinthians 12:10, ὅταν γὰρ ἀσθενῶ τότε δυνατός εἰμι (for "when I am weak, then I am strong").

Mastricht was buried on February 24 in the Catherine church, the resting place of his teacher Gisbertus Voetius, his colleague and friend Gerhardus de Vries, and his acquaintance Jacobus Koelman.[99] Oomius noted that not many ministers were, like he and Mastricht, given a long life.[100]

---

95. From November 11, 1700, onwards, Mastricht held public lectures twice a week. Cf. Kernkamp, *Acta et Decreta Senatus*, 2:176.

96. Jacob van Sluis, *Herman Alexander Röell*, (Leeuwarden: Fryske Akademy, 1988); idem, "De Cartesiaanse Theologie van Herman Alexander Röell," in *Vier eeuwen Theologie in Utrecht*, 141–50; Cramer, *De Theologische Faculteit*, 18*; cf. Kernkamp, *Acta et Decreta Senatus*, 2:199.

97. Pontanus, *Laudatio Funebris*, 21.

98. Kernkamp, *Acta et Decreta Senatus*, 2:207, notes that the vroedschap places on March 15 and 22, 1707 a "verbod aan de boekverkoper van de Water om de lijkrede van Prof. Pontanus op Mastricht te verkopen of te verspreiden, omdat deze is opgedragen aan Gerard van Mastricht, syndicus in Bremen, wien de titels worden gegeven, die alleen aan H.ed.Achtb. toekomen, de reeds verspreide exemplaren moeten worden opgehaald. Pontanus, die in goede trouw heeft gehandeld, heeft exuses aangeboden" (the publisher [bookseller] van de Water is forbidden to sell or distribute the funeral oration of Mastricht by Prof. Pontanus, because this was dedicated to Gerard van Mastricht, syndicus at Bremen, who was given its title, which belonged to the honorable, and the distributed copies must be picked up. Pontanus, who dealt in truth, did offer his apology).

99. Mastricht is registered on March 1, 1706, in the list of deceased persons. Tellingen, *Het leven en enige aspecten*, 33: "Aenbracht den 1 Maert 1706 d'Heer Professor Petrus van Mastri[ch]t, bejaerd Heer...." Cf. Pontanus, *Laudatio Funebris*, 5.

100. S. Oomius, *Cierlijke Kroon des Grysen Ouderdoms* (Leiden: Daniel van den Dalen, 1707), 336: "Op den eersten Maart [1706] nu aanstaande, sal ik treden, soo het den Hemel behaagt, uit mijn leven seven en seventigste jaar; van deese hebb' ik op den Predik-Stoel mijne Stemme doen hooren. In den Kerkelyken dienst nu in de vier en vyftig jaren, een weldaae seeker, welke de Heere aan weinige bewijst. Hij heeft met deselve begunsigt dese Vermaarde Mannen, Petrus van Mastrigt (die agt maanden en vier dagen jonger was doe hy onlangs stierf als ik), Witsius, Joh.

Mastricht, being unmarried, left in his oleographic will a considerable estate for the study of Reformed theology by students at Utrecht, which served its purpose for nearly 250 years, stating: "Genegeegen en sich obligeerende particulierlijk tot het studeeren in de practycale Godsgeleerdtheit en dies te bequamer te worden Godt in sijn kerke dienst te doen." (Inclined and obliged in particular to the study of practical theology to become competent to serve God in his church.)[101] It took the university and city council of Utrecht nine years to fill the vacancy left by Mastricht.[102]

Mastricht's Theology

Theology in the Service of Preaching

Mastricht's articulation of theology was a homiletical, theological, and philosophical endeavor of three decades that culminated in the *TPT*. Treatises written at Glückstadt and Frankfurt an der Oder, as well as disputations held at the universities of Duisburg and Utrecht, contributed to the formation of Mastricht's definitive thought on theology. His works of philosophy, moreover, not only showed continuity with the pedagogical tradition of Aristotelian philosophy, but also offered a philosophical-theological response to the new philosophy, identifying Cartesianism as neither adiaphora nor advanced Reformed orthodoxy.

The formation of Mastricht's theological thought commenced in Utrecht — the summit of theoretical-practical Reformed orthodoxy and Protestant scholasticism — with an unwavering approval of the authority of Scripture as the norm for human reason. The latter continued in Mastricht's philosophical treatise *Vindiciæ veritatis et authoritatis sacræ scripturæ* (1655),[103] which resonated later

---

Vollenhovius...." (On the coming first of March, I will leave, if it pleases heaven, my seven and seventieth year; from this pulpit, my voice was heard. In the service of the church, now fifty-four years, a privilege certainly, which the Lord has given a few. The same he has granted to the famous men, Petrus van Mastricht [who was eight years and four days younger than me, when he recently died], Witsius, Joh. Vollenhovius...).

101. M. J. A. de Vrijer, *Ds. Bernardus Smytegelt en zijn "Gekrookte Riet"* (Vianen: De Banier, 1968), 9, 10. Van der Zee, *Vaderlandse Kerkgeschiedenis van de Hervormede Kerk*, 3:142, also mentions 24,000 guilders. An average month's wages was thirty Dutch guilders in 1700. Isaac le Long, *Hondert-Jaarige Jubel-Gedachtenisse der Academie van Utrecht* (Utrecht: M. Visch, 1736), xii. The following works mention 20,000 guilders: *Biographisch Lexicon voor de geschiedenis von het Nederlands Protestantisme* (Kampen, 2001), 5:362; Kernkamp, De Utrechtsche Universiteit, 1:175. Cf. Vrijer, *Ds. Bernardus Smytegelt en zijn "Gekrookte Riet,"* 10. In the 1920's students received bursaries. Cf. Van der Linde, "Mastricht, Petrus van," in *Christelijke Encyclopaedie*, 4:250: "waaruit nog steeds studenten in de theologie te Utrecht een welcome ondersteuning in hun studie intvangen."

102. Pontanus, *Laudatio Funebris*. On the succession of Mastricht, see Tellingen, *Het leven en enige aspecten*, 36.

103. Cf. Aza Goudriaan, *Reformed Orthodoxy and Philosophy, 1625–1750. Gisbertus Voetius, Petrus van Mastricht, and Anthonius Driessen* (Leiden: Brill, 2006).

in Mastricht's thought on the doctrine of Scripture as found in the prolegomena of the *TPT* (1682, 1699)[104] just as the various disputations of Duisburg and Utrecht became part of the *TPT*. Furthermore, Mastricht's writing about the creation of man (*De creatione hominis*) in the *Prodromus* (1666) was largely used in his discussion about the divine works,[105] while the chapters of the *Prodromus* on the obedience and exercise of faith resonated strongly in his theology of ethics (*Idea theologicæ moralis*, 1699) and ascetics (*Hypotyposis theologiæ asceticæ*, 1699). In other words, Mastricht's theological project comprehensively consists of systematic, moral, and ascetical theology.

The ultimate aim of Mastricht's lifelong development of systematic theology, however, is most clearly articulated in the disputation *De optima concionandi methodo* (*The Best Method of Preaching*), which was intended as a guide for using Mastricht's magnum opus on theology. Mastricht notes in the preface that he writes "so that you may have the usefulness of our work in your sermon [preparation]." This perspective—placing theology into the service of preaching—is important for Mastricht, and he outlines this approach more fully in the preface of the final edition (1699). First, the text of Scripture and its exegesis are foundational for the formulation of doctrine, so that the students of theology, "our Nazarites, are familiar with the fundamental parts of Theology."[106] Secondly, the elenctic part provides exposition of controversies related to the doctrine, arranged in the form of *quæstiones*, so that the "middle position" of orthodoxy can be discerned.[107] However, related to its use for preaching, Mastricht counsels that controversies should not be sought out unnecessarily, but only for equipping the hearers when there is an imminent doctrinal danger to the churches.[108] Lastly, Mastricht points out that the concise sections of practical observations are supported with testimonies

---

104. Mastricht, *Theoretico-practica theologia* (1682), I.2, *De Scriptura*.

105. Mastricht, *Theoretico-practica theologia* (1682), III.9, *De Homine et Imagine Dei*.

106. Mastricht, *Theoretico-practica theologia*, præfatio, "Etenim in *exegeticis*, Scripturae textus, capitibus Theologiae, pro fundamento substructi, ad compendium spacii, priori editioni, non paulò aridius praefixi; hîc non nihil explicatius, ex philologiâ, praemissi comparent, ad hoc ut Naziraei nostri, superstruendis capitibus Theologicis, Scripturae fundamentis adsuescerent."

107. Mastricht, *Theoretico-practica theologia*, præfatio, "In *Elenchticis*, omnes controversias, ad quaestiones redegimus, ut singularum historiam commodius tangeremus, eorum πρῶτον Ψεῦδος, sententiarum divortia, & medium orthodoxiae locum, inter declinantes ab utrâque parte, sententias heterodoxas, facilius assequeretur lector, & ab hoc utriusque exorbitantis extremitatis difficultatibus, facilius ac solidius occurreret."

108. Mastricht, *De Optima Concionandi Methodo*, [10], "Controversiae citra necessitatem, cum dispendio temporis, non *quaeruntor*. Nec tamen è contrario, ubi Ecclesiae ab illis imminet periculum, adeoque auditores armandi sunt, *negliguntor*." Cf. Mastricht, *The Best Method of Preaching*, 52.

from the Scriptures.[109] Thus, the praxis of theology is bound to Scripture. Mastricht advises preachers, then, to observe and comprehend the content of the text of Scripture, and to use the *TPT* for their homiletic exposition.[110]

Distribution of Theology

Mastricht's overall arrangement and divisions of theology consist in faith and obedience—following a similar division as proposed in the *Medulla theologiæ* (*The Marrow of Theology*) of William Ames and resting on Scripture's testimony in 2 Timothy 1:13.[111] As such, Mastricht's arrangement of theology differed from other Reformed systems, such as the *Synopsis purioris theologiae* (1625), Bucanus's *Institutio theologica* (1658), Hoornbeeck's *Theologia practica* (1663), Burman's *Synopsis theologica* (1676), Turretin's *Institutio theologicae elencticae* (1686–1689), Leydecker's *Synopsis theologiae Christianae* (1689), and Braunius's *Doctrina foederum sive systema theologiae* (1691). Mastricht's divisions of theology consisted of systematic theology (faith) and moral and ascetic theology (obedience). He placed his exposition of the doctrine of faith (*De fide salvifica*, 1671), written at Duisburg, in summarized form into the first chapter of book 2, dealing with the doctrine of God (theology proper). Placing the doctrine of faith near the opening of his theological enterprise, immediately after the prolegomena of theology, differed from most of his contemporaries, who placed their discussions of faith within the context of the ordo salutis in soteriology. The importance of faith over reason, and therefore as requisite for the covenant of grace, underscores that the centrality of faith in theology cannot be overlooked. Natural theology, he argued, is useful for attesting to God to unbelievers, but is not salvific.[112] His definition of saving faith remained the same between 1671 and 1699: "Saving faith is nothing other than an act of the whole rational soul, by which it receives God

---

109. Mastricht, *Theoretico-practica theologia*, præfatio, "In *practicis* rarior accidit amplificatio, ne in nimiam molem degeneraret Theologia nostra, ne in plura volumina se diffunderet, & ex eo scopo brevitatis frustrarer; cum praesertim lector attentus, amplificationes, ex congestis Scripturae testimoniis, paulò attentiùs expensis, non magno negotio adornare possit, si comprimis observet, non omnia, demonstrationi; sed nonnulla illustrationi tantum fuisse adiecta."

110. Mastricht, *Theoretico-practica theologia*, **2, "Tandem, ut & usum nostrorum, in homileticis pro concione habeas, id unum moneo, ut cautè observes, praedominans argumentum textus tui; tum nostra, per sua capita conferas, ea quae in rem tuam erunt commodissima, arrectis tantum animi viribus, ut Scripturae locorum vim & efficaciam, cùm ad amplificandum; tùm ad demonstrandum, assequaris quantum satis. His praelibatis, iam ad ipsum opus, te dimitto."

111. William Ames, *Medulla theologiæ*, "Theologiæ duæ sunt partes: fides et observantia, 2 Tim. 1:13" (Hold fast the form of sound words, which thou has heard of me, in faith and love which is in Christ Jesus). From Lib. I, Cap. II.

112. Mastricht, *Theoretico-practica theologia*, 1.1

as its highest end, and Christ as its only Mediator, to this end, that we may be united with him, and so united obtain communion in all his benefits."[113]

Method of Theology

Mastricht advocates a proper and orderly method according to which theology must proceed. Resting on divine revelation, that is, Scripture, theology should be taught in accordance with 1 Timothy 6:2–3, should be ordered according to the covenant of grace (2 Sam. 23:5)—both thoughts which resonate with Cocceius—and should be understood, according to Mastricht, as a reasonable service (Rom. 12:1)—this latter notion is reflected in the title of the magnum opus of Wilhelmus à Brakel (1635–1711), *The Christian's Reasonable Service in which Divine Truths Concerning the Covenant of Grace are Expounded, Defended against Opposing Parties, and their Practice Advocated as well as the Administration of this Covenant in the Old and New Testaments.*[114] Hence, for Mastricht, the method according to which theology proceeds is four-fold: exegetical, doctrinal, elenctical, and practical. This is characteristic for his theological reflections, which commenced in Glückstadt, continued in Duisburg, and were completed in Utrecht. For him, theology begins with a philological-etymological, grammatical, and syntactical analysis of the text of Scripture—the *explicatio*: an explanation of the meaning of words. Doctrine thus arises and is formulated on the basis of biblical exegesis—the *dogmatica* or *didactica*, the *doctrina*, is the right teaching: an assembling of the parts and meaning of the biblical text. The third approach to theology is the refutation of opponents, though he counsels that controversies should not be sought, and should not be revived, when they are already "dead and buried." In fact, though Mastricht sees the elenctic part of theology entailing the refutation of teachings that do not accord with Scripture and Reformed orthodoxy, he also maintains that it should lead to a positive statement of orthodoxy that strengthens piety. Finally, theology should lead to the *praxis pietatis*. The true nature of theology is not knowledge in itself, but is directed to God, in Christ.

Definition of Theology

Mastricht defined theology, then, as Christian theology *theoretico-practica*,[115] a

---

113. Mastricht, *De fide salvifica syntagma theoretico-practicum*, 27, xiiiC. f. Ibid., *Theoretico-practica theologia*, 2.1.iii, 51, "...fides salvifica nihil aliud sit, quam actus totius animae rationalis, quo Deum accipit, quà summum finem; & Christum, quà unicum Mediatorem, ad hoc, ut cum eo uniamur, & uniti, communionem consequamur, omnium eius beneficiorum."

114. Wilhelmus à Brakel, *The Christian's Reasonable Service*, trans. Bartel Elshout, ed. Joel R. Beeke, 4 vols. (Grand Rapids: Reformation Heritage Books, 1999).

115. Mastricht, *Theoretico-practica theologia*, 1.1.ix, 4.

doctrine of living to God through Christ, a doctrine that accords with piety.[116] The latter part of the definition resonates with Cocceius's definition: *theologia est doctrina secundum veram pietatem*.[117] However, Mastricht's definition also displays elements of two other trajectories concerning the definition of theology or divinity. First, Petrus Ramus (1515–1572) defined the "what" of divinity or theology in his *De religione Christiana* as: "*Theologia est doctrina bene vivendi*,"[118] which was echoed by William Perkins in *A Golden Chain* as "The body of Scripture is a doctrine sufficient for living well" (*est doctrina bene vivendi*).[119] In turn, Perkins's student William Ames (1576–1633) followed his teacher in this and provided a concise definition of theology in the *Medulla S.S. Theologiae*: "*Theologia est doctrina Deo Vivendi*," rendered in the English edition as "Divinity is the doctrine of living to God."[120] Mastricht was the only seventeenth-century Reformed scholastic to expand Ames's definition of divinity to *Theologia est doctrina Deo vivendi per Christum*.[121] This is, for him, not just an addition, but makes his articulation of theology Trinitarian and Christocentric. Thus, Mastricht provides a long-standing definition of the *quid sit* of theology that reaches back to Ramus.

Secondly, Mastricht's defining of theology as *theoretico-practica* was a result of his inquiry as to whether theology is speculative or *practica*. On the one hand, Mastricht and Protestant scholastic theologians, such as Johannes Cloppenburg (1592–1552), Johannes Cocceius (1603–1669), Hoornbeeck, and others,[122] recognized theology as being a mixed discipline, both *theoretica* and *practica*, though leaning toward the *practica*—but they rejected its anthropological character, as proposed by the Remonstrants. Moreover, Francis Turretin (1623–1687)

---

116. Mastricht, *Theoretico-practica theologia*, 1.1.xxxvi, 12, "Theologia ista Christiana, theoretico-practica, non est, nisi doctrina vivendi Deo per Christum; seu doctrina, quæ est secundum pietatem."

117. Johannes Cocceius, *Opera Omnia Theologia* (Amsterdam: P&J Blaev), 7.3 §1.

118. Petrus Ramus, *Commentariorum de religione Christiana libri quatuor* (Frankfurt: A. Welchem, 1576), Cap. I *Quid Theologia sit*, 6.

119. William Perkins, *A Golden Chain* (1592), Chap. I *Of the bodie of Scripture and Theology*, A3.

120. William Ames, *Medulla S.S. Theologiae* (1627), Cap. I *De Theologiae definitione vel natura*, 1; idem, *Marrow of Sacred Divinity* (1642), Chap. I *Of the Definition, or Nature of Divinity*, 1.

121. Mastricht, *Theoretico-practica theologia*, Cap. I.iii *De Definitione Theologiae*, 12, "Theologia ista Christiana, theoretico-practica, non est, nisi doctrina vivendi Deo per Christum."

122. Johannes Cloppenburg, *Theologica opera omnia Tomus prior* (Amsterdam: Gerardus Borstius, 1684), 600; Johannes Coccejus, *Summa theologiae ex scripturis repetita. Editio secunda…* (Geneva: Sumptibus Samuelis Chouët, 1665), 65; Johannes Hoornbeek, *Theologiae practicae partes duae* (Utrecht: Iohannem & Guilielmum van de Water, 1689), na; Johannes à Marck *Compendium theologiae Christianae didactico-elencticum. Immixtis problematibus plurimis, & quaestionibus etiam recentioribus adauctum* (Amsterdam: Adrian. Douci & Abr. A Paddenburg, 1749), 13.

explicitly raised the question, "Is theology theoretical or practical?"—inquiring not only about the understanding of the essence of theology but also the controversies "of this time," such as "the Remonstrants and Socinians"[123]—a concern that Mastricht shared.[124] Turretin asserted, furthermore, that a theoretical or speculative system is occupied in contemplation alone with knowledge as its object, contrary to a practical theology, which has activity for its object.[125] Therefore, the Genevan theologian concludes: theology is neither theoretical nor practical but a mixed discipline, and yet more practical than speculative, which appears, Turretin explained, "from its ultimate goal, which is praxis…indeed nothing in theology is theoretical to such as degree and so remote from praxis that it does not bring about the admiration and worship of God; nor is a theory salvific unless it is referred to praxis."[126]

On the other hand, Mastricht and his contemporaries revisited the medieval scholastic discussion on whether the character of theology is theoretical or practical. With the thirteenth-century rise in interest in Aristotle's writings, the discussion of the nature and the extent of theology was formed in part by the philosopher's classification of the forms of knowledge, science (*scientia*) and wisdom (*sapientia*).[127] Franciscans such as Alexander of Hales (ca. 1183–1245) and Bonaventure (1221–1274) insisted on the affective, practical, and experiential character of theology—excluding it from consideration as *scientia* in the

---

123. Turrettini, *Institutio theologiae elencticae*, 22, I.vii, "An Theologia sit theoretica, an practica?;" Theologiae naturam; sed etiam propter Controversias huius temporis, maximè contra Socin. & Remonstrantes, qui Theologiam ita strictè practicam dicunt, ut nihil in ea praecisè ad salutem necessarium sit, nisi quod pertinet ad praecepta morum & promissione." Cf. Francis Turretin, *Institutes of Elenctic Theology*, trans. George Musgrave Giger, ed. James T. Dennison, Jr. (Phillipsburg, NJ: P & R Publishing, 1992), vol. I, 21, I.vii.

124. Mastricht, *Theoretico-practica theologia*, 6, I.1.xx, "nec *Practica* tantum, quae veritatis *cognitionem*, susque deque habeat (quam Sociniani vellent & Arminiani, quo commodius fidem in Christum, aliaque Religionis fundamentalia, negligant & eliminent."

125. Turrettini, *Institutio theologiae elencticae*, 23, I.vii, "*Disciplina theoretica* dicitur, quae in sola contemplatione occupatur, & finem alium non habet à cognitione; *Practica*, quae non subsistit in solâ rei noritiâ, sed naturâ suâ & per se tendit ad praxim, & pro fine habet operationem." Cf. Turretin, *Institutes of Elenctic Theology*, vol. I, 22, I.vii.

126. Turrettini, *Institutio theologiae elencticae*, 23, I.xv, "Theologiam tamen magis esse practicam quàm speculativam patet ex *fine ultimo* qui est praxis; licèt enim omnia mysteria non sint regulativa operationis, sunt tamen impulsiva ad operationem; Nullum enim est tam θεωρητόν & à praxi remotum, quin incitet ad Dei admirationem & cultum; nec Theoria salutaris est nisi ad praxim revocetur, Ioan. 13:17, 1 Cor. 13:2, Titus 1:1, 1 Ioan. 2:3–4, Titus 2:12." Cf. Turretin, *Institutes of Elenctic Theology*, vol. I, 23, I. xv. See also Richard Muller, *Post-Reformation Reformed Dogmatics* (Grand Rapids: Baker Academic, 2003), 1:353–54.

127. In this paragraph I follow Muller's discussion in part on the development of theological prolegomena as found in Muller, *Post-Reformation Reformed Dogmatics*, 1:88–96.

Aristotelian sense of a rational or speculative discipline.[128] Aquinas, on the other hand, not only argues in the *Summa Theologica* that "sacred doctrine is a science,"[129] but also raises the question whether sacred doctrine is a practical science—to which Thomas, reflecting Dominican theology, replied, "It is not a practical but a speculative science."[130] These fairly broad outlines of the character of theology find their culmination in Duns Scotus's (†1308) formulation of theology. Scotus not only resonated with Franciscan theology, though he integrated more Aristotelian philosophy than was previously accepted, but also considered theology as a discipline oriented toward the ultimate goal of humanity in God: in essence, *praxis*—that is to say, a knowledge not known for itself but directed to God.[131]

Mastricht, then, also discussed whether theology is *theoretico-practica*.[132] Although he does not reject the Thomistic position altogether, Mastricht is inclined to follow a modified Scotist position on the issue, proposing that the *praxis* is defined as *doctrina*, known for the sake of the end toward which it directs the knower. In other words, Mastricht aims to maintain a balance between the speculative and *practica*, expressed in the conjunction *theoretico-practica*,[133] yet oriented to the practical.

Mastricht's Reception

Despite Mastricht's beneficence and academic attentiveness to his international group of divinity students, few of them seem to remember their teacher, or, at least, they do not refer to him in their published writings. These include students from

---

128. Alexander of Hales, *Summa universae theologiae* (Cologne: Agri., 1622), quaestio 1, cap. 1–2; quaestio 2, memb. 3, cap. 3; St. Bonaventure, *Commentaria in quator libros Sententiariam*, (Quaracchi edition, 1882), prologus, quaestio 1.

129. Aquinas, *Summa Theologica*, prima pars, quaestio 1, secundo, "Utrum sacra doctrina sit scientia...Respondeo sacram doctrinam esse scientiam" (Whether sacred doctrine is a science...I respond, Sacred doctrine is a science).

130. Ibid., quarto, "Utrum sacra doctrina sit scientia practica.... Non ergo est scientia practica, sed magis speculative" (Whether sacred doctrine is a practical science...[I respond] Therefore it is not a practical science, but speculative).

131. Johannis Duns Scotus, *Ordinatio* (Rome: Polyglottis Vaticanis, n.d.), 1, Prologus, pars prima, "Primum est de necessitate huius doctrinae.... Quartum et quintum pertinet ad genus causae finalis, et est quartum: utrum theologia sit practica; quintum: utrum ex ordine ad praxim ut ad finem dicatur per se scientia practica." Cf. http://www.franciscan-archive.org/scotus/opera/dun01001.html (accessed March 9, 2015) (The first concern the necessity of this doctrine...the fourth and fifth pertain to the genus of the final cause, and the fourth is: whether theology is practical; the fifth: whether from its order to praxis as to its end it is called a practical science per se).

132. Mastricht, *Theoretico-practica theologia*, 15, I.1.xlvii, *Tertio* sitne habitus *theoreticus?* an *practicus?* an *theoretico-practicus?*"

133. Mastricht, *Theoretico-practica theologia*, 15, 1.1.xlvii, "Quin & negamus, esse *Theoretico-practicam*, proprie & in se; quamvis, ex *modo tractandi*, ita eam in signiverimus: sed *practicam* dicimus, & εξοχως practicam."

Zeeland, such as Drywegen, De Clyver,[134] Jacobus Fruytier (1659–1731), and
Bernardus Smytegelt,[135] as well as others, such as Petrus Immens (1664–1720)
and the later scholar of Islam, Adrianus Reland (1676–1718). Like Henricus
Nahuys, the father of Petrus Nahuys (1692–1766), they all seem primarily to
esteem Witsius, as does another student, Petrus Dinant (1663–1724).[136] It
also seems that Mastricht's Hungarian students, such as Samuel Kaposki and
Johannes Pelsöczi, neglected to mention their teacher[137]—though Mastricht's
disputations and the *TPT* were found in the libraries of Transylvania. As for his
Scottish students, only James Hog appealed to his teacher, doing so during the
Marrow controversy.[138]

Despite a lack of direct mention by his students, the reception of Mastricht's
works on homiletics, philosophy, and theology was influential, international, and
transatlantic. *De optima concionandi methodus* became known primarily through
the printing and distribution of the *TPT*, and while *De fide salvifica* remained
the least-known work, *Novitatum Cartesianarum gangraena* became one of the
most influential anti-Cartesian works of the late seventeenth century.

The appreciation of Mastricht's magnum opus of philosophy was shared
by Roman Catholics, Lutherans, and the Reformed alike. Already in 1680,
Gisbertus Cocquius (ca. 1630–1708) lauded the *Gangraena* in his *Anatome
Hobbesianismi*, a critique of the philosophy of Thomas Hobbes (1588–1679).
This work was commended by Mastricht on behalf of the faculty at Utrecht.[139]
The Italian Jesuit Giovanni B. De Benedictis (1622–1706) vehemently approved
Mastricht's view against the new philosophy.[140] Michael Foertstius (1654–1724)

---

134. De Cluyver came from the congregation of Wemelding, which was served by Wilhelmus
Eversdijk (1653–1729), a representative of the *Nadere Reformatie* (Dutch Further Reformation).

135. Smytegelt came in 1683 to Utrecht, the year Mastricht was rector. Smytegelt defended
for his cousin Melchior Leydekker in November 1686 a number of propositions of Augustine's
De unitate ecclesiæ.

136. See, for example, Petrus Dinant, *De Brief van de H. Apostel Paulus aan die van Efeze*,
2d ed. (Rotterdam: Jan Daniel Beman, 1726), vol. 1, preface (3): "Herm. Witsius, weleer myn hoog
geachte Meester in de Akademie te Utrecht" (Herm[an] Witsius, previous my highly esteemed
professor at the Academy of Utrecht).

137. Petrus van Mastricht, *Disputationum practicarum de desertione spirituali*, pars quarta;
Samuel Kaposi (Utrecht: Meinardi a Dreunen, 1683); idem, *Dissertationis historico-philologico-
theologicae, tremendum vindictae divinae monumentum, in perennem memoriam, Ananiae et Sapphirae
Actor. Ca v vs. 1.–12. miraculose erectum exhibentis*, pars prior; Johannes Pelsöczi (Utrecht: Francisci Halma, 1699).

138. Edward Fisher, *The Marrow of Modern Divinity*, 346.

139. Gisbertus Cocquius, *Anatome Hobbesianismi* (Utrecht: Franscus Halma, 1680).

140. Giovanni B. De Benedictis, *Difesa della terza lettera apologetica di Benedetto Aletino,
divisa in tre discussioni, una teologica, l'altra filosofica della filosofia cartesiana, la terza critica* (Rome:
Antonio DeRossi, 1705), 45, 46.

of the Lutheran University of Jena identifies Mastricht as the most commanding seventeenth-century critic of the "detestable" Cartesianism[141]—a thought echoed by the German historian of philosophy, Jacob Brucker (1669–1770). He noted the importance of Mastricht in the seventeenth-century Cartesian debate and the Bekker controversy in his *Historia critica philosophiae*.[142] The laudable reception of the *Gangraena* in Lutheran circles was evidenced at the University of Uppsala, Sweden, which prescribed Mastricht's work in the curriculum of philosophical studies far into the eighteenth century.[143] However, the Dutch Reformed pastor Jacobus Fruytier (1659–1731) wrote in 1715: "The godly Maastricht has published a work in his life, entitled *Gangraena philosophiae Cartesianae*: in it he discovered and foretold many things resulting from philosophy; however, no one paid attention, no one wanted to read the book, because he was not a man of the new era."[144]

The neglect signaled by Fruytier was balanced, however, by continuing interest from a number of quarters, including the reprint of the work in 1716,[145] its use by the Scottish minister and colleague of James Hog, Ralph Erskine (1685–1752), who described Mastricht as "a learned divine and philosopher both,"[146] and in the work of Bernardus de Moor (1710–1765), who positively cites the *Gangraena* in his massive commentary on Johannes à Marck's *Compendium Theologiæ* (1761).[147]

While the reception of Mastricht's anti-Cartesian work was noted in the Dutch Republic, Germany, Italy, and Sweden, his magnum opus of theology

---

141. Michael Foertstius, *Selectorum Theologorum Breviarium, id est decussio principalium punctorum theologicorum nostro tempore maxime controversorum* (Jena, 1708), 32.

142. Jacob Brucker, *Historia Critica Philosophiae* (Leipzig: Reichi, 1766), 4:265, 720.

143. Sten Lindroth, *A History of Uppsala University, 1477–1977* (Stockholm: Almqvist & Wiksell international, 1976), 73.

144. Jacobus Fruytier, *Sion's Worstelingen of historische samenspraken over de verscheide en zeer bittere wederwaardigheden van Christus Kerke, met openbare en verborgene vyanden: in de reformatie, ten tyde der Remonstranten, in deze onze dagen* (Rotterdam: Johan van Doesburg, 1715), 659, "De godvruchtige Maastricht he(e)ft in zijn leven een boek uitgegegeven, getiteld: *Gangraena Philosophiae Cartesianae* : daar heeft hij vele dingen in ondekt en voorzegd, die uit die wijsbegeerte zullen voortvloeien; doch daarop is geen acht geslagen, men wilde dat boek niet eens lezen, omdat het geen man van den nieuwe tijd was."

145. Petrus van Mastricht, *Theologia cartesiana detecta, seu gangraena cartesiana, nobiliores plerasque corporis theologici partes arrodens et exedens* (Deventer, 1716).

146. Ralph Erskine, *Faith No Fancy: Or, A Treatise of Mental Images Discovering the vain Philosophy and vile Divinity of a late Pamphlet* (Philadelphia: William M'Culloch, 1805), 239.

147. Bernardus de Moor, *Commentarius perpetuus in Johannis Marckii Compendium Theologiæ Christianæ didactico-elencticum* (Leiden: Johannem Hasebroek, 1761). Except the reference to the *Theoretico-practica theologia*, I:796, all other references are made to the *Novitatum Cartesianarum Gangraena*, I:49, 53, 70 (2x), 90, 318, 321(3x), 322, 410, 414, 416, 436, 468(2x), 589, 590, 591, 600, 601, 603, 630, 657, 672, 714, 796, 833, 883, 889.

(1699; reprinted in 1715 and 1724) found its way throughout eighteenth-century Europe in the Dutch Republic, England, Germany, Scotland, and Switzerland as well as to the New World.

The Continent

Mastricht's first volume of the TPT (1682) was critically and extensively reviewed in the *Acta eruditorum* of Leipzig (1694), which was the first of several cofounded by Gottlieb Leibniz (1646–1716).[148] Already in 1698, Heinrich L. Benthem stated in *Holländischer Kirchen- und Schulen-Staat*: "Although his work was not held in high esteem, he did not permit himself to deviate but maintained his opinion, which here and there still finds devotees."[149]

Pontanus, however, elaborates on the TPT in Mastricht's funeral *Laudatio*, asserting that he never saw a work like it before: precise, succinct, and expository on the matters of theology—a work commended by "many theologians" and in such high demand that "the publishers are considering a third edition." This was "a work," he continued, "that always will remain famous and highly regarded."[150] In 1710, Johannes d'Outrein (1662–1722) noted that Mastricht combines the *theoretica* and *practica* of theology[151]—an appraisal echoed in 1730 by Johann Franz Buddeus (1667–1729) of the Lutheran University of Jena. He argues that the TPT of Mastricht is a laudable work that brings together theology as *theoretico-practica, ascetica,* and *morali.*[152] This assessment was shared by Buddeus's student and son-in-law, Johann Georg Walch (1693–1775),[153] a church historian— but also by the Cocceian theologian Salomon van Til (1643–1713) and by De Moor, who recommended the reading of the TPT for practical theology.[154]

---

148. *Acta eruditorum Lipsiensia* (Leipzig: Christian Goezl, 1694), 348–56.

149. Heinrich L. Benthem, *Holländischer Kirchen- und Schulen-Staat* (Frankfurt an der Oder: Förster, 1698), 2:460, "Obschon seine [Peter van Mastricht 1630–1706] Arbeit wenig geachtet wird, lässet er sich doch solches nicht irren, sondern bleibet bey seiner Meynung, welche hie und da ihr Liebhaber noch finden."

150. Pontanus, *Laudatio Funebris*, 23–24.

151. Johannes D'Outrein, *De Droefheid die naar God is, werkende een Onberouwelijke Bekeeringe tot Zaligheid. Mitsgaders de ware Selfs-Verloochening* (Amsterdam: Jacobus Borstius, 1710), Aen de Leeser, 5.

152. Johann Franz Buddeus, *Isagoge Historico-Theologica ad Theologiam universiam* (Lipsea: Thomas Fritschi, 1730) 1:595, 596. Cf. C. van der Kemp, voorrede, in Petrus van Mastricht, *Beschouwende en Praktikale Godgeleerdheid,waarin alle godgeleerde hoofdstukken hen, het Bijbelverklarenden Leerstellige, Wederleggende en Praktikale deel, door eenen onafgebroken schakel onderscheidelijk samengevoegt, voorgestelt word* (Rotterdam: Hendrik van Pelt; Utrecht: Jan Jacob van Poolsum, 1749), ***3.

153. Johann Georg Walch, *Miscellanea sacra, sive commentationum historiam ecclesiasticam sanctioresque disciplinas pertinentium collecti* (Amsterdam: Zachariae Rombergii, 1744), 706.

154. Salomon van Til, *Methodus concionandi: illustrata commentariis et exemplis. Quibus additae sunt Eiusdem auctoris bibliotheca theologica, et aliae dissertat* (Traiectum ad Rhenum, 1727),

In addition to general praise of the work, Salomon Deyling (1677–1755) of the University of Leipzig specifically appealed to Mastricht concerning Cocceianism,[155] and the former lecturer at the University of Jena, Johann Friedrich Cotta (1701–1779), approvingly cites *TPT* in a disputation on the unforgiveable sin against the Holy Spirit (Tübingen, 1753).[156] In Spain, moreover, the Jesuit Lorenzo Harvás (1735–1809) referred to the *TPT* and asserted that Mastricht "fleeing scholasticism, propounded theology with theses and antitheses."[157] The Cistercian and dogmatician of the University of Ingolstadt, Stephan Wiest (1748–1797), in sketching the Calvinist position on the doctrine of the satisfaction of Christ, specifically cited the *TPT*.[158]

Scotland

With respect to Scotland, the "Marrow-men,"[159] such as Ralph Erskine (1685–1752)[160] and John Brown (1722–1787),[161] were favorable toward Mastricht's

---

bibliotheca theologica; Bernardus de Moor, *Commentarius perpetuus in Marckii Compendium Theologiæ Christianæ*, vol. 1, præfatio.

155. Salomon Deyling, *Observationum sacrarum pars prima* (Leipzig: Frid. Lanckisch, 1708), 233.

156. Johann Friedrich Cotta, *De peccato in spiritum sanctum irremissibili*, disputabit Wilhelm Friedrich Hochstetter (Tübingen: Christian G. Cotto, 1753), 11, 43.

157. Lorenzo Hervás, *Historia de la vida del hombre* (Madrid: De Villalpando, 1794), 4:312, "Van Mastrich[t] huyendo del escolasticismo, propuso la teologia con theses y antitheses."

158. Stephan Wiest, *Institutiones Theologicæ, Dogmatum Catholicorum in specie Doctrina De Deo Salutis auctore* (Ingolstadt: J. Wilhelm Krüll, 1789), 250, 261.

159. John Macleod, *Scottish Theology, In relation to Church History* (Edinburgh: Knox Press, 1974), 152.

160. Ralph Erskine, *Faith no Fancy, or, A treatise of mental images: discovering the vain philosophy and vile divinity of a late pamphlet entitled [sic] Mr. Robe's fourth letter to Mr. Fisher, and showing that an imaginary idea of Christ as man (when supposed to belong to saving faith, whether in its act or object), imports nothing but ignorance, atheism, idolatry, great falsehood, and gross delusion* (Philadelphia: William M'Culloch, 1805), 31. On the theological relationship between seventeenth and eighteenth century Scotland and the Netherlands, see Robert H. Story, ed., *The Church of Scotland, past and present: its history, its relation to the law and the state, its doctrine, ritual, discipline, and patrimony* (London: William Mackenzie, 1890), 216: "...a deeper study of the Covenant theology which had been imported from Holland, and was destined to occupy a prominent place in the orthodox school in Scotland"; John Kennedy, *The Days of the Fathers in Ross-shire* (Inverness: Christian Focus Publications, 1979), 134: "They [the Ross-shire fathers] had no difficulty in regarding the Sacrament of the Supper, as intended by the Lord, specially to seal something other and higher than that which is specially sealed by baptism. They called it, with Mastricht, 'sacramentum nutritionis'"; Keith L. Sprunger, *Dutch Puritanism: A History of English and Scottish Churches of the Netherlands in the Sixteenth and Seventeenth Centuries* (Leiden: E. J. Brill, 1982), 435, "At Utrecht Voetius, Nethenus, and van Mastricht showed favor to Scottish Presbyterians, and van Mastricht went so far as to praise the discipline of the Church of Scotland as 'the purest that had been since the apostles' days.'"

161. John Brown, *The Systematic Theology*, intro. by Joel R. Beeke and Randall J. Pederson (Grand Rapids: Reformation Heritage Books, 2002), [j].

thought on the doctrine of the covenant—a probable influence of Mastricht's student, James Hog.[162] The Scottish interest continued into the nineteenth century, as attested by Donald Fraser's notes in 1823 to his English translation of Witsius's *Exercitationes sacrae in symbolum apostolorum* (1681), which identify the *TPT* as "that truly valuable work."[163]

New England

The most important and immediate reception of the *TPT*, however, occurred in colonial New England, commencing with the admiration of Cotton Mather (1663–1726), the first admirer outside the European continent, and lasting over a hundred and fifty years in New England. Writing to Jacob Wendel in May 1720, a Dutch merchant in Albany, New York, the learned pastor of Boston requested twelve copies of the *TPT*, noting: "The World has never yet seen so valuable a system of divinity.... 'Tis orthodox, 'tis concise, 'tis complete. In one word, it is everything.... In these two volumes, our young ministers would have a rich library.... Happy would our churches be, if they were fed from the stores, and with the admirable spirit of the most vital piety, all along breathing therein, which are to be found in Dr. Mastricht."[164] Mather would repeat his generous praise of the *TPT* six years later in his handbook for students studying for the ministry, *Manuductio ad ministerium* (1726), stating: "But after all there

---

162. David C. Lachman, *The Marrow Controversy* (Edinburgh: Rutherford House, 1988), 125, 126.

163. H. Witsius, *The Apostles' Creed*, translated from the Latin and followed with notes, critical and explanatory by Donald Fraser (1823; Escondido: Den Dulk Christian Foundation, 1993), 1:379: "See also some short historical notes on the Arminian controversy in that truly valuable work, *Theol. Pet. Van Mastricht*, lib. viii. Cap.3. sect. xliii. P.1152, et seq."; ibid., 1:441, "Calvin, Mastricht, Guthrie and many other excellent Divines have styled faith the condition of the covenant"; ibid., 1:455: "The judicious *Mastricht* may be mentioned as furnishing another [after discussing Witsius's position, AN] example of the unfavorable sentiments with which even well-informed Christians at first regarded the system maintained by the celebrated Newton (who, by the way, was a decided believer of the Scriptures) with his predecessors and followers. That excellent Theologian, when taking notice of the system of the world, has the following observation; 'The Reformed ascribe the lowest place to this earth, which according to the uniform tenor of sacred writ, is contradistinguished from the heavens and stars, and which beginning in a manner the centre of the universe, remains unmovable, Eccles i.4, *Theol*. Lib.iii. cap. vi. Sect. 19;' ibid., 2:551: "The reader who is disposed to study this subject [the argument for the divinity of the Spirit] may consult...Owen's Exposition of the Hebrews, Ch. vi.4–6. x.26–29, and Mastricht's Theology, lib. iv.cap.3.sect.16, 17"; ibid., 2:554, "On the reality, nature, and importance of the unions between Christ and believers, the reader may consult Maestricht, *Theolog*. lib.vi.cap.5." Note, Mastricht is missing in the "index of authors quoted by Witsius," ibid., 2:598–628.

164. American Antiquarian Society, MSS Cotton Mather, U/AAS, May 10, 1720. Cf. Kenneth Silverman, *Selected Letters of Cotton Mather* (Baton Rouge: Louisiana State University Press, 1971), 306–7.

is nothing that I can with so much Plerophorie Recommend unto you, as a *Mastricht*, his *Theologia Theoretico-practica*. That a Minister of the Gospel may be *Thoroughly furnished* unto every *Good Work*, and in one or two *Quarto* Volumes enjoy a *well furnished Library*, I know not that the Sun has ever shone upon an Humane Composure that is equal to it."[165]

In fact, with Ames's *Medulla* as the principal textbook required among New England's colleges in the American Colonial Period, Mather's praise was echoed throughout eighteenth-century New England, for Mastricht's work was highly valued by Benjamin Colman (1673–1747),[166] Joseph Seccombe (1706–1760),[167] Mastricht's editor and translator of "On Regeneration," a chapter in *TPT*,[168] Samuel Hopkins (1721–1803),[169] and Joseph Bellamy (1719–1790).[170] And if the words of Edwards Amasa Park (1808–1900)[171] can be relied upon, Jonathan Edwards Jr. (1745–1801) read Mastricht's *TPT* seven times. However, it is Jonathan Edwards, America's philosopher and theologian, who bestowed the highest praise on Mastricht's work: "But take Mastricht for divinity in General, doctrine, practice & Controversie; or as an universal system of divinity; &

---

165. Cotton Mather, *Manuductio ad Ministerium. Directions for a candidate of the ministry: Wherein, first, a right foundation is laid for his future improvement; and, then, rules are offered for such a management of his academical & preparatory studies; and thereupon, for such a conduct after his appearance in the world; as may render him a skilful and useful minister of the Gospel* (Boston: Thomas Hancock, 1726), 85.

166. Benjamin Colman, *A Dissertation on the Image of God wherein Man was created* (Boston: S. Kneeland and T. Green, 1736), 27, 28.

167. Joseph Seccombe, *Some Occasional Thoughts on the Influence of the Spirit with Seasonable Cautions against Mistakes and Abuses* (Boston: S. Kneeland and T. Green, 1742), title page "oportet intelligentem, phantasmata speculari. Van Mastricht."

168. Peter van Mastricht, *A Treatise on Regeneration. Extracted from his System of Divinity, called Theologia theoretico-practica; and faithfully translated into English; With an APPENDIX containing Extracts from many celebrated Divines of the reformed Church, upon the same Subject* (New Haven: Thomas and Samuel Green, [n.d]), v; reprint, ed. Brandon Withrow (Morgan, Pa.: Soli Deo Gloria Publications, 2002).

169. Samuel Hopkins, *The System of Doctrines: Contained in Divine Revelation, explained and defended: showing their consistence and connection with each other: to which is added, A treatise on the millennium* (Boston: Isaiah Thomas and Ebenezer T. Andrews, 1793), 769.

170. *The Works of Joseph Bellamy, D.D.* (Boston: Doctrinal Tract and Book Society, 1853), I.xiv,n*. Tyron Edwards (1809–1894) notes that Jonathan Edwards lent a copy of Mastricht's work to Bellamy. Cf. Michael A.G. Haykin, ed., *A Sweet Flame. Piety in the Letters of Jonathan Edwards* (Grand Rapids: Reformation Heritage Books, 2007), 85n2.

171. Edwards Amasa Park, "New England Theology," in *Bibliotheca Sacra*, 9 (January 1852). Cf. Douglas A. Sweeney, Allen C. Guelzo, *The New England Theology. From Jonathan Edwards to Edwards Amasa Park* (Grand Rapids: Baker Academic, 2006), 261.

it is much better than Turretine or any other book in the world, excepting the Bible, in my opinion...."[172]

Edwards's admiration is demonstrated throughout his work from 1725 to just before his death in 1758. Mastricht's work, moreover, heads (the second part of) Edwards's reading list in his catalog, and was his chief book in systematic theology. He frequently refers[173] to the *TPT* in his reflections on the Sabbath, covenant, fall, predestination, Trinity,[174] humility,[175] sin, and Christ's ascension.[176] His major work, *A History of the Work of Redemption*, is modeled after the eighth book in Mastricht's *TPT*, *De dispensatione foederis gratiæ*. Following his sermon series on redemption in mid-1739, Edwards preached an extensive treatment of the text of Hebrews 5:12 in November at Northampton, addressing the question, "What divinity is" (*Quid sit theologia*). He defined it thus: "Divinity is commonly defined, the doctrine of living to God; and by some who seem to be more accurate, the doctrine of living to God by Christ"—the latter definition found only in Mastricht's *TPT*.[177] Edwards's appreciation for Mastricht's work, to which his wife Sarah may have introduced him,[178] is echoed by his students—Samuel Hopkins (1721–1803) of Rhode Island and Joseph Bellamy (1719–1790), the pastor of the Congregational church in Bethlehem, Connecticut for fifty years. The latter refers to the "celebrated Mastricht,"[179] while the former notes in his treatise on saving faith: "That great, learned, and accurate Dutch divine, Van Mastricht, whose body of divinity perhaps excels

---

172. Jonathan Edwards, *Letters and Personal Writings*, Georges S. Claghorn, ed., *The Works of Jonathan Edwards*, vol. 16 (New Haven, London: Yale University Press, 1998), 216, 217. Edwards also mentions Mastricht in two other letters written on June 11, 1747 and January 9, 1748/9 to Bellamy (see respectively Edwards, *Letters and Personal Writings*, 223, 266).

173. Yale Beinecke Rare Book and Manuscripts, *Edwards collection*, Gen. MSS 151, box 22, folder 1316. The *TPT* heads (the second part of) Edwards's list of reading in his catalog and was his chief book in systematic theology, as Poole was his favorite biblical commentator.

174. *The Works of Jonathan Edwards*, ed. John E. Smith, vol. 13, *The Miscellanies*, ed. Thomas A. Schafer (New Haven, London: Yale University Press, 1994), 319 (Sabbath), 382 (fall), 384 (predestination), 524 (Trinity).

175. *The Works of Jonathan Edwards*, ed. John E. Smith, vol. 2, *Religious Affections*, ed. John E. Smith (New Haven, London: Yale University Press, 1994), 337.

176. *The Works of Jonathan Edwards*, ed. John E. Smith, vol. 15, *Notes on Scripture*, ed. Stephen J. Stein (New Haven, London: Yale University Press, 1998), 298.

177. Jonathan Edwards, *Practical Sermons never before published* (Edinburgh: M. Grey, 1788), 5. Cf. *The Works of Jonathan Edwards*, vol. 22 (New Haven, London: Yale University Press, 2003), 86. See Mastricht, *Theoretico-practica theologia*, 12, 1.iii (*definitione theologia*).

178. Elisabeth D. Dodds, *Marriage to a Difficult Man. The Uncommon Union of Jonathan and Sarah Edwards* (Philadelphia: Westminster Press, 1971; reprint, Laurel, Miss.: Audubon Press, 2003), 21.

179. Joseph Bellamy, *True Religion Delineated* (Boston: S. Kneeland, 1750), 58.

all others that have yet been written, and is, in my opinion, richly worth the repeated perusal of every one who would be a divine…."[180]

The interest in Mastricht's works continued into the mid-eighteenth century in New England, exemplified by a translation into English, announced in the *Connecticut Journal, and New Haven Post-boy* on Friday, August 24, 1770: "In the Press and in few Days will be published A Treatise on REGENERA-TION by *Peter Van Mastricht*, A.M, Professor of Divinity in the Universities of Francfort, Duisburg and Utrecht. Extracted from his System of Divinity, call[ed] Theologia theoretico-practica…."[181]

While Edwardsean theology was debated in America, the translator of Mastricht's chapter of the *TPT* "On Regeneration"[182] asserted that both parties "manifest their entire approbation of, and concurrence with van Mastricht," and hopes that the treatise will "put a stop to the controversy, which seems to be growing among us, relative to regeneration; whether it be wrought by the immediate influences of the divine Spirit, or by light as the means? And happily, to unite us in the truth."[183]

In addition to the translation of a chapter of the *TPT* into English, the Dutch translation of the entire work was announced in the *Boekzaal der Geleerde Waereld* (*Bookroom of the Learned World*), a literary journal, in October 1748; the description identified the rector of the Latin School at Woerden, "Boudewyn ter Braak, V.D.M." as translator.[184] This journal, moreover, published an extensive

---

180. Samuel Hopkins, *The system of doctrines: contained in divine revelation, explained and defended: showing their consistence and connection with each other: to which is added, A treatise on the millennium* (Boston: Isaiah Thomas and Ebenezer T. Andrews, 1793), 769.

181. *The Connecticut Journal, and New Haven Post-boy*, Friday August 24, 1770, no. 149, 3. See also, *The Connecticut Journal, and New Haven Post-boy* Friday August 31, 1770, no. 150, 4, "To Morrow Will be Published A Treatise on REGENERATION by *Peter Van Mastricht…*; Ibid., Friday, September 7, 1770, no. 151, 3, "Just Published by the Printers hereof A Treatise on REGENERATION by *Peter Van Mastricht* with an Appendix, containing Extracts from many celebrated Divines of the Reformed Church." The appendix contains statements from Charnock, Twisse, Flavel, Witsius, Ames, and Rutherford.

182. Petrus van Mastricht, *Treatise on Regeneration, Extracted from His System of Divinity, Called Theologia theoretico-practica* (New Haven: Thomas and Samuel Green, in the Old Council Chamber, 1770).

183. Petrus van Mastricht, *Treatise on Regeneration*, preface. Another New England acquaintance with Mastricht is also noted on the title page of the anonymous work, *Some Occasional Thoughts on the Influence of the Spirit, with seasonable cautions against mistakes and abuses* (Boston: S. Kneeland and T. Green, 1742), title page.

184. *Maandelyksche uittreksels of boekzaal der geleerde waereld* (Amsterdam: Dirk onder de Linden en Zoon, 1748), 67:424–25.

review in June 1749. The *Beschouwende en Practicale Godgeleerdheid*[185] is a much-desired work by the Dutch *Bybel-oeffenaren* (Bible-devotees), according to the reviewer, asserting that this exceptional book of divinity is rooted in none other than the Scriptures.[186]

The entire work, then, was translated from 1749 to 1753 and published as *Beschouwende en praktikale godgeleerdheit* (Theoretical and Practical theology), with a preface by Cornelis van Kemp (1702–1772) stating that the parts of theology are joined in such a way "as never seen before; why, this book is a complete summary of the divine theology, yes, a treasure book, a store-house…that perfect[s] theologians."[187]

The laypeople of the Dutch Reformed congregations read Mastricht's *Beschouwende en praktikale godgeleerdheid*, as attested by the Dutch ministers, Alexander Comrie and Nicolas Holtius, who noted concerning Mastricht's work: "His system, of which an equal, I think, cannot be found, has been translated into our own language and is in everyone's hand."[188]

The sixty-five-year-old Pieter Morilyon Jacobszoon wrote in his daily journal on June 15, 1769: "I have been allowed to enjoy much, much benefit, especially from the old theologians, both in France, England, Scotland, as well as in the Netherlands. The writing of later theologians, such as those of…Mastricht…and many others, has been very beneficial to me."[189]

A declining but varied interest in Mastricht's work of theology can be noted in the nineteenth century, though the Dutch neo-Calvinist Abraham Kuyper recommended Mastricht's work for his students, asserting it as the "de zuiverste en best verkrijgbare" (purest and best obtainable) work of Reformed orthodoxy. Continental systematic and historical theologians rarely refer to Mastricht but do so with various appraisals, such as "a typical Reformed medieval" (Eduard

---

185. Petrus van Mastricht, *Beschouwende en Praktikale Godgeleerdheit, waarin alle godgeleerde hoofdstukken hen, het Bijbelverklarenden Leerstellige, Wederleggende en Praktikale deel, door eenen onafgebroken schakel onderscheidelijk samengevoegt, voorgestelt word*, Hendricus Pontanus (Rotterdam: Hendrik van Pelt; Utrecht: Jan Jacob van Poolsum, 1749–53).

186. *Maandelyke uittreksels, of Boekzaal der geleerde waerelt* (Amsterdam: Adriaan Wor en Erven G. onder de Linden, 1749), 68: 603–30.

187. Mastricht, *Beschouwende en Praktikale Godgeleerdheit*, preface.

188. [A. Comrie, N. Holtius], *Examen van het ontwerp van tolerantie* (Amsterdam: Nicolaas Byl, 1756), 352, 409, "…en Doctor Mastricht, uit welke laatsten ik geen uitreksel behoeve te geeven, wyl zijn Systema, wiens weerga ik denke dat niet te vinden is, in onze taal overgezet en in ieders handen is."

189. Middelburg, *The Netherlands, Regional Archive Zeeland*, archive Steenbakker, number 3, "Ik hebbe uit vele, veel nut mogen genieten, bijzonder uit de oude godgeleerde, zo wel in Frankrijk, Engeland, Schotland, als in Nederland. De Schriften van latere Godgeleerde, als die van…Mastricht,…en vele andere zijn mij zeer nuttig geweest." S. Post is acknowledged.

Böhl), as one who used "the scholastic method very cautiously" (A. Ypey), and as an important opponent of the Cocceians (L. Diestel, H. Heppe, A. Ritschl).[190] The assertion of H. Visscher about Mastricht's dependency on William Ames,[191] moreover, was continued by W. Goeter and K. Reuter in the next century.[192]

The twentieth century, furthermore, witnessed appeals to Mastricht's theology in controversy, as well as continuing interest by systematic theologians. In matters of theological controversy, Mastricht's authority is sometimes noted, as it was in eighteenth-century New England; in addition, at the Synod of 1924, the Christian Reformed Church in North America referenced Mastricht concerning the doctrine of common grace. The Synod differed with the Revs. Hoeksema and Danhof, who appealed to Mastricht more than to Calvin, to assert the Reformed understanding of the doctrine.[193] In the works of systematic theology from Dutch theologians such as Herman Bavinck, Louis Berkhof, E. C. Gravemeijer, Herman Hoeksema, and G. H. Kersten, but also from the Swiss Karl Barth, the *TPT* is cited favorably, but usually only in the footnotes.[194]

---

190. Eduard Böhl, *Von der Rechtfertigung Durch den Glauben. Ein beitrag zur rettung des Protestantischen Carkinaldogmas* (Leipzig: K. Gustorff, 1890), 55; A. Ypey, *Algemeene Kerkelijke Geschiedenis* (Haarlem: F. Bohn, 1816), 25:170; H. Heppe, *Geschichte des Pietismus und der Mystik in der Reformirten Kirche* (Leiden: Brill, 1879), 164; idem, *Reformed Dogmatics*, trans. G. T. Thomson (London: Allen & Unwin, 1950), 12, 20, 62, 81, 83, 91, 92, 93, 95, 96, 99, 108, 152, 196, 220, 226, 229, 236, 240, 266, 270, 308, 317, 351, 361, 366, 367, 375, 381, 385, 493, 510, 546 (the majority of citations are found in the doctrine of God); L. Diestel, *Studien zur Föderaltheologie, Jahrbücher für deutsche Theologie*, 10 (1865): 209–76; A. Ritschl, *Geschichte des Pietismus* (Bonn: Marcus, 1880–1886), 3:451.

191. H. Visscher, *Guilielmus Ames* (Haarlem: J. M. Stap, 1894), 212.

192. W. Goeters, *Die Vorbereitung des Pietismus* (Leipzig: J. C. Hinrich, 1911), 56; K. Reuter, *Wilhelm Ames, des führende Theologe des erwachenden reformierten Pietismus* (C. Brugle: Ansbach, 1940), 35.

193. *Acta der Synode 1924 van de Christelijke Gereformeerde Kerk.* Gehouden van 18 Juni tot 8 Juli, 1924 te Kalamazoo, Mich., U.S.A, 127–29 (Calvin), 128, 130, 133–34 (Mastricht).

194. Karl Barth, *Die Kirchliche Dogmatik* (Zürich: EVZ-Verlag, 1970), I/1:5, 199; I/2:310; II/1: 369f., 373, 404, 508, 516, 592, 601, 646, 731f.; II/2:83, 122, 142, 150, 371; III/2:456; III/3:72, 75, 107, 118, 178, 186, 333; IV/2:115; IV/3:17. Works with no reference index will be cited with page number; Herman Bavinck, *Gereformeerde Dogmatiek* (Kampen: Kok, 1921); Louis Berkhof, *Systematic Theology*, with a new preface by Richard A. Muller (Grand Rapids: Eerdmans, 1996); E. C. Gravenmeijer, *Leesboek over de Gereformeerde Geloofsleer* (Utrecht: H. Ten Hove, 1896), 1:118, 194, 254, 256, 263, 283, 293, 319, 334, 338, 342, 344, 349, 351, 362, 368, 370, 374, 376, 379, 393, 402, 408, 410, 414, 421, 422, 455; Herman Hoeksema, *Reformed Dogmatics* (Grand Rapids: Reformed Free Publishing Association, 1966), 61, 287, 447; G. H. Kersten, *De Gereformeerde Dogmatiek* (Utrecht: De Banier, 1988, zesde druk), I:15, 25, 43, 94, 96, 97, 100, 110, 148, 150, 164, 179, 197, 207, 216, 228, 230, 244, 251, 326, 394, 412, 415; II:5, 11, 13, 14, 16, 19, 25, 26, 28, 29, 34, 39, 42, 45, 56, 237, 255, 301, 346.

At the opening of the twenty-first century, both a renewed academic and non-scholarly interest is evident in the reprint of *A Treatise Concerning the Regeneration* and the *Beschouwende en Practicale Godgeleerdheid*, as well as in various scholarly publications.[195]

In retrospect, the emerging portrait of Mastricht contains three main and consistent characteristics: theology, Hebrew, and anti-Cartesianism, to which can be added, to a certain extent, homiletics. With respect to theology, Mastricht's theological formation from catechism class to his graduation from the University of Utrecht consisted of thoroughly Reformed orthodox and Protestant scholastic training, combined with piety. Both theory and practice—of theology and of the theologian—became a central theme of Mastricht's intellectual development. The "Utrecht emphasis" on *theologia practica* was advanced and codified by Mastricht in *TPT*, a pinnacle of Protestant scholastic theology: exegetical, doctrinal, elenctical, and practical. With respect to Hebrew, Mastricht's teaching of this Semitic language cannot be viewed independently of the Renaissance humanist concern for the study of original languages. Furthermore, his acquaintance with rabbinic literature provided him with a solid linguistic foundation and exegetical aids for theology. In respect to anti-Cartesianism, Mastricht was very attentive to the philosophical developments of his time. His excellent reputation in this field was known throughout Europe.

In addition, this emerging portrait of Mastricht contains two other elements. First, the social and ecclesiastical context of his life and work was largely international and ecumenical. It was international in that it included French Huguenots, English Reformed and Presbyterians, and the Reformed church of the Dutch Republic. The ecumenical aspect, although less noticeable, is most prominent in the union of Lutherans and Reformed at Frankfurt an der Oder. Moreover, his presence in the predominantly Cocceian classis of Cleve should not be ignored. The second prominent element in Mastricht's life is his concern for the students of divinity or ministry. This concern was expressed in the

---

195. Petrus van Mastricht, *A Treatise on Regeneration*, ed. Brandon Withrow (Morgan, PA: Soli Deo Gloria Publications, 2002); idem, *Beschouwende en Practicale Godgeleerdheid* (Ermelo: F. N. Snoek, 2003); idem, *On the Justification of the Redeemed*, trans. Brannan Ellis (Escondido: Westminster Theological Seminary, 2006); Martijn Bac, "De Philosophia Christiana. De interactie van klassiek gereformeerde theologie en cartesiaanse filosofie (1639–1677)" (ThM thesis, Utrecht University, 2001); J. C. van Burg, "Extern en intern: Uitwendige en inwendige roeping bij Petrus van Mastricht (1630–1706)" (ThM thesis, Utrecht University, 2010); Jan Adriaan Schlebusch, "Cartesianism and Reformed Scholastic Theology: A Comparative Study of the Controversy between Christoph Wittich and Petrus van Mastricht" (ThM thesis, University of the Free State, 2013). See also footnote 1.

Prodromus and repeated in the *Methodus, De optima methodus concionandi,* and *TPT*—theology in the service of preaching.

In conclusion, the influence of Protestant Scholasticism and Renaissance humanism contributed to Mastricht's status as a seventeenth-century post-Reformation Reformed theologian, Christian Hebraist, homiletician, and philosopher. Mastricht's personal motto, as well as the deficiency of autobiographical material in his works, reinforces the belief that his "true image is revealed when one lives by his book."[196]

---

196. Cf. Petrus van Mastricht, *Beschouwende en praktikale godgeleerdheid,* op de afbeeldinge. The motto is 2 Corinthians 12:10b, "for when I am weak, then I am strong."

Funeral oration on the death of
Petrus van Mastricht[1] by Henricus Pontanus

24 February 1706

With unbounded zeal the Egyptians, Phrygians, Greeks, and finally the Romans worshiped Earth, the bride of Heaven, the mother of all things and of the gods themselves. After Publius Cornelius Scipio Nasica received from sailors an image of her that had been transported from Phrygia up the Tiber and delivered it to the noble matrons (among whom Claudia Quinta, a daughter of Claudius Appius Caecus, was preeminent) so that it might be transferred to the temple of Victory, the image earned the honor of standing as a statue in that temple's vestibule. The Romans imagine that Earth's statue remained intact, even when the temple burned down twice.[2] So if wretched human beings, carried away with blind and base superstition, so greatly venerated that mother from whom they supposed the nourishments of the body originated, it is all the more right that not only all the good leaders of our republic, but also all the citizens and inhabitants of this city of Utrecht, love and revere their academy, their alma mater, whom the fathers of the fatherland have raised up within these walls to be a fruitful trainer not only of the body but also of the mind, useful and necessary for divine and human affairs, nay indeed, even a channel of salvation to the city and to the world! But how much greater does love and godly reverence for the common mother of us all bind us and guide us; how right and just it is that we suffer all the

---

1. This oration was first published as Henricus Pontanus, *Laudatio funebris in excessum doctissimi et clarissimi senis, Petri van Mastrigt...XXIV Februarii postridie sepulturae dixit Henricus Pontanus* (Utrecht: Guilielmus vande Water, 1706). Mastricht's funeral oration is included in the first printing of the third edition, Petrus van Mastricht, *Theoretico-practica Theologia...editio nova*, 2 vols. (Utrecht, Amsterdam, 1715), foll. *4v-§***3v. On Henricus Pontanus, see "Henricus Pontanus" in *Nieuw Nederlandsch Biografisch Woordenboek* (*NNBW*), eds. P. C. Molhuysen and F. K. H. Kossman, 10 vols. (Leiden: A. W. Sijthoff's Uitgevers-Maatschappij N. V., 1911–1937), 10:748.

2. See 1.8.11 in Valerius Maximus, *Memorable Doings and Sayings*, ed. and trans. D. R. Shackleton Bailey (Cambridge, Mass.: Harvard University Press, 2000), *Loeb Classical Library* (*LCL*) 492:115.

more sorely, when we experience her distresses and disasters, and especially when we either hear of or ourselves begin to sense her impending decline.

This filial affection has been fixed most firmly in my heart from the time that I became one of the public teachers, whom the nobles, through their care and benevolence, have made responsible to instruct the youth, so that they would not pass through life without letters, which would be nothing less than burying a man alive.[3] If any blessings or joys have befallen our Muses, for me, they were exquisite delights, and more so than any bodily ones. But when adversities came, I groaned under them in anguish, no less than I would under the griefs and sorrows of my own mother. Alas, in recent years events have been of the latter kind. So many and such grave occurrences are laid upon us that I could scarcely recount them without tears. Now certainly, by kindness of the Supreme Divinity, our academic affairs, and especially theological ones, have not been so disturbed, nor has our calamity progressed as far as the false accusation liars have spread far and wide would have it, as if the long-established large attendance of our lectures had passed into sheer solitude. Disparagements of this sort shame the most crowded lecture halls of other professors. And if you permit, I would in this number include my own lectures, which have been filled in the past semester by over fifty of the most distinguished youths, not only from these shores, but also from England, Scotland, Ireland, Germany, Silesia, Prussia, and Hungary. But even given these blessings, I cannot deny the wounds inflicted on us and the deaths that have threatened us.

I do not want to stray too far from our subject, but recall how the incomparable Johann Georg Gräve died three years ago.[4] Even his despisers did not deny what a great and irreparable loss we suffered along with the whole world in his death. Most truly did the renowned Pieter Burmann, as he sought to pay him deserved praise, exclaim with Metellus Macedonicus, "Rally citizens! The walls of our city and academy have been overthrown."[5] And however much we hope

---

3. Pontanus's phrase "ne vitam sine literis transigat, quae nihil est, praeterquam vivi hominis sepultura," resembles a common proverb taken from Seneca the Younger, *Ad Lucilium Epistulae Morales*, 82.3: "Otium sine litteris mors est et hominis vivi sepultura" (Leisure without literature is death and the burial of a person still living).

4. Johann Georg Gräve (1632–1703) served at Utrecht University from 1662 until his death. He was Utrecht's first chair of rhetoric and in 1667 was also a professor of politics and history. He was also known for several works illustrating his classical scholarship in critical editions. See "Graevius, Johannes Georgius" in *Biografisches Archiv der Antike*, Microfiche (Munchen, 1996–1999), no. 191:79–80.

5. Petrus Burmannus, *Oratio funebris viri clarissimi Joannis Georgii Graevii, Magnae Britanniae Regis historici, politices, historiarum & eloquentiae professoris ordinarii* (Utrecht: Guilielmus vande Water, 1703), 7. Cf. Petrus Burmannus, *Petri Burmanni orationes antea sparsim editae et*

that this prophets' song, which they sang at our jubilee, will be proven false, that this illustrious academy would die with the illustrious Gräve, yet these are the times that we should rightly tremble at omens and auguries of this sort. Three years ago Gräve died, three months ago, Gerardus De Vries.[6] By your faith! What a gem that adorned our profession! He stipulated in his will that none of his colleagues were to offer a memorial service for him. But far be it from me, having received such a suitable occasion as this, to pass over in ungrateful silence the man's most excellent merits, by which he bound our academy to himself. De Vries had outstanding predecessors—Reinerius,[7] Schotanus,[8] Goorius,[9] Senguerdius,[10] Berckringer,[11] Paul and Daniel Voetius,[12] Ravensperg,[13] Bruinius,[14] Mansveldius[15]—among whom you would find those who excelled in fame and merits. I will not delve into their praises. I would not want to seem to fawn over these most honorable men with base flattery, since there are those here who are connected by the closest bond of blood and kin, and survive their ancestors in this city.

I would like to remember just one, Ravensperg, who in his early youth, having far surpassed his Steinfurter parent, the Groningen theologian, Hermann

ineditis auctae (The Hague: P. G. van Balen, 1759), 85. For the original reference in Latin and its English translation, see Maximus, *Memorable Doings and Sayings*, 4.12, LCL 492:348.

6. Gerardus De Vries (1648–1705): in 1674 he was appointed to a chair in philosophy, in 1685 he was appointed to a chair in theology; *NNBW* 10:1140.

7. Henri Reneri (1593–1639), professor of philosophy at Utrecht, 1636–1639. For information on his life, see Antonius Aemilius, *Oratio in obitum…Henrici Renerii, liberalium artium magistri & philosophiae in academia Ultrajectina professoris* (Utrecht, 1639).

8. Meinardus Schotanus (1593–1644), professor of theology at Utrecht, 1637–1644. See *NNBW* 9:1000.

9. Arnoldus van Goor (fl. 1607–1638), professor of philosophy at Utrecht, 1638. See A. J. van der Aa, *Biographisch Woordenboek der Nederlanden (BWDN)* (Haarlem: K. J. R. van Hardewijk & G. D. J. Schotel, 1852–1878), 7:287–88.

10. Arnoldus Senguerdius (1610–1667), professor of metaphysics and physics at Utrecht, 1639–1648. See *BWDN* 17-1:613.

11. Daniel Berckringer (1598–1667), professor of practical philosophy at Utrecht, 1640–1667. See *BWDN* 2-1:359.

12. Paul Voetius (1619–1667), professor of metaphysics and logic at Utrecht, 1641–1654. See *BWDN* 19:304.

13. Jacobus Ravensperg (1615–1650), professor of philosophy at Utrecht 1641–1650, see *NNBW* 2:1169.

14. Johannes de Bruyn (1620–1675), professor of physics and mathematics at Utrecht, 1652–1670, see *NNBW* 4:328.

15. Regnerus van Mansveld (1639–1671), professor of logic and metaphysics at Utrecht, 1660–1671, see *BWDN* 12-1:155.

Ravensperg,[16] became quite famous by reputation for his ability, especially in his attack on Spinoza, despite the fact that most of his writings are no longer extant. I know not by what misfortune this happened, but it has certainly been to the manifest detriment of the good of the republic and posterity.[17] Then, furthermore, when the immortal men Johann Heinrich Bisterveld[18] and Johann Heinrich Alsted[19] built the new academy at Alba Iulia, in Transylvania of Romania, under the auspices of the prince, George I Rákóczi, Ravensperg was called there to teach philosophy on terms so lavish that I doubt whether any professor in our Netherlands enjoys such a great wage. But whether he refused the offered position because he would be painfully wrenched from our most beautiful Utrecht, or was prevented by fate so that he could not accept, I dare not say. As to what records remain of him, I know them well. For when in Meppel in the countryside of Drenthe I took my first call to ecclesiastical ministry (a most sweet time that I will never forget), I found in the house of the judge, Sciccardus, the erudite elderly uncle of our Ravensperg, the accounts of Ravensperg's calling and most eagerly read them with great admiration.

After such great men, de Vries followed. But unless I am much mistaken, he either equaled or exceeded all of them with respect to the celebrity of his name, his facility in teaching, his care and perseverance in his labor (even though afflicted with suffering from chronic disease), and finally, the size of the crowds who heard him. Such great love for his homeland and his homeland's academy animated him that during its most difficult times, when the French had barely left the city and the public treasury was in miserable ruin,[20] when he was called (with a less than lavish offer) from Leiden University to this Athenaeum, he

---

16. Jacobus Ravensperg's father was Hermann Ravensperg (1586–1625), who was a theologian at both Steinfurt and at Groningen. See *BWDN* 16:104–105; *NNBW* 2:1167–69.

17. Cf. Jacobus Ravensberg, *Centuria quaestionum philosophorum quam Dei gratia auxilante sub praesidio D. Iacobi Ravensberg* (Utrecht: Joannes Waesberg, 1649).

18. Johann Heinrich Bisterveld (1605–1655), *ADB* 2:682–83; *Biographisch-Bibliographisches Kirchenlexikon (BBKL)*, ed. Friedrich Wilhelm Bautz (Hamm, Herzberg, and Nordhausen: Traugott Bautz, 1990–2006), 20:215–16.

19. Johann Heinrich Alsted (1588–1638), *ADB* 1:354–55; *BBKL* 1:124–25; *NDB* 1:206.

20. Resulting from the death of the last Hapsburg king of Spain, King Carlos II, the Spanish War of Succession (1701–1714) plunged almost the whole of Western Europe into a war over the possibility of a unification of Spain and France under one Bourbon king. The combatants were divided thus: a Spanish faction, France, and Bavaria being in favor of the unification, another Spanish faction, England (which became Great Britain in 1707 with the English-Scottish unification), the Netherlands, Portugal, the Holy Roman Empire, and the Duchy of Savoy being against the unification. The failure of Bourbon ambition terminated in a treaty at Utrecht (1713) and Rastatt (1714), which Spain did not formally ratify with Austria until 1720. In the meantime, the Netherlands were the scene of constant fighting between 1702 and 1707, with significant tracts of territory in the Low Countries passing back and forth between the combatants.

could not be kept in Leiden, not by money, nor by the offer of an ordinary professorship in philosophy, nor by any other promises. Afterward, when he was
flourishing here and adorning the Utrecht chair, again he was invited to the
Leiden academy with an honorable stipend. And when our most distinguished
senate feared the departure of a citizen so beloved by them and so devoted to
them, they permitted him to name whatever terms he wanted so that he would
stay. Content with his fair and equitable arrangements, he continued to devote
himself to his most beloved homeland. Though in his last six years he walked
around like a dead corpse, even so he could not abandon his chair, since a whole
crowd of students were calling for their teacher. Although the poor custom had
prevailed even among us that citizens of the academy pursue their own schools at
home and spurn the public ones to their own great loss, even so that man enjoyed
a packed auditorium all the way to his last lecture. He could so soothe and rouse
the ears and minds of his hearers, as if by enchantment (a praiseworthy and most
useful enchantment, that is), that they clung to him with great devotion—a characteristic that Hendrik Boxhorn[21] lavishly praised in Justus Lipsius.[22]

Are there any supporters and lovers of their alma mater and their academy
who do not grieve over these turns of events and do not lament this misfortune? Chief among the mourners are the noble magistrates of our city, who with
the utmost reluctance and difficulty agreed to forego a funeral eulogy for such
a great man. They would not have changed their mind except that in the end,
their reverence for the last will of the deceased had greater weight, which is but
one more proof of their honor and love for him. I hope that I will to some extent
satisfy these men with this fitting eulogy. Indeed I attribute to the fathers of
the fatherland and of the academy that laudable generosity of the sons of the
Roman general Pomponius, who when they had set up three columns for their
victorious father—one for the fighter, another for the victor, and a third for the
conqueror—and their father in modesty declined this honor, they added a fourth
for Pomponius the humble man. At a time when Gräve lived among us hale and
healthy and the strength of De Vries was giving way, Gräve's sorrow was frequently in my ears (for he was, as you no doubt know, most amiable toward me),
lamenting that adversity of every sort would befall our Athenaeum, if the sick
man were to die. While I have this memory in mind and while I think of each
man—both Gräve, whose eulogists' predictions have been fairly well fulfilled in

---

21. Hendrik Boxhorn (ca. 1545–1631), see *BWDN* 2:1120–22; *Biographisch Woordenboek
van Protestantsche Godgeleerden in Nederland* (*BWPGN*), ed. Jan Pieter de Bie et al. ('s-Gravenhage,
1907–1949), 1:549–53; *NNBW* 2:236–37.

22. Justus Lipsius (1547–1606), see *BWDN* 11:507–19; *NNBW* 3:775–82.

the fate of the Academy, and de Vries, because of whose fate Gräve grew fearfully apprehensive and bemoaned future changes to the academy—please do not accuse me of madness if I should find myself in the same fear and panic. For when I consider that students from either of the top two classes will not be coming to the schools of the theologians, lawyers, and doctors properly prepared to enter them, I tremble all over. If, contrary to all these things that do not disagree with the truth in the least bit, Envy dared to open her mouth (which I scarcely believe would happen), she would harm herself, and not our dead hero, who has risen above all envy. Therefore as De Vries is now silent in the nearby tomb, Wisdom has departed from the nearby lecture hall. There would be no measure or end to our sorrow, if there were not still living very learned and diligent men who will act bravely and manfully to detain Wisdom as she departs and flees, and to bring her back to her former abode.

While we are grieving that De Vries was taken from us, behold, our long-lived elder Petrus van Mastricht dies! We buried his perishable remains yesterday in the same tomb with De Vries, so that those closest in mind also might be joined in body in the crypt, and so that holding hands they might rise up together and run to meet their Savior when he returns in judgment. But we have come together now to contemplate the gifts and the deeds of a godly and erudite mind. Antiquity afforded this honor to its own heroes, to men and to women, those renowned in peace and war, and especially to the learned. Likewise the church to her martyrs. This praiseworthy custom, based on these examples, has continued up to the present, that those still living might gaze into the lives of the dead as into a mirror, and learn to ardently conform their words, deeds, and thoughts to their example. I would have preferred, because of the weight of more than one serious reason, to be exempt from this duty, but after I learned that the last will of the dying man and the wish of our university senate together agreed that this honorific duty would fall to me, considering that only the glory of obedience remained for me, I took up the task willingly. But just as I am girding myself for the task, another adornment to our rank meets his day, Paul Bauldri d'Iberville, whose bones and ashes we committed to the earth just three days ago, and who was a greatly beloved and close friend to me.[23] And this man, how well-known, and how well-pleasing, did he become by his erudition among the leading men in Italy and France, namely, Cardinal Enrico Noris and Bishop Pierre Daniel Huet.[24] Moreover, as a victim of French cruelty, out of love for the true religion

---

23. Paul Bauldri d'Iberville (1639–1706), professor of church history at the University of Utrecht from 1685–1706, *BWDN* 2-1:186–87.

24. For the life of Cardinal Enrico Noris (O. S. A.) (1631–1704), see *H. Norisii...opera*

he exchanged Croesus's wealth, which he possessed, for exile in poverty. By his excellent holiness of life he shined brightly before all his own countrymen and ours, and most especially before me, so that by his most excellent worth he ought to be counted among the number of the martyrs and confessors. Thus he is most worthy of the eulogy soon to be given by my most renowned colleague and dear friend, Adriaan Reeland.[25]

Therefore, having mentioned this, I return to my Petrus.[26] And in order to celebrate him I begin with the fatherland that made Mastricht renowned, for his home was Köln. If we were to turn our attention to the ancient Ubii, to Nero's mother who was born among them, under whose auspices a colony of Romans was afterwards led across to those shores, who gave the city its name, and changed the *Ubii* to the *Agrippinenses*;[27] if I were to mention all the real and imagined glories of this most prosperous city; if I would pause to consider the archbishop and reformer Hermann, the learned men, and the theologians whom that city birthed from her prolific womb, not those fools and sophists of ancient times who imprisoned and ruined the youth with scholastic barbarities and useless precepts, but the better ones who happily devoted themselves to good literature and the exposition of Greek and Latin writers, among whom Mauritius the Count of Spilenberg, the canon of the Köln Basilica, is eminent, who with Rudolph Agricola and Langenius, a knight of Münster, Francisco Philelphus, and Theodore of Gaza, and other restorers of both languages in Italy, gave themselves to their work; if, I say, I wanted to treat these and other similar topics thoroughly, when would I ever stop speaking?

---

omnia nunc primum collecta atque ordinata...praefationes, vitam auctoris...dissertationes indicemque, 4 vols. (Verona, 1729–1734), 4:XIII–XLII; for Bishop Pierre Daniel Huet (1630–1721), see *Memoirs of the Life of Peter Daniel Huet written by himself,* trans. John Aikin, 2 vols. (London: Longman, Hurst, Rees and Orme, 1810).

25. Adriaan Reeland (1676–1718) was professor of oriental languages (1701–1713) and professor of sacred antiquities (1713–1718) at the University of Utrecht, *BWDN* 16:145–51.

26. For information on Petrus van Mastricht's life in biographical and bibliographical dictionaries see *BWDN* 12–1:361–62; for a relatively recent and brief bibliography of scholarship on Mastricht up to 2001, see Willem van Asselt, "Petrus van Mastricht" in *Biografisch lexicon voor de geschiedenis van het Nederlands protestantisme* (Kampen: Kok, 1978–2006), 5:360–61. Also see Adriaan C. Neele, *Petrus Van Mastricht (1630–1706): Reformed Orthodoxy: Method and Piety* (Leiden: Brill, 2009), 27–62, and biographical material in this volume.

27. Nero's mother, Julia Augusta Agrippina the Younger, was born at *Oppidum Ubiorum* (circa 38 BC), which was subsequently named *Colonia Claudia Ara Agrippinensium* in 50 AD. It is sometimes known variously in subsequent literature as *Agrippina, Colonia,* or *Ubiopolis.* See J. G. T. Grässe, Helmut Plechl, Friedrich Benedict, Günter Spitzbart, *Orbis Latinus: Lexikon lateinischer geographischer Namen des Mittelalters der Neuzeit* (Klinkhardt & Biermann, 1971).

There is not only cause to praise Mastricht's homeland: if Köln produced good men, it also produced bad ones. Such was Theodoricus, *doctor theologus*, who was present at the Council of Constance, and in session thirteen gave a speech to the fathers, who also impiously harassed that most innocent martyr Jan Hus. Another such person was Conrad Vorstius.[28] Of his two greatest disciples, Johannes Piscator customarily called Vorstius his worst student,[29] whereas Johann Heinrich Alting was his best one.[30] Vorstius abused his most genteel nature and extensive learning and miserably afflicted the Steinfurt school (my alma mater) as well as the whole Reformed world, and would have afflicted it more if he had obtained the Leiden chair of theology, that is, if the most distinguished magistrates of Amsterdam and all those in the Dutch Republic who held fast to the catholic truth, together with foreign princes and kings committed to orthodoxy, did not strongly and manfully intervene against this wretched plot hatched by a few men.[31]

I would freely pardon even the foulest errors of this most learned man, if he had admitted frankly what he kept unspoken in his heart. But who does not become angry at the hypocrisy by which, throughout his whole life, he decieved the unsuspecting? Indeed, that man once, then twice, took the oath at Heidelberg that he would die for the catechism of the Palatinate. That man, in speech and writing, in words and tears, testified so many times to the nobles of Holland that he differed from any of the Reformed churches only on the doctrine of predestination and its related heads, agreeing from his heart with every other point. Indeed, the apostate Petrus Bertius wrote an epitaph for that man, whose sum was this: the Reformed Church was and has remained most unfair to Vorstius

---

28. Conrad Vorstius, *BBKL* 13:84–90; *BWDN* 19:373–78; *NNBW* 3:1342–44.

29. Johannes Piscator was a professor at the Herborn Academy from 1584–1625 where he trained both Conrad Vorstius and Johann Heinrich Alting, *ADB* 26:180–81; *BBKL* 7:640–44. At one point, Vorstius and Piscator were engaged in a significant disagreement on predestination, in which Vorstius stridently attacked the views and character of his former professor. See Conrad Vorstius, *Parasceue ad amicam collationem cum Joh. Piscatore* (Gouda: Jasper Tournay, 1612), and Piscator's response, *Ad Conradi Vorstii, S. Theol. D. Parasceuen Responsio apologetica Johan. Piscatoris, Professoris Sacr. Litt. In Illustri Schola Herbornensi: Qua is defendit suas notas contra examen illius. Ubi multa Scripturae dicta, ac inprimis ea quae loquuntur de divina praedestinatione, accurate explicantur* (Herborn, 1613).

30. Johann Heinrich Alting (1583–1644), *ADB* 1:367–68; *BBKL* 1:132.

31. Pontanus is referring to the actions and diplomatic interventions and threats against the Dutch Republic, for example, of King James I, in the appointment of Vorstius to Leiden University. For samples of the diplomatic correspondence and declarations see King James 1 of England, "A Declaration Concerning the Proceedings with the States Generall, of the United Provinces of the Low Countreys, in the cause of D. Conradus Vorstius" in *The Workes of the Most High and Mightie Prince Iames* (London: Barker & Bill, 1616), 354; see 347–80.

and yet was and remained most beloved by him.[32] Indeed, that man confessed several times the Triune nature of the one God, condemning Arius as well as Socinus. That man offered to the Synod of Dordt the views he had previously expressed in a noteworthy book, refuting Socinus,[33] and yet now only a malevolent man would doubt that he was in fact an adversary of the three hypostases of the Godhead, which Christoph van den Sand Jr.,[34] a learned and noble man, realized and did not disguise like Vorstius did. Of such stuff was that Köln

32. The adjective "apostate" could refer to several issues surrounding Petrus Bertius (1565–1629). First, Bertius's critique of the Dutch Reformed Church in the funeral oration for Jacobus Arminius was a continuing point of contention with Franciscus Gomarus after 1609. The oration is *Petri Bertij Oratio in obitum reuerendi & clarissimi viri D. Iacobi Arminij, Sacrosanctae Theologiae Doctoris & Professoris in Academia Lugdunobataua habita post exsequias in auditorio theologico XXII Octobr. anno 1609* (Leiden: Joannes Patius, 1609); in Dutch, *Liick-Oratie over de doot van den Eervveerdighen ende vvytberoemden Heere Iacobvs Arminivs, Soctor ende Professor der H. Teologie inde Hooghe Schole tot Leyden: De welcke by hem is ghedaen inde latynsche tale terstont nae de begraeffenisse in het auditorium der Theologie op den XXIJ Octobris Anno 1609, Ende namaels door een liefhebber verduyst* (Leyden: Jacobszoon, 1609); in English as *The Life and Death of James Arminius and Simon Episcopius, professors of divinity in the University of Leyden in Holland: both of them famous defenders of the doctrine of Gods universal grace and sufferers for it: now published in the English tongue* (London: Thomas Ratcliff and Nathan Thompson for Francis Smith, 1672). The subsequent issue with Gomarus is evidenced by Petrus Bertius, *Aen-Spraeck aen D. Fr. Gomarum op zijne Bedenckinghe over de Lijck oratie ghedaen na de Begraefenisse van D. Jac. Arminius* (Leiden: Jacopszoon, 1609, 1610); see also Franciscus Gomarus, *Proeve van M. P. Bertii Aenspraeck. Ter eeren der waerheydt, tot toutsinge van de geesten, die in de ware Religie, verandering soecken in te bringen, ende tot stichtinge der Gemeynte, uytgegeven*, 2nd ed. (Leiden: J. Jeanszoon Orlers, 1609, 1610). Second, in 1615, Bertius was stripped of his teaching position at Leiden University for, among other things, his pro-Arminian work *Hymenaeus desertor, sive de sanctorum apostasia problemata duo* (Leiden: Joannes Patus, 1601) and its Dutch translation, *Hymenaeus desertor, ofte tweevragh-stucken van den afval der heylighen* (n.p.: n.n., 1613). Third, later in life, while employed in the French court as a royal cartographer, Bertius converted to and later died in the Roman Catholic faith. For his life and works, see *ADB* 2:509–10; *BWDN* 2:446–50; *NNBW* 1:320–23.

33. For an example of Vorstius's defense of the Reformed before moving to Leiden, see Conrad Vorstius, *Apologia pro ecclesiis orthodoxis; in qua tres primi fidei nostrae articuli plenius examinantur. Opposita thesibus Iesuitarum, Monasterii nuper excusis, hoc titulo: Credo Caluini-sequarum* (Steinfurt: Guielmus Antonius, 1607). For an example of Vorstius's orations to the Synod of Dort, see Vorstius, *Oratio apologetica habita in pleno concessu Hollandiae et Westfrisiae Ordinum* (J. Patius, 1612); for a Dutch translation, see *Oratie tot Verantwoordinghe. Ghedaen in de volle vergaderinghe der...Staten van Hollandt ende West-Vrieslandt. In s'Graven-haghe den 22 martij stilo novo* (Hillebrandt Jacobsz, 1612). For the sentence of the Synod of Dort against Vorstius, see Synod of Dort, *Sententia synodi nationalis Dordrechtanae de doctrinâ Conradi Vorstii [in d. 4 mei]...Simulque decretvm...Ordinum Hollandiae & West-Frisiae quod est illam subsecutum [in d. 27 junij]*. (Hagae-Comitis: Ex officina Hillebrandi Iacobi, 1619).

34. Christph van den Sand, Jr. (1644–1680) was a follower of Spinoza, an anti-Trinitarian, and one who promoted Arianism as a high point in Christian theology and history. His *Bibliotheca Antitrinitariorum* (Freistadt, 1684) was edited by Fausto Sozzini's grandson, Benedyt Wiszowaty. For Sand's life and work, see *BWDN* 17–1:88–91; *NNBW* 10:869–70; *ADB* 30:338–39.

theologian that I thought it worthwhile to explain in an excursus, so that those who today take up Vorstius's cause, and who loudly gripe against the bravest and most praiseworthy men who took action in the republic and church so that Vorstius would not be foisted upon Leiden University, may be filled with shame and forget how to curse.

Moreover, since the excellence that a fatherland confers on a citizen may be meager, I say this of our Kölnian, that his ancestors were residents and guests, and not citizens born in Köln, for just like Bauldri is today, in the same way at that time these men were most glorious confessors who had fled to Köln so that they might enjoy liberty of conscience and religion, a liberty that in their homeland the executioners of the Roman persecution cruelly sought to destroy. Without a doubt, Mastricht's ancestors preferred to be sojourners and guests in Köln with holy Christians than to rejoice in the right of citizenship and to glow with consular dignity.

Certainly Mastricht's great-grandfather and great-grandmother were among the first illumined by the light of the rising gospel. In the year 1577,[35] in the first and cruelest siege of Maastricht, his great-grandfather, because he could not be rescued quickly enough by his children from the hands of the Spaniards, was drowned in the waters of the River Maas, which run next to the city. However, in 1583, his grandfather Cornelius and his grandmother, whom he married in the same year, with his only sister at the time of Alva's persecution, fled Maastricht for Köln after he purchased with gold the license to leave. It was at that time, he and his posterity adopted the family name of "Mastrigtius" or "van Mastricht," even though they had come from the Schoning clan, which was held in high honor at that time in Maastricht.[36] His father, Thomas, following in the footsteps of his

---

35. The Siege of Maastricht occurred in 1579; however, there was an uprising of Maastricht against the Spanish in October 1576, and there was also a subsequent "Spanish Fury" in Maastricht in 1576 that resulted in a great amount of bloodshed and pillaging. "Spanish Furies" occurred within the context of unpaid Spanish troops and mercenaries and the sack of Dutch towns in which Spanish troops were given free reign to slaughter the garrison and civilians in addition to plunder. Several notable Spanish Furies occurred at Mechelen (1572), Zutphen (1572), Haarlem (1573), Maastricht (1576), and Antwerp (1576).

36. For example, in connection with his family's previous surname and the place in which he was born, Petrus van Mastricht on occasion employed the Latin pseudonym Cephas Schuenenus Agrippinas, as in his work against his fellow Dutch Reformed pastor Petrus Allinga: Cephas Schuenenus Agrippinas, *Cartesianismi gangraena insanabilis duodecim erotematum illustrium decadibus, frustra curata per D. Petrum Allingam, pastorem in pago Widenes prope Hoornam enneade erotematum vulgarium demonstrata a C. Schuenenus Agr. S. Literarum Studioso* (Utrecht: Franciscus Halma, 1680).

ancestors,[37] at that time nourished and governed a congregation secretly gathered in that locale as an assistant to the pastors of the Presbytery of Köln.

His maternal grandfather was Nicolas Planque, commonly known as de la Planque, a consul in Aath. Planque's own grandmother is buried in a rather large tomb on the same hill in that place with her twenty-two children, and today over her tomb she can be seen depicted in bronze-covered stone in the habit of a nun, covering all her children with her sacred garment. But Planque, sick of the Roman superstition because of the countless recent examples of French cruelty, abandoned not only his consulate but also his wife and children, who did not want to follow him, and fled to Antwerp, which at that time was an asylum for refugees. Afterwards, Planque induced his wife to come to him by feigning sickness, and he brought her unwillingly and weeping with their four children to Köln. Although their fertile marriage added five more to that number, his business happily prospered, and God so abundantly blessed him through it that it was not necessary to grieve and pine over their lost ancestral wealth.

From this clan of nine children, Johanna married Thomas van Mastricht, and blessed him with numerous offspring, of which, now that Petrus has died, only Gerhard is still living. Although Gerhard is ten years younger than Petrus, yet by no means is he inferior in piety and learning, for he has shown uncommon evidence of both, previously at Duisburg, where he was preeminent in the chair of jurists, then at Bremen, of which city he is an advisor and orator, eminent for many diplomatic missions and writings that will stand the test of time.[38] I do not dare to add several other things, so that I do not burden his modesty as he sits here with us.

From these details it is established from what sort of stock our Petrus arose, and in what likeness to his ancestors he might boast. He himself was born in the month of November, 1630, from which it is evident that it is true what he said to me while I was assisting him on his sickbed, that he was farther from seventy than he was from eighty. So he reached the upper limit of an ordinary life and earned the white and glittering crown of old age. This seems like a miracle that in the fragility of human nature it happens in the case of many outstanding theologians that they have quite a long life, even though by perpetual care and ceaseless effort, they exhaust their bodies of strength and vigor, and extinguish the lamp of life through excessive use. Peter, Paul, John, Titus, Polycarp, Epiphanius, Athanasius, Jerome, and countless other ancients; the venerable Beza, Du Moulin,

---

37. The 1749–1753 Dutch translation expands *avitis vestigiis insistens* as *die het voetspoor van zyne Godsvruchtige Voorouderen drukkende* (pressing on in the footsteps of his godly ancestors).
38. See "Mastricht, Gerhard von" in *ADB*, 20:579.

Pareus, both of the Rivets, Maresius, Heidanus, Spanheim—and it would be a sin to forget Gisbertus Voetius, the immortal pillar of this Academy—even though they were daily broken by astounding burdens, nevertheless they either attained eighty years or nearly approached this high summit. As divine Providence chastises the sins of the church by frequently snatching away from her the greatest men who have not yet worn out the vigor of youth, so he provides outstanding proofs of his goodness and power whenever he to such a great extent lengthens the years of its masters.

"An old man in the house is a good sign," as the Jewish sages said, because they often buttress teetering households by their prudence and piety. Surely for the same reasons we could say that an old man is a good sign in the house of God, where those who rule are called presbyters (that is, old men), and their gathering a presbytery, not because rule ought to be committed only to the old men of the churches, but that it should be committed only to those who evidence a similar gravity, prudence, and piety. If indeed an old man is a good sign in the house of God, necessarily it would be a bad one whenever the house of God is deprived of elders and their counsel. Some of these same Jewish masters called old men the staffs of families.[39] If we apply this again to the church of God, who would not fear, if her walking sticks were broken, that she should soon fall to ruin? Of course, just as there are indignities in every stage of life, so there are also in old age, even among churchmen, and they grow worse year by year. But we will pay such indignities no heed, because those who gain the garland of old age, provided they walk in the paths of righteousness and die faithful to the work of their supreme Master, as our Petrus did, are most worthy of manifold honor, and are to be revered as though divine, because they defer their departure to the heavenly country for our sake.

But our Petrus did not rely upon his own birth or that of his parents, but labored by the strength of his own character, and because he did not take credit for what he did not accomplish himself—his ancestry, his great-grandparents, or anything else—let us therefore now carefully consider those matters that are properly his. He spent his childhood in the school of Duisburg, where he met his outstanding classmate Theodor Undereyck,[40] who later was an eminent servant of God in the ministry at Kassel and Bremen and was also renowned for his most useful writings. After he left adolescence behind, and after exceptional

---

39. *scipiones familiarum*: Among the Greeks, a σκίπων was a walking stick or even a crutch, but a *scipio* for the Romans at various times was a baton carried as a sign of wealth, rank, honor, or official station, such as for nobles, consuls, or emperors (e.g. Livy, *The History of Rome*, 5.41).

40. See W. Raup, "Theodor Undereyck" in *BBKL* 17:1439. Cf. Neele, *Petrus van Mastricht*, 29n14.

progress in Greek and Latin literature, he was sent to an academy. Petrus preferred Utrecht above all others, not only on account of the renown of its teachers but also because of its most famous Scottish surgeon, whose help his parents sought for the purpose of healing a deformity in Petrus's foot and hips, which had befallen their son in an accident, not by any defect of nature, but by the carelessness of a maidservant when he was an infant. But even though hope eluded the doctor, and he could not remedy the limping of his body, the doctors that had been placed in charge of forming his mind—Voetius,[41] Hoornbeeck,[42] de Maets,[43] worthy of eternal remembrance—shaped his soul in such a way that he excelled all other alumni of the Academy. He also visited Leiden University as well as Heidelberg. He also crossed once into England for the sake of studying language and improving his practice of holiness, but when his fortunes changed, he hurried back to his old teachers. Thus, if we count the months and days, he spent nearly five whole years here, though they were not continuous.

In 1652, he was registered as a candidate for the holy ministry by the venerable Classis of Utrecht, and well equipped with the most honorable academic and ecclesiastical testimonies, he returned to his homeland. A short while afterwards Mastricht provided pulpit supply for a considerable time in the church of Xanten near Wesel. Next he declared the gospel in Glückstadt, because at that time the Reformed were not permitted anywhere else in the whole of Denmark. But when by the remarkable godliness of the great Queen Charlotte Amalie of Hesse-Kassel, who visited Glückstadt the previous summer, a church for the Reformed religion was opened in the royal capital,[44] counsel was taken in the Danish royal court so that Mastricht might be called from the neighboring environs to Copenhagen. But in these matters the most serene and powerful Brandenburg Elector, Frederick Wilhelm the Great, with no greater titles and trophies than that of a lover of true religion and godliness, intervened. Moved by the reputation of this man, the Elector placed him with the theological doctors in his own academy at Frankfurt an der Oder, and furthermore called upon him to teach Hebrew, indeed for this most rare example of Christian manhood he

---

41. Gisbertus Voetius (1589–1687) was professor of theology at the University of Utrecht from 1634–1687. See "Voetius, Gisbert" in *TRE* 35:181–84; *BWDN* 19:296–303; *NNBW* 7:1279–82.

42. Johannes Hoornbeeck (1617–1666) was professor of theology at the University of Utrecht from 1644–1654. See *BWDN* 8:1230–34; *NNBW* 8:843–44; *BWPGN* 4:277–86.

43. Carolus de Maets (1597–1651) was professor of theology at the University of Utrecht from 1639–1651, see *BWDN* 12–1:64–66; *NNBW* 8:1094–96.

44. On Mastricht and the royal residence at Glückstadt-Holstein, see Neele, *Petrus van Mastricht*, 34n38.

created a professorship of practical theology. He did all this by a series of splendid commands, which because they breathe of pure piety, I have reviewed eagerly, and with great delight.[45]

It has often been considered on these shores, not only by godly and learned men, but also by entire classes, synods, and even Dordrecht itself, whether or not practical theology could be profitably entrusted in our academies to one of the theologians, who would then lecture on vices and Christian virtues, and on what they call cases of conscience, who would distinguish the lawful from the unlawful, the praiseworthy from the contemptible, and who would teach youths to serve God and his church not by disputing about holy things, but by living well, and would instruct them in the method of preaching reverently and fruitfully to the people of God, and of rightly approaching the other aspects of their future office. But these most desirable measures have long since ceased to be implemented in our land. Yet in the duchy of Cleves Mastricht began to work in this allotted field, and already in his second year of cultivating and enlarging it, he could not but be accorded the titles and honors of doctor. Thus he hastened on to Duisburg in Cleves, his childhood residence and lodging, and in a public disputation strenuously and happily defended the theoretical-practical nature of theology, and gave an oration concerning the name and nature of a doctor of theology.

In 1669, in a traditional ceremony held in the great auditorium before a crowded gathering, he was solemnly declared by the distinguished Crellius to be a doctor of both theology and of philosophy. All these trappings he would perhaps have spurned, even to death, if good order and the laws of the academy had allowed him to abstain from them. And thus Mastricht was equipped at Frankfurt, so that at last he might that much more fruitfully devote himself to us. That Academy of Groningen did once snatch up the Utrechter, Marten Schoock,[46] and recently took from us the illustrious Cocceius, but Mastricht stayed with us; for such are the turns of fate in academies, that they rise and fall by mutual losses and gains. Yet he did not return to Utrecht to teach, where he had previously studied, until after he finished his course at Frankfurt and spent seven years at the Academy of Duisburg.

As fate would have it, the outstanding theologian and most eloquent preacher of the divine word, Martin Hund (who baptized me while pastoring

---

45. Cf. Neele, *Petrus van Mastricht*, 39n69, "The universities of Duisburg, Frankfurt an der Oder, and Halle belonged to the elector of Brandenburg."

46. Marten Schoock was professor of literature and rhetoric at the University of Utrecht (1638) and then became professor of logic and physics at the University of Groningen (1640–1666), see *BWDN* 17:396–403; *NNBW* 10:889–91.

the congregation at Steinfurt) had passed away.[47] This man, with help from the celebrated Cocceius's book on the covenant,[48] had unlearned Amyraut's method of ordering the divine counsels, which he had imbibed in France, and he was so fruitful in both understanding and explaining Cocceius's reflections on these subjects and others, which at that time were understood by very few people, that the academy mourned the death of their dear Hund no differently than as that of a most beloved brother or son. For on account of his lovable docility there arose a sort of family relation or affinity by which they embraced him. And when a successor had to be sought for this man that had brought great renown to the new academy in the duchy of Cleves, Mastricht alone seemed worthy to the Elector Prince to restore to them the image of their lost professor Hund. For although Duisburg did not surpass the glory of the Frankfurt Athenaeum, yet attracted by a love for his fatherland, he preferred to teach at Duisburg, where he had grown up, and where not long before he had obtained the highest honors in theology and philosophy. Moreover, he found his dearest brother flourishing there in the academic order of jurists. Nor did he deny these motivations in his oration upon the obligation of academic oath-taking, which he recited in 1670 when he was inaugurated as professor of theology and Hebrew.[49]

But after these seven years he spent in Duisburg had elapsed, only Frans Burman[50] of our theologians was still living, and although the renown of his name had filled the earth, and would be even more eminent by my praises, yet he could not sustain the theological task alone. Thus since the Academy needed to be restored after its Gallic captivity, and a successor for the great Voetius was being considered, all were pleased to find in Mastricht a disciple and hearer of Voetius, who had given such great proofs of learning and piety near and far in the mouth and eyes of all, that one could hope to see in him the grand old Voetius himself come to life again. Soon after Voetius and Burmann, a third man who

---

47. Martin Hund (1624–1666) was professor of theology at Duisburg (1655–1666); *ADB* 13:392.

48. Johannes Cocceius, *The Doctrine of the Covenant and Testament of God* (Grand Rapids: Reformation Heritage Books, 2016). Cocceius was a professor of theology variously at Bremen (1630–1636), Franeker (1636–1650), and Leiden (1650–1669) respectively. See *BWDN* 3:518–28; *BWPGN* 2:123–48; *NNBW* 1:615–16; *ADB* 4:376–78; *Neue Deutsche Biographie* (*NDB*), 25 vols. (Berlin: Duncker & Humblot, 1953–present), 3:302.

49. Cf. Neele, *Petrus van Mastricht*, 39.

50. Frans Burman (1628–1679), professor of theology at Utrecht (1662–1671) and professor of church history at Utrecht (1671–1679); *BBKL* 1:822–823; *NNBW* 4:351–352; *BWPGN* 1:702–11; *BWDN* 2:1592–94.

survived them came to us, Melchior Leydekker,[51] our colleague most close to us. Though I fear to praise him to his face, even so because I am already embellishing so many others with true and deserved eulogies, it would be a sin to leave unmentioned that he so thoroughly bound himself to this academy by the labor of many years, and is so overflowing and distinguished in his diverse knowledge and in his grasp of many languages, arts and sciences, that he is second to none of us, indeed that he surpasses most, if not all of us. How fortunate was the college to be led and commanded by these three!

Certainly the college has been fortunate: Mastricht, who spent nearly thirty years here, while he was leading the Academy in 1682, saw such a numerous student body, such as no one had seen before, which is clear from this, that in the same year we graduated more than sixty doctors. If in the most recent times he could not confer as much for public advantage by teaching, let us consider his body's debilitation and ill health, which, by the indications of doctors, harried him for a long time with an apoplexy. Let us consider his stage of life: what more could we fairly demand from an old octogenarian, one who in church and school for such an extended period of time broke the strength of his body and mind? Especially if we would inspect these two huge volumes[52] in which he covers practical theology, which he not only revised while in this city, but enriched with a third part and then some, then we will recognize that he adorned our academy by his writing even while his strength to walk, to speak, and to teach was fading. Certainly if he had devoted his whole life to begetting, birthing, bringing forth, fondling, cherishing, and adorning this most beautiful offspring, he would have accomplished more than enough, and would have lived for the church, the academy, and posterity. I did not ever happen upon any other books of his, of which several, as I now understand, have been copied not only in print, but even by hand. But I confidently affirm concerning this corpus, that it has been so logically arranged, that it is so pregnant and full with such a great weight of material, that it is packed with such great and diverse erudition, that I do not know whether in all the world there could ever exist anything more accurate and elaborate. And if someone should attempt to deny this, oh how he would scratch his poor empty head and gnaw his nails, if he were told to attempt something similar or greater, to put such an unfair burden on his own shoulders.

---

51. Melchior Leydekker (1642–1721) was a professor of theology at the University of Utrecht from 1676–1721, see *BWDN* 11:387–92; *BWPGN* 5:775–85; *NNBW* 4:910–13.

52. The first edition of the *Theoretico-Practica Theologia* was published in two volumes, 1682 and 1687.

But why should I pour forth my own words to uphold the honor and authority of this book? For some time now the most equitable judgments of the most erudite theologians have established its worth, and it is so eagerly purchased everywhere, so that quite deservedly the printers have formed a plan to prepare a third edition. Indeed its honor and glory will abide, even when the names of its spiteful critics[53] lay buried in darkness, forgotten by everyone, and their peevish scribblings have become wrappers for incense and pepper, if not used for worse purposes.[54] Now, the ardor of my speech in praise of this one book has so carried me away that it is not necessary to add anything about its erudition. No one, I should think, will deny that certain men hide in the shadows, wrapped in dirty clothes, whose teaching ought even so to be lifted on high and adored by all. On the contrary, many advance to the highest honors and the rewards of those honors even though they are not worthy of them in the least degree. But our Petrus, insofar as he has obtained great honors in so many academies and churches, has acquired and obtained those honors by persistent labor, the sweat of his brow, and extraordinary skill. This also among his praises must not be left unmentioned, that as he neared the end of his life, he was the greatest stranger to a zeal for parties and factions, loathing all those who through the cause of truth forget Christian charity.

It is true that charity is twisted into vice when a man has become too hostile to reason and has cast it from its throne under the pretext of religion. Indeed, many matters hotly disputed today in this cause of truth turn aside and degenerate into wranglings about phrases and terms. In recent years Werenfels, who adorns the academy of Basel, published the most beautiful little book on contests over words,[55] to which if one would add all the ways people everywhere sin in this regard, into how vast a volume would it grow? If anyone finds fault with any use of human reason in theology, he must be banished from human society into the company of brute beasts. Indeed, the Sacred Letters were written for men, not beasts.

---

53. *nomina Zoilorum*: Zoilus (400–320 BC) was a cynic and critic in the time of Ptolomaeus Philadelphus whose name became synonymous with a malignant and spiteful critic; cf. Ovid, *Remedia Amoris*, 367–70, "But envy did the wit of Homer blame. Malice gave obscure Zoilus a name. Thus sacrilegious censure would destroy, the pious muse, who did her heart employ." Cf. Ovid, *Remedies of Love* in *LCL* 232:202–203; this translation is Garth's from Horace and Ovid, *The works of Horace…also the works of Ovid* (London: Doig and Sterling, 1815), 659.

54. Cf. Martial, *Epigrams* 3.2.5.

55. Samuel Werenfels, *Samuelis Werenfelsi Basiliensis Dissertatio de logomachiis eruditorum* (Amsterdam: Henricus Wetstenius & Rod. Et Gerh. Westenii FF., 1702). On Werenfels's life and works, *ADB* 42:5–8.

The Reformed Church from its earliest beginnings has thought differently, and by countless examples has shown how much she has accomplished with the assistance of a sober and modest philosophy. For this reason in all its schools it created philosophers as much as theologians, just as the wise mistress depends on the help of her handmaiden. One of this innumerable host, the renowned Maresius,[56] whom they even often number among the enemies of reason, gave a serious and elegant oration on the use of reason in theology on the day he was crowned with the doctor's laurel by the great Rivet.[57] Therefore if there is no disagreement on these matters, then where is it? In this perhaps: some thought Maresius was lying, and others on the contrary acquit him of this blemish. For indeed truly, since all not only acknowledge that reason is finite, but vitiated, corrupted, and blinded by the crime of our first parents (which was recently driven home here in a splendid speech), what sort of person would dare to pronounce blind reason free from the danger of error? But perhaps you will say, "Reason as far as it is reason does not deceive, conscience as far as it is conscience does not lead astray, for insofar as it errs and cheats, it is not reason and not conscience, but madness, temerity, and prejudice." I am not so picky about jots and tittles, and I prefer to speak from the divine oracles, that all men, now that their nature is corrupted, are fools, not wise. Born in dense darkness, they are mere shadows, not the light they were at first. Their heart is deceptive, not upright; impure, not pure; their conscience sordid, not undefiled; indeed their religion itself is a confession of their idolatry.

If on the contrary you should argue, "To the extent that we are wise we are not fools, and conscience to the extent that it is vitiated is not, by definition, conscience," and such things of this kind. O what charming subtlety! Doubtless, they say, an eye is not an eye to the extent that it is blind, an ear is not deaf to the extent that it is an ear, a soul is not a soul to the extent that it sins and rebels, an angel is not evil to the extent that it is an angel. But by that logic blind eyes do not exist, nor deaf ears, nor sinning souls, nor evil angels. Now certainly right reason, that lamp and image of God, does not deceive—who denies this except a fool? But whenever it deceives, it turns from its uprightness. Then, you ask, where does that right reason exist except in God and heaven's angels? Moreover, corrupted reason is thoroughly deceived. So if you do not want to call it reason, but rather the fault or defect of reason, that is fine by me.

---

56. Samuel Desmarets (1599–1673), see "Maresius, Samuel," *ADB* 20:313–15.
57. André Rivet (1572–1651) was a professor of theology at Leiden University from 1620–1646, see *BWDN*, 16:358–66; *NNBW* 7:1051–52.

Furthermore, seeing that we agree on this point, where is the core and marrow of the disagreement? We sharply contend with Socinus that finite and corrupt reason must not be made the rule of believing, or what amounts to the same thing, that we must not trust in reason if the sacred page contradicts it. Such a hideous error we all abhor, but many among us—some knowingly, others incautiously and ignorantly—follow in the footsteps of Socinus, although from this source comes every deformity of religion. What a miserable little manikin that has more faith in himself than in God! The divine oracles teach that in the beginning all things were created from nothing, which finite and vitiated reason does not accept. They depart from us, who teach not only with Socinus that there was matter before the world existed, but also that from that matter this universe came together according to the natural laws of motion, a conclusion which frightened even Socinus. And when they were pressed that all this could not naturally happen in the space of six days, they promptly responded that six days are six periods of time, ages or perhaps myriads of ages, forgetful that the divine Moses speaks about evenings and mornings separated one from another by nights, and that the rest of the days were no longer than the seventh day of the Sabbath. Because the history of Moses concerning Paradise and the cherubim that expelled our first parents from that most beautiful garden with a flaming sword, is not according to the taste and character of such kind of rational persons, they converted Paradise into the fruitful fields of Arabia and the cherubim into Canaanites. Because it displeased them that every animal was named by Adam, they invented the idea that all the brute beasts were not gathered together for this reason, but so that he might consider that there were none among them that he could take into the partnership of the marriage bed and could name with his own name. And when he did not find any one at all suitable, Eve was formed and joined to him by God. Because the transformation of the wife of Lot does not correspond to the laws of their physics, they invent that she was terrified and therefore grew stiff as a stone, or that on the journey she was suffocated by the sulfurous smoke, or that returning to Sodom she was burned with the city, and posterity, to commemorate the affair, erected a statue, which is called a pillar of salt on account of the bitumen used in its mortar. By the same audacity and from the same principles they transmuted the pillar of cloud and fire into a portable burning altar that was carried before the army of Israel, which spewed forth a cloud of smoke by day and a fire by night. The crossing of the Israelites through the Red Sea they attributed to the aid of the ebb and flow of the tide. They have so diminished the stupendous miracles of manna that nothing beyond a natural dew remains.

If the holy codex proclaims something in lofty tones, it does this because it is recounting the history and operations of various angels and demons; divine truth is constrained to follow this method because Sacred Reason does not perceive the operations of minds upon bodies. But this is hardly different than denying, as the Saducees did, that angels and demons even exist. And whatever God, or Jesus Christ, or the prophets and apostles speak is nothing but a crass shadow of heavenly realities, a certain accommodation of God to man, by which the deity is likened to an earthly king, as if he were sitting on a throne, surrounded by a great entourage. Demons do not wander around, seduce, harass, or destroy human beings, they are not cast out from the possessed, but rather, those who suffer from epilepsy or some other disease are set free. Thus men divinely inspired, as well as our Lord Jesus himself, speak falsehood to the common people. They take counsel from their own imaginings, not from right reason, as often as they testify that those things actually happened. Of course, God and his Son and Spirit did not desire, and neither did the divine prophets, to teach the church these monstrous errors, but they had to wait to receive this recognition until this modern age, when natural theologians would educate the human race.

The catholic church sees nothing clearer in the divine books than that God, just as surely as he is the one and only God, is also three in number, and that the Father, Son, and Holy Spirit are not only one essence, but are one God, and one only, and that man, having become an enemy of God, and hated on account of his sins, could not return to his holy and worthy communion with God, except through the bloody death of the Son, and that this death can save no one who is not gifted and filled with the breath of the Holy Spirit. But this the goddess Reason is in no way willing or able to swallow and stomach. The mystery of the Father, the Son, and the Holy Spirit, and the mystery that rests on it, that of redemption, of Christ, she mocks as stupidity—to her it is a perpetual stumbling block.

This is why these heretical buffoons hiss at the triune God and the expiation of divine wrath, as if a triple God, who gave to man a law that he could not keep, and who was so implacably angry at man for transgressing it that he doomed him with his entire posterity to the eternal flames, turned nonetheless upon himself so that he could spare the guilty and vented his wrath on account of another's guilt upon his very own son, and crushed him even to death, so that anyone who would believe that such had been done would obtain a relaxation of their penalty. This is almost word for word how in Amsterdam Andrzej Wiszowaty Sr.,[58] a grandson of Socinus from his only daughter Agnieszka, threw down the

---

58. Andreas Wissowatius or Adrzej Wiszowaty, Sr. (1608–1678) was a Socinian theologian

gauntlet and upbraided the pious old Johannes Amos Comenius.[59] So then in the very bosom of our mother, the Reformed Church, they were sure they had beautifully explained the holy Triad when they taught a mere threeness of name (which is nothing less than a pure Sabellian Trinity). They were sure, moreover, that they believed and defended the satisfaction of the Savior when they taught that, according to the eternal counsel or the eternal ordering of history, he had so made satisfaction that even his traitor Judas and his executioners satisfied God. On account of this method, a certain worldly philosopher is causing our own methods to stray: I have seen another man from Wiesbaden going entirely to the other extreme and crossing into the camp of Johannes Philoponus, having defected to the Tritheists out of fear of the error of Sabellius.[60] In the same way at the first dawn of the Reformation, Servetus and Gentilis, both obeying corrupt reason, embraced absurdities: the former that of Sabellius, the latter of Philoponus. But what at last will be the end, if I were to keep enumerating these things and more? Let me put it all in a few words: men of this sort are so desperately in love with their reason that they do not admit any miracles or mysteries that are not conformable to their own reasoning, as if the Creator of nature had so bound himself to the laws of nature that he could neither will nor do anything apart from nature or contrary to it, despite the fact that before nature even existed he brought forth all things from nothing. And if it is true that there are no miracles at all, and that nothing ever occurs or has occurred in the world apart from natural causes, then by this logic there is no more proof of the Christian religion in the miracles of Christ and the apostles than in the rising and setting of the sun. Indeed, these miracles were nothing but snares set for the gullible. This is to adore Mother Nature and to consign the Father God to oblivion. Indeed at bottom, if this is not a wicked attempt to confuse nature with God, it nonetheless thoughtlessly aids such attempts.

If we all praise the use of reason and detest this execrable abuse of it, again I ask you, what is it in which we differ? In answer I add this one thing: when Pelagius was blamed because by his sacrilege he snatched glory from God and conferred it upon man, he complained that such a charge was unfair, responding that he attributed all things to God and to divine assistance, from which and

and the editor of the *Bibliotheca Fratrum Polonorum quos Unitarios vocant*, 8 vols. (Amsterdam: Frans Kuyper, 1665, 1668, 1692).

59. Johannes Amos Comenius (1592–1670) or Jan Amos Komenský, see *NNBW* 8:302–5.

60. Johannes Philoponus (490–570) was condemned posthumously in 680–681 with the charge of tritheism. Cf. T. Hainthaler, "Johannes Philoponus, Philosoph und Theologe in Alexandria" in *Jesus der Christus im Glauben der Kirche*, 4 vols., *Die Kirche von Alexandrien mit Nubien und Athiopien nach 451*, ed. A. Grillmeier (Frieburg: Herder), 2:109–49.

by which we exist, live, and move. But Augustine took most diligent care not to confuse the blessing of nature with the gift of grace. Indeed whatever a person has, he receives from God by creation, but on account of the fall, this is not sufficient for him to return to God: he needs the Holy Spirit and the grace of the Redeemer, and if devoid of these, he together with his natural blessings perishes in eternity. Whoever has a soul, certainly has it from God. If however a person has only that and not the Spirit of God, he is a natural man,[61] not a spiritual one,[62] and would be more blessed if he had never existed. If finally we also agree in this and distinguish the strength of grace from the strength of nature, and the Spirit of God from our own soul, therefore, again I cry out, what reason remains for quarrels? None, surely, that is not empty and unimportant. Indeed, there is only one good reason: if in the quarrel, universal doubt, the cause of so many contentions, is taken as an opportunity to do nothing other than to inquire into the things that are most true, certain, and well-known, in order more surely to confirm them, that even the most obstinate skeptics might be satisfied. This is exactly what I recently saw, to my mind's great delight, when our excellent Mastricht held forth in the oration with which he bid his academic labors goodbye, having been most honorably discharged from duty. On the other hand, if anyone opposes his own reason and wisdom to God's, if anyone corrects God as he speaks and twists God's oracles to fit his reasoning, if anyone argues in this way, then we cannot but charge him with inciting the corruptors of the Christian religion. If Petrus van Mastricht opposed such men in youth and old age, God forbid that we would count this opposition among his errors and vices. I openly count it among his praises, and I have hope that with him and committed to his principles I will die and appear before God, the author of his Word and of the Christian religion.

Since Christ's birth no method of philosophy has been maintained whose abuse did not harm holy Christians. That this is true regarding Platonism, only a stranger to the ancient church would doubt. The scholasticism of Aristotle that followed miserably corrupted not only proper theological terms, but also the truths they signified. Granted, the modern method of the well-known philosopher Descartes has brought much light to certain arts and sciences, yet whoever denies seeing that these bold inventions are misused to destroy the Christian religion is either dishonest, denying what he sees with his own eyes, or he excels the mole in blindness. Heidanus saw it.[63] Cocceius saw it. In an earlier time,

---

61. ψυχικός

62. πνευματικός

63. Abraham van der Heyden or Abraham Heidanus (1597–1678) was professor of theology at Leiden University from 1648–1676. See *ADB* 11:292; *NNBW* 7:587–88.

they were the grand lights of our neighboring academy, and they intervened with their counsel in the year 1666. Heidegger saw it.[64] Suicerus saw it.[65] They were the Zürich theologians, and what great and good men they were. The first, after writing so many synopses, by the advice of Fabritz,[66] the extraordinary theologian and philosopher in the Palatinate, composed his *Marrow of Theology* at the end of his life.[67] This work was later published in a large volume and had in it no trace of any philosophy, whether ancient or new, in order that he might strike down all the monsters rising in the church which threaten disaster for God and his Word, as he said in an oration concerning the internal enemies of the Reformed Church. But this man—O what sorrow!—was recently snatched from the Palatinate churches, over which he had been appointed to guide and reform. But the same danger that Fabritz saw, all my preceptors also saw, the shapers of my youth, the greatest among whom were the most eminent men Jacob Alting[68] and Reinoldus Pauli.[69] The illustrious orders of Holland saw it as well, those who used their most sacred laws more than once to curb the unbridled sophists. The powerful orders of this city saw it, magistrates we revere to the utmost, who by a praiseworthy decree in 1695 sanctioned anyone from examining and arranging the heads of divine revelation according to the rule of their own reason. The whole Christian world saw it—the godly Christian world, that is—and moaned.

Anyone would think that the deceased has been given enough praises, after we have celebrated his country, lineage, age, honors, and erudition, but these are merely disgraces and splendid vices if to them is not added an unfeigned love of God and neighbor. What good is a proven argument concerning secret and obscure matters, the ignorance of which will not harm us in the last judgment? What good is it to be most diligent in asking and answering questions but most negligent in rooting out vices and cultivating virtues? What good is an arduous

---

64. Johann Heinrich Heidegger (1633–1698) was a professor of theology at Steinfurt (1659–1665) and at Zürich (1667–1698). See *ADB* 11:295–96; *NDB* 8:244.

65. Johann Caspar Schweizer (1619–1684) was a professor at Zürich variously of Hebrew, catechetical theology, and Greek and Latin. See *ADB* 37:141–43.

66. Johann Ludwig Fabritz (1632–1697) was the professor of Old and New Testament at Heidelberg (1661–1696), Johann Heinrich Zedler, *Grosses vollständiges Universal-Lexicon aller Wissenschafften und Künste*, 68 vols. (Halle, Leipzig: 1731–1754), 9:46–48; *ADB* 6:516–18.

67. Johann Heinrich Heidegger, *Joh. Henrici Heideggeri Medulla theologiae Christianae corporis theologiae praevia epitome* (Zurich: Heinrich Bodmer, 1696).

68. Jacob Alting (1618–1679) was a professor of Hebrew at Groningen (1643–1677). See *BWDN* 1:214–18 ; *BWPGN* 1:120–27; *NNBW* 1:96–97.

69. Reinoldus Pauli (1638–1682) was a professor of theology at Steinfurt (1666–1670) and at Marburg (1674–1682). See Zedler, *Universal Lexicon*, 26:1456.

disputation about the Trinity if we lack submission and displease the Trinity? One day before the divine tribunal the doctor of theology will not be asked so much what he read and how elegantly and neatly he spoke and wrote, but what he did and how he lived. O how greatly on that fearful day will he excel in understanding the penalty due to sinners, how well will he grasp its most accurate definition! All those who are swollen with the vanity of knowledge and seek to be called doctors, magistrates, and great, illustrious, and honored men, but are devoid of Christian charity, are the most foolish of all mortals and will be rejected and mocked by God and the inhabitants of heaven. That man alone is great who thinks often of his own smallness, and has great charity. That man is truly learned who pursues the will of God and neglects his own. The only knowledge worthy of love is to know and esteem Christ and him crucified, and to condemn all earthly things as loss and dung. To fear Jehovah, that alone is wisdom, and to depart from evil, that alone is understanding. If therefore I have not vindicated the godliness of our departed brother, all my praise becomes reproach. Conversely, only once I have defended his godliness has my praise put the finishing touch on this portrait of his glory.

Mastricht is unique among Reformed doctors that I have known in that he was distinguished by the name and title of Professor of Practical Theology. He alone published a corpus of practical theology worthy to be preferred before all other efforts in this genre. And indeed, the model he constructed for shaping the character of Christians was the same model to which he conformed himself his whole life long. I do not assert that he possessed the spotless perfection that the godly long for in this life and will possess in the life to come; we all stumble in many things. He was a human to whom no part of human experience was unfamiliar.[70] But if he is best who exerts himself even in the smallest details of life, if he truly is godly who walks with integrity before God and constantly desires to be godly with an unremitting zeal, then without any hesitation we should ascribe godliness to Mastricht, since he was intent upon it from his childhood to his last moment. I call all the godly who knew him, I call the ungodly, the enemies of Mastricht, of godliness, and even of God himself, to testify—was Mastricht not preeminent among the godly? How chastely he always and everywhere spent his life as a single man, not only above reproach, but above the suspicion of reproach! How holy and blameless he dwelt in his house! How religiously he attended to the daily exercises of godliness, how he was less likely to neglect them than to neglect his nightly rest, his breakfast, and dinner (humble as it was), his household knows well! With what zeal he attended public worship, we all saw! When

---

70. Cf. Terence, *Heauton Timorumenos*, act 1, scene 1, line 25 (77).

in this last year on account of the diminution of his strength, he suspended his public lectures and did not appear in the Academic Senate, when at last he even ceased from all private duties, yet he most constantly clung to the holy assemblies. Wherever he was and lived, with great strength of heart, despising rewards and punishments that were offered him, he proved himself just as fierce in opposing vices as in conquering errors. I have read many magnificent testimonies about him from doctors, pastors, classes, synods, churches, and academies from his first youth to his old age, but there is not one in which his remarkable godliness was not commended as exemplary. When we have such testimonies to the facts, what is the use of saying more?

But just as the middle part of his life corresponded with its beginning, so also the end corresponded with the middle. You will agree with me on this, if by your leave I may now with a few words portray his last moments. At length weighed down with years, broken by various diseases and by great travail, he awaited his last hour. Finally on Friday, January 29, when in evening time as he was going down the stone steps into his kitchen, with a sudden fall he dropped to the ground. Whether he fell down because of a vertigo of the brain, a kind of debility he had often experienced previously, or because of the deformity of his lame foot, or because of some other cause, without doubt it happened because of divine providence. The wound, moreover, had struck the very same foot that was weak, and in the same place where he used to strengthen and nurse it using a poultice smeared with ointment from Nürnberg, but as he did not feel it, so he revealed it too late. As he was recovering, fever attacked his weakened body and gangrene his foot. And although the most learned and experienced doctors — our Leusden colleague together with Dr. Wagtendorp, and even Dr. Zijpenstein, a man of consular rank who had grown old in the medical art, consulted even by princes and kings — devoted all their attention so that he might recover, and happily not only overcame the fever and the pains in his left side, but even checked the gangrene of the wound so that it did not spread more extensively, nevertheless, step by step the embers of life failed, and on Tuesday, February 9, at nine in the evening, he died peacefully.

It would take a long time to tell of all the proofs of godliness that he exhibited even during this last sickness. I will speak of what happened when I was present before him, either because I had come out of duty, or because he had repeatedly summoned me, together with the others whom, with me, he had entrusted to execute the articles of his last will. It is worth recalling how on a Lord's Day Petrus Eindhoven (a man not only venerable for his gray hair, but also for his teaching and holiness, just a few years older than our deceased brother), together with the whole church, commended this man who was like him in both name and age with the most fervent prayers to God as he approached his death. And when those who gathered were dismissed, except for our illustrious colleagues Leidekker and Luitsius, I approached our dying brother's bed, and on bowed knees I led him and the others there in prayer, and as I did, he by his voice, by his gestures, and by his doubled "amen, amen" approved of the prayer. With the holy things completed he openly professed that he was dying faithful to the doctrine he had taught, and that he was now headed to the tribunal of the supreme Judge to render him proof of that fact. Furthermore he also added in his loudest voice that in no place and in no way did he make a defense of the truth which sincere godliness and holiness of life did not inseparably accompany. At the same time he praised divine providence for his recent fall, and signified the most ready compliance of his will to depart immediately, or even to remain. Then he added again that he wanted to fall again and to endure all other evils that he had ever endured, if it would so please his heavenly Father, the highest judge of all his and others' affairs, and that he would do it without any sigh or evidence of sadness or grief. This is the sort of constancy that he also demonstrated in the year 1682 when he was tormented by intestinal pain and there was fear that he would vomit his insides out. It was from this disease that André Rivet, who must never be remembered without praise, perished, though the divine hand prevented him from vomiting up his entrails, so that his most pure mouth, from which flowed the sweetest eloquence of speech and words, would not be befouled by his own excrement (just as Crucius the doctor attested, though a Romanist by religion). And during the whole time that Mastricht suffered the same disease he neither complained nor sighed, until by divine kindness his bowels relaxed at the very moment when the church publicly prayed to God for his deliverance. And when soon after he had recovered to some degree, and scarcely after leaving his bedroom, he was handed the leadership of the academy, in a thanksgiving speech, which I saw, given before our great consuls, he recalled both the greater and the lesser of these two unexpected divine blessings, and added to the praise of our most excellent and great triune God, that in the overwhelming attack of such a painful disease he was flooded with such great joy and such great light and comfort from the divine communion that he did not even perceive the pangs of this little fever. These sorts of privileges belong to very few; we normally admire them in martyrs.

Finally, when each of us had given him the right hand of fellowship to say goodbye for the last time until the heavenly palace should unite us again, he heaped upon us and others his fullest thankgivings and prayers. And in an outpouring of every kind of divine felicity, both at that time and at others, he was so generous to the most honorable Consul Quintius and the whole of his family and posterity that you would say that abundant streams were flowing from the mouth of the one dying. He prayed the kind of prayers that no Christian could disregard; thus we hung on his every word, and we did not depart without weeping. At another time I was present with him almost alone and I was praising his good fortune, that he could, mindful of his own sincerity, say with King Hezekiah, "Jehovah, remember that I have walked before thee in truth and in integrity of heart." At this his brow furrowed and he rejected it due to the danger of pride, and when I added that I was not celebrating his strength but the divine power, and after I cried out more than once, "You are what you are by the grace of God!" he acquiesced. If in these accounts we do not find remarkable proofs of his patience, constancy, and Christian trust, where else could they be found? If indeed we have been convinced by such arguments of his true godliness, who will doubt the reward that our most truthful and just God has prepared for him?

Therefore, now discharged from all care and toil, Petrus van Mastricht delights among the inhabitants of heaven and enjoys his Creator and Savior, while we groan like slaves in prison during these cloudy and uncertain times in our church and republic. So then, let us all and especially you, his brother Gerhard, and you Petrus, the image and copy of your father and of the uncle who was your namesake, wipe away our tears and rest in the divine will without murmuring. Let us praise our most merciful God that he granted us the enjoyment of this man for so long, until the day his strength was spent and he was no longer fit for the labor God has laid on his servants in this life, but nonetheless became perfectly fit for performing heavenly duties among the choirs of angels. Let us reverently honor his works, which this city and academy will never be ashamed to remember. Let us admire greatly his exceptional talents and virtues, which the divine indulgence granted with a bountiful hand to him, and let us imitate them, and if our strides be not as great as his,[71] yet may they be certain and continuous, all the way until with him we reach that goal for which we long. Until then, O Jehovah, regard the wounds and woes of our academy and intervene so that we may not perish, but stand and flourish forever for thy glory, for the increase of the church and republic, and for the eternal salvation of many.

---

71. cf. Virgil, *Aeneid* 2.724.

The Best Method of Preaching

Preface

I. In the eighty-first year of this century, in the year of our Lord, on the seventh of December, I had produced disputations on the use of the *Theoretical-Practical Theology* that was about to be published, and I placed them in the front of that theology.[1] I did not produce those disputations in haughtiness, for I cheerfully and frankly confess that they do not possess anything from their learning and erudition that could commend them to anyone—especially not in this most self-indulgent age—or that could demand any praise, but I did this so that I might present in abbreviated form[2] the method of that theology that would follow it, and that I might acquaint my readers a little with it. Indeed, I designated it as "best," not because I imagined that what I advanced could be good even in a moderate sense, much less the best. In fact, it is not even my method, but that which, not only the great men—William Perkins, William Ames in his *Marrow*, Oliver Bowles, Guilelmus Saldenus in his brilliant *The Preacher*, and especially the celebrated Johannes Hoornbeeck in his six or seven disputations "On the Method of Preaching," as well as several others—had shortly before made known, but also the whole British nation, so that I do not need to mention our Utrecht; indeed, all those more devoted to practice and practical things throughout the whole world happily observed it for the great good of the church, such that I could not claim with any appearance of truth that it was mine. Therefore, I called it "best" because, compared with any other method, it especially seemed to serve the edification of the church. I have found it, through the seventeen years of my ecclesiastical office, not only the most convenient to me as the one preparing to preach, but also the easiest and least cumbersome to my hearers, seeing that among the catechumens there are those who by its aid are able aptly to repeat the outline of my sermons, and their listeners openly profess that they perceive at least the same degree of usefulness from these repetitions as from the sermons themselves. Not only this, but also by its use our Utrecht church has lifted up its head above the others "as do cypresses among the bending shrubs,"[3] so that there is no need to mention anything concerning the British churches, which have flourished with such great care under its use.

I have also touched upon four reasons for my opinion regarding the goal of this method, but I have only touched upon them briefly here, as I would speak more copiously if such a short space would bear it.

---

1. That is, the first edition of *TPT* (1682/1687). This preface was added in the second edition (1698).

2. ὡς ἐν ἐπιτομῇ

3. Virgil, *Eclogues*, 1:26.

First, it is advantageous for a minister's preparation for preaching that he tie his reflections to its few but universal precepts and by their aid discover an abundance of things to say, from which he may later select those that are most useful for the church. For with respect to a sermon, one ought not to think that there is anything that cannot be referred back to its topics, nor in fact that there can be anything found while reading the writings of others, no matter how scattered, that you could not refer back to its laws, rationale, character, motive, means, mode, and so forth.

Second, it is advantageous for the hearers who, once acquainted with this method, can conveniently follow the thread of the sermon, commit it to memory, and review it at home with their families, without which, as Ames wisely admonishes, all the usefulness of the sermon dies.

Third, it is advantageous with respect to the very things that will be said, which will everywhere obtain their order and place. This order will procure both brilliance and elegance for the things that will be said, connect them to the things that have been said, and from this supply perspicuity.

But especially, fourth, it is advantageous for the practice of piety, which is the soul of a sermon, so that by its assistance, virtues and vices as well as other things are displayed from their very foundational principles throughout all their essentials. From this it will be observed that, as long as this method was in use among the British and our Utrechters, praxis flourished as happily as possible and practical writings were published day by day. Whereas on the contrary, when that method expired, gradually the precision[4] of practice subsided, and on account of this, it appears that at one time an Amsterdam printer published for our Dutch people I do not know how many practical writings translated from the English language, one year after another, but now in several years he scarcely publishes one practical book.

To all these things is added the brevity of the method, which has a few universal precepts that can easily be applied to every argument, such that these precepts may always be present to your memory, direct your preparation for preaching, and assist your hearers. For I have never been able to approve the practice of those who compose dense volumes concerning the method of preaching, the perusal and reading of which demands as much time of theology students as a proper syntagma of theology. This is not to mention that in committing them to memory and bringing them into praxis, and in addition applying them to the text, they are so worn out that at last becoming exhausted, they cast aside all concern for method. Moreover, they devote whole hours to the exposition of

---

4. ἀκρίβεια

the words, such that they are forced to send away hungry and starving hearers without any practice, without any longed-for nourishment of the soul, with the bald excuse of the lapse of time, even if they may have this one thing in their favor, that they have supplied a learned and elegant sermon. Finally, such preachers comment on the individual expressions of the text in such a way that they are not able to elaborate any argument, whether a theoretical or practical one, as it deserves, with great loss both to their hearers and to their practice.

Therefore, I claimed, and still claim, that this method alone, which is quite brief, is full and complete,[5] and it alone has universal precepts that can be applied to every ecclesiastical argument. Furthermore, I will claim that it is the best method until I am convinced by arguments to the contrary, and just as I am sincerely prepared to yield to such arguments, so also I am ready to uphold against anyone that this is the best method. And thus now that you have had a taste of what is to come, I will affix this appendix on the best method of preaching, formerly prefixed to the system of theology, without adding anything, lest I should fall into the same Scylla that I have pointed out in others. I will speak about the parts of preaching, and in the parts, their parts and arguments, as well as about the rules by which we are directed in each part, and about the affections that should be stirred in each part; finally, I will illustrate all the points in an example by means of an exposition of Colossians 3:1.

The Parts of Preaching

II. There are four things that must be observed in preaching: invention, arrangement, elaboration, and delivery, which, in turn, faithfully extend outstretched, helping hands to each other.

Twofold invention

III. Invention is the discovery either of the argument to be made to the people, or of a text suitable for the argument. The argument will be supplied from the condition of the church, and also from its time, place, and other things carefully noted by the one who is to speak. In selecting the argument it must be observed:

A. That one would not search for something obvious, familiar, or of interest only to the speaker; or

B. That which seems intended to attract the applause of the common people, but rather what is most suitable for edifying the church, which should be the guiding star of the entire sermon.

---

5. ἄρτιος

For example, someone observing in his church an excessive zeal for this world and a lukewarmness toward spiritual piety might undertake an argument concerning a heavenly manner of life. A suitable text for the selected argument should: (1) be taken from only the canonical books of Scripture, which are the most effective in convicting the conscience; (2) not be excessively prolix, so that the time for the argument not be snatched away first by a rather prolix explanation of the words; and (3) not be excessively brief, so that the preacher not make his argument less clearly and plainly, and even produce in his hearers a suspicion of affected brevity.

For example, an argument chosen regarding a heavenly manner of life could be built upon the text of Colossians 3:1: "And so if you have been resurrected with Christ, seek the things above, where Christ is, seated at the right hand of God."

The arrangement of a sermon and its laws

IV. The arrangement[6] is that by which the things invented or to be invented are reduced, for the sake first of the intellect and then of the memory, into an order analogous to the subject matter. The rules of arrangement shall be these:

A. The absence of confusion, in which there is not any order preserved.

B. An absence of a cryptic order,[7] in which at least some order is preserved, but at every point hidden in such a way that none is apparent to the people, with no other result than that the preacher becomes an orator, whose business is to conceal his art.

C. An absence of inconsistency, by which in individual sermons the preacher follows a different order, so that it happens that the hearers—especially the less educated—cannot become familiar with his method and take away the contents of the sermon in their memory, without which, as Ames observes, all the fruit of the sermon perishes.

D. It will be helpful in this matter to make known to one's hearers formulas of connections and transitions, unless consideration of a more advanced and polite audience, in order to prevent their disgust, suggests something different. Although also at this point consideration for the less educated, who are the greatest and majority in number, must be observed, since the more erudite can accommodate themselves more easily to the capacity

---

6. *dispositio*
7. *ordo* κρυπτικός

of the less educated than vice versa, the less educated to the capacity of the erudite.

An inquiry into the introduction

V. We make an elaboration concerning the individual parts of the sermon, and individually the ingredients of the parts, among which there is, first, the introduction,[8] which for orators is a less important part of the oration, and thus more frequently neglected by the most outstanding masters of the art. Yet it is useful, first, for the preparation of the hearers, by which they gradually gather the resources of innate ability and memory for hearing, and for calling them to attention, which occurs by the explanation of the majesty, necessity, and usefulness of the argument to be declared.

The introduction is customarily constructed in various ways by various preachers. In my opinion, it is for many reasons especially fitting when it is derived from the coherence of the text, first its coherence with the matters in a theological syntagma that most closely precede or follow its own matter. This, first, should especially be used when the text is disconnected, and when it does not show any connection to the context, which is especially common in Proverbs and Ecclesiastes. Or, second, it may be derived from coherence with the words in its context that precede or follow it.

Both of these are accomplished, first, partly by an investigation of some appropriate thesis, and by a proof, made by some saying of Scripture, and by confirmation through a certain solid and evident rationale; and second, partly by a conversion of the same into a hypothesis, which expresses the previously investigated connection.

The laws of the introduction

These rules of introduction must be especially observed:

A. There should be nothing either prideful, such that it would move your hearers to suspicion of arrogance at the very beginning, or base, so that it would not prove inadequate to arouse their attention.

B. It should not be far-fetched or long, so that the mind of the listeners, suspended throughout the introduction in expectation of the argument to be delivered, might not be excessively wearied, and their attention flag at the beginning.

---

8. *exordium*

C. It should not be something foreign to the text or argument, because this would be unsuitable for the purpose of preparing them and calling for their attention.

D. It should not be matter intrinsic and essential to the text or argument, so that it prematurely takes up matter that will then be repeated idly afterward or disregarded in its proper place with loss.

E. For this reason, I would think it most useful to construct for the introduction a brief and meaty analysis of the whole chapter from which the text was taken, so that in this way your hearers would not only more easily comprehend the coherence of the text, but also would obtain a summary of the whole of some chapter.

The affections of the introduction

In the introduction, the affections, although they ought not to be aroused as much as in the argument, should nevertheless not be entirely absent, since the mind of your hearers needs to be prepared, and their attention stimulated, which will hardly be achieved without the use of any affections. Therefore, such affections that can procure their attention must be admitted in the introduction—the sort that call forth all those things that unfold the majesty, necessity, and utility of the impending argument.

For example, concerning the passage of Colossians 3:1, in searching for an introduction let this connection be observed: after the apostle had taught heads of doctrine in the preceding chapters, he now prepares himself for the heads of practice. Therefore, there should be the following:

Thesis: A preacher not only must declare the heads of doctrine, but also the heads of practice. For Scripture is useful not only for doctrine, but also for rebuke and correction, and so forth (2 Tim. 3:16), and the Christian religion is doctrine according to godliness (1 Tim. 6:3). And this is especially true since the Savior likewise and even more hangs the salvation of hearers upon their practice than upon their knowledge (John 13:17).

Hypothesis: In this way, the apostle, after he has spoken about the heads of doctrine, progresses to practice in our text.

Or, if you prefer to construct the introduction from the connection with what follows, you will observe by the same method that the apostle, who would explicate Christian practice to the Colossians, places the foundation of the whole business in a heavenly manner of life, and thus:

The thesis would be: A heavenly manner of life is the basis and foundation of all Christian duty, which is proven from Scripture and confirmed by reason, in the way that we have said.

And the hypothesis: So then, the apostle, who is about to explain Christian duties, starts from a heavenly manner of life.

The content of the text

VI. Second, the summary or content of the text follows, so that the entirety is readily available to us, which afterward will properly be separated into its parts. Concerning this it must be observed:

A. That it should exhaust the text and be adequate for the parts to be treated, and should neither exceed them nor be exceeded by them.

B. That what has been investigated should be characterized with a suitable description, through which, for example, it is called a consolation, censure, or exhortation. When this has been done, the parts of the text will flow forth more conveniently, as is evident throughout the individual chapters of our theology.

For example: This text contains a most serious apostolic exhortation regarding a heavenly manner of life.

The analysis and the exposition of the text, and their rules

VII. Third, the exposition of the text follows, which includes two things:

A. The analysis, in which the content is divided into its own parts and the members of the parts, so that the function of each may come into full view. Concerning this it should be observed:

1. That the immediate parts should be adequate to the content and entirely exhaust it. However, the mediate parts should not be given with such formality to the hearers, that is, not so much by points as by paraphrase, so that their memory may not be excessively burdened by the most minute divisions.

2. The immediate parts should be expressed by substantive terms analogous to the content, and not by interrogatory particles—who, what, why, how, when, and others—just as we demonstrate in the individual chapters of our theology.

3. The parts should not be superfluous.

B. The exegesis intertwined with the parts, which reveals and untangles obvious obscurities, textual controversies, and hidden meanings,[9] however much is needed. In this matter it must be observed:

1. That textual obscurities and controversies should not be sought out zealously, but should be obvious in such a way that you could suppose by just reasons that hearers are ready for an examination of them, which accordingly could not be forgone without the loss of edification.

2. That the preacher should not strive to explain things that by themselves are clear and perspicuous enough, for in so doing, not only would he steal time away from argument, but would also further obscure the text in his desire to elucidate it, and in fact would discredit Scripture with perpetual obscurity.

3. Thus, the preacher should take the measure of a sufficient explanation from his intended argument, the foundation of which the explanation of the text labors to lay down; accordingly, when this is done, the explanation is sufficient.

4. Finally, the explicated parts should be tied together again in a certain paraphrase so that the doctrinal argument emerges more easily.

Helps for exegesis are drawn from: (1) the analogy of faith; (2) the analogy of the context; (3) things that are extrinsic to the text—first philological, next philosophical, and then historical; and (4) the most excellent commentators, not only critical and verbal ones, but also analytical and substantial ones, such as Calvin, Piscator, Poole, and so forth.

The affections of the exegesis
At this point, the affections should not be so vigorous, nor in general should they be stirred, unless they are the sort that arise from conviction, for example, the love of the divine truth, and then the hatred of falsity, distortion, and any misinterpretations.[10] Thus, whatever is solidly apt to convince, that is, whatever is spoken solidly and with evidence, is useful for stirring them.

For example:

In the exhortation of the text Colossians 3:1, four parts are obvious:

A. The foundation of the exhortation: "For if you have been resurrected together with Christ." First, union with Christ is indicated, then

---

9. ἐνεργείας
10. παρερμηνειῶν

communion, both with his death, and with his resurrection and life itself in verse 3 (cf. Rom. 6:5).

B. The duty built upon the foundation: Ζητεῖτε τὰ ἄνω, "Seek the things above." Ζητεῖτε is either in the indicative, "you seek," such that it signifies the character and practice of those who have been resurrected with Christ, how they act; or, in the imperative, "seek," such that it expresses their duty. You may prefer to conjoin both, what they seek and also ought to seek: τὰ ἄνω, that is, heavenly things. Thus the duty has been prescribed that a heavenly manner of life must be lived on the earth.

C. The implicit double motive:

1. That Christ in this passage is the alpha and omega[11] of all a person's love and desire.

2. That in this passage he is seated at the right hand of God, that is, in glory and not in misery, and accordingly he is the one who is able and willing one day to glorify our humble body (Phil. 3:21).

D. The inseparable connection of the duty with its foundation in the expression: εἰ οὖν, "But if therefore."

Thus the sense is: if that antecedent "you have been resurrected with Christ" is true, that is, you have been united with Christ, and have the communion of both death and life in him, then it is also true that you seek those things that are above; or if the consequent should not be true, then the antecedent is not.

Five parts of the doctrinal argument
VIII. Fourth, then follows the doctrinal argument made in the sermon, gathered from the text, to which belongs:

A. Its investigation and proposition, in which two things must be observed:

1. That it should certainly be in the text, or be brought forth from it by irrefutable consequence, so that the preacher does not say just any word of God, but precisely the particular word that is in his text.

2. That this also should be evident to his hearers, and the rationale of the deduction or consequence should be so plainly rendered, that the hearers cannot doubt that the doctrine is in the text.

---

11. α καὶ ω

B. Its proof, made in parallel or equivalent[12] passages, for the reason that the hearer may be all the more persuaded that this is the constant and perpetual thought of God. In this it must be observed:

1. That it should solidly demonstrate what must be proven.

2. That the proving passages should not only be cited in a plain manner, but in proving they should also be applied with brevity and vigor.

3. That nevertheless the texts should not be abused by artificial or excessive evidence of proof.

4. That parallels should not be amassed without necessity, and steal away the time for speaking, when two or three can ordinarily suffice, because by the mouth of two or three witnesses every truth is established.

C. Its confirmation through reasons, by which what has been proven obtains the evidence that, when joined to the testimonies, completely convinces. Moreover:

1. The reasons should be solid and evident, suitably designed that they may convince naysayers.

2. They should be carefully distinguished from motives, which look to practice, with which they often share a great affinity. They differ, however, because the former concern convincing the intellect regarding the truth; the latter concern moving the will to do its duty. And if ever in practical arguments you are not able to distinguish them enough, at least you must take care that you do not say the same thing twice.

3. Those reasons are sought either from the nature and properties[13] of the subject in our argument, which have a certain connection with its predicate; or from the nature and properties of the predicate, which equally are allotted a connection with its subject; or from an immediate coherence of both. Let me say nothing regarding logical topics: with respect to cause, effects upon the subject, adjuncts, consistencies, inconsistencies, and so forth.

D. Its vindication, if ever our observation is liable to scruples and objections. And since:

---

12. ἰσοδυναμοῦσι
13. *affectiones*

1. Out of a zeal for brevity, they must not be searched for, thus

2. Obvious ones must be solved briefly and thoroughly.

E. Its explanation, in which either the part of both arguments, the subject and the predicate, or at least the more important one, is distinctly represented by its parts and ingredients, so that the majesty and fruitfulness of the undertaken argument may be more clearly perceived. In it:

1. A verbal explanation must be carefully distinguished from a real one, because the former does not exert itself further than to obtain the genuine and literal sense of the text; however, the latter exerts itself to obtain the nature of the thing signified by the words. Although I am not ignorant that these are everywhere confused, yet they are more rightly distinguished so that each may have its rightful place.

2. We must take heed, especially in somewhat more theoretical arguments, that we would not digress into commonplaces (unless perhaps the sermons are catechetical), but we should select only the apposite ones.

3. Finally, we must take heed that we be not excessively lengthy here also, and steal away our time from application, which is the soul of preaching.

Since the goal of the whole doctrine is nothing but the conviction of the mind and the knowledge of the truth that is according to godliness, no other affections can be roused here, except those that derive their origin from here, that is, a love of truth and a despising of falsehood, for the rest are revealed in the application.

The example of all these, according to the text of Colossians 3:1, proceeds in this way:

Here is the doctrine: those who are united to Christ and obtain the communion of Christ's death and life abide in the heavenly way of life.

For, the apostle says, those who have been raised with Christ seek heavenly things, and those who have been raised with Christ certainly are none other than those who have been united with him, have died with him, and have been raised from death.

A. He says the same thing elsewhere—for example, in Ephesians 2:1, 5–6—that those made alive with Christ, and raised with him, and thus united with him and having acquired the communion of spiritual life, are said to be seated with him ἐν ἐπουρανίοις, "in the heavenlies";

therefore, what would hinder from this being understood as a heavenly way of life?

B. Again in Romans 6:5, where σύμφυτοι τῷ Χριστῷ, those "united to Christ" like branches to a root, and thus ὁμοιωθέντες, "made like to him," as much with respect to his death as with respect to his resurrection, are said in verse 11 to live to God in Christ. Now, in what way is that different from the heavenly way of life?

C. In addition, in Philippians 3:9, he says that, united with Christ and a partaker of his righteousness, he forgets those things that are behind, without a doubt earthly things, and strives for those things that are ahead, pressing on toward the goal, to the prize τῆς ἄνω κλήσεως, "of the upward call" (vv. 13–14), and what, if not this, is it to have one's manner of life in the heavens? Nor does he attribute this to himself only, but whoever may be τέλειοι, "mature" (v. 15) like himself, having their citizenship with him in the heavens (v. 20).

There are many reasons for this.

First, those who have been united with Christ, who is from heaven (1 Cor. 15:47), and through a spiritual and heavenly generation have received a heavenly character that pursues heavenly things—these, without a doubt, live a heavenly way of life.

Second, those who have been imbued with a heavenly calling are being brought toward a heavenly goal, that is, they live a heavenly way of life (Phil. 3:14). Now, those who have been united with Christ are imbued with that heavenly calling, because calling of this sort is the unique cause of this union, and thus...[14]

Third, those who have been united with Christ hold their chief treasures in heaven (Matt. 6:21–22); accordingly, also their mind, thought, and desire are in heaven.

If you should say: at the same time, those who have been united with Christ, just like all others, are human beings, consist of body and soul, are on the earth, and use earthly things; accordingly, it is also fitting that they are concerned with earthly things, for which reason even the patriarchs—Abraham, Isaac, and Jacob—the prophets—Samuel, David, and Solomon—and believers in the New Testament—Joseph of Arimathea, Cornelius the Centurion, and so forth—are read to have been concerned with earthly things, and thus to have lived an earthly manner of life. I would answer: certainly they had—and it is

---

14. Mastricht simply wrote *etc.*, omitting the expected conclusion: "...they live a heavenly life."

lawful to have—a concern for earthly things. However, (1) they were not without a concern for heavenly things (Ps. 10:4); (2) nor was the concern for earthly things more important (Matt. 6:33–34); (3) nor would it be opposed to a concern for heavenly things and extinguish it (Rom. 13:14); (4) nor did they care for earthly things for their own sake but for the sake of heavenly things, so that we may be conveyed by earthly things to celestial ones, to be made rich in God and good works (1 Tim. 6:17–18).

Furthermore, the argument asserted to this point specifies two things:

A. Those who have been united with Christ also have communion with him, first in his death (v. 3), then in his resurrection, which we will not address specifically out of a desire for brevity.

B. Their heavenly way of life, which:

1. Generally is nothing other than to live a heavenly life here on earth, so that we may attain in the future a heavenly glory in heaven.

2. Specifically requires:

   a. A heavenly soul, that is, one endowed with a spiritual nature, which understands spiritual things (Rom. 8:6–7), a heavenly and divine nature (2 Peter 1:4), the sort that is suitable for those things that are in heaven.

   b. A heavenly goal, that is, the goal the heavenly calling marks out (Phil. 3:14) and which the blessed inhabitants of heaven pursue.

   c. Heavenly occupations of the soul, as much of the intellect, to think, to meditate, and to set the mind upon (φρονεῖν, Rom. 8:6) heavenly things, as of the will, to seek and pursue (Col. 3:1–2) such sorts of things by which the inhabitants of heaven are marked out.

   d. A heavenly norm for our occupations (Matt. 6:10), by which we live not according to the flesh or examples of this world, but according to the spirit (Rom. 8:1; 12:3) by which the inhabitants of heaven live.

   e. A heavenly fellowship with heavenly people (Ps. 16:3)—not with the worldly, but the sort of fellowship we will have in heaven in the future.

   f. A heavenly zeal, by which we do willingly the things that are done in heaven, for example, seeing God, that is, knowing him (1 Cor. 13:12; John 17:3), enjoying God, rejoicing and delighting in him (Ps. 16:11), and glorifying God (Isa. 6:3, etc.).

Rules for the informatory use

IX. Fifth, a twofold application of the explained argument: the dogmatic, which concerns the truth of the argument, and the practical, which concerns its goodness. Again, the dogmatic either pursues another truth to be confirmed by our argument, or a falsehood to be refuted by its assistance. From the prior arises the informatory use, which employs dogmatic argument for the purpose of strengthening another certain dogma of religion. Regarding the informatory use, these will be the chief rules:

A. This use should be rarer—indeed, the rarest—nor, in general, should it be wrested from us except by evident necessity or extraordinary advantage. This is so because time is short, and the application of the argument is more necessary and useful; accordingly, to snatch any of it away would seem to manifest the barrenness of the speaker.

B. The truth to be confirmed ought to be momentous, and the effectiveness of its confirmation ought to be solid and evident.

The goal of this use is the conviction and instruction of your listeners; accordingly, the affections to be stirred that result from this, or that look to it, are those concerning which we have already spoken in §§V, VII, and VIII.

For example, with regard to the text:

If those united with Christ live a heavenly manner of life, then faith and zeal for good works cannot be separated. The reason is that faith and union and communion with Christ cannot be separated. For this reason, Christ is said to have been made for us not only our justification, but also our sanctification (1 Cor. 1:30). And he is said to have given himself for us so that he might deliver us from all unrighteousness and cleanse us for himself as his own special people, zealous for good works (Titus 2:14).

The ingredients and rules of the elenctic use

X. Sixth, from the refutation of falsehood arises the elenctic or refutatory use, which includes three things:

A. A legitimately formed state of the controversy, so that we would not vainly box the air or argue laboriously about something that is uncontroverted.

B. Constructive reasoning,[15] in which truth is established by (a) the Scriptures, (b) reasons, and (c) the consensus of antiquity, especially against those who seem to want to depend upon this consensus.

---

15. Κατασκεύασιν

C. Deconstructive reasoning,[16] in which the objections of adversaries are blunted.

The rules here shall be:

A. Controversies shall not be sought out without necessity, because of the loss of time.

B. Yet, on the other hand, when there is an imminent danger to the church from these controversies, and thus your hearers must be equipped, controversies shall not be neglected.

C. Those controversies that have been buried shall not be exhumed, and those that are unknown shall not be made known, lest in refuting them we teach them.

D. We should not employ any arguments and solutions except solid ones, suitable for bringing a man to conviction, willing or not.

E. We should not be excessively laborious in this business, so that practice is not suspended or excluded.

F. Let us exert ourselves so that even the elenctic part, however much it can be done, is handled in a practical manner, that is, so that it is made manifest that the emphasis and power[17] of the truth to be defended and the falsehood to be refuted is either to promote or to hinder piety, as well as eternal salvation.

For example, in the argument of Colossians 3:1:

If those united with Christ and participants in his death and resurrection cannot but live a heavenly manner of life, then they strenuously slander the orthodox who proclaim that the doctrine of the orthodox concerning justification through faith alone steers people toward sluggishness and carnal security. For those who have been endowed with saving faith have been united with Christ and obtain a communion in both his death and his resurrection, and thus they ultimately cannot but live a heavenly manner of life. Accordingly, those who are in Christ are said to bear much fruit (John 15:5), and those who have been crucified with him do not themselves live, or live for themselves, but Christ lives in them (Gal. 2:20). If they should say that even so, by "faith alone," good works are excluded, we respond that they certainly are excluded from justification, but are not excluded from exercise or from salvation. And yet we agree that if good works were not excluded from justification, those same works would exclude us

---

16. Ἀνασκεύασιν
17. ἐνέργεια

from participation in Christ (Gal. 5:4), and at the same time from participation in salvation (Rom. 10:3).

The ingredients, rules, and affections of the consolatory use

XI. Seventh, the practical application follows, which respects either (1) evil, first sorrowful evil, against which the consolatory[18] use strives, then shameful evil, which the reproving[19] use remedies, or (which coincides with it) the admonitory use; or (2) good, whether the good is to be explored, to which the exploratory[20] use tends, or to be stirred up, to which the hortatory[21] use inclines. We will pursue each of these individually. Therefore, the first in the practice shall be the consolatory, in which a vexing evil is destroyed or alleviated.

Three things could be included in this use:

A. An enumeration of the evils that our dogmatic argument could heal: spiritual evils, bodily evils, and so forth.

B. Comforting arguments, which could apply our argument to each evil.

C. An anticipation and removal of objections by which an anxious mind customarily strives to blunt and weaken those consolatory arguments.

The following rules guide this use:

A. I think that the first place in practice must be given to consolation, not so much because our first and foremost concern ought to be for the pious who are afflicted, but so that it does not blunt the sharpness and efficacy of the preceding practice by being put in the last place.

B. Consolation should be less frequent than the rest of the practical uses, because the spiritually afflicted are less common in any church, and to those who are afflicted, consoling arguments can be more properly applied in private.

C. Consoling arguments shall not be poured out promiscuously, so that, having been snatched up by the impious, they should be used incorrectly, to their own hardening and ruin (Matt. 7:6), but rather let those be carefully distinguished from the others to whom consolation is spoken.

The affections that predominate in a consolation are, at least with respect to the one speaking, love toward the afflicted and sadness concerning his affliction,

---

18. παρακλητικός
19. νουθετικός
20. πειραστικός
21. παραινετικός

that is, compassion. Those affections to be awakened with respect to the afflicted, and in him, are hope and patience, which are stirred up in demonstrating: either (1) that what presses is not in fact evil; or (2) if it may be evil, it is not so great; or (3) if it is grave, yet it is not going to continue perpetually, or even for a long time; also (4) it will have its uses according to the paternal providence of God, which uses are able abundantly to offset the sadness; and in addition, (5) by the just judgment of God for our sins much graver things are owed; and (6) by his power the eternal tortures are turned away; and so forth.

For example, from the stated argument, for these whose manner of life is in the heavens, in a variety of cases, a diverse consolation is able to be supplied:

A. Generally, in every evil, of whatever sort and however much it may be, that such persons are free from all evil. For just as those who have been united to Christ live a heavenly manner of life, so also those who live a heavenly manner of life have been united to Christ, and thus are in him; accordingly, in the judgment of Paul, there is now no longer any condemnation upon them (Rom. 8:1).

B. Specifically, in any lack, because, being united to Christ, in him they may receive grace for grace (John 1:14, 16) in such a way that they become complete in him (Col. 1:28; 2:10), inasmuch as he is the one who for them is all in all (Col. 3:11).

C. In the anxieties of sin, because, united with Christ, they have died with him, and their life has been hidden with Christ in God (Col. 3:3), they have been crucified together with him, and in him they live free from guilt (Gal. 2:20).

D. In earthly poverty, insofar as: (1) those who live a heavenly manner of life also revere God, and to such persons there is promised no want (Ps. 34:9); (2) in any need there is a better substance for them in heaven (Heb. 10:34; Ps. 73:25).

E. In death itself, insofar as: (1) not only have those who have a manner of life in heaven, and who look not toward visible things but invisible things, been persuaded that when this their earthly tabernacle has been destroyed, they will have a dwelling not made with hands[22] in the heavens (2 Cor. 4:18; 5:1); but also (2) they know that as they have been made like to him with respect to his death, so also they will be made like to him with respect to his resurrection (Rom. 6:5); indeed (3) having a

---

22. ἀχειροποίητον

manner of life in heaven, from there they look for Jesus Christ, who will glorify their humble bodies (Phil. 3:21).

If they should say, (1) meanwhile I am pressed with so many and such great evils, internally and externally, I respond: (a) neither are they as many and as great as the things by which Christ, the one to whom they have been united, was pressed (Matt. 26:37–38); (b) nor are they perhaps as many and as great as the things by which Paul was pressed (2 Cor. 11:23); indeed, (c) this also is an argument for you, that your hope is not confined to this life (1 Cor. 15:19), and that is so because your manner of life is in heaven.

If they should say, (2) if only my manner of life truly were in heaven, then I respond: (a) at least you seriously will and desire it to be so, and accordingly it is so, and you will be satisfied (Rev. 22:17; Isa. 55:1). In the meantime, (b) measure yourself by those marks that we will discuss further on.

The ingredients of the rebuking use

XII. Eighth, upon sorrowful evil follows shameful evil, for which the cure is rebuke, denoted by other names according to the different manner of treatment—sometimes admonition, sometimes dissuasion, sometimes accusation. Its ingredients are:

A. Evils to be rebuked, whether they are habits, which are called vices, or operations, which are designated as evil works, to be recounted in order.

B. Rebuking arguments, which especially suggest themselves

   1. Either from the indecency of the things that must be rebuked, to the extent that they are adverse to the law, to right reason, to good custom, and so forth.

   2. Or from the divine threats, by which evils are pronounced upon these evils.

   3. Or from judgments, by which the evils pronounced also are read to have been inflicted.

C. Remedies, or causes of the evils to be removed through correction. For example, ignorance and blindness of mind, a perverse inclination and disposition of the will, depraved customs, the examples of others, and so forth.

Its affections

The affections to be roused here are especially: (1) shame arising from the indecency of the reprehended evil; (2) fear, from the communication of penalties;

and (3) a hatred and detestation of both, emerging from both the threats and the contemplation of divine judgments.

Let there be an example from the text. The doctrine mentioned marks out the following:

A. Those whose manner of life is so far from heaven that it is in hell itself, namely, those who indulge in hellish vices, hatreds, curses, blasphemies, jealousies, or who in whatever way are openly impious, upon which account Judas is said to have departed to his own place (Acts 1:25).

B. Those whose manner of life is in any event set upon the earth, whom the text notes in the following verse as those who devote themselves totally to earthly things, wealth, honors, and desires (Col. 3:2; Phil. 3:19; 1 John 2:16).

C. Those whose manner of life is neither in heaven nor completely in hell, but who, as it were, are suspended between heaven and hell, neither truly pious nor entirely impious, but participate in both, such as are hypocrites (2 Tim. 3:5).

D. Those whose manner of life is not with God, the inhabitants of heaven, or heavenly things; for example, those who do not delight in the exercises of the inhabitants of heaven: knowledge, celebration, enjoyment of God, and so forth (Job 21:14–15).

All these:

A. As they are strangers from heaven and heavenly things (Eph. 2:12), so they reveal their earthly, infernal, and diabolical character (John 8:44), inasmuch as they are the ones in whom the god of this age works (Eph. 2:2).

B. Have been separated from union with Christ, inasmuch as the Spirit of Christ is not in them (Rom. 8:9, 14) and Christ does not live in them (Gal. 2:20).

C. Do not have communion with the benefits of Christ: neither with his death, inasmuch they are its enemies (Phil. 3:18), nor with his resurrection, inasmuch they are still dead in sins (Eph. 2:1, 3, 5), nor accordingly with his justification, glorification, and so forth.

D. Finally, who do not delight in heaven and heavenly things, in the just judgment of God, will be sent away with Judas into a place analogous to their own character, desires, and devotions (Acts 1:25).

So that we may cure those evils, it is necessary to inquire into their causes that should be removed, such as:

A. Blindness of the mind, which does not recognize spiritual, divine, and heavenly things as they are in themselves, but holds them to be foolishness (1 Cor. 2:15; 1:23).

B. An aversion of the heart to heavenly things and a propensity for earthly ones, by which we do not set our mind on anything except carnal things (Rom. 8:5–7; Phil. 3:19).

C. An excessive care and concern for earthly things, by which the soul is loaded down and suppressed (Luke 21:34), and all spiritual and heavenly things are suffocated (Matt. 13:22).

D. Unbelief, by which we inadequately believe those things that the Scriptures declare regarding God, the excellence of spiritual and heavenly things, and the weight of heavenly glory. For this reason, the apostle teaches that we should not have a wicked and unbelieving heart that turns away from the living God (Heb. 3:12).

E. The perverse examples of this world, everywhere watching us and most powerfully enticing us (1 John 5:19; Rom. 12:2).

The ingredients of the exploratory use: motives, signs, and affections
XIII. Ninth, the exploratory use follows, by which we investigate virtue or vice, a good or evil work, or the state of grace or sin, so that a conscience established in virtue, good works, and the state of grace can be quieted, rejoice, glory, and be confirmed, and on the contrary, that a conscience established in vice, sin, and the state of sin can be touched by a saving perception, fear, and concern, and allured and drawn from the state of sin to the state of grace. Thus, this use generally has three ingredients:

A. The moving arguments, by which a conscience could be roused to the most wearisome and difficult task of examination, which generally are suggested from two things:

1. From the affinity that the things to be explored have with certain emulators, who by disguise imitate and feign their nature, from which the danger of seduction comes most easily.

2. From the excellence, usefulness, and necessity of certainty, which we pursue by examination; from the ease by which we may work to achieve certainty; from the consequences of the certainty born from examination, peace, tranquility, joy, spiritual boasting, and so forth;

and likewise from the danger and destructiveness of deception and error in a matter of such great importance, namely, from carnal security, hardening of heart, strengthening in evil, and at last, eternal destruction.

B. The signs by which we certainly and infallibly pursue the truth sought in the examination. Concerning which:

1. What is explored must be cautiously observed as to whether it is a virtue or vice, a good or evil work; whether the true spiritual state of a person before God is that of sin or of grace. These different things likewise must be investigated by different marks.

2. Likewise, a twofold truth must be carefully distinguished in virtues and vices, as well as in good and evil works. First comes physical truth, whether or not with respect to essence, there is a particular virtue or vice truly present in us, for example, any true love of God. This truth is discerned partly from its causes, effects, and adjuncts, and accordingly, in investigating it there is not as much difficulty and trouble. And next is moral or spiritual truth, whether a virtue whose presence we have come to discern is a common or saving virtue, and whether a vice is such that would separate us from a state of grace, or not. This surely is not as readily distinguished for certain, nor are there as many and as evident marks for making distinctions.

3. Accordingly, in discerning the state of a man, or the virtue or vice that reveals the state, one must proceed slowly, so that, from one perspective, we would not without cause lead the consciences of the pious into doubts and anxieties from which afterward we could not so easily lead them out; from another perspective, so that we would not also strengthen hypocrites and harden them in their carnal security.

4. For which reason, in the examination of the state or of the virtue or vice that reveal the state, no other signs should be proffered than those that are certain, universal, reciprocal,[23] and properly fortified from the consensus of Scripture.

5. Yet it is not absolutely unprofitable, especially in the investigation and discerning of virtues and vices, that those signs be consulted that argue only from one perspective: either only negatively, that he who

---

23. That is, not only must the sign always imply the state, but the state must always imply the sign.

does not have these or those signs is not endowed with this or that virtue or vice, or only affirmatively, that he who shows these or those signs shows without doubt that he is so endowed, although these may not be true vice versa.

C. The goal of the examination is that when the investigation has been completed, those who are endowed with saving virtue and who by that fact have discerned that they are in the state of grace may be strengthened, and on the contrary, that those who labor in vices, especially in deadly ones, are forcibly drawn to a concern, fear, and care for their correction.

The affections that must be moved in the examination are: first, a fear of deceit and deception, which can be evoked by the impression of the weight that deceit can have in disturbing someone's peace of conscience, tranquility, and joy, and in impeding his conversion and eternal salvation. Second, the love and desire to be sure of the healthiness[24] of our spiritual state, which similarly is stirred up by the consideration of its excellence and usefulness in procuring tranquility of conscience, glorying, and eagerness in any spiritual exercise. Third, boldness and effort in applying ourselves to all devotions and exertions, so that we may achieve certainty of our good state. And for this end it is effective to recognize the certainty of success by the grace of God, and the facility of the means, considered together with the importance of the certainty that is sought in the examination.

For example, if those who are united to Christ and obtain the communion of his death and resurrection have their manner of life in heaven, then surely it is the case that we should earnestly examine ourselves as to whether such a heavenly manner of life belongs to us. Here,

A. The motives are:

1. That without this examination, we cannot be certain that we have been united with Christ and made participants in his death and resurrection. And finally, what solid peace of conscience can be present to us without certainty in this matter (cf. Rom. 5:1–3)?

2. That also in this matter, error so easily and readily arises, since there is no lack of those who, instead of a heavenly manner of life, applaud themselves for some sort of civil and honorable manner of life, as is seen in the case of the Pharisee (Luke 18:11–12) and the church of Laodicea (Rev. 3:17).

---

24. εὐεξίαν

B. The signs, certainly adequate and abundant ones, could be gathered from the very explanation of the doctrinal argument, which is in §VIII; yet for the sake of an example, we will add:

1. He whose manner of life is in heaven, both whose treasure and whose soul are, by that fact, in the same place, spurns earthly things (Matt. 6:19–21; cf. Heb. 11:24–26) and knows how, as it were, to trample them underfoot (Rev. 12:1).

2. He whose manner of life is in heaven considers himself a pilgrim on the earth (Heb. 11:8–10; 13:14; Ps. 39:12), and can bear every condition on earth with a calm mind (Phil. 4:11–13; cf. 3:20). He can undergo the plundering of all earthly goods and all the worst afflictions, even the most dreadful death, with a calm mind (Heb. 10:34; 2 Cor. 4:17–18).

3. He who can consider death itself as of no consequence, indeed, even embrace it with a desire for heavenly things, without doubt has his manner of life in heaven (2 Cor. 4:18; 5:1–5; Rev. 22:17; Ps. 42:2–3), although this may not be reciprocal.[25]

4. Those who have their manner of life in heaven overcome the world (1 John 5:4–5), certainly not as much externally as internally, that is, they prefer God and the Mediator, spiritual and heavenly things, to any sort of worldly things, wealth, desires, and honors; and this is true vice versa (Matt. 10:37–39; 6:19–21; cf. 6:33).

The ingredients and affections of the hortatory use
XIV. Tenth, the hortatory use is next, in which attention is paid to the doctrinal argument for the purpose of exciting a zeal for virtue or any good work. Four things could be advanced here:

A. The duty that is recommended, the virtue or good work, to be delineated by particulars with respect to its acts or objects.

B. The arguments that urge the duty, out of the commonplaces of the orators,[26] to be taken from that which is upright, pleasant, useful, necessary, and easy, as well as from the baseness, perniciousness, and so forth, of the contrary.

---

25. That is, although some with their manner of life in heaven may still be excessively concerned about death. Cf. n. 23, above.

26. This could be a reference to, among others, Protagoras, Gorgias, Isocrates, Cicero, Quintilian, and Aristotle. Cf. Aristotle's *The Art of Rhetoric*.

C. The means by which the duty could be obtained, if virtue is what is urged. These means are sought from its causes, both the principal ones and the instrumental ones, as much external ones (such as the Holy Spirit's operation, exercise, reading and hearing of the Word, living with the pious, prayers, and other things that are common and everywhere obvious) as internal ones, which are sought from the nature and character of the very duty that is urged. These sorts of things especially must be sought out here.

D. The manner by which the duty must be exercised, if a good work—for example, the reading of Scripture—is what is urged, where it is not a means but a mode of acting that is sought. The manner will be supplied from the affections or adjuncts of that good work itself, for example, that it should be done sincerely, diligently, constantly, everywhere, and toward everyone.

E. Still, it must be observed that there are things that are set forth under the terms *action* or *good work*, while at the same time they intend a habit or skill, such as, in our example, a heavenly manner of life represents. And thus here, just as with respect to virtue, the supports must be sought by which we might acquire the faculty of that skill for ourselves and others.

The principal affections that must be stirred in the exhortation are a love and a desire for the virtue or good work, which the magnified excellence, sweetness, and usefulness of the duty are able to stir up; hope and courage, which the certainty and facility of accomplishment are able to stir up; and fear, which the usefulness and necessity of the duty, considered together with its lack, are able to stir up.

For example, if all who have been united with Christ and obtain communion with him in his life and death live a heavenly manner of life, then certainly we who profess and desire to be united with Christ and have communion with him must strive in every way that we should have our manner of life in heaven.

The motives could be:

A. We profess that: (1) We are united with Christ, we are in him, belonging to him as members to a head, belonging to him who came from heaven (John 6:41), who is the Lord from heaven (1 Cor. 15:47) and lives a heavenly life; therefore, surely is it not fitting for us to live the same life with our head? As members of the heavenly Christ, will we become members of this world, or of hell, or of a harlot (cf. 1 Cor. 6:15)? (2) We have died with him, and our life has been buried with him in God (Col. 3:3); we have been crucified and live with him, or rather, Christ lives in us (Gal. 2:20), and therefore the world has been crucified to us and in turn we to the world (Gal. 6:14); without a doubt for this reason, that as he gave up life in this world by his death so that he might enter life in heaven, so also we have died with him to earthly things so that we may live to heavenly ones (cf. Rom. 6:10–11). (3) We have been resurrected with him undoubtedly for this reason, that instead of an earthly life we might live a heavenly life hereafter. Indeed, (4) we have been raised with Christ, already placed with him in the heavenly places (Eph. 2:6). Therefore, by all these things, is it not most fitting that we would live a heavenly life?

B. What could be thought of as sweeter than to live in heaven with Christ, whose yoke even here is so sweet (Matt. 11:30), and with God, whose kingdom is not food and drink, but peace and joy in the Holy Spirit (Rom. 14:17)? If to live in heaven would not be to live sweetly and bless-edly, then what would it be?

C. Furthermore, the heavenly manner of life is most effective: (a) for call-ing us to piety, that is, while we are continuously eager for heaven and heavenly things (Phil. 3:14); (b) for turning away the temptations of Satan—when in our souls we are in heaven, filled with heavenly delica-cies, indeed, satisfied with them, why would we be captivated with the husks of sinners and of this world (cf. Luke 15:16)? Occupied with the most serious matters of heaven, what would call us back to earthly, vain, and childish things?. And (c) for destroying or mitigating the bitterness of whatever sort of affliction, great as it may be, to think of the rest that is stored up for us in heaven (Heb. 4:9–10; 12:2).

D. Finally, whoever does not begin a heavenly life here, will he continue it in the hereafter (cf. 1 John 3:15; John 3:36)? Whoever will not delight in heavenly things here, will he delight in them in the hereafter? Indeed, whoever lives an earthly, carnal, hellish life here, will such a person ever gain a spiritual, divine, and heavenly life in the hereafter?

Therefore, so that we may be rendered more ready for a heavenly manner of life:

A. Let us be frequent in the contemplation of heavenly beatitude and of those things that produce this (Col. 3:1), for there is no desire for a thing unknown.

B. Let us pray to God, that he may confer a spiritual and heavenly character and inclination upon us by his Spirit (cf. John 3:5), that he may bless us with heavenly gifts in Christ Jesus (Eph. 1:3), indeed that he may place us—even while we are here—in the heavenly places with Christ (Eph. 2:6).

C. Let us become accustomed to what is heavenly, and to the heavenly way of life, with continued heavenly exercises. For example, let us become accustomed to contemplation, divine glorification, the heavenly Sabbath, and so forth, so that we may forget the world and worldly things.

D. Let us embrace heavenly fellowship, the sort we will possess in heaven in the future (Heb. 12:23), so that by its help we may be built up and shaped in a heavenly life and manner of life (cf. Heb. 10:24–25).

And if you should also desire the manner of this heavenly way of life:

A. Let it be genuine, sincere, with no hypocrisy, which outwardly imitates the heavenly form, but inwardly is worldly, indeed hellish (1 Tim. 1:7).

B. Let it be constant and perpetual (Gal. 3:3).

C. Let it be heavenly everywhere, not only publicly, but also privately as well; not only with the pious and heavenly present, but also the impious, hypocrites, and worldly.

D. Let it be universal, that is, heavenly not only in heavenly things, such as in divine worship, but also in our earthly affairs, such that: (a) we can always acknowledge something spiritual in earthly things; for example, in the sweetness of food and drink, the sweetness of the heavenly banquet (Matt. 8:11), in the brightness of the sun and the stars, the brightness of the sun of righteousness, and so forth; and (b) we would strive through earthly things to be led to heavenly ones, and so forth.

Some cautions

XV. Therefore you have all the parts of the sermon, the ingredients of the individual parts, the rules, the affections, and one example in which we attempted to convey not only the substance but also the form. Here three things must be observed:

A. All texts do not admit each and every one of these parts. Thus, the informational use, likewise the refutational one, indeed, perhaps even the consolatory one, are not as suitable for our text, as certainly the three latter ones are.

B. Nor also, if perhaps a text should admit all of them, does either the time or the capacity of the hearers always admit all the uses; accordingly, the selection is here to be committed to the prudence of the preacher.

C. Nor in the individual parts can all the ingredients be admitted, nor if they could, ought they always to be admitted. Nor ought those that are admitted be admitted with the same effort and length, because sometimes one thing is more useful than another to the hearers.

How the more lengthy texts should be handled
XVI. The more lengthy texts, as far as the sum of their matter is concerned, can and ought to be interpreted in the same way. Namely, in such a way that:

A. Either it is briefly explained according to the laws of textual exposition, then the goal of the entire text is accurately investigated, and from there one doctrinal argument is constructed, and next all things that are in the text are referred to their own place, such that one thing is referred to the confirmation or exposition of the doctrine, the other to the ingredients of consolation, or rebuke, or examination, or exhortation. And this can be done in an extremely useful way. I have constantly observed this practice on most Lord's Days, but not without effort.

B. Or if you do not prefer this, you could work through the passage by a brief analysis and exegesis, according to the aforementioned laws of textual exposition, and when that is done, bring out its chief doctrines, and from them, pursue one or another that would be especially advantageous to the church, and through them, pursue the parts that especially regard edification.

C. Or in the individual parts of the text, you could mix in your own observations or applications, selecting from all the parts of the text those that are most useful and especially necessary for the church, which is a most commonly received method.

Delivery
XVII. Up to this point, we have mentioned invention, arrangement, and elaboration; there remains only delivery, which includes these three things:

A. Style, which:

1. As much as can be done, must be purified of all foreign expressions and terms from the arts, so that everything can be understood by everyone. For God, whose person a preacher represents, does not will that anything should be said in vain.

2. Should not be pompous, courtly, or long-winded;[27] nor excessively common and lowly, so that it would be despised, but it should be manly and spiritual.

3. Should be clear and perspicuous, suitable to express the matters in a manner suited to their importance.

B. Voice, which:

1. Should be sonorous, distinct, and sufficient to satisfy every hearer, and neither excessively slow nor excessively fast.

2. Should be adapted to the matters and to the affections, and accordingly: (a) neither too high nor too low, but in the middle, so that it can be raised or lowered as circumstances require; and (b) not monotone, whether hovering around one tone throughout the whole sermon, or with a fluctuating tone but still after a few clauses and sentences receding to the same point, for by such monotone expression most of the grace and efficacy of the sermon departs.

C. Gestures, which should properly be:

1. Neither excessively affectionate nor placid.

2. Nor histrionic, suitable to move to laughter rather than to pious affections.

3. Spiritual, adapted to the things that are declared and to the affections that are intended to be moved.

The reasons why this is the best method

XVIII. This, at last, is the method of preaching that we judge to be not simply good (a description I would not want to take away from all others, on account of the variety of their churches, places, and times), but best. It is:

A. Best for the preacher, who by its help will be able to take anything that comes to him, both in meditation and in reading, no matter how scattered, and refer it to its place, and likewise commit it to memory.

B. Best for the hearers, who will be able more easily to follow what has been said and what will be said, commit it to memory, recall it, and repeat it to themselves or with their families, upon which generally all the effectiveness of the sermon depends.

---

27. *sesquipedalis*, lit., "a foot and a half long."

C. Best for the things that will be said, all of which, whatever kind they are, or to whomever they come, can be recalled according to their topics without any trouble.

D. Best especially for practice, which by the help of this method can be, from its very foundations and according to all its parts, most suitably built up and equipped. Assenting to this fact are the great number of those most practical writings,[28] of the English as well as of the Dutch, that are equipped by the benefit of this method.

---

28. *scriptis* πρακτικωτάτοις

Part One

PROLEGOMENA
AND FAITH

Book One

Prolegomena of
Theoretical-Practical Theology

Theoretico-Practica
THEOLOGIA,

QUA,

Per singula capita Theologica, pars exegetica, dogmatica, elenchtica & practica, perpetuâ successione conjugantur.

EDITIO NOVA,

Priori multo emendatior, & plus quam tertiâ parte auctior.

ACCEDUNT:

Historia Ecclesiastica, plena quidem; sed compendiosa : Idea
Theologiæ Moralis: Hypotyposis Theologiæ Asceticæ &c.
Proin opus quasi novum.

AUCTORE

PETRO van MASTRICHT,

SS. Theol. in Academiâ Ultraj. Doctore & Professore.

TOMUS PRIMUS.

TRAJECTI ad RHENUM,
Ex officinâ THOMÆ APPELS, Bibliopolæ.
Anno cIↄ Iↄ c xcIx.

The Theoretical-Practical Theology

in which
Throughout every theological head, the exegetical,
dogmatic, elenctic, and practical parts are united
in continual succession,

The New Edition,

which is much more correct than the previous
one and is augmented by more than a third.

There Have Been Added:

A complete but succinct Church History, an Outline of
Moral Theology, and a Sketch of Ascetic Theology, and
other things, and thus it is like a new work.

By the author

Petrus van Mastricht

Doctor and Professor of Sacred Theology
at the Utrecht Academy

Tome One

Utrecht: Thomas Appels,
1699

1699 Dedication

To the most noble and renowned consuls, Mr. Everardus van Sypesteyn[1] and Mr. Arnoldus Spoor,[2] as well as to the whole senate of the renowned Commonwealth of Utrecht, preservers of the church and curators of the academy.

From the day I was brought by a singular fate to your city, O most renowned sirs, and devoted myself to the reputation of your academy, I developed such a great love of both, that I prefer them well above my own homeland. This is due not only to the reputation this city has among all the cities of the Netherlands as the most elegant and wholesome, but especially because the academy maintains professors in every faculty who are most learned and most famous for their fervency of study. I say this especially of the theological faculty, the celebrated Voetiuses, De Maetses, Hoornbeecks, and others who with one mind and with one hand so joined together the old Reformed theology with its genuine practice that both your church and academy lifted their heads above all others, and those who held these two things dear flocked from far and wide to you. For these reasons, I not only rejoiced over my own fate, but I also devoted my whole career of theological study only to your academy, even though for a brief time, after I was registered among the candidates for ecclesiastical ministry by

---

1. Cf. The Université d'Angers (founded 1356) promoted Everardus van Sypesteyn to *doctor medicinae* in 1657, see the "loose" collection of the Utrecht Municipal Archive (*Verzameling losse aanwinsten van de Gemeentelijke Archiefdienst Utrecht*): item 49, *Bul van de universiteit van Anjou, waarbij Everardus van Sypesteyn promoveert tot doctor in de medicijn*, 1657.

2. Arnoldus Spoor was appointed to the city council of Utrecht on April 25, 1674 and Everhardus van Sypesteyn was appointed to the magistracy at the same time. In a proclamation dated April 20, 1674 (enacted in Utrecht April 25, 1674), William III settled and appointed the government of these liberated provinces after the Anglo-French invasions of 1672, the *Rampjaar* (the Year of Disaster). See *The Netherland-historian containing a true and exact relation of what hath passed in the late warrs between the king of Great Britain and the French king with their allyes against the States Generall of the United Provinces from the beginning thereof anno 1671…to the end of 1674* (Amsterdam: Stephen Swart, 1675), 1:424–39. Sypesteyn and Spoor are mentioned specifically in various lists of appointed officials in the city and provincial government on 1:434.

the venerable classis of Utrecht, I departed for a time to Leiden, Heidelberg, Groningen, and Oxford.[3] After this little academic diversion, upon returning to my homeland, I hid away with my parents for a whole three years, during which I felt compelled to draw up a sort of outline of the theology, O noblest sirs, that you have before you. From there, after I was led to the pastorate at Glückstadt-Holstein, on the advice of my Utrecht preceptors[4] I published my *Prodromus of Theoretical-Practical Theology* so that I might know the judgments of learned men regarding the full theology that was to come.[5] I was called from there by the most serene Elector of Brandenburg to Frankfurt an der Oder, and after fulfilling a vocation as much ecclesiastical as academic for about three years,[6] I went to the church and academy at Duisburg. And there over a period of seven years I published the *Syntagma on the Nature and Practice of Saving Faith* and also the *Gangrene of the Cartesian Innovations*.[7]

Scarcely after the latter had left the womb, I was called by your kindness, O most distinguished sirs, to the Utrecht academy, and I am glad to say that after every hindrance was removed, led by the inborn love of which I spoke previously, I took up the charge. Once here there was nothing I prayed for more than that I would fulfill my duty to God, the church, and my vocation with a good conscience, and in order that I might obtain this more fully, I decided that my

---

3. Mastricht is referring to his own *peregrinatio academica* that took place after his graduation. Cf. Giese, Simone, "Peregrinatio academica," in: Enzyklopädie der Neuzeit Online, ed. Friedrich Jaeger (2014); A. Frank-Van Westrienen, *De Groote Tour. Tekening van de educatiereis der Nederlanders in de zeventiende eeuw* (Amsterdam: Noord-Hollandsche Uitgeversmaatschappij, 1983), 13–48.

4. Mastricht previously identified Gisbertus Voetius and Johannes Hoornbeeck as instrumental in his decision to publish. See Petrus van Mastricht, *Theoretico-practica theologia: qua, per capita theologica, pars dogmatica, elenchtica et practica, perpetua sumbibasei conjugantur; praecedunt in usum operis, paralipomena seu sceleton de optima concionandi methodo* (Amsterdam: Henricus et Vidua Theodori Boom, 1682), fol. ** recto, "…diu promisse Tomum-primum, cuius iam tum a MDCLXV (cum, consilio celebb. theologorum Voetii et Hoornbeekii, eius prodiret *Prodromus*)."

5. Petrus van Mastricht, *Theologiae didactico-elenchtico-practicae Prodromus tribus speciminibus* (Amsterdam: Johannes van Someren, 1666), henceforth *Prodromus*, which means "precursor," "forerunner," or "firstfruits."

6. Mastricht served as a professor of Hebrew and practical theology at the University of Frankfurt am der Oder from 1667–1670. See Adriaan C. Neele, *Petrus van Mastricht (1630–1706): Reformed Orthodoxy: Method and Piety* (Leiden: Brill, 2009), 35–39.

7. Petrus van Mastricht, *De fide salvifica syntagma theoretico-practicum in quo fidei salvificae tum natura, tum praxis universa, luculenter exponitur: cum praefatione de membris ecclesiae visibilis seu admittendis, seu rejiciendis: oborienti scismati moderno applicanda* (Duisburg: Typis Francenis Sas, 1671); Petrus van Mastricht, *Novitatum Cartesianarum gangraena, nobiliores plerasque corporis theologici partes arrodens et exedens, seu theologia Cartesiana detecta* (Amsterdam: Jansson & Waesburg, 1677). *Syntagma* means "orderly arrangement" or "treatise."

pen should be yoked together with my tongue so that what one lacked the other would supply. Therefore I selected for my pen a subject chosen not for boasting but for usefulness, namely, a theology that was complete, joining practice with theory, which the *Prodromus* had already promised and my Utrecht preceptors had early on commended. The first part of this I published in 1682, and the second part in 1687. And when this edition was so widely distributed that a copy, or at least a whole one, could not be found for sale, I undertook this second edition, not only that it might present the previous one again, but also clean it up, augment it throughout, and join to it, in place of the outline of church history, a full history, albeit abridged, and moreover, that it might add an Outline of Moral Theology in three books and a Sketch of Ascetic Theology in four books. And by these designs it grew so much that it evolved into a new work, and it would have evolved even more if I had been given the strength, at almost seventy years old, to work the moral and ascetic part into the same shape as the rest. In my retirement, due to such an advanced age, for more than three years I have been burdened by a great loss of my vital spirits and the near ruin of my health and life. And I would have succumbed—indeed that is what the first stages of my affliction threatened—if God by extraordinary grace had not then supported my tottering hope and raised it up by the promise of some return from these labors, for the glorification of his name and the edification of the church, which, I can genuinely say, has been the supreme desire of this endeavor.

To whom ought such a progeny, born as it was under your auspices, protection, and benevolence, be presented if not to you, especially since so many and weighty reasons have come before me in favor of this idea? Indeed, on more than one occasion I had desired an opportunity in which I might offer you, O noblest sirs, an accounting of my affairs, but for reasons I know not, I have so far been hindered. By this accounting I would have you understand that, although I could not do all I wanted, yet I have offered what I could, and have not wasted my time with you in leisure and laziness. Above all, I was encouraged to dedicate the work to you because I observed that your academy—since it conjoins[8] pristine Reformed theology with its practice (which my present work strives for)—has from its very founding flourished so far above others that any student that wanted theology and practice joined together passed over the others and for his studies chose yours. Therefore, O conscript fathers, accept with your accustomed courtesy this child that I offer to you with heartfelt reverence. I in turn will pray to God that he would amply bless your civic

---

8. *a* συμβιβάσει

leadership, your persons, and your families with every kind of grace and blessing, spiritually as well as bodily.

The fourteenth day of February, 1698.
My lords, I have nothing left to add but farewell and goodbye,[9]
Your most devoted servant,
Peter van Mastricht

---

9. *N.N.A.A.V.V.*, that is, *Nil Nisi Avete Atque Valete, Viri.* This is a common closing in the seventeenth-century period and is probably derived from Catullus's Poem 101 which closes with the famous remark: *ave atque vale.* David C. Noe offered instrumental assistance to the translator in tracking down this abbreviation. His assistance at this point is acknowledged with thanks.

1699 Preface

I will detain you on this threshold, not with too many words, but also not with too few, dear reader, for I want you to perceive the character of this second edition.

If you should be surprised that I used smaller type for this edition than for the first, realize that I did so in order to spare you some expense. Even though this plan failed because of all of the added material, this at least should satisfy you, that now you have in two volumes what otherwise you would have had in three. And if the type should hinder the acuity of your eyes, I thought this trouble was easily compensated: the young have sharp eyes, and the old have glasses.

At the same time, in this edition you will have all that you had in the previous one, not only much more corrected but also, at least by a third, more substantial.

For example, in the exegetical sections of the prior edition I supplied the texts of Scripture, the foundation on which the heads of theology are built, fairly sparsely in order to save space. But here, for learning's sake, the previously omitted texts appear. In this way our Nazarites[1] might become accustomed to building their theological heads upon the foundations of Scripture. In these sections, as much as could be done, we refrained from the terms of the art of logic, insofar as they are not useful for the students, and drew our terms instead from the text itself, so that here also they might become accustomed to the nature of the topics.

In the elenctic sections, we reduced all the controversies to questions so that we might more easily touch on the history of each one, that the reader might more easily comprehend the primary error,[2] the differences of opinion, and the golden mean of orthodoxy between the heterodox opinions that turn aside in either direction. Then from this vantage point the reader might more solidly and easily oppose the problems of both deviant extremes. For I thought that the

---

1. *Naziraei*, those set apart or consecrated (see Numbers 6), that is, pastors or seminarians.
2. πρῶτον ψεῦδος

best way to save time in judging controversies was for you to perceive clearly the deviations on both sides of the truth.

In the practical sections there was less amplification, so that our theological system would not degenerate into a hulking mass, so that it would not overflow into more volumes, and so that I would not disappoint in aiming for this goal of brevity, especially since an attentive reader can without great difficulty provide his own elaborations from the compiled testimonies of Scripture by giving them a bit more careful thought, particularly if he notes that I have not sought to include everything for the purpose of demonstration, but only several things for the purpose of illustration.

In the eighth book, on the dispensation of the covenant of grace throughout all the ages of the church, we have included an ecclesiastical history. It is quite full, albeit abbreviated, and in it you will find the leading figures,[3] both political and ecclesiastical, of each of the ages of the church: patriarchs, judges, and kings of both kingdoms, Judah and Israel, and the most remarkable deeds of each one, with respect to the Old Testament. With respect to the New, Roman emperors and popes, each described through his remarkable deeds, will be presented to you, then the stages of development in theology as well as the heresies and errors deviating from it at each point, then the stages of the church and those who advanced it—the patriarchs, prophets, apostles, and evangelists, each of whose history is thoroughly interwoven—and the things that aided in its advance, namely, ecclesiastical writers, synods, schools, form of church order,[4] persecutions, martyrdoms, and various other topics regarding the church. I believe that from these things can be drawn whatever could be desired for a full church history, though it was written in an abbreviated fashion, because otherwise I would have run over into many volumes, and large ones at that. At first I began in the style of a commentary upon the shorter summary in the previous version, a work quite copiously addressing the circumstances of the church, and I had advanced as far as a history of the patriarch Isaac, but when I noticed it growing into an excessive bulk, and I compared it with my rather advanced age, and because other things more advantageous for the church would have to have been excluded, I gave up hope and replaced it with this compendium that you see here. If in the meantime you are eager to have a whole treatise of church history, I know that the famous Frédéric Spanheim Jr. in his historical works, which are now bearing fruit from the Leiden printing presses, will satisfy more than many others.[5] May God breathe

---

3. προεστῶτας
4. *regiminis forma*
5. This is probably a reference to the various editions of Frédéric Spanheim Jr., *Brevis*

upon these works with his blessing, that they may soon enjoy public light! In the meantime, so that you may follow the order and coherence of our synopses more closely throughout their somewhat longer paragraphs,[6] I will try to assist you: prefixed to the eighth book of the church history is an outline of the book. I do not wish to mix myself up in the innumerable controversies of the chronologers, so instead I am content to follow the more received opinion.

In this edition, for the sake of the integrity of the theological system, an "Outline of Moral Theology"[7] is added, dealing with the simple Christian virtues, where I have placed under distinct heads their nature, marks, goods, and helps, as much as possible in a succinct style, since they require an attentive reader. I have followed the method of the renowned Dr. William Ames, in his *Marrow* and *Cases of Conscience*, which seemed to me so profitable that I did not want— nor ought I—to substitute another. In these matters, I certainly planned at first to say more, as is evident from the three disputations held just on the obedience of faith.[8] But afterward, spread thin by age, I lapsed into the other extreme, that is, I was exceedingly concise to the point that I contracted those three

---

introductio ad historiam sacram utriusque testamenti ac praecipue christianam ad a. MDXVII inchoata jam Reformat. (Leiden: Joannes Verbessel, 1688, 1694, 1695). There were also editions published in Utrecht (Utrecht: Balthazar Lobet and Otto de Vries, 1696) as well as in Frankfurt and Leipzig (Frankfurt and Leipzig: Samuel Garman, 1698). This work was also entitled: Frédéric Spanheim Jr., *Summa historiae ecclesiasticae a Christo nato ad seculum XVI inchoatum* (Leiden: Joannes Verbessel, 1688, 1689).

6. "somewhat long paragraphs": Part 1, book 8, chapters 1–4 is a history of the dispensations of the covenant of grace under the patriarchs, Moses, Christ, and eternity. For example, in 1.8.3, Mastricht divides the seventh dispensation of the covenant of grace under Christ into six ages of the New Testament through the opening of the sixth seal in Revelation 6:12. The doctrinal section of 1.8.3 (§§IV–XLIV) extends to approximately 174,000 words and covers the period between the first century and the close of the seventeenth century.

7. Part 2 is entitled *Idea Theologiae Moralis*.

8. Petrus van Mastricht presided over three disputations in 1691, parts 1 and 2 were defended by the respondent Joachimus Witzonius and part 3 was defended by Johannes a Breen. In part one, on the first page of the text, the disputation begins: "*Theologia Moralis, Liber Primus, De observantia Christiani in genere, Caput primum de Obedientia Fidei*" in *Disputatio theologica de obedientia fidei pars prima...sub praesidio D. Petri van Mastricht...publicis tueri conabitur Joachimus Witzonius...a. diem 23 Maiis* (Utrecht: Franciscus Halma, 1691), fol. A2 recto. The first disputation handles the exegetical section and part of the dogmatic section (§§1–6). The second disputation, *Disputatio theologica de obedientia fidei pars secunda...sub praesidio D. Petri van Mastricht...publicis tueri conabitur Joachimus Witzonius...a. diem 27 Maiis* (Utrecht: Franciscus Halma, 1691), picks up *in medias res* in the dogmatic section, and continues through the elenctic section (§§7–18). The third disputation, *Disputatio theologica de obedientia fidei pars prima...sub praesidio D. Petri van Mastricht...publicis tueri conabitur Johannes a Breen...a. diem 10 Juniis* (Utrecht: Franciscus Halma, 1691), by a different student, concludes the treatment of the topic with the practical section (§§19–25). This indicates quite succinctly that these student disputations fit into the professor's much larger publication plan. These three disputations can be found in a bound collection

disputations into a few brief lines. Finally, as I kept going forward, I reached the mean, so that they would neither be excessively dry nor help the reader too little.

I also added a "Sketch of Ascetic Theology"[9] on how to practice virtues, that is, on the exercises of piety in every circumstance of life, altogether in four books, which would have been presented in more detail, with more chapters (reduced together now), if fear of prolixity had not constrained me. Yet you will have before you the important points, which can be expanded into more without any trouble, if the case demands it. I was convinced to tread this path of ascetic theology, one not well worn by Protestants, because when fighting with the adversaries of the truth, we must stand against them at every point in the line of battle. The British theologians, whom I entirely commend to you for consultation, occasionally supplied several points.

In the moral and ascetic sections alike I ought to have been more expansive, but this could not have been done, because I am nearly seventy years old and this edition would have been excessively prolonged. Therefore I wish nothing more than that learned men, whom our age nourishes with such great abundance, might devote their energy, which they now spend on less necessary and useful things, to these more practical matters.[10] They would discover that as much difficulty as there is, there is just as much usefulness, and accordingly they could guarantee for themselves no less glory than they could from their present idleness. Indeed, it would bring much greater gain for God's glory and for the edification of the church.

Finally, as for the indices: the one that collects the Scripture references from their abundant supply I committed fully to the care of a most equipped and erudite young man, Mr. William Muller, shortly to be a candidate for the most holy ministry. I prepared the rest myself, with his collaboration.

At last, in order that you may use our theology homiletically for your sermons, let me advise you of one thing: you should first carefully observe the predominant argument of your text and then consult the topics throughout our work that will be most appropriate for your argument. Next, your mind will thus be strengthened to comprehend sufficiently the force and efficacy of the Scripture passages, so that you may first build your argument, then prove it. And now that you have had a taste of what is to come, I dismiss you to the work itself.

---

entitled, *Theological Tracts 17–28*, shelfmark 491.b.19 at the British Library, specific shelfmarks of the disputations respectively are: 491.b.19.(26), 491.b.21.(4), and 491.b.21.(5).

9. Part 3 is entitled *Hypotyposis Theologiae Asceticae.*

10. πρακτικώτερα

Methodical Arrangement of the Whole Work

The index of topics and terms in this edition removes the necessity of the analytical index which we adjoined to the prior edition, insofar as its contents are easier to locate since you have here a methodical arrangement of the whole work.[1]

The outline of the whole work

The whole of theology is summed up into:

I. The prolegomena of theology (Part 1, Book 1: *TPT* 1.1):
   A. The nature of theology (Part 1, Book 1, Chapter 1: *TPT* 1.1.1)
   B. The principle of the same, or Scripture (*TPT* 1.1.2)
   C. The distribution into its parts (*TPT* 1.1.3)

II. The system (*TPT* 1.2–3.4) in which is explained:
   A. Faith (*TPT* 1.2), with respect to its:
      1. Nature (*TPT* 1.2.1)
      2. Primary object, God (*TPT* 1.2–8)
   B. Observance
      1. Moral matters (*TPT* 2.1–3) regarding virtues and their opposing vices, in three books
      2. Ascetic matters (*TPT* 3.1–4) regarding the exercise of virtues, or the practice of piety and impiety, in four books

---

1. As Mastricht's original outline extended to fifteen levels deep at points, it seemed more profitable to segment the outline into more manageable portions. Furthermore, the original schema is inconsistent in its numbering, indicating the early modern printer's difficulty to accommodate Mastricht's complex outline. In this edition, measure has been taken to bring a degree of scale and utility to the outline. All of the original wording has been retained though some of the headings are repeated at the beginning of their own outline. It is hoped that this will maintain the spirit of Mastricht's outline although it is readily acknowledged it does not maintain the historical letter of the 1699 edition.

The outline of Part 1, Book 2, Chapters 1–27

II.A.2 – Faith's primary object, God, is explained with respect to his:

    a. Existence and knowledge (*TPT* 1.2.2)

    b. Imperceptible essence, in his independence (*TPT* 1.2.3), which is noted by

        (1) The divine names (*TPT* 1.2.4)

        (2) The attributes, which are treated:

            (a) Generally (*TPT* 1.2.5)

            (b) Individually, with respect to his:

                i. Primitive attributes, by which are represented:

                    (α) What God is,[2] namely an independent Spirit,[3] which concerns

                        I' God's spirituality and simplicity (*TPT* 1.2.6)

                        II' God's immutability (*TPT* 1.2.7)

                    (β) How many is God,[4] with respect to quantity that is

                        I' Discreet, and thus, God's unity (*TPT* 1.2.8)

                        II' Continuous, which is considered

                            (A') Absolutely, in his infinity (*TPT* 1.2.9)

                            (B') Relatively, with respect to:

                                (1') His presence, or where God is, which is called his immensity (*TPT* 1.2.10)

                                (2') His duration, which is called his eternity (*TPT* 1.2.11)

                    (γ) What kind of God is he.[5] Here is explained:

                        I' God's life and immortality (*TPT* 1.2.12)

                        II' God's intellect, and therein his omniscience (*TPT* 1.2.13)[6]

                        III' God's will (*TPT* 1.2.15), and then is explained

                            (A') His acts, in which are his affections (*TPT* 1.2.15)

                            (B') His virtues, through which his will is considered as:

---

2. *Quid sit*: i.e. questions with respect to essence and substance, whereas *an sit?* would address a being's existence.

3. *Spiritus a se*

4. *Quantus sit*: i.e. with respect to quantity. For comparison, the *quid sit* and *quantus sit* are frequently combined in treating the *attributa negativa* among Protestant scholastics, whereas the *attributa positiva* are linked to discussions of *qualis sit*, that is, qualitatively. Cf. Adriaan Neele, *Petrus Van Mastricht (1630–1706): Reformed Orthodoxy: Method and Piety* (Leiden: Brill, 2009), 76; Richard A. Muller, *Dictionary of Latin and Greek Theological Terms* (Grand Rapids: Baker Book House, 1996), 50.

5. *Qualis sit*: i.e. qualitatively.

6. Mastricht's outline leaves out 1.2.14, on God's truthfulness and faithfulness.

(1′) Desirable in itself, hence God's goodness (*TPT* 1.2.16)

(2′) Communicative, through which:

(a′) God is favorable toward his own, in grace, mercy, patience, etc. (*TPT* 1.2.17)

(b′) God acts according to a rule, hence his righteousness (*TPT* 1.2.18)

(c′) God is pure in himself, that is, his holiness (*TPT* 1.2.19)

(C′) God's authority and power,[7] namely his omnipotence (*TPT* 1.2.20)

ii. Derivative attributes, namely:

(α) God's omnisufficiency and perfection (*TPT* 1.2.21)

(β) Majesty and glory (*TPT* 1.2.22)

(γ) Blessedness (*TPT* 1.2.23)

c. Subsistence

(1) The Trinity of persons in general (*TPT* 1.2.24)

(2) The persons of the Trinity:

(a) The Father (*TPT* 1.2.25)

(b) The Son (*TPT* 1.2.26)

(c) The Holy Spirit (*TPT* 1.2.27)

d. Efficiency (*TPT* 1.3-8)

The outline of Part 1, Books 3–8

II.A.2.d. – Faith's primary object, God, is explained with respect to his efficiency, which is treated:

(1) Generally

(2) Specifically, with respect to God's operations:

(a) The internal operations, namely the decrees, of which are displayed their:

i. General nature (*TPT* 1.3.1)

ii. Parts or kinds, such as: Predestination (*TPT* 1.3.2), in its kinds:

(α) Election (*TPT* 1.3.3), and

(β) Reprobation (*TPT* 1.3.4)

(b) The external operations, which includes:

i. Creation, of which are noted:

(α) Its general production (*TPT* 1.3.5), or nature

(β) The things produced, or creatures: first

---

7. *potestas et potentia*

    I' Irrational ones (*TPT* 1.3.6): (A') The universe,
      (B') heaven, (C') earth
    II' Rational ones:
      (A') Angels: (1') good ones (*TPT* 1.3.7), and (2') evil
      ones (*TPT* 1.3.8)
      (B') Men and their: (1') Creation, and
      (2') Excellence in the image of God (*TPT* 1.3.9)
  ii. A twofold Providence:
    (α) A physical, or general one (*TPT* 1.3.10)
    (β) An ethical, or special one concerning man in his threefold
     state:
     I' Of nature, wherein is the covenant of works
      (*TPT* 1.3.11)
     II' Of sin, wherein is noted:
      (A') The violation of the covenant of works
      (*TPT* 1.4.1)
      (B') The consequences of its violation, namely:
       (1') Sin: (a') Original (*TPT* 1.4.2), and
       (b') Actual (*TPT* 1.4.3)
       (2') The penalty and state of sin (*TPT* 1.4.4)
     III' Of grace, wherein is treated:
      (A') Redemption, and its:
       (1') Norm in the covenant of grace (*TPT* 1.5.1)
       (2') Procurer, Christ (*TPT* 1.5.2), with respect
       to his:
       (a') Names (*TPT* 1.5.3)
       (b') Person (*TPT* 1.5.4)
       (c') Office, of which must be maintained:
        (i') Its trinity (*TPT* 1.5.5)
        (ii') Its threefold function:
         (α') Prophetic (*TPT* 1.5.6)
         (β') Priestly (*TPT* 1.5.7)
         (γ') Kingly (*TPT* 1.5.8)
       (d') Twofold State:
        (i') Of humiliation, of which are taught:
        (α') Its nature in general (*TPT*
        1.5.9)
        (β') Its four degrees:
         I" Incarnation (*TPT* 1.5.10)
         II" Life (*TPT* 1.5.11)
         III" Death (*TPT* 1.5.12)

IV" Descent (*TPT* 1.5.13)

(ii') Of exaltation, of which are taught:

   (α') Its nature in general
(*TPT* 1.5.14)

   (β') Its degrees:

     I"   Resurrection (*TPT* 1.5.15)

     II" Ascension (*TPT* 1.5.16)

     III" Session at the right hand
of God (*TPT* 1.5.17)

(3') Procurement or redemption (*TPT* 1.5.18)

(B') Redemption's application and its:

  (1') Nature in general (*TPT* 1.6.1)

  (2') Acts:

    (a') Calling (*TPT* 1.6.2)

    (b') Regeneration (*TPT* 1.6.3)

    (c') Conversion (*TPT* 1.6.4)

  (3') Foundation in union with Christ
(*TPT* 1.6.5)

  (4') Applied benefits:

    (a') Justification (*TPT* 1.6.6)

    (b') Adoption (*TPT* 1.6.7)

    (c') Sanctification (*TPT* 1.6.8)

    (d') Glorification (*TPT* 1.6.9)

  (5') Subject, the church (*TPT* 1.7.1)

  (6') Instruments of application such as:

    (a') The ministry of the Word (*TPT* 1.7.2)

    (b') The sacraments: (*TPT* 1.7.3)

      (i') Of spiritual generation (*TPT* 1.7.4)

      (ii') Of nourishment (*TPT* 1.7.5)

    (c') Ecclesiastical discipline (*TPT* 1.7.6)

    (d') Governance of the church (*TPT* 1.7.7)

  (7') Various dispensations, namely:

    (a') Under the patriarchs (*TPT* 1.8.1)

    (b') Under Moses (*TPT* 1.8.2)

    (c') Under Christ (*TPT* 1.8.3)

    (d') Under eternity (*TPT* 1.8.4)

The outline of Parts 2 and 3[8]

II.B. – The system of theology, in which its second part is observance, which is occupied with:

   1. Moral things, concerning virtues and the vices opposed to them, in three books, namely:

      a. Generally, concerning the observance of faith, of which is explained by:

        (1) Its nature (*TPT* 2.1.1), with respect to:

          (a) Obedience, and its:

            i. Definition

            ii. Distribution

            iii. Affections

            iv. Marks

            v. Exercise,[9] where must be maintained its: (α) Origin, (β) Benefits, (γ) Supports

          (b) Disobedience, and its:

            i. Nature and acts

            ii. Evils

            iii. Restoration, which has: (α) causes, and (β) remedies

        (2) Its twofold norm:

          (a) Primarily, the law of God (*TPT* 2.1.2), and its:

            i. Use, and its:

              (α) Nature

              (β) Distribution

              (γ) Obligation

              (δ) Exercise, and its: (I') Acts, (II') Benefits, and (III') Affections

            ii. Neglect, and its: (α) Nature, (β) Evils, (γ) Causes, and (δ) Remedies

          (b) Secondarily, conscience (*TPT* 2.1.3), and its:

            i. Oversight,[10] and its: (α) Nature, (β) Species, (γ) Oversight, (δ) The process of oversight,[11] (ϵ) Benefits, and (ζ) Supports

            ii. Neglect, and its: (α) Vices, (β) Evils, (γ) Causes, and (δ) Remedies

---

8. Mastricht titled Part 2 *Idea theologiae moralis* (Outline of Moral Theology), and Part 3 *Hypotyposis theologiae asceticae, de exercitio pietatis* (Sketch of Ascetic Theology: The Exercise of Piety). Note that though compared to his above outline of Part 1, his below outline of Parts 2 and 3 is longer and more detailed, even so these two parts together make up less than one tenth of the whole work. Cf. the brief outline in 1.1.3 §X.

   9. *studium*

   10. *cura*

   11. *actus curandi*

(3) Its properties, with respect to:

    (a) Intellect (*TPT* 2.1.4), wherein concerns:

        i. Knowledge and its: (α) Nature, (β) Distribution, (γ) Marks, (δ) Benefits, and (ε) Exercise

        ii. Ignorance, and its: (α) Nature, (β) Evils, (γ) Causes, and (δ) Remedies

    (b) Will (*TPT* 2.1.5), in which is:

        i. Humility toward God, and its: (α) Nature, (β) Distribution, (γ) Marks, (δ) Benefits, and (ε) Supports

        ii. Pride, and its: (α) Nature, (β) Evils, (γ) Causes, and (δ) Remedies

    (c) Affections, wherein are treated:

        i. Fear and despising of God (*TPT* 2.1.6), treated individually:

            (α) Fear of God, and its: (I') Nature, (II') Distribution, (III') Marks, (IV') Benefits, and (V') Supports

            (β) Despising of God, and its: (I') Nature, (II') Evils, (III') Causes, and (IV') Remedies

        ii. Zeal and lukewarmness (*TPT* 2.1.7), here is treated:

            (α) Zeal, and its: (I') Nature, (II') Distribution, (III') Marks, (IV') Benefits, and (V') Means

            (β) Lukewarmness, and its: (I') Nature, (II') Evils, (III') Causes, and (IV') Remedies

    (d) The entire person (*TPT* 2.1.8), in sincerity and hypocrisy, here are treated:

        i. Sincerity, and its: (α) Nature, (β) Distribution, (g) Marks, (δ) Benefits, and (ε) Means

        ii. Hypocrisy: (α) Nature, (β) Evils, (γ) Causes, and (δ) Remedy

(4) The Parts of the observance of faith, namely:

    (a) Virtue and vice (*TPT* 2.1.9). Here are:

        i. Virtue, and its: (α) Nature, (β) Distribution, (γ) Marks, (δ) Benefits, and (ε) Means

        ii. Vice, and its: (α) Nature, (β) Evils, (γ) Causes, and (δ) Remedies

    (b) The properties of virtue, namely:

        i. Prudence and imprudence (*TPT* 2.1.10), wherein are explained:

            (α) Prudence: (I') Nature, (II') Distribution, (III') Benefits, and (IV') Means

            (β) Imprudence: (I') Nature, (II') Marks, (III') Evils, (IV') Causes, and (V') Remedies

    ii. Watchfulness and laziness[12] (*TPT* 2.1.11), separately:

        (α) Watchfulness, and its: (I') Nature, (II') Distribution, (III') Benefits, and (IV') Supports

        (β) Laziness, and its: (I') Nature, (II') Evils, (III') Causes, and (IV') Remedies

    iii. Courage,[13] which is treated:

        (α) Generally (*TPT* 2.1.12), and then:

            I' Courage,[14] and its: (A') Nature, (B') Distribution, (C') Marks, (D') Benefits, and (E') Means

            II' Weakness, and its: (A') Nature, (B') Evils, (C') Causes, and (D') Remedies

        (β) Specifically, namely:

            I' Confidence and fearfulness (*TPT* 2.1.13):

                (A') Confidence, and its: (1') Nature, (2') Distribution, (3') Benefits, and (4') Means

                (B') Fearfulness, and its: (1') Nature, (2') Evils, (3') Causes, and (4') Remedies

            II' Constancy and fickleness (*TPT* 2.1.14), individually

                (A') Constancy, and its: (1') Nature, (2') Distribution, (3') Benefits, and (4') Means

                (B') Fickleness, and its: (1') Nature, (2') Evils, (3') Causes, and (4') Remedies

            III' Patience and impatience (*TPT* 2.1.15), namely:

                (A') Patience, and its: (1') Nature, (2') Distribution, (3') Marks, (4') Benefits, and (5') Means

                (B') Impatience, and its: (1') Nature, (2') Evils, (3') Causes, and (4') Remedies

    iv. Temperance and intemperance (*TPT* 2.1.16), individually:

        (α) Temperance, and its: (I') Nature, (II') Distribution, (III') Marks, (IV') Benefits, and (V') Means

        (β) Intemperance, and its: (I') Nature, (II') Evils, (III') Causes, and (IV') Remedies

    v. Good and evil actions (*TPT* 2.1.17), namely:

        (α) Good action, and its: (I') Nature, (II') Distribution, (III') Benefits, and (IV') Mode of operation

        (β) Evil action or sin, and its: (I') Nature, (II') Evils, (III') Causes, and (IV') Remedies

  b. Specifically, on the observance of faith, concerning namely:

---

12. *somnolentia*: lit. "drowsiness" or "sleepiness."
13. *Fortitudo*
14. *Fortitudo*

(1) Religion, namely concerning:
- (a) Godliness and ungodliness (*TPT* 2.2.1), specifically:
    - i. Godliness, and its: (α) Nature, (β) Distribution, (γ) Benefits, and (δ) Means
    - ii. Ungodliness, and its: (α)Nature, (β) Evils, (γ) Causes, and (δ) Remedies
- (b) Faith and unbelief (*TPT* 2.2.2)
    - i. Faith, and its: (α) Nature, (β) Distribution, (γ) Marks, (δ) Benefits, and (ε) Means
    - ii. Unbelief, and its: (α) Nature, (β) Evils, (γ) Causes, and (δ) Remedies
- (c) Profession and denial of faith (*TPT* 2.2.3), namely:
    - i. Profession, and its: (α) Nature, (β) Distribution, (γ) Benefits, and (δ) Affections
    - ii. Denial, and its: (α) Nature, (β) Evils, (γ) Causes, and (δ) Remedies
- (d) Hope and hopelessness (*TPT* 2.2.4)
    - i. Hope, and its: (α) Nature, (β) Distribution, (γ) Marks, (δ) Benefits, and (ε) Means
    - ii. Hopelessness, and its: (α) Nature, (β) Evils, (γ) Causes, and (δ) Remedies
- (e) Love and hatred of God (*TPT* 2.2.5), separately:
    - i. Love, and its: (α) Nature, (β) Distribution, (γ) Marks, (δ) Benefits, and (ε) Means
    - ii. Hatred, and its: (α) Nature, (β) Evils, (γ) Causes, and (δ) Remedies
- (f) The hearing and neglect of the divine Word (*TPT* 2.2.6)
    - i. Hearing, and its: (α) Nature, (β) Distribution, (γ) Marks, (δ) Benefits, and (ε) Means
    - ii. Neglect of hearing the Word, and its: (α) Nature, (β) Evils, (γ) Causes, and (δ) Remedies
- (g) Prayer and its neglect (*TPT* 2.2.7)
    - i. Prayer, and its: (α) Nature, (β) Distribution, (γ) Benefits, (δ) Method, and (ε) Supports
    - ii. Neglect of prayer, and its: (α) Nature, (β) Evils, (γ) Causes, and (δ) Remedies
- (h) Confession and the suppression of sins (*TPT* 2.2.8), namely:
    - i. Confession, and its: (α) Nature, (β) Distribution, (γ) Benefits, (δ) Affections, and (ε) Supports
    - ii. Suppression of sins, and its: (α) Nature, (β) Evils, (γ) Causes, and (δ) Remedies

(i) Vows, their use and abuse (*TPT* 2.2.9), especially:
   i. The use of vows, and its: (α) Nature, (β) Distribution, (γ) Benefits, and (δ) Method
   ii. The abuse of vows, and its: (α) Nature, (β) Evils, (γ) Causes, and (δ) Remedies

(j) Oaths and perjury (*TPT* 2.2.10), namely:
   i. An oath, and its: (α) Nature, (β) Distribution, and (γ) Use
   ii. Its abuse, and its: (α) Nature, (β) Evils, (γ) Causes, and (δ) Remedies

(k) The use and abuse of lots (*TPT* 2.2.11)
   i. The lot, and its: (α) Nature, (β) Distribution, and (γ) Use
   ii. Perjury, and its: (α) Nature, (β) Evils, (γ) Causes, and (δ) Remedies

(l) Communion with God and alienation from him (*TPT* 2.2.12), specifically:
   i. Communion with God, and its: (α) Nature, (β) Distribution, (γ) Marks, (δ) Benefits, and (ε) Means
   ii. Alienation from God, and its: (α) Nature, (β) Evils, (γ) Causes, and (δ) Remedies

(m) The instituted worship of God and superstition (*TPT* 2.2.13), specifically:
   i. The worship of God, and its: (α) Nature, (β) Distribution, (γ) Benefits, and (δ) Exercise
   ii. Superstition, and its: (α) Nature, (β) Evils, (γ) Causes, and (δ) Remedies

(n) The use and abuse of instituted worship (*TPT* 2.2.14), namely:
   i. The use of instituted worship, and its: (α) Nature, (β) Distribution, and (γ) Benefits
   ii. The abuse of instituted worship, and its: (α) Nature, (β) Evils, (γ) Causes, and (δ) Remedies

(o) The sanctification and profanation of the Sabbath (*TPT* 2.2.15), specifically:
   i. The sanctification of the Sabbath and its: (α) Nature, (β) Distribution, (γ) Sanctification, and (δ) Benefits
   ii. The profanation of the Sabbath, and its: (α) Nature, (β) Evils, (γ) Causes, and (δ) Remedies

(2) Justice and injustice toward our neighbor, specifically:
  (a) Justice and injustice, in general (*TPT* 2.3.1), namely:
   i. Justice, and its: (α) Nature, (β) Distribution, and (γ) Benefits
   ii. Injustice, and its: (α) Nature, (β) Evils, (γ) Causes, and (δ) Remedies

(b) Love and malevolence toward our neighbor (*TPT* 2.3.2), namely concerning:

    i. Love, and its: (α) Nature, (β) Distribution, (γ) Marks, (δ) Benefits, and (ε) Means

    ii. Malevolence, and its: (α) Nature, (β) Evils, (γ) Causes, and (δ) Remedies

(c) Honor and spite toward our neighbor (*TPT* 2.3.3), especially:

    i. Honor, and its: (α) Nature, (β) Distribution, (γ) Benefits, and (δ) Supports

    ii. Spite, and its: (α) Nature, (β) Evils, (γ) Causes, and (δ) Remedies

(d) Humanity and homicide (*TPT* 2.3.4), namely:

    i. Humanity, and its: (α) Nature, (β) Distribution, (γ) Benefits, and (δ) Supports

    ii. Homicide, and its: (α) Nature, (β) Evils, (γ) Causes, and (δ) Remedies

(e) Chastity and indulgence (*TPT* 2.3.5), especially:

    i. Chastity, and its: (α) Nature, (β) Distribution, (γ) Benefits, and (δ) Supports

    ii. Indulgence, and its: (α) Nature, (β) Evils, (γ) Causes, and (δ) Remedies

(f) Commutative justice and theft (*TPT* 2.3.6)

    i. Commutative justice, and its: (α) Nature, (β) Distribution, (γ) Benefits, and (δ) Supports

    ii. Theft, and its: (α) Nature, (β) Evils, (γ) Causes, and (δ) Remedies

(g) Truthfulness and lying (*TPT* 2.3.7), especially:

    i. Truthfulness, and its: (α) Nature, (β) Distribution, (γ) Benefits, and (δ) Means

    ii. Lying, and its: (α) Nature, (β) Evils, (γ) Causes, and (δ) Remedies

(h) Contentment and covetousness (*TPT* 2.3.8), especially:

    i. Contentment, and its: (α) Nature, (β) Distribution, (γ) Benefits, and (δ) Means

    ii. Covetousness, and its: (α) Nature, (β) Evils, (γ) Causes, and (δ) Remedies

2. Ascetic things, concerning the exercise of virtues, or the practice of piety and impiety, in four books, namely:

  a. Generally, namely:

    (1) Concerning the practical nature of piety and laziness (*TPT* 3.1.1), especially:

       (a) The practice of piety, and its: i. Nature, ii. Benefits, and
          iii. Supports
       (b) Impiety, and its: i. Nature, ii. Evils, iii. Causes, and iv. Remedies
    (2) Progress in the practice of piety and being self-satisfied[15]
      (*TPT* 3.1.2)
       (a) Progress, and its: i. Nature, ii. Benefits, and iii. Supports
       (b) Spiritual self-satisfaction, and its: i. Nature, ii. Evils, iii. Causes,
          and iv. Remedies
    (3) The practice of impiety and its denial (*TPT* 3.1.3), specifically:
       (a) The practice of impiety, and its: i. Nature, ii. Evils, and iii. Causes
       (b) The denial of impiety
  b. Specifically concerning the practice of piety:
    (1) Toward God, wherein these are treated:
       (a) The reception[16] and rejection of God (*TPT* 3.2.1), specifically:
         i. The reception of God, and its: (α) Nature, (β) Benefits, and
           (γ) Supports
         ii. The rejection of God, and its: (α) Nature, (β) Evils,
           (γ) Causes, and (δ) Remedies
       (b) The seeking of God and flight from God (*TPT* 3.2.2)
         i. The seeking of God, and its: (α) Nature, (β) Distribution,
           (γ) Benefits, (δ) Method and means
         ii. The flight from God, and its: (α) Nature, (β) Evils,
           (γ) Causes, and (δ) Remedies
       (c) Pleasure and displeasure in God (*TPT* 3.2.3)
         i. Pleasure in God, and its: (α) Nature, (β) Benefits, and
           (γ) Supports
          ii. Displeasure in God, and its: (α) Nature, (β) Evils,
           (γ) Causes, and (δ) Remedies
       (d) Walking with God and wandering from him (*TPT* 3.2.4),
         especially:
         i. Walking with God, and its: (α) Nature, (β) Marks,
           (γ) Benefits, (δ) Method, and (ε) Supports
         ii. Wandering from him, and its: (α) Nature, (β) Evils,
           (γ) Causes, and (δ) Remedies
       (e) Benevolence and malevolence toward God (*TPT* 3.2.5), namely:
         i. Benevolence, and its: (α) Nature, (β) Benefits, and
           (γ) Supports

---

15. *satietas*
16. *agnitio*

       ii. Malevolence, and its: (α) Nature, (β) Evils, (γ) Causes, and
          (δ) Remedies

(f) Private worship to the glory of God (*TPT* 3.2.6)

(g) Public or ecclesiastical worship (*TPT* 3.2.7)

       i. Generally, and its ingredients

       ii. Specifically, with respect to all its duties

       iii. Most specifically with respect to:

          (α) The hearing of the divine word

          (β) Prayers

          (γ) Psalm singing

          (δ) Sacraments in general: I' Baptism, and II' Lord's Supper

          (ε) Alms

(h) Household worship and its neglect (*TPT* 3.2.8), especially:

       (α) Household worship, and its: I' Nature and ingredients,
          II' Benefits, and III' Supports

       (β) Its neglect, and its: I' Nature, II' Evils, III' Causes, and
          IV' Remedies

(i) Daily worship and its neglect (*TPT* 3.2.9), especially:

       (α) Daily worship, and its: I' Nature, II' Benefits, and
          III' Supports

       (β) Its neglect, and its: I' Nature, II' Evils, III' Causes, and
          IV' Remedies

(j) The worship of God in fasting (*TPT* 3.2.10), and its: I' Nature,
    II. Benefits, and III' Method

(k) Thanksgiving worship, and its (*TPT* 3.2.11): I' Nature, II' Ben-
    efits, and III' Supports

(l) Examination of oneself and its neglect (*TPT* 3.2.12):

       (α) Examination, and its: I' Nature, II' Benefits, and
          III' Supports

       (β) Its neglect, and its: I' Nature, II' Evils, III' Causes, and IV'
          Remedies

(2) Toward our neighbor, wherein these are treated:

    (a) The use and abuse of solitude (*TPT* 3.3.1), namely:

       i. Its use and: (α) Nature, (β) Benefits, and (γ) Method

       ii. Its abuse and: (α) Nature, (β) Evils, (γ) Causes, and
          (δ) Remedies

    (b) A godly and ungodly manner of life[17] with our neighbor
       (*TPT* 3.3.2), in general, especially:

---

17. *conversatio*

      i. A godly one, and its: (α) Nature, (β) Benefits, and
         (γ) Supports

     ii. An ungodly, one and its: (α) Nature, (β) Evils, (γ) Causes,
        and (δ) Remedies

(c) Specifically, concerning our manner of life in:

      i. Our feasts (*TPT* 3.3.3) and their:

         (α) Use, and its: I′ Nature, II′ Benefits, and III′ Supports

         (β) Abuse with respect to its: I′ Nature, II′ Evils, III′ Causes,
           and IV′ Remedies

     ii. Our commerce (*TPT* 3.3.4)

         (α) Just commerce, and its: I′ Nature, II′ Benefits, and
           III′ Supports

         (β) Unjust commerce, and its: I′ Nature, II′ Evils, III′ Causes,
           and IV′ Remedies

    iii. With the afflicted through consolation (*TPT* 3.3.5), of which
       consolation is mentioned:

         (α) Its exercise with respect to its: I′ Nature, II′ Benefits, and
           III′ Supports

         (β) Its neglect, and its: I′ Nature, II′ Evils, III′ Causes,
           and IV′ Remedies

    iv. With the lapsed and their reprimand and partaking in their
       sins (*TPT* 3.3.6), especially:

         (α) Their reprimand, and its: I′ Nature, II′ Benefits, and
           III′ Supports

         (β) Partaking in their sins, and its: I′ Nature, II′ Evils,
           III′ Causes, and IV′ Remedies

     v. With good persons, through love and friendship (*TPT*
       3.3.7), of which is treated its (i.e. manner of life): (α) Nature,
       (β) Benefits, and (γ) Supports

    vi. With evil persons and enemies (*TPT* 3.3.8), and its:
       (α) Nature, (β) Benefits, and (γ) Supports

   vii. With superiors, inferiors, and equals (*TPT* 3.3.9), specifically
       among:

         (α) Equals

         (β) Those unequal in their status, such as:

           I′ Economic status, such as in the duties:

              (A′) Of a husband toward his wife

              (B′) Of a wife toward her husband

              (C′) Of parents toward their children

              (D′) Of children toward their parents

              (E′) Of masters toward their servants

(F') Of servants toward their masters

II' Political status, here are treated such duties:

(A') Of magistrates toward subordinates

(B') Of subordinates toward magistrates

III' Ecclesiastical status, namely:

(A') Of pastors toward their hearers

(B') Of ruling elders

(C') Of their hearers and subjects, in which are handled:

(1') The benefits of this manner of life

(2') The supports of the same

(3) Toward ourselves, and that:

(a) In life, concerning its duties

i. More generally, in relation to its:

(α) Occupation and leisure (*TPT* 3.4.1), especially concerning:

I' The occupation of life, and its: (A') Nature, (B') Benefits, and (C') Supports

II' Leisure, and its: (A') Nature, (B') Evils, (C') Causes, and (D') Remedies

(β) Sustenance, or of provisions (*TPT* 3.4.2)

I' Their use, and its: (A') Nature, (B') Benefits, and (C') Supports

II' Their abuse, and its: (A') Nature, (B') Evils, (C') Causes, and (D') Remedies

(χ) Protection, or of clothes (*TPT* 3.4.3)

I' Their use, and its: (A') Nature, (B') Benefits, and (C') Supports

II' Their abuse, and its: (A') Nature, (B') Evils, (C') Causes, and (D') Remedies

(δ) Refreshment, or of recreation (*TPT* 3.4.4)

I' Their use, and its: (A') Nature, (B') Benefits, and (C') Supports

II' Their abuse, and its: (A') Nature, (B') Evils, (C') Causes, and (D') Remedies

ii. More specifically, in relation to:

(α) A prosperous state, wherein regarding prosperity:

I' In general (*TPT* 3.4.5), with respect to its:

(A') Use, and its: (a') Nature, (b') Benefits, and (c') Supports

(B') Abuse, and its: (a') Nature, (b') Evils, (c') Causes,
(d') and Remedies

II' In particular (*TPT* 3.4.6), with respect to the world
and worldly things:

(A') Their use and abuse, particularly:

(1') Use of the world, and its: (i') Nature, (ii')
Benefits, and (iii') Supports

(2') Abuse of the world, and its: (i') Nature,
(ii') Evils, (iii') Causes, and (iv') Remedies

(B') The vanity of human affairs, and its: (a') Nature
and (b') Use.

(β) An adverse state, and its:

I' Nature (*TPT* 3.4.8), wherein consists cross-bearing,
and its: (1') Nature, (2') Benefits, and (3') Supports

II' Origin, from trials (*TPT* 3.4.9), wherein are
explained:

(A') Their use, and its: (a') Nature, (b') Comfort, and
(c') Supports

(B') Their abuse, and its: (a') Nature, (b') Evils,
(c') Causes, (d') and Remedies

III' Kinds of crosses:

(A') Bodily ones (*TPT* 3.4.10), and their (a') Nature,
(b') Arguments for consolation, and
(c') Supports

(B') Spiritual ones, specifically

(1') Confounding and melancholic terrors
(*TPT* 3.4.11), and their: (i') Nature,
(ii') Causes, and (iii') Remedies

(2') Blasphemous suggestions (*TPT* 3.4.12),
and their: (i') Nature, (ii') Causes, and
(iii') Remedies

(3') Spiritual desertions (*TPT* 3.4.13), and
their: (i') Nature, (ii') Treatment,[18] and
(iii') Comfort

(4') Various kinds of doubt (*TPT* 3.4.14) and
their: (i') General remedies and (ii') Species.

(b) In death, wherein is treated the art of dying well (*TPT* 3.4.15),
and its: (a) Nature, (b) Benefits, and (c) Supports

---

18. *cura*

CHAPTER ONE

The Nature of Theology

Teach and exhort these things. If anyone teaches a different doctrine, and it does not agree with the sound words of our Lord Jesus Christ and with the doctrine that is according to godliness, he is puffed up, knowing nothing.

—1 Timothy 6:2–3

The first of the prolegomena of theology concerns the nature of theology.

I. We will demonstrate our theoretical-practical theology, consistent with the nature of any discipline, in two parts: the prolegomena and the system. Thus, with respect to the prolegomena, three are set forth in the first book: the nature, rule, and distribution of theology. And since the nature of something is not made known to us in any way more clearly than in its exact definition, which presupposes that which is defined (*definitum*),[1] in this chapter, after a preliminary discussion of the method of teaching theology, we will contemplate the

---

1. The issues involved in the distinction are found in, among others: Aristotle's discussion of "first principles" or "basic truths," definition, and demonstration, Aristotle, *The Organon: Posterior Analytics | Topica* (Cambridge, Mass.: Harvard University Press, 1960), 4.1–10; Boethius in *De Topicis Differentiis* in Migne, *Patrologia Latina (PL)*, ed. Jacques-Paul Migne (Paris, 1841–1855), 64.1173–1216, for a critical English translation with notes and commentary, see Boethius, *De Topicis Differentiis*, trans. Eleonore Stump (Ithaca: Cornell University Press, 1978); also note Stump's essay, "Dialectic and Boethius's *De Topiciis differentiis*," 179–204; see "The eight properties of the definitum and of the definition" in Jean Buridan, *Summulae de dialectica: An Annotated Translation with a Philosophical Introduction*, trans. Gyula Klima (New Haven, Conn.: Yale University Press, 2001), 8.2.1. There is a broad history of scholarship, discussion, and debate on how one correlates the necessary and accidental attributes in the *definitio* and the *definitum* as it correlates to logical extension and comprehension, especially as to whether these are *in ipsa re* or simply *in nostra cognitione*. It is sufficient for our purposes to state that a definition is the criteria of predication or a list of essential, delimiting attributes, and a *definitum* is that to which the definition applies. In short, the underlying reality is the *definitum* and the terminological criteria is the *definitio*. In this chapter, Mastricht engages the classical distinction between the definition and the thing defined, that is, the *definitio* and its *definitum*. The Dutch translation seeks to convey the distinction with the terms *beschryve* and *beschryving*.

definitum, which is theoretical-practical Christian theology,[2] and then its definition by which it is "the doctrine of living for God through Christ." We will lay as the foundation for all these things the exegesis of the aforementioned text, 1 Timothy 6:2–3.

The Exegetical Part
It is built upon the text.

II. In this text, the apostle, who is about to put the finishing touch on this epistle, gives Timothy a most serious admonition regarding true and false theology: encourage the former and flee the latter. In this the following points are clear:

A. A certain exhortation concerning the good that must be pursued: "teach and exhort these things."[3] In this two things are shown:

1. The subject encouraged,[4] namely, "these things"[5]—which is to say, "those things that I have taught you, not only in the immediately preceding words, but throughout this entire epistle, and indeed throughout the entire course of my ministry, while I declared the entirety of sacred theology, as much with my living voice as in my writing" (see Acts 20:27). Here the whole of Christian theology is commended to Timothy, which is indicated not only by the antithesis in the following phrase ("if anyone should teach otherwise"),[6] but also by the parallel of 2 Timothy 1:13.

2. The duty of exhortation,[7] which concerns how theology must be related, is twofold, namely:

a. He should "teach,"[8] that is, he should inform the intellect, in part by the exposition of true dogmas and in part by the refutation of false ones.

---

2. Given the interplay and discussions throughout medieval logic up to Mastricht's time on the nature of the relationship between the *definitio* and the *definitum*, for lack of a better term in English for "that which is defined," *definitum* will be utilized as a technical term from this point forward.

3. ταῦτα δίδασχε καὶ παρακάλει

4. παραινετικόν

5. ταῦτα

6. εἰ τὶς ἑτεροδιδασκαλεῖ

7. παραινέσεως

8. δίδασκε

b. He should "exhort,"[9] that is, by moving the will, so that what the intellect perceives is carried over into practice, for it is the chief end of theology and its highest apex. For the root word παρακαλεῖν means to call someone to his duty. And since I chiefly call someone in order to rouse him from his lethargy, to spur him on when he is sluggish, to lead him with gentle words, or to comfort him in his grieving, so then the word frequently means "I exhort," "I plead," and "I comfort." And the "Paraclete"[10] is the one who does all these things (John 14:16). Johann Tarnov says in his *Four Books of Biblical Exercises*, "All these sorts of things breathe the spirit of praxis, yet at this point one should note that the twin duty the apostle desires to be carried out concerning the same object is plural in number: ταῦτα, 'these things.' That is, one should point out that theory and praxis must be conjoined not only in the entire body of theology, in such a way that these two, as it were, should constitute the two essential parts of theology, but also in each of its integral parts, in such a way that each article of theology has its own theory as well as its own praxis."[11]

B. An admonition concerning fleeing evil, namely, false teachers and false doctrines. Here the apostle notes three things:

1. False doctrine, of which he teaches four chief criteria[12] by which one may distinguish it from true doctrine:

a. False doctrine teaches something erroneous,[13] that is, it teaches something different or in a different manner than what he in fact personally taught along with the other apostles. That is, false doctrine is whatever is contrary to the apostles and the prophets (Isa. 8:20; Eph. 2:20; Gal. 1:8–9; 6:16).

---

9. Παρακάλει
10. παράκλητος
11. See Johann Tarnov, *D. T. O. M. A. Johannis Tarnovii…Exercitationum biblicarum libri qvatuor, quorum III. Miscellaneorum Et IV. Dissertationum: in quibus verus et genuinus sensus locorum Scripturæ multorum ex verbo Dei, textuq[ue] authentico diligentius inquiritur ac defenditur; Cum Indicibus* (Lipsiae: Ritzschius, 1640).
12. κριτήρια
13. ἑτεροδιδασκαλεῖ

    b. It does not remain in the things they taught[14] (the Vulgate: "it does not rest"),[15] that is, it changes them by adding to them or subtracting from them (Deut. 4:1–2; 12:32; Rev. 22:18–19).

    c. It fails to teach the sound words of Christ or about Christ. This occurs either when it simply does not teach Christ as the power and wisdom of God (1 Cor. 1:24) or, if it does teach Christ, when it does not do so soundly, but by peddling the word (2 Cor. 2:17), whether concerning his person, his offices, or his benefits.

    d. It does not deliver a doctrine that is "according to godliness." By contrast[16] to these points, Paul teaches a careful definition of true theology, in which:

        i. The genus is "doctrine" because it ought to be taught, by appropriation (John 6:45), while not only any other kind of science but even natural theology is rather learned than taught. And it ought to be taught, I say, not only by men but also by God, not only externally by the Word but also internally by the Spirit, and for this reason let us listen as those taught by the Lord (Isa. 54:13).[17]

        ii. The difference is in the words "according to godliness."[18] You might call it the doctrine of rightly worshiping God, which is elsewhere expressed synonymously[19] as living for God through Christ (Rom. 6:11), for which reason theology is called "the word of life" (Acts 5:20). Therefore, it appears that Christian theology is best defined as the doctrine of living for God through Christ. Several things will be said about this in their places.

2. False teachers: "He is puffed up, knowing nothing," and so forth (1 Tim. 6:4).

3. The fruits and effects of both false doctrines and false teachers: it is from them that envy, contentions, and the like occur, concerning which we have no need to say more in this place.

---

14. Μὴ προσέρχηται
15. *non acquiescat*
16. κατ᾽ ἀντίθεσιν
17. למודי יהוה
18. κατ᾽ εὐσέβειαν
19. συνονύμως

FIRST THEOREM—The Method of Theology

The Dogmatic Part

Theology must be taught in a certain order.

III. From what has been said, it is apparent by way of introduction, that theology must be taught according to a certain method, and it must be the kind of method in which theory and practice always walk in step together. In fact, they must walk together in such a way that theory precedes and practice follows in every one of theology's articles. For the apostle commands Timothy (1) to teach just as much as to exhort all the heads of theology. First he should certainly teach, and then he should exhort. For this reason, (2) the covenant is spoken of as a "covenant ordered in every respect"[20] (2 Sam. 23:5); not only is it called such because the covenant of grace is itself most well ordered,[21] but also because its records,[22] in which theology is preserved, present themselves as set down in a most suitable manner. For this reason, (3) the apostle says that the approved "worker"[23] is the one who "rightly divides the Word of truth"[24] (2 Tim. 2:15). But one cannot rightly divide what has not been rightly constructed. (4) The worship that theology propounds is called "reasonable"[25] (Rom. 12:1) because it has been arranged according to the laws of right reason. (5) Many illustrious and remarkable examples of methodical arrangement found throughout the Scriptures argue this main point. If you want to contemplate what must be done, consider the Decalogue, which is striking for its amazing method. If you want to look for what must be petitioned, consider the Lord's Prayer. If you want to seek what must be believed, then consider not only Hebrews 6:1–2 as a brilliant catechism, but the entire system of theology in most of the Pauline epistles. I would add (6) that the whole biblical text, without doubt, is a "covenant ordered in every respect." And (7) since the heads of theology are scattered throughout the whole corpus of Scripture, it is surely necessary to gather and arrange them according to a suitable order and method. For this reason, (8) from the very first beginnings of the Christian church, when doctrinal heresies began to creep in, Christian theology immediately began to be arranged methodically into a system, as is evident not only in the more illustrious creeds—the Apostles', the Nicene, the Ephesian, the Chalcedonian, and others—but also in the individual writings of the first

---

20. ברית ערוכה בכל.
21. εὐτακτότατον
22. Latin: *instrumenta*; Dutch: *denkeschriften*.
23. ἐργάτην
24. ὀρθοτομοῦντα τὸν λόγον τῆς ἀλεθέιας
25. *rationalis*, λογικός

fathers; for example, in the eight books of Clement of Alexandria's *Stromata*, the four books of Origen's *On First Principles*, the seven books of Lactantius's *Divine Institutes*, the five books of Gregory of Nazianzus's *On Theology*, the books of Augustine's *On Christian Doctrine* and his *Enchiridion*, Rufinus's *Commentary on the Apostles' Creed*, Theodoret's *Epitome of Divine Dogma*, Prosper of Aquitaine's little book of *Sentences*, the four books of John of Damascus's *On the Orthodox Faith*, the four books of Peter Lombard's *Sentences*, and what commentators on those books have written, such as Albert the Great, Thomas Aquinas, Scotus, Bonaventure, and others; see especially Thomas Aquinas's *Summa Theologiae*. And, finally, see the work of those theologians who escaped from the papacy: Zwingli, Luther, Melanchthon, Calvin, Bullinger, Musculus, Aretius, Vermigli, Ursinus, Zanchi, and a thousand others who were occupied to the utmost with rendering the heads of theology into systems.

The need for method in theology is confirmed by three reasons.
IV. In addition to the reasons from Scripture, method in theological matters is urgently demanded for the following reasons: (1) The nature of God, who, since he is not a "God of confusion,"[26] has conducted and does conduct all his works in the most orderly way possible, and desires all things to be done "decently and in order"[27] (1 Cor. 14:33, 40). Surely for this reason he conferred on rational creatures the principles of order and method, that he might show that he is the author of all order and method, and also that he might direct us to preserve order and method, certainly in general, but especially in matters of great importance. And without a doubt, theological matters are of this sort. To that end, he also inspired the writing of his Scriptures by amanuenses in an order according to his choice, and yet certain and logical. This order has been shown, by the logical analysis of both testaments provided by learned men, to be clearer than the sun. (2) The nature of this theology, which, since it embraces diverse dogmas scattered throughout the vast corpus of Scripture that are among themselves mutually consistent, ordered, and aiming at the same goal, certainly requires those dogmas to be collected and constructed in a manner mutually consonant with one another. Method consists in this sort of activity. (3) The benefits of this method, which, if they belong to any science, at the least belong to the most outstanding science of all. Then what is a method for? A method brings clarity to the topics that must be taught, and produces understanding when, through a knowledge of logical consequences, it makes it easy to remember since it strings

---

26. ἀκαταστασίας θεός
27. εὐχημόνως καὶ κατὰ τάξιν

together subjects as with a chain by which something may be recovered easily enough if it should drop out. Additionally, a method produces brilliance and elegance in argument. For without method, there arises, according to Philo, "knowledge without knowledge."[28] Would you have any right to deny such benefits to theological matters?[29]

The sort of method that must be employed is explained.
V. You might ask, by what method, then, is theology most suitably taught? A method is nothing but an apt arrangement of the different topics according to the dependence they have upon each other, first with respect to themselves in how they mutually coexist, and then with respect to us in how we understand them. This is necessary so that the method of theology corresponds not only to the topics that must be taught—by it, for example, more general matters are placed ahead of specific ones and simpler matters ahead of complex ones—but that it corresponds also to the comprehension and use of the students. At this point, different people follow a different method, which we will not criticize. We approve, out of all methods, the one that the apostle not only commends in this text to Timothy, when he wishes that theological matters first be taught and then admonished, that thereby practice be perpetually joined to theory, but also employs everywhere throughout his epistles, especially those he wrote to the Romans, Ephesians, Hebrews, and others. By this method, I say again, practice should be joined to theory, not only in the whole corpus of theology, in such a way that the first place is especially reserved for the things that must be believed and the second for the things that must be done, but also that in each member of theology, practice should walk in step with theory in a continuous agreement.[30] Let me say more precisely what I desire and will pursue, God willing, to the best of my ability, namely, that the heads of theology should be (1) positively proved from the Scriptures, confirmed by reasons, and explicated in all their members, which is like a solid foundation for the entire structure; (2) elenctically vindicated against the artifices of all opponents, for without that

---

28. ἐπιστήμη ἀνεπιστημόνως: cf. Philo, "Peri to Ceiron twi Kreittoni | *Quod eo deterius potiori insidiari soleat*" in Philo of Alexandria, *Philonis Alexandrini Opera quae supersunt*, ed. Leopoldus Cohn (Berlin: Georg Reimer, 1896), 1.241 §7. Colson and Whitaker render the fuller phrase οὐδ᾽ ἄλλην τινὰ κατ᾽ ἀρητὴν ἐπιστήμην ἀνεπιστημόνως as "or any other virtue-governed knowledge in a spirit of ignorance," Philo of Alexandria, "The worse attacks the better" in *Philo: Volume II*, trans. F. H. Colson and G. H. Whitaker (Cambridge, Mass.: Harvard University Press, 1929), 214–15.
29. θεολογουμένοις
30. συμβιβάσει

vindication the constructed foundation neither stands sufficiently on its own nor becomes sufficiently rooted in the hearts of those who theologize;[31] and (3) practically applied, without which the prior points will be entirely and plainly useless.[32] For just as practice without theory is nothing, so theory without practice is empty and vain. For that reason, in his most wise counsel, the Savior joins them together: "If you know these things, you will be blessed if you do them" (John 13:17).

The Elenctic Part

Must theology be taught according to a certain method?

VI. It is asked, must theology be taught according to a certain method? As an example of excess, the Scholastics, according to their philosophical theology, loved the philosophical method of Aristotle—whether it was his analytic or synthetic method—to the point of distraction. As an example of deficiency, the Anabaptists, enthusiasts, and fanatics, due to ignorance and hatred of philosophy, reckon that all method should be eliminated from theological matters. One after another of our Reformed theologians, in proving their own points, opposed such persons. The Reformed, against the Anabaptists and enthusiasts,[33] demand a method, but not, precisely speaking, a philosophical one. They demand a natural method, that is, a method that is suitable for theological matters, and for assisting the judgment and strengthening the memory—however much that method might otherwise depend on the discretion of the writer. We have previously demonstrated such a method in §§III–V, and in this method we are supported by the continual practice of the God-breathed[34] Scriptures, which follow diverse methods according to the matters arising in them. The enthusiasts raise the following objections: (1) Theology surpasses the capacity of reason and thus also a logical method. I respond that it does indeed surpass the capacity of a corrupted reason, but not the capacity of a reason illuminated by the Word and Spirit, which judges spiritually, and thus also orders and arranges spiritual things (1 Cor. 2:10, 12, 13, 15). (2) Theology transcends all the sciences, and likewise transcends the laws of method. I respond that it does transcend the natural sciences, but does it therefore also transcend all order? Does theology really exclude order? (3) Method detracts from the simplicity of theology, as does the subtlety of artificial logic. I respond that, first, this objection does indeed

---

31. *animis* θεολογούντων
32. ἄχρηστα
33. Latin: *Anabaptistas et Enthusiastas*; Dutch: *Wederdopers en Quakers*
34. θεοπνεύστων

refute the excess of the Scholastics, but it does not, however, refute the method that is natural to theological matters.[35] Second, this objection is false, for order does not change the matter ordered or detract in any way from its perfection. If the order detracts from theology, it is not the method that is at fault, but the ignorance of the artisan who contorts theology to his own perverse rules rather than prudently adapting his method to theology.

The Practical Part

The first use is for censuring, noting: 1. Those to be censured

VII. Now we turn to practice. In the first place, the sort who deviate from the right path are (1) those who teach theological matters,[36] whether from a professor's chair or a preacher's pulpit, without any method; or (2) those who, though they have some kind of method, work hard to hide it, and therefore act as if they have none at all; or (3) those who, although they show some method, it is not suitable to the topic; or (4) even if it is suitable to the topic, nevertheless it is not suitable for the student; or, finally, (5) even if it is suitable for the student, nevertheless it is suitable only to his intellect for speculation, but not to his will for action.

2. Arguments for censuring

Those who deviate in these ways (1) incur the mark of disorder[37] and confusion, which is hated by God (1 Cor. 14:33, 40); (2) deprive their theological discourses of charm and elegance; and (3) render themselves useless[38] to their hearers when they simultaneously hinder their intellect and memory by their lack of method.[39]

The second use is for exhortation. 1. The duty

VIII. In the second place, the apostle rightly exhorts all Timothys (that is, all doctors and ministers) to pursue a method by which they equally teach and apply the heads of religion, and moreover that they first teach, then apply. In this manner, (1) they prove that they are sons of God, inasmuch as they are his imitators, since he is the God of order, not of confusion, whereas those of the

---

35. θεολογουμένοις
36. θεολογούμενα
37. ἀταξίας
38. ἀκάρπους
39. ἀμεθοδείᾳ

contrary view prove that they are agents of Satan, who is the author and patron of confusion.

2. Motives

(2) These Timothys show themselves to be workers approved and unashamed,[40] since they can rightly divide[41] the Word of truth (2 Tim. 2:15). (3) By a brilliant and elegant method, they render the doctrine of God pleasing to their hearers. As Philo said in his treatise, *The worse attacks the better*, "work is not good of itself, but, adorned with art, it is good."[42] (4) They make the doctrine of God not only pleasing and welcome, but also useful and fruitful. For by the precision[43] of their method, they assist the intellect of their hearers, strengthen their memory, kindle their zeal, and so forth. "For," according to Fulgentius, "an investigation of the truth deserves a high regard, or at least it does not fail to achieve its desired effect, if the mind strives toward understanding along the right lines."[44]

3. Mode

So that teachers may pursue the method more properly, I would recommend that three things must be observed, namely, that the method be consistent with the following: (1) The topic to be handled. (2) The capacity of the hearers. Thus, a topic is treated in one manner with beginners, using a catechetical method, and in another manner with the more advanced, using a systematic method—that is, partly constructively[45] (by definitions, divisions, canons, and arguments) and partly deconstructively[46] (by the refutation of objectors). It is treated in one way with the mature, using an exegetical and textual method in which catechetics and

---

40. Δοκίμους *item* καί ανεπαιξύντους ἐργάτας

41. ὀρθοτομεῖν

42. Mastricht cited as: Ὅτι ὀυχ ὁ πόνος κατ᾽ αὐτὸν, ἀλλά μετὰ τέχνης ἀγαθὸς, *Tract. quod deterius potiori insidietur.* cf. Ὅτι ὀυχ ὁ πόνος κατ᾽ αὐτὸν, ἀλλ᾽ ὁ μετὰ τέχνης ἀγαθὸν in "Peri to Ceiron twi Kreittoni | *Quod eo deterius potiori insidiari soleat*" in Philo of Alexandria, *Philonis Alexandrini Opera quae supersunt*, ed. Leopoldus Cohn (Berlin: Georg Reimer, 1896), 1.241 §7.

43. ἀκριβείᾳ

44. Cited in Mastricht simply as "in Fulgentius, book 1, chapter 3." "S. Fulgentii ad Trasimundum regem Vandalorum Libri Tres," *PL* 65.227. Fulgentius's Latin reads, "Magnum bonum confert inquisitio veritatis, quae tamen tunc desiderato non frustratur effectu, si rectis ad veri cognitionem lineis animus innitatur." (The investigation of the truth confers a great good, or at least it does not fail to achieve its desired effect, if the mind strives for a knowledge of the truth along the right lines.) Mastricht's citation differs at these points: "Magnum enim locum meretur inquisition veritatis…si rectis ad cognitionem lineis, animus annitatur."

45. κατασκευαστικῶς

46. ἀνασκευαστικῶς

systematics are applied for searching out the sense of Scripture, and in another way with beginners, that is, only catechetically. (3) Usefulness and godliness, such that all things are carried over into practice and end up there (2 Tim. 3:16).

SECOND THEOREM—The *Definitum*[47] of Theology

The Dogmatic Part

Only a theoretical-practical Christian theology must be pursued.

IX. Using this very method, we will first investigate the nature and character of theology by its exact definition. Yet before doing so we must set out its *definitum*, which is Christian theology that is theoretical-practical, which alone is to be taught among Christians. For the apostle commands Timothy to teach "these things,"[48] namely, what he himself taught together with Christ, the prophets, and the other apostles (specifically, Christian theology). He also commands that what can be taught should also be applied, and that doctrine should be according to godliness,[49] that is, theoretical-practical. He also prohibits Timothy from teaching in any other way.[50]

It is proved from the Scriptures.

X. The Scriptures everywhere urge the same. Since they commend walking according to this rule (Gal. 6:16), they forbid any other gospel (Gal. 1:6–9). They stress that one is not to turn aside from the true gospel, either to the right or to the left, whether by addition or subtraction (Deut. 4:1–2; 12:32; Rev. 22:18–19; 2 Tim. 1:13), for otherwise God is worshiped in vain (Matt. 15:9), nor can the "dawn" of grace be obtained in any other way (Isa. 8:20).

It is confirmed by three reasons.

XI. (1) For the only theology worthy to offer to Christians is what belongs to the one who alone is the head of his communion (Eph. 1:22–23), who brought his theology down from heaven, from the bosom of the Father (John 1:18), who understands perfectly the method[51] of worshiping God (John 1:18) and who has the power of eternal life (Rev. 1:18), which Christians seek by theology. (2) On the contrary, another theology or that of any other person than Christ

---

47. See n1.
48. ταῦτα
49. κατ᾽ εὐσέβειαν
50. ἑτεροδιδασκαλεῖν
51. *ratio*

is neither heard nor recognized by Christians (John 10:5, 8–10, 12). Specifically, Christ's theology does not originate from reason, which is blind (1 Cor.
2:14), nor from any man whatsoever (Matt. 23:8; 1 Cor. 3:5–7), for all men are
liars (Rom. 3:4). Finally, (3) only his theology must be pursued, into whom Christians are baptized (1 Cor. 1:13) and by whose name they are called Christians
(Acts 11:26), and their church and religion are called the sect of the Nazarenes
(Acts 24:5). Therefore, he alone is the self-authenticating[52] and infallible[53]
Teacher[54] of Christians (Matt. 23:7–8).[55]

That theology is given

XII. Moreover, (1) not only does the universal consensus of all nations (Rom.
2:15) declare that a certain theology is given, but (2) nature itself teaches that
God exists and that he must be glorified (Ps. 19:1; Rom. 1:19–21), and that he
in turn will be a rewarder[56] of those who seek him (Heb. 11:6), the method
of whose worship we proclaim in theology. (3) Nature teaches that the soul is
immortal, burning to have its immortal desire for perpetual beatitude satisfied,
and theology is believed to open the path to this satisfaction. (4) Nature also
teaches that the rational creature, having been created by God, strives toward
God, so that he is satisfied in God alone, to whom theology leads. So then
theology is, in our opinion, nothing other than speech about God,[57] about the
divine worship, about the immortal blessedness of the immortal soul, and about
the method of coming to God and living for him.

Its name

XIII. As to the origin of the term *theology*, it is without a doubt owed to the
pagans. For among the pagans, Pherecydes of Syros, who lived in the time
of Cyrus, is considered to be the first to have treated theology. His disciple
Pythagoras, and Pythagoras's own followers, hail Pherecydes as the preeminent[58]
theologian. (See Pliny's book *Natural History*, ch. 7, and Diogenes Laertius's life
of Pherecydes.)[59] Others point to Musaeus the son of Eumolpus, whom the

---

52. αὐτόπιστος
53. ἀσφαλλής
54. *doctor*
55. Dutch: *de door zich zelven geloofwaardige en onfeilbare Leermeester der Christenen is.*
56. μισθαποδότην
57. *sermo de Deo*
58. ἐξόχως
59. Pherecydes of Syros (Φερεκύδης) was a Greek philosopher (c. 600–550 BC) who
wrote *Pentemychos*. See also G. S. Kirk, J. E. Raven, and M. Schofield, *The Presocratic Philosophers*

Platonists emphatically called "the Theologian."[60] Philostratus testifies in his *Heroics* that Homer surpassed Orpheus himself in many things pertaining to theology. These pagans[61] call those who discourse about God theologians;[62] what they discuss they call theological matters;[63] and the science of those matters they call theology.[64] These theologians, however, were poets, as Aristotle testifies in his *Metaphysics*,[65] and Clement of Alexandria in his *Stromata*.[66] Generally they were writing symbolically,[67] enigmatically,[68] or cryptically concerning the births of their gods, for they asserted that their gods were born. Whatever its origin, the term is not written[69] in the Scriptures. It appears there neither expressly[70] nor by way of analogy.[71] It is uncertain when the term entered the Christian community. It is set forth in the inscription of the book of Revelation, though it is doubtful whether that inscription has canonical authority. This title of theologian is attributed to John for another reason, and in another sense, namely, because he bore witness to the Word of God (Rev. 1:2),[72] or to the deity of Christ. Dionysius the Areopagite uses this term "theologian" in a familiar way, as if it were quite common in his own time, but nearly all agree that that writer was actually from a later time.[73] It first occurs in Origen. Nevertheless, although it is not expressly written[74] in the Scriptures, it should not be immediately eliminated just yet from Christian topics (as many would like), because it conveys what it means with sufficient vigor, and it endures from the very first beginnings of Christianity. Furthermore, it should be retained especially since

---

60. τὸν θεολόγον: This may refer to Musaeus of Athens, who was considered a pre-Socratic theologian, prophet, and philosopher by among others, Herodotus, *The Histories*, 7.6; Plato, *Protagoras*, 316d; Euripides, *Rhesus*, 915.

61. *Gentiles*

62. θεολόγους

63. θεολογούμενα

64. θεολογίαν

65. Cited as Aristotle, *Metaphysics*, book 3.

66. Cited as Clement of Alexandria, *Stromata*, book 3.

67. συμβολικῶς

68. αἰνιγματικῶς

69. ἄγραφος

70. αὐτολεξεί

71. κατ᾽ ἀναλογίαν; Dutch: *Wat 'er ook van zy het woordt is onschriftuurlyk, en wordt in de H. Schrift noch woordelyk, noch by wyze van evenredigheid gevonden.*

72. ἐμαρτύρησε τὸν λόγον τοῦ θεοῦ

73. ὑπερβολιμαῖον

74. ἄγραφος

the derivative[75] "theologian" is attributed to John in the inscription of Revelation, which comes without a doubt from the term *theology*. The term's ingredients, *God* and *word*,[76] also occur in combination in the Scriptures (Rev. 19:13; 1 Peter 4:11; Rom. 3:2). Moreover, it is designated such because it is not only speech about God but speech that proceeds from God (2 Peter 1:20)—thus also John Owen, *On the Nature of Theology*, book 1, chapter 1.[77]

Its synonyms

XIV. Its synonyms among the Hebrews are "the wisdom of God,"[78] "legal knowledge,"[79] and "the study of the law";[80] in the Church fathers, "the wisdom of God,"[81] "the fear of God,"[82] and sometimes "the work of God;"[83] in the Scriptures of the Old Testament, "service" or "worship,"[84] that is, of God (Ex. 12:26); in the Scriptures of the New Testament, "the oracles of God"[85] (Rom. 3:2; 1 Peter 4:11; Heb. 5:12), "godliness"[86] (1 Tim. 3:16), "the pattern of sound words" (2 Tim. 1:13),[87] and "the sound words of Christ" (1 Tim. 6:3);[88] in both testaments, "the way"[89] of God (Ps. 25:4, 12; Matt. 22:16; Acts 24:14); and among the Latin fathers, "religion," either from "re-reading" (*relegendum*) or from "binding fast" (*religandum*).

Homonyms

XV. However, the term *theology* provides the basis for more than one homonym, insofar as it sometimes denotes the archetype of God's own knowledge concerning himself and other times its ectype, or a sort of copy of the former. Again, theologians separate ectypal theology into that which belongs to those who comprehend, who are in the home country (that is, in heaven), and that which

---

75. παρόνυμον

76. θεὸς et λόγος

77. John Owen, ΘΕΟΛΟΓΟΥΜΕΝΑ ΠΑΝΤΟΔΑΠΑ, *sive de natvra, ortv, progressv, et stvdio verae theologiae libri sex* (Oxoniae: Henry Hall for Thomas Robinson, 1661), 1–5.

78. חכמת האלהים

79. דעת התורה

80. תלמוד תורה

81. θεοσοφία

82. θεοσέβεια

83. θεουργία

84. עבדה

85. λόγια τοῦ θεοῦ

86. εὐσέβεια

87. ὑποτύπωσις ὑγιαινόντων λόγων

88. ὑγιαίνοντες λόγοι τοῦ Χριστοῦ

89. דרך, ὁδός

belongs to pilgrims, who are on earth. Furthermore, the theology of those on earth is either natural or revealed. Concerning these matters, the observations of the common places are readily available.

Christian theology
XVI. But the task at hand for us is not to consider bare theology, but rather to consider specifically Christian theology. This sort of theology is called "revealed theology," which has been revealed by him who is in the bosom of the Father (John 1:18). Our text (1 Tim. 6:3) speaks synonymously[90] of this theology, calling it "the word of our Lord Jesus Christ."[91] In this designation is included whatever is theological, whether it is made known to us by pure divine inspiration[92] or is taught additionally by nature, though it already is present in the Scriptures. For natural theology does not include anything that Scripture does not include.

Christian theology does not exclude natural theology, of which are taught:
A. Its parts
XVII. So Christian, revealed theology does not exclude natural theology, but includes it just as a larger quantity includes a smaller one. Therefore, just as revealed theology is summed up as those matters that must be believed[93] and those that must be done,[94] natural theology, which displays nothing but bits and pieces of revealed theology, consists in things that must be known[95] (which philosophers embrace in their metaphysics and spiritual writings) and things that must be done (which they consider in their ethics, economics, and politics). Therefore, natural theology is on the one hand partly in the intellect, which recognizes a true or false theological point, either theoretically or practically. Scripture grants this recognition even to the most depraved, who have been blessed with some use of their reason (Rom. 1:19–20; Ps. 19:1–2; Acts 17:27; Rom. 2:15). On the other hand, natural theology is partly in the will, which is inclined to the good, understood as such, which, as experience declares, not

---

90. συνονύμως
91. λόγον τοῦ κυρίου ἡμῶν Ἰησοῦ Χριστοῦ
92. θεοπνευγία. The 1749–53 Dutch translation renders the phrase as *ene zuiver Goddelyke Ingeving*. It should be noted, however, that the Dutch translation intentionally does not include the Greek word in the text next to the Dutch translation as it normally does for other Greek words, perhaps indicating the difficulty or obscurity of the Greek term.
93. *credenda*
94. *agenda*
95. *scienda*

even savages themselves reject. Nevertheless, natural theology must be carefully distinguished from pagan theology as such, because the latter is false and the former is true.

B. Its fourfold use
XVIII. We note that natural theology has four chief uses. (1) The first has to do with God, who by means of it renders the impious without excuse[96] (Rom. 1:20). (2) The second has to do with the pagans and atheists, who are most powerfully refuted by it (Acts 17:24–26; Ps. 8:2–3; Matt. 6:26). (3) The third has to do with revealed theology, which, at least with regard to us, is confirmed to an amazing degree when we discover that it agrees completely with natural theology. (4) The fourth has to do with us, who root ourselves chiefly in the recognition of revealed truth, that we discern that nature itself applauds it. And this is so even in our pursuit of the good, where nature itself calls us in the same direction as revelation.

C. A threefold abuse
XIX. At the same time, a threefold abuse threatens[97] its use whenever: (1) natural theology replaces revealed theology as the foundation and norm, and thus the mistress is subjugated to her handmaiden when the latter ought to be directed by the former (2 Cor. 10:5–6); (2) a kind of natural theology is devised that suffices for salvation, even though no hope of salvation is revealed outside of Christ, of whom natural theology is ignorant (Acts 4:12); and (3) some kind of common theology is devised by which everyone, even apart from Christ and faith in him, can be saved by the help of reason and nature only. Christ himself contradicts this point (John 14:6; 15:5).

Theoretical-practical theology
XX. For this reason, a Christian theology is required that embraces Christ (John 17:3; Isa. 53:11) and is theoretical-practical. That is to say, it is not theoretical only, resting in some sort of contemplation of the truth, nor practical only, considering the knowledge of the truth to be indifferent (which the Socinians and Arminians maintain, whereby they more conveniently neglect and eliminate faith in Christ and the other fundamentals of religion; in turn, they lure into their society whoever might be devoid of the knowledge of Christ and of Christian fundamentals). Rather, Christian theology unites theory with practice, and

---

96. ἀναπολογήτους
97. προσέρχεται

is "a knowledge of the truth that is according to godliness"[98] (Titus 1:1). And the doctrine according to godliness, by which we know and do (John 13:17), is composed of faith and love (2 Tim. 1:13), in agreement with the fathers. Cyril of Jerusalem writes: "The method of divine worship consists in these two things: careful concern for pious doctrine and for good works."[99] Thus, the layman confessor in the Council of Nicaea says, "Simple-mindedness[100] must be preserved by faith and good works."[101] Even more, each and every part of theology requires its own work, by which, according to the thought of our Savior, whatever we know, we do. "Because," according to Lactantius, "religion cannot be separated from wisdom, nor wisdom severed from religion, because it is one and the same God who ought to be understood (which is wisdom) and honored (which is religion). But wisdom precedes, then religion follows, because the first thing is to know God, and the result is to worship God. Thus, in these two things there is one driving force, however much they appear to be separated."[102]

The distribution of false religions

XXI. Every false theology and so-called[103] theology is opposed to Christian theology in that it is either ignorant of Christ or speaks falsely about him. The former is professed by unbelievers,[104] such as (1) the pagans, whom Paul separates into barbarians and Scythians (Col. 3:11); (2) the modern Jews, who also hatefully persecute Christ (I say modern, for in reality the ancient Jews thought the same thing concerning Christ as we do); and (3) the Muslims,[105] who are aware of Christ and receive him, but only as an extraordinary prophet, not as the God-man[106] Redeemer, over whom they even prefer that most crafty impostor Muhammad, and substitute his tenets found in the Qur'an for the divine oracles of Christ. The latter is professed by heretics, both the ancient ones,

---

98. ἐπίγνωσις ἀληθείας τῆς κατ᾽ εὐσέβειαν

99. Mastricht cites as Cyril of Jerusalem, *Catechesis* 4, "τῆς θεοσεβείας τρόπος, οὐκ [read ἐκ] δύο τούτων συνέστηκε, δογμάτων εὐσεβῶν ἀκριβείας, καὶ πράξεων ἀγαθῶν."

100. γυμνὴν γνώμην

101. Mastricht cites as "πίστει καὶ καλοῖς ἔργοις φυλαττομένην" from Socrates, *Ecclesiastical Histories*, bk. 1, ch. 5, cf. *Nicene and Post-Nicene Fathers*, Series II (NPNF2), ed. Philip Schaff and Henry Wace (New York: Christian Literature Co., 1890–1900; reprint Peabody, Mass.: Hendrickson, 1994), 2:9, Socrates, *Ecclesiastical Histories*, bk. 1, ch. 8.

102. Mastricht cites as Lactantius, bk. 4, ch. 4, cf. *Ante-Nicene Fathers* (ANF), ed. Alexander Roberts and James Donaldson (New York: Christian Literature Co., 1885–1896; reprint Peabody, Mass.: Hendrickson, 1994), 2:104.

103. ψευδόνυμος

104. *infideles*

105. *Muhammedani*

106. θεάνθρωπον

whom Augustine, Epiphanius, Daneau, Schlüsselburg, and others examine, and the more recent and modern ones. Among these modern heretics, (1) the first place belongs to the Socinians, who are the closest to unbelievers and Muslims, because the Socinians attribute to Christ just as much as unbelievers and Muslims do, for both of them deny his deity and satisfaction; (2) the second place belongs to the Anabaptists, who insult the true humanity of Christ and have not quite made up their minds concerning his satisfaction, and who likewise deny baptism to infants and sometimes repeat it for adults; and (3) the third place belongs to the papists,[107] who follow the Antichrist. They generously grant to Christ his deity, of course, and his satisfaction, at least in word, but in substance they more than adequately overthrow the latter when they pile up mediators in his place, and when they substitute their own satisfactions, the merits of good works, papal indulgences, and other similar things for his satisfaction. We add to these heretics the schismatics, who usually end up in heresy. Of this kind are: (1) those who call themselves Lutherans, who state that they chew in their mouths the human nature of Christ, which is either present everywhere, or at least in the elements of the holy synaxis,[108] and (2) those who follow Arminius, also known as Remonstrants, but only the five article men,[109] for we place the Socinianizers[110] or their apologists with Socinus. We do not even enumerate the fanatics, enthusiasts, libertines, and others of that sort because they have a form of atheism rather than a theology.

The Elenctic Part

1. Is the theology of the pagans true?

XXII. First, it is asked whether the theology of the pagans, which we have distinguished from natural theology, is true. The pagan writers who taught about theology and theological matters—Julian,[111] Porphyry, and Celsus being emi-

---

107. *Pontificii*

108. Mastricht utilizes a Latin term, *Synaxeos*, for the historic Greek one, συνάξεως, which in Eastern Orthodoxy could mean a eucharistic assembly, but in the Latin West was a synonym for the Mass. In either case, it emphasizes the presence of Christ in the elements during the liturgical assembly.

109. Latin: *quinquarticulani*; Dutch: *doch die alleen welke Voorstanders van de beruchte vyf Artikelen zyn* (but only those who are proponents of the infamous five articles). The *quinquarticulani* were those committed to the five articles of remonstrance. For an English translation see Philip Schaff, *The Creeds of Christendom* (New York: Harper & Brothers, 1877), 3:545–49.

110. *Σοcινιζοντες*

111. This is most likely the Roman Emperor Flavius Claudius Julianus (331–363), known colloquially as Julian the Apostate because he sought to overturn the establishment of Christianity in the Empire. In his writings he expressed a form of pagan Neoplatonism. His most direct attack

nent among them—without hesitation answer in the affirmative. Christians, Jews, Muslims, and all those who receive some sort of canonical scripture deny it with one voice. Although we grant that (1) pagan theology contained some true things about God and about divine worship (Rom. 1:19–20; 2:14–15), nevertheless, it did not have the true God, that is, the triune God, and the majority of the things that it held concerning the one God were not true. Also, the common people of the pagans used to enumerate, instead of one God, nearly an infinite number of gods, among whom—besides the sun, moon, and stars—were mere men. Now and then these men were illustrious, but frequently they were the worst and most wicked sorts of people—even devils! We also grant that (2) pagan theology recognized that God must be worshiped and his will obeyed, yet the way of worshiping God, and the will of God that they were responsible to obey, were thoroughly hidden from it. For this reason, it devised for itself childish, impure, and plainly horrendous ways of worshiping God. We grant that (3) it taught some of the virtues, yet it was ignorant of their nature, purposes, and essential ingredients—namely, that they should be devoted to the glorification of God, the advantage of one's neighbor, and one's own salvation; that they ought to be arranged according to the prescription of the divine will; and that they ought to be performed not in one's own strength but in that strength conferred by the grace of God. Instead, pagan theology regulated the virtues for one's own glory and advantage, according to the prescription of a blinded mind, and in the strength of one's own nature. We grant that (4) pagan theology had some sort of conception of human misery. Nevertheless, it was plainly ignorant of the origin of this misery and ran after the worst remedies in sacrifices (even human sacrifices!) and the worst sorts of other things. There is hardly anything that the pagans may allege for their theology but that it arose from nature and reason, and coincides with it. But we oppose them: (1) They freely presuppose for no reason that pagan theology corresponds to natural theology, while we have distinguished natural theology from pagan theology by this: the former is true and the latter is false. (2) Even if we should grant that it emanated from nature and reason, we deny that it flowed from uninjured nature and right reason, but rather from corrupted nature and blind reason. Indeed, (3) on the contrary we assert that nature contradicts polytheism, and that right reason does not allow people to have any gods they please, to claim religious worship for them, or to worship their gods in the way that pagan theology prescribes, all of which we have taught before.

---

on Christianity is found in *Julian, Volume III: Letters, Epigrams, Against the Galilaeans, Fragments,* trans. W. C. Wright, *LCL* 157 (Cambridge, Mass.: Harvard University Press, 1923, 1989).

2. Is any kind of natural theology allowed? The divergence of opinions

XXIII. Second, it is asked whether any natural theology, whether innate or acquired, is allowed. Some, who attribute too much to natural theology, err in excess at this point, just as the Scholastics among the papists do when, since they are helpless to sustain their doctrine of transubstantiation and other super-stitions by revealed theology, they flee to their own philosophical theology, the closest thing to natural theology. We will treat these things a little further on. Others dream of a kind of common theology by which anyone can be saved in his own religion. For an example of this, see Tomasso Campanella, from whom the Socinians do not differ very much when they require that a per-son must believe only a very few things about God and Christ in order to be saved.[112] There are others who, drawing on Plato, teach that the ideas of all things, even theological things, are innate in man. They direct all our study toward the contemplation and awakening of those ideas in such a way that, as they suppose, nothing is to be admitted as truth that is not found in those ideas by clear and distinct perception. We have disputed with them elswhere in our *Gangrene of the Cartesian Innovations*.[113] The Socinians, on the other hand, err in defect on this point. Socinus, Ostorodt,[114] and others absolutely deny all natural theology, whether innate or acquired, for this reason, so that they would not be compelled to admit that man had an original righteousness which involved a knowledge of divine things (Col. 3:10). Here also, in agreement with Socinus, Jan Crell (and many others of the same persuasion) denies innate the-ology. However, he not only acknowledges acquired theology but painstakingly

---

112. Mastricht does not cite a specific work of Campanella, but a work that could be in view, which maintains primarily that true religion is natural and universal, is chapter nine in Tomasso Campanella, *Atheismus Triumphatus, seu reductio ad religionem per Scientiarum veritates* (Paris: Tussanus Dubray, 1636), 94–104.

113. See Mastricht's *Novitatum Cartesianarum gangraena: nobiliores plerasque corporis theologici partus arrodens et exedens: Seu Theologia Cartesiana detecta* (Amstelodami, 1677), 2:153–56. Writ-ing under the pseudonym Cephas Scheunenus, he published a similar version in 4° as *Cartesianismi Gangraena insanabilis. Duodecim erotematum illustrium decadibus, frustra curata per P. Allingham pastorem…enneade erotematum vulgarium, demonstrata a C. Scheuneno*. (Ultrajecti, 1680).

114. For the chief theological work of Christoph (or Christoff) Ostorodt, see *Unterrichtung Von den vornemsten Hauptpuncten der christlichen Religion, in welcher begriffen ist fast die gantze Confession oder Bekentnis der Gemeinen in Königreich Polen, Grossfürstenthumb Littawen un[d] anderen zu der Kron Polen gehörenden Landschafften, welche, weil sie bekennen, das allein der Vater unsers Herren Jesu Ch[r]isti der Einige Gott, Iesus Christus aber von Nazareth, welcher vond der Jungfrawen Maria geboren ist, und kein ander, vor ausser ihm sein eingeborner Sohn sey verächtlicher weise, wiewol mit höchster unbilligkeit, Arrianer un[d] Ebpionite[n] genennet werde[n] / geschrieben: Durch Christoff Ostorodt von Goslar* (Rackaw: Sebastian Sternatzki, 1612 and 1625). Ostorodt's work entered into Dutch translation in 1689 by Hendrik van Heuven as *Onderwyzinge van de voornaamste hooftpunkten der christelyk religie* (S.I., 1689).

defends it with heaped-up arguments.[115] The Reformed certainly accept both innate and acquired natural theology, but in this way: they neither mean that such theology is actual (that is, actually present in each and every person, including infants and the mentally handicapped), nor that it is sufficient for salvation. Rather, by natural theology they mean a theology that arises spontaneously, without any revelation, from the rational nature concreated in all, in much the same way that reasoning is said to be innate to human beings. The following four things refute those who deny this sort of natural theology: (1) Scripture (Rom. 1:19–20; 2:14–15; Ps. 19:2–3; 104; Acts 14:15), whenever it teaches that divine things are observed by pagans by their reason apart from revelation; (2) conscience, naturally excusing and condemning either good or evil deeds (Rom. 2:15); (3) the consent of the nations, which is most evident from the voyages of the Portuguese, the English, and the Dutch; and (4) experience, which is obvious in the great many spiritual, ethical, economic, and political writings of the pagans. The objections of opponents[116] refute only the kind of natural theology that would actually and always exist in each and every person by nature, or the kind that would be sufficient for salvation, but even we do not accept such a natural theology. Or, the objectors, when they hear of a mouth that denies the existence of God, a heart that desires his nonexistence, and a life that rejects God, deduce that it is a given that all are completely devoid of a sense of deity (cf. Ps. 10:4; 14:1;[117] Titus 1:16).

3. Is natural theology sufficient for salvation?
XXIV. Third, someone may ask whether natural theology is sufficient for salvation. There are those on one side who do not think it is useful at all. Thus Socinus, together with his followers, denies natural theology, and the Anabaptists are in basic agreement with him through their hatred of philosophy. There are those on the other side who make so much of natural theology that it is seen as sufficient for salvation. In this group are the pagans, and formerly the Pelagians, since they taught that the patriarchs were saved by natural law alone, and Campanella, as well as the Libertines, who openly profess it. The Reformed certainly acknowledge that natural theology is useful for refuting atheists, for demonstrating a deity, for some kind of worship of God (Rom. 1:19–20), and

---

115. Mastricht does not cite a reference here, however, see "Liber de Deo et eius attributis" in Jan Crell, *Joannis Crelli Franci Operum Tomus Quartus Scripta eiusdem Didactica & Polemica Complectens* (Irenopolis [Rakow]: post annum Domini, 1656).
116. ἀντιλεγόντων
117. Latin: Ps. XI.I; Dutch: Ps. XIV.I.

for rendering the pagans, including the philosophers, without excuse[118] (Rom. 1:21–24, 32; Acts 17:24ff.; 1 Cor. 11:13–14), but they consider it in no way sufficient for salvation. They hold this because (1) a knowledge of Christ is required for justification (Isa. 53:10), and likewise (2) for eternal life (John 17:3), such that (3) outside of Christ, there is no salvation (Acts 4:12; John 14:6); and (4) insofar as Paul condemns and rejects philosophy as vain deception[119] (Col. 2:8), the spirit of this world (1 Cor. 2:12), worldly wisdom proper to natural men[120] who do not understand the things of the Spirit of God (1 Cor. 2:13–14), and the wisdom of the flesh[121] (1 Cor. 2:14), which does not submit itself to the divine law and cannot do so (Rom. 8:6–7). Moreover, (5) what is born of nature and reason, which is corrupted, dim-sighted, and blind, cannot offer us a theology that is sufficient for salvation. Nevertheless, the same Reformed do not deny that natural theology as it existed in the state of man as originally instituted, or in the state of integrity, was sufficient for the attainment of eternal life by the covenant of nature, because at that time human nature was still whole, owing to the wisdom of original righteousness. Nor also do they deny that while sin was absent, a mediator who is revealed by theology was not necessary.

Objections

If the Libertines could say anything to the contrary, it would be (1) that Acts 10:35 says, "Anyone from whatever people who fears God is accepted by him," including the one who is imbued only with natural theology. But it would have to be demonstrated that one can truly fear God apart from Christ (who is offered only in revealed theology) since without Christ we can do absolutely nothing (John 15:5). If they should stand on (2) the example of Cornelius the centurion, arguing that a Gentile, while yet outside of Christ, is called a pious person who feared God, abundantly gave alms, and constantly called upon God, then we will respond that he was indeed by nationality a Gentile, but by profession he was a Jew who believed in the Messiah by means of the revealed theology of the Jews, although he was yet ignorant of who that Messiah was, about whom Peter would thoroughly instruct him. (3) Natural theology, they say, is true and good; and of course, it originates from God. We will repeat that, in itself, it is not at all sufficient for the salvation of a sinner.

---

118. ἀναπολογησίαν
119. κενὴ ἀπάτη
120. ψυχικοῖς
121. φρόνημα σαρκός

4. What should we think about scholastic theology?

XXV. Fourth, someone may ask what we should think about scholastic theology, which is a middle way between natural and revealed theology inasmuch as it teaches revealed things by natural method and arguments. By "scholastic theology" we do not understand here revealed theology as it is taught in the familiar manner of the schools—which is the sense our Alsted meant when he published his scholastic theology—but rather that philosophical theology that is held in the schools of the papists in order to sustain their doctrine of transubstantiation and other sorts of superstitions. This philosophical theology was born under Lanfranc of Pavia while he was contending with Berengar over transubstantiation. In that dispute, at every point Lanfranc lacked the authority of both Augustine and Scripture, insofar as nothing in Augustine or Scripture presents itself in favor of transubstantiation. At least at that time this philosophical theology was more modest, but afterward, when quite dreadful philosophical terms were contrived, gradually it became more impudent, all the way up to Peter Lombard in his *Four Books of Sentences*, and from there to Albert the Great and his disciple Thomas Aquinas. By Aquinas, without any shame, not only were those quite dreadful philosophical terms augmented to an enormous extent, but also, disregarding the Scriptures, the heads of the faith began to be demonstrated by philosophical reasons, and even Aristotle, Averroes, and others began to be considered equal to the Scriptures, if not preferred over them. Concerning this kind of scholastic theology, it is now asked, what should we think?

Confirming arguments

Since the papists generally find nothing in the Scriptures to reinforce their positions on transubstantiation, the absolute rule[122] of the pope, their own satisfactions and merits, and all other kinds of papal doctrines, they commonly flee to philosophical subtleties and to the thickets of quite dreadful terms. The Reformed generally think, for the reasons already noted, that the aforementioned type of scholastic theology ought to be rigidly proscribed, and in substance agree with the more discriminating of the papists, such as Desiderius Erasmus, Melchior Canus, Denis Pétau, and others. Nevertheless, there are among the Reformed those who think we should take the middle way, that scholastic theology ought to be neither entirely preserved nor entirely eliminated, but that it ought to be purged of its blemishes, and only then can it be preserved.

---

122. *monarchia*

The sources of the solutions

Scholastic theology is useful (1) in controversies with the papists, since you cannot engage very soundly and fruitfully with them if you are unfamiliar with their style, tricks, and thickets; (2) in refuting pagans and atheists; (3) in building up souls concerning revealed truth itself; and especially (4) in those questions that border on theology on one side and philosophy on the other.

The Practical Part

The first point of practice, examination. Its motives

XXVI. Therefore, since only Christian theology ought to be impressed upon Christians, and since so many kinds of false theology and so-called[123] theology surround it on all sides,[124] it is, in the first place, a duty incumbent on us that we cautiously distinguish the latter from the former. This duty is (1) prescribed by Scripture (1 Thess. 5:21; 1 John 4:1; Heb. 5:14; Phil. 1:9–10); (2) recommended by the matter itself, inasmuch as it is most shameful, and equally pernicious, to be deceived and swayed in a matter of such great importance (Eph. 4:14); and (3) induced by the danger of error and of seduction, which threatens on every side. This threat of danger comes from Satan the seducer, who blinds (2 Cor. 4:4; 11:3); from false prophets, who are the agents of Satan (Matt. 7:15); from the inconstancy, blindness, and sluggishness of one's own mind (1 Cor. 2:14; Eph. 4:14); and from the variety and deceit of errors, which bear a "form of religion"[125] or of genuine theology (2 Tim. 3:5). So the most disciplined senses are required here to discern good from evil[126] (Heb. 5:14), as well as "knowledge and all discernment for testing those things that differ"[127] (Phil. 1:9–10). (4) We also are bound to this duty by the importance of distinguishing between true and false theology, upon which hangs either the eternal destruction or the eternal salvation of the soul (2 Peter 2:1; John 6:68).

The signs and mode of examination

But that this scrutiny might happen as desired, it is required first that we have Scripture at hand as our touchstone (Isa. 8:20; Gal. 6:16), and, second, the analogy of faith (Rom. 12:6) and "the pattern of sound words"[128] (2 Tim. 1:13).

---

123. ψευδόνυμος
124. εἰ εὐπερίστατος sit
125. μόρφωσιν εὐσεβείας
126. πρὸς διάκρισιν καλοῦ τε καὶ κακοῦ
127. ἐπίγνωσις, καὶ πᾶσα αἴσθησις πρὸς τὸ δοκιμάζειν τὰ διαφέροντα
128. ὑποτύπωσιν ὑγιαινόντων λόγων

In addition, we should have, third, certain particular criteria,[129] which hardly anyone has described more accurately than our text (cf. II.B.1), compared with which any so-called[130] theology will be discovered to be (1) unscriptural or "teaching differently,"[131] or (2) inadequate, not "agreeing with the sound words of Christ,"[132] either by addition, which is the chief reason that popery collapses, since it has added to these sound words an infinite number of traditions, or by subtraction, which is the reason Socinianism fails, since it takes away the Trinity, satisfaction, and other fundamentals. Or, false theology will be (3) apart from Christ, that is, not teaching the words about Christ,[133] for which reason heathenism, Judaism, and Islam fail, since they do not hold to the words about Christ. Or, it will be (4) insufficiently "according to godliness,"[134] which is especially problematic for the schismatic theology of the Lutherans and Arminians, since they either excessively extol man and his will, his works, his perfection, and disparage God's grace and mercy in Christ—which Arminianism does along with the Pelagians, papists, and Socinians—or they present an opportunity for despairing by setting up, in their teaching on absolute perfection[135] and the total apostasy of the saints, perpetual doubts about salvation. Even Lutheranism participates in this last error: along with what was just pointed out, at least regarding the total apostasy of the saints, they also give rein to carnal security either by a universal grace of God, a universal satisfaction of Christ—which they apply to all equally, for which reason, with the rest, the Lutheran faith is especially troubled—or by widening the path of salvation, which agrees little with either the justice or mercy of God. In this way, by setting mercy against justice, Lutheranism follows the Socinian path to its own ruin. Therefore, Reformed theology is the most exact of all in agreeing[136] with those apostolic marks of orthodoxy, as what is evident to our eyes testifies. For more on the truth of the Christian religion, see Pierre Mornay, Juan Luis Vives, Hugo Grotius, and recently Pierre-Daniel Huet in his *Evangelical Demonstration*.[137]

---

129. κριτήρια

130. ψευδόνυμος

131. ἄγραφος *seu* ἑτεροδιδασκαλῶν

132. προσερχομένη ὑγιαίνουσι λόγοις Χριστοῦ

133. λόγους τοῦ Χριστοῦ

134. κατ᾽ εὐσέβειαν

135. Latin: *omnimoda perfectione*; Dutch: *een alleszins volmaaktheit*.

136. προσέρχεται

137. Pierre-Daniel Huet, *Petri Danielis Huetii Demonstratio euangelica ad serenissimum Delphinum*, 2 vols., 2nd edition (Amsterdam: Jansson-Waesberg & Henricus & Theodorus Boom, 1680).

The second point of practice: shunning any false theology

XXVII. But since it is not sufficient merely to have distinguished true theology from a spurious one, it is necessary, in the second place, for everyone, when he has discovered any so-called[138] theology, to strive according to his station to cast it out. As for what we understand by *false theology*, we presuppose here the definition from the preceding paragraph, namely, "any different doctrine."[139]

Who is obligated?

This duty is incumbent on (1) preachers of Christian truth (Titus 3:10–11; Acts 15:2; Gal. 2:11, 14); (2) the magistrate (2 Kings 10:25), to whom it was formerly prescribed to resist false theology, even with capital punishment (Deut. 13:5; 18:20; 1 Kings 18:40); and (3) whoever has professed Christian truth (Matt. 7:15; Rom. 16:17; 2 Thess. 3:14; 2 Tim. 2:16–17; Titus 3:10–11; 2 John 10).

Reasons for these things

Indeed, false theology must be resisted because it (1) strives to overturn the gospel of Christ (Gal. 1:7); (2) blasphemes the way of truth (2 Peter 2:2); (3) bewitches people so that they do not yield to the truth (Gal. 3:1); (4) ransacks churches (Acts 15:24; Gal. 1:7; 5:10, 12); (5) is destructive (2 Peter 2:2–3); and (6) is hateful to Christ (Rev. 2:6, 15).

The mode and means by which it is shunned

For this reason, it is especially incumbent upon ministers to watch over the flock (Acts 20:29–31; Rev. 2:2, 6) by (1) refuting those who teach different doctrines[140] (2 Tim. 2:16, 25; Titus 1:9), according to the examples of Stephen (Acts 6:9ff.), Paul (Acts 9:22), Paul and Barnabas (Acts 15:2), Apollos (Acts 18:28), and Peter (2 Peter 3:4ff.); (2) strengthening their own flock in Christian truth (Acts 14:19, 22); and (3) calling back home those who have been led astray (Gal. 1:6–7).[141] It is incumbent upon magistrates to restrain false theology by political authority and force, as we taught above, and act as nursing fathers of the church (Isa. 49:23). Finally, it is incumbent upon all to guard themselves carefully (Matt. 7:15) and to fix their minds in the truth against errors, so that they may not, like children, vacillate and be carried about by every wind of doctrine (Eph. 4:14). Let them keep in mind the analogy of faith, the "pattern of sound

---

138. ψευδόνυμον
139. ἑτεροδιδασκαλίαν
140. ἑτεροδιδασκαλοῦντας
141. *retrahendo seductos*: Classically, to reclaim, recall, or even drag back fugitives, e.g. Cicero, *Pro Caelio*, §§63–64.

words,"[142] and the catechetical heads well fortified by passages of Scripture (2 Tim. 1:13, etc.).

The third point of practice: the study of true theology, in which there are degrees of knowledge

XXVIII. Third, when any false theology has been cast out, it is then necessary that an indefatigable concern for and study of true Christian theology should advance among all who profess Christ. For although the knowledge of theological matters that anyone obtains now, at least compared to the knowledge obtained in the future, is only "in part"[143] and as if "in a mirror, in an enigma"[144] (1 Cor. 13:12), nevertheless it admits of degrees. According to these degrees of knowledge we are called infants or adults (1 Cor. 3:1–2; Heb. 5:12–14), that is, in proportion to (1) times and degrees of illumination, for which reason a higher degree is demanded now under the New Testament than formerly under the Old Testament (Joel 2:28–29; 1 Cor. 3:12–13; Isa. 11:9; Jer. 31:34, 36);[145] (2) the means of gaining knowledge, in which one location surpasses another (Col. 3:16; Heb. 5:12–14), for which reason a higher degree of knowledge is demanded of us Europeans than of the Indians, or of the Reformed than (for example) the papists; (3) persons and offices; a greater and higher degree is demanded among teachers and pastors than among others (Mal. 2:7; Hos. 4:6); and finally, (4) theological matters themselves, since some are clearly more fundamental than others (Heb. 6:1; 1 Cor. 3:1–2). For this reason theological matters are separated into the heads of faith, which concern *being* a Christian, and the heads of theology, which promote a Christian's *well-being*. Although I assert for these reasons that we must by all means grant that there are degrees of knowledge, yet it is incumbent upon each and every person to consider and to gain for himself a knowledge of the fundamental and catechetical heads of doctrine (Jer. 31:34), and to strive more and more to make progress and to be rooted in these doctrines (Col. 2:6–7; Heb. 5:12; 1 Cor. 14:20).

Its quality
But not just any sort of knowledge of Christian matters will suffice. For there exists (1) a perverse knowledge (1 Tim. 1:4; 6:20) that is born for contention (1 Tim. 6:4–5); (2) a vain, bookish, speculative knowledge that only wanders

---

142. ὑποτύπωσιν ὑγιαινόντων λόγων
143. ἐκ μέρους
144. δί ἐσόπτρου, ἐν αἰνίγματι
145. Latin: Jer. XXX. 34. 16; Dutch: Jer. XXXI. 34. 36.

about in the brain and does not penetrate into the heart, except perhaps to puff it up (1 Cor. 13:1; 8:1); and (3) a saving, experimental, practical knowledge that strives earnestly for the inner man so that from there it might bring forth the practical application of what is known (John 13:17; Phil. 3:8, 10; 4:9; Col. 1:9–10), in the words of the apostle, the "knowledge of the truth according to godliness"[146] (Titus 1:1).

Its subjects: (1) Ministers

Therefore, everyone should strive toward this knowledge with all his strength. By "everyone" I mean the following: Teachers and ministers, who should preserve theology (1 Cor. 2:2; Mal. 2:7; Hos. 4:6), teach theology (1 Tim. 6:2; 2 Tim. 4:2), expound theology (2 Tim. 2:15), defend theology (Titus 1:9), and apply theology (1 Tim. 4:2), according to the variety of persons and situations (Titus 2:2; 1 Tim. 6:17).

(2) Magistrates

Magistrates, who should know theology and should have the law before their eyes (Deut. 17:18–20; Josh. 1:8; Psalm 19), prescribe it for their subordinates (2 Chron. 17:7–9; Josh. 24:14ff.), protect it against enemies, as nursing fathers of the church (Isa. 49:23; 60:16) and as guardians of both tables of the law, and propagate it (Gen. 18:19).[147] In sum they should, in all these ways, kiss Christ (Ps. 2:10–12), so that their polity becomes a theocracy, that is, a Christocracy.

(3) All Christians

Finally, all Christians, who should acknowledge Christian truth (Col. 3:16), take care to advance in it more and more (John 5:39; Ps. 1:2), to rest upon it (2 Peter 1:19), and, each according to his ability, to offer it to others (Col. 3:16).

Motives for the study of Christian theology
XXIX. The most effective reasons to persuade all to study theology are:

Its excellence

First, the excellence of theology, in which it leaves any other discipline behind by a thousand miles (Eph. 3:19; 1 Cor. 2:2). It obtains this excellence: (1) From its own heavenly and divine birth and origin (Gal. 1:1), for it is "the wisdom from

---

146. ἐπίγνωσις ἀληθείας τῆς κατ᾽ εὐσέβειαν

147. Latin: *Gen. XVIII.12*. The 1699 Latin text, the 1715 and 1724 reprints, and the 1749–53 Dutch translation contain this reference. It is unclear, however, how this citation applies, and if it is an error, the proper citation should probably be Gen. 18:19.

above"[148] (James 3:17); even more, from the mode of its birth, which is plainly glorious (2 Cor. 4:6). (2) From the majesty of its subject matter, which is God and Christ, for which reason it is called the "wisdom of God"[149] (1 Cor. 2:6–7; Prov. 2:5) and "the surpassing greatness of the knowledge of Christ,"[150] on account of which the apostle counted all things as loss and dung[151] (Phil. 3:8) and also viewed all other knowledge with indifference (1 Cor. 2:2). Furthermore, it is the method of living for God (Rom. 6:11), for which reason it is called the words of life (Acts 5:20; John 6:68). (3) From its end and use, since it directs a person to live for God, to glorify God, and to pursue blessed immortality, and since it directs all the particular ends of all things to the one common and highest end, without which everything would fly off track. (4) From its unmoved certainty, which indeed itself rests on the faithfulness of the God who never lies[152] and embraces all things according to their formal cause (as they say), their infallibility (1 Cor. 15:15; John 3:33), since all other kinds of knowledge are acquired and advanced by experience and reasoning, which are frequently uncertain. (5) From its purity and holiness (James 3:17), which is so great and of such a kind that it also renders the possessor of it holy and pure (Ps. 19:8–9).

Its delightfulness

The second reason is the sweetness and pleasantness of theology, with which the mind is marvelously flooded when it possesses it (Ps. 19:8; 119:103; Prov. 2:10; 24:13–14; Job 23:12), and which arises first from the excellence of its object, and then from the certainty of its knowledge.

Its usefulness

The third reason is the usefulness of theology, which is so diverse and distinguished that here you could use Christ's maxim: theology is the "one thing necessary"[153] (Luke 10:42); or the apostle's: it is "useful for all things," indeed, "having promise for this life and the life to come"[154] (1 Tim. 4:8).

---

148. ἡ ἄνωθεν σοφία
149. σοφια τοῦ Θεοῦ
150. τὸ ὑπερέχον τῆς γνώσεως Χριστοῦ
151. ζημίωσιν καὶ σκύβαλα
152. *Dei* ἀψεύστου, cf. Titus 1:2
153. ἑνὸς χρεία
154. πρὸς πάντα ὀφέλιμος...ἐπαγγελίαν ἔχουσα ζωῆς, τῆς νῦν, καὶ τῆς μελλούσης

Its necessity
The fourth reason is the plainly absolute necessity of theology, to the extent that without it, you are not able to obtain either justification here (Isa. 53:11) or life hereafter (John 17:3). On the contrary, any of your studies, if they wander away from their highest goal, will prove entirely useless. In this way, it is not without cause that the psalmist makes every kind of human happiness depend upon this study (Ps. 1:1–2).

The evils of ignorance
The fifth reason is the evils of the ignorance of theology, by which we are rendered strangers to the life of God (Eph. 4:18–19) and to the covenant of grace (Jer. 31:33–34), and made liable to divine wrath (Ps. 79:6), likewise to the most serious temporal judgments of God (Amos 4:6), and even to eternal condemnation (2 Thess. 1:8–9; 2 Cor. 4:3).

Examples
All of these reasons motivated the saints in both Testaments. By their study of divine matters, the patriarchs and prophets under the Old Testament (1 Peter 1:10–11), and the apostles and evangelists under the New Testament (2 Tim. 3:15; Acts 18:24)—indeed even the heavenly angels (1 Peter 1:12; Eph. 3:10)— light the way by their own example.

The means of obtaining theology
XXX. But, in order that, given such a great mass of reasons, we may not recommend the study of theology or religion in vain, we must explicitly add the means of acquiring it.

1. Let us seek it from its author.
Therefore, first and foremost it must be recognized that theology's supreme author and first source is: God (James 3:17), for which reason theology is the "wisdom of God"[155] (1 Cor. 2:6–7) because it is first about God, and then from God; Christ, for which reason theology is called the "words of Christ"[156] (1 Tim. 6:3); and the Holy Spirit, for which reason he is called "the Spirit of wisdom" (Isa. 11:2; Eph. 1:17). From these designations we gather that theology exists by the revelation of the Father (Matt. 16:17), the Son (John 1:18), and the Holy Spirit (2 Peter 1:21), by illumination for perceiving revealed truth (Eph. 1:18),

---

155. σοφία τοῦ Θεοῦ
156. λόγοι τοῦ Χριστοῦ

and by guidance in the truth that has been perceived (John 16:13; Ps. 25:5; 143:10). Therefore, let us entreat him with the most fervent prayers (James 1:5; 1 Kings 3:9), that he would give the Spirit to us (John 16:13) and anoint the eyes of our minds with salve (Rev. 3:18), that thus we might see marvelous things in the law of God (Ps. 119:18, 27).

2. Let us be instructed in the things that theology requires.
Then, second, in order to pursue theology more certainly, let us attend to ourselves as we give our attention to theology so that we may be reconciled to God as his friends (John 15:15), be God-fearers (Ps. 25:12), humble in heart (1 Peter 5:5; Ps. 25:9; Matt. 11:25), and fools to this world (1 Cor. 3:18).

3. Let us keep the instruments in view.
Being prepared in this way, third, let us keep the instruments in view: the book of nature that is spread out before us, inwardly through the conscience (Rom. 2:14–15) and externally through the contemplation of created things (Rom. 1:20; Ps. 19:1); the book of Scripture that will spread theology before us, specifically Christian and revealed theology (Ps. 19:7–8); and the ministry of scholastic and ecclesiastical instruction (Mal. 2:7; Eph. 4:11–14).

4. Let us use them carefully, guarding against these things.
Then, fourth, let these be banished: (1) contrived ignorance (2 Peter 3:5; Prov. 1:22; 29:7); (2) vain curiosity and "what is falsely called knowledge"[157] (1 Tim. 6:20; 2 Tim. 2:23; Titus 3:9), by which, on the one hand, we would wrongly concern ourselves with investigating the secret things of God (Deut. 29:29), or the things that do not concern us (John 21:22; Acts 1:6–7), or that are less necessary to know (1 Cor. 14:1), or on the other hand, we neglect the basics to pursue deeper things (Heb. 6:1), or we do not rest in those things God has said unless they agree with our reason (Luke 1:34; Rom. 9:19–20); (3) pride (1 Cor. 8:1); (4) fleshly wisdom (1 Cor. 2:14; 3:18–19); (5) and fleshly desires that blind the mind (Eph. 4:18) by disturbing, enticing, and darkening it.

Things to be employed
Finally, the following should be employed with regard to the divine Word (Ps. 19:7–8; 119:130; 2 Tim. 3:15–17): reading it (1 Tim. 4:15), hearing it (Luke 11:28), meditating upon it (Ps. 1:2), discussing it with others (Luke 24:15), and

---

157. ψευδώνυμος γνῶσις

practicing it (John 7:17; James 1:25; Ps. 119:99–100; Rev. 22:7; John 13:17; cf. William Ames, *Cases of Conscience*, bk. 3, ch. 2).[158]

Eleven Rules of Academic Study

XXXI. Regarding the academic study of theology, we will touch, as with a pin, on only a few particulars: (1) Both from what has been said and what will be said, we plainly presuppose the excellence, usefulness, necessity, sanctity, grandeur, and even the difficulty of theology. (2) In the student, the requisite theological character[159] is to be teachable, industrious, pious, and suitable for theology. This character results from a skillfulness of judgment, which can discern[160] spiritual things; a reliability of memory, in which so many and such a variety of things can be grasped; and an orderliness[161] of affections in purity and constancy, with which one inclines toward holy things not reluctantly, but with a certain holy proclivity. (3) The student has a theological goal set before him, not wealth, glory, pleasures, or leisure, but rather the glory of God, the edification of the church, and his own salvation. Additionally, (4) in his own study, a three-part introductory curriculum ought to come first: philology, consisting of the Greek, Hebrew, Aramaic, and Latin languages; philosophy, consisting of logic, physics, metaphysics, mathematics, and practical philosophy; and history, which includes geography and chronology as if they were its two wings. (5) Biblical study should follow these preparations, or rather join them. It should be as much a cursory study constantly sprinkled into other studies as an exegetical and careful one— in which the context is investigated, the difficulties are noted and clarified, and conclusions are drawn, both theoretical and practical. At the same time, (6) a dogmatic and positive theology should be added, just as much a catechetical theology as a systematic theology of commonplaces. (7) An elenctic theology should follow. This consists of both a general polemic, which engages with many opponents, and a particular one, which engages with each individually—with unbelievers (pagans, Muslims, Jews, and atheists), heretics (Socinians, Anabaptists, papists, and fanatics), and schismatics (Arminians, Lutherans, Brownists, Independents, Colemanists, and others). And there should also be (8) a practical theology that is moral (concerning virtues and vices), ascetic (concerning the

---

158. In a more widely available edition, see "De Scientia" in William Ames, *De conscientia et ejus jure vel casibus, libri quinque* (Amsterdam: ex Officiana Boomiana, 1670), 3.2, 106–108. Cf. the 1631 Jansson edition printed at Amsterdam, 3.2, 99–101. See "Of Knowledge" in William Ames, *Conscience with the power and cases thereof* (London, 1639), 3.2, 49–51.

159. εὐφυΐα

160. ἀνακρίνειν

161. εὐταξία

exercises of piety), casuistic (concerning cases of conscience), and political (concerning the government of the church). Next is (9) antiquarian theology, which traces ecclesiastical history and considers the church fathers and the councils, each in their own time. Furthermore, (10) in all these things, let the student occupy himself with hearing, reading, meditating, praying, and disputing. And (11) this study should divide up the duties according to a certain order through the years, days, and hours. It should suffice to have touched on these things that are explained in their proper breadth[162] by others, such as Erasmus, Hyperius, Crocius, Alsted, and the one to be considered above all, Voetius.

The fourth use: the study of practical theology

XXXII. Indeed, the study of theology, to the extent that it is true theology, is not sufficient, unless, fourth, it is earnestly devoted to practical theology and to practice. For this reason our theorem does not urge a merely Christian theology, but rather a specifically theoretical-practical theology. By this, however, we understand that this theology is not any of the following: the pagan theology of Socrates, Plato, Scipio, Aristides, Cato, or Seneca; the philosophical theology that is summed up in the exercises of ethics, economics, and politics; the Pharisaical theology (about which Josephus remarks in *Jewish Antiquities*) which professed celibacy, frequent fasts, prayers, alms, and which abstained only from shameful acts and was vigilant in the external exercises of godliness with great austerity;[163] the Essene theology, which even surpassed the Pharisaical theology in precision[164] (as a witness see Josephus, bk. 18);[165] the monastic and eremitic theology; or any sort of hypocritical theology. All of these have a "form of religion but deny its power"[166] (2 Tim. 3:5). We will perhaps treat this expressly in a chapter concerning hypocrisy.[167]

Marks

XXXIII. But for practical theology, in all these and infinite other duties, and especially those that are internal, to be truly "according to godliness,"[168] it must: (1) not

---

162. κατὰ πλάτος

163. Cited as: *Josephus Arch. lib. XIII cap 18.* Since book 13 does not have 18 chapters, see instead Josephus, *Josephus...in ten volumes, Jewish Antiquities, books 12–14,* trans. R. Marcus (Cambridge, Mass.: Harvard University Press, 1957), 13.5.9, 13.10.6.

164. ἀκριβείᾳ

165. Cited as *Josephus XVIII cap 2.* See instead Josephus, *Josephus...in ten volumes, Jewish Antiquities, books 18–19,* trans. L. H. Feldman (Cambridge, Mass.: Harvard University Press, 1981), 18.1.5.

166. μόρφωσιν εὐσεβείας, δύναμιν ἠρνημένα

167. Cf. *TPT* 2.1.8.

168. κατ᾽ εὐσέβειαν

stop at externals, but flow from the inner heart (Ps. 51:6; Rom. 2:28–29), which must indeed be endowed with a true and living faith (Rom. 14:23; Gal. 5:6); (2) strive not for its own advantages, honor, and wealth (Matt. 6:1–5), but rather for the glory of God (1 Cor. 10:31), the edification of its neighbor (Matt. 5:16), and its own salvation (1 Peter 1:9); (3) proceed not according to its own pleasures (Matt. 15:9), but according to divine precept (Gal. 6:16); finally, (4) not be produced by the strength of nature (John 3), but by the Spirit of God (Gal. 5:22).

Motives

XXXIV. Many things urge the serious study of practical theology and theological practice. (1) Christian theology is not theoretical, or theoretical-practical (though because of how we discuss it we do designate it that way), but rather, it is purely and preeminently[169] practical. This presupposition will be demonstrated and proved in its own place.[170] (2) Not only is the whole of theology said to be the "doctrine according to godliness"[171] (1 Tim. 6:3) and the "knowledge of the truth according to godliness"[172] (Titus 1:1), and to pertain to teaching, correction, and training in righteousness, that the man of God may be perfectly equipped[173] for every good work (2 Tim. 3:16–17), but also, its individual parts are each joined together with their own practice, as we will show, Lord willing, throughout the whole corpus of theology, such that "faith and love"[174] (2 Tim. 1:13), hearing and doing (James 1:22–23)[175] agree, and the end of the "commandment"[176] is said to be charity that comes from a pure heart, a good conscience (1 Tim. 1:5), and the "obedience of faith"[177] (Rom. 1:5) arises; it then in practice becomes the "power of godliness"[178] (that is, of theology), since bare theory offers nothing but its "form"[179] (2 Tim. 3:5). (3) On practice hangs salvation, which is denied to bare theory (John 13:17; James 1:22).[180] (4) On practice likewise depends the refutation of gainsayers,[181] more than on theory (James 2:18–19), and this is true even with regard to their conversion (1 Peter 3:1–2),

---

169. ἐξόχως
170. §XLVII
171. διδασκαλία κατ᾽ εὐσέβειαν
172. ἐπίγνωσις ἀληθείας τῆς κατ᾽ εὐσέβειαν
173. ἐξηρτισμένος
174. πίστις καὶ ἀγάπη
175. ἀκρόασις καὶ ποίησις (a paraphrase). Originally cited as James 2:22–23.
176. παραγγελίας
177. ὑπακοὴ πίστεως
178. δύναμις εὐσεβείας
179. μόρφωσιν
180. Originally cited as James 2:22, 29.
181. ἀντιλεγόντων

and indeed, conversion is more safe, proven, and stable, when it is born from love of practice than from theory alone. I will not press the point that (5) by the study of practical theology and of theological practice, we check as effectively as possible the calumnies of the Arminians and the papists by which our theology is accused of being useless, vain, and merely theoretical. And, furthermore, (6) Satan and his followers resist matters of practice with a no less vigorous attack than matters of theory. In fact, day by day he hatches all kinds of new and novel plans (1 Tim. 3:6) to shut off practical study and the practice of study.

The means of obtaining a practical theology

XXXV. The supports for obtaining and propagating this practical theology may be found, with the necessary changes being made, in §XXX. Nevertheless, let us add a few more that are more specific to practical study.

First

First, an assiduous and practical study of the divine word is exceedingly conducive to this end, that the man of God may be perfectly equipped[182] for every good work (2 Tim. 3:17), if by this study one seeks most of all not merely a knowledge of the truth, but also its force and efficacy, and if in addition one reads certain authors, both old and more recent ones, especially the most practical[183] Dutch and English authors, and arranges them into common places.

Second

The second support is an experimental study of theology in which we not only understand, but also experience the force and efficacy of each theological head. For this reason the apostle conjoins "knowledge and all insight"[184] (Phil. 1:9), by which we taste and see how good the Lord is, and how blessed the one who hopes in him (Ps. 34:8). Nor do I think that the masters of theology have pursued practice more successfully than when they have rightly equipped their minds with the experience of theological truths, compared what they experienced with Scripture, and then put down both on paper. For this reason, Luther declared those sermons best in which the preacher experiences what he says and says what he experiences.

Third

The third support is an exemplary study of theology, in which you not only experience it for yourself, but also set an example for others so that they also

---

182. ἐξηρτισμένος
183. πρακτικωτάτων
184. ἐπίγνωσιν καὶ πᾶσαν αἴσθησιν

may experience it. This is what the apostle commends to ministers especially, that above all they should present themselves as an example of good works in their teaching (Titus 2:7). Nor does anything, according to Luther, penetrate the heart more deeply than that which springs from the depths of the heart.

Fourth
Fourth, in their expositions of the theological heads, theologians should expressly teach not only dogmatic and elenctic matters, but also practical ones.

Fifth
I will add, fifth, that in the examinations of candidates, we should require evidence not only of dogmatic and elenctic theology, but also of practical theology and of practice.

THIRD THEOREM – The Definition of Theology

The Dogmatic Part
Theology is the doctrine of living for God through Christ.
XXXVI. This theoretical-practical Christian theology is nothing less than the doctrine of living for God through Christ, in other words, the doctrine that is according to godliness (1 Tim. 6:3), and likewise the knowledge of the truth that is according to godliness (Titus 1:1). For this reason in the church fathers it is sometimes also called "the fear of God,"[185] "the life of God,"[186] and even "the work of God,"[187] in accord with Scripture, since:

It is proved from the Scriptures.
(1) It calls theology the words of life (John 6:68; Acts 5:20). (2) It portrays habitual theology or theological skill by the phrase "living for God"[188] (Rom. 6:11; 2 Cor. 5:15; Rom. 14:7–8; Col. 3:3–4; Phil. 1:20–21). (3) The entirety of this theology is occupied in forming the life of a person and directing it toward God insofar as everything encountered in the Scriptures flows together and aims at this end, as if at a central point, and that this becomes, as it were, their broadest possible theme. From all this it follows that theology is most correctly defined as the doctrine of living for God through Christ.

---

185. θεοσέβεια; Dutch: *Godsdienstigheit of Godvruchtigheit*
186. θεοζωία
187. θεουργία
188. τὸ *vivere Deo*

It is confirmed by reasons: First

XXXVII. In proof of this, first we will presuppose: (1) Every knowable complex[189] that admits of an orderly arrangement[190] of a great number of conclusions pointing in the same direction, constitutes a science or discipline. (2) In accordance with the preceding paragraph, living for God[191] is a knowable complex of this sort. (3) Yet, "living for God" is not comprehended within the object of just any discipline. For there is no science that teaches how to live for God through Christ except Christian theology. For this reason we understand that this is, without a doubt, its true and proper business. And because nothing is offered in theology that does not incline to this point, namely, that a person's life should be directed toward God, then whether on account of its end or on account of its means, either way it remains certain that this is its adequate object, and therefore theology is nothing other than the doctrine of living for God through Christ.

Second

Second, we likewise presuppose: (1) Since God made all things for the sake of man, and man for God, so that God is the ultimate end of man and of all human actions, it is necessary that some teaching be given that directs man and all he has to that point. (2) There is no discipline that assumes to do this for itself, since every discipline is committed to its own peculiar end, for example, medicine to the happiness of the human body (that is, to health), ethics to the moral blessedness of individuals, politics to the social blessedness of the state, economics to that of the household, and so on in all other disciplines. From this we conclude that theology alone directs the ends of all, proper to each, to a certain common and highest end, which is God, so that in this discipline, God indeed might receive his own glory, but in God and his glory, we might receive perfect blessedness. And these two come together, if we live for God.

Third

To these things we could add, third, that in this definition all the laws of definition coincide. For "living for God" explains the very essence of the *definitum*, theology, and is adequate for it, since there is nothing in theology that does not concern this, nor does anything concern this that does not belong to theology. For this reason, it must emerge that the doctrine of living for God through Christ supplies the most genuine definition of theology.

---

189. *scibilis complexus*
190. σύνταγμα
191. τὸ *vivere Deo*

That it is termed doctrine, and why

XXXVIII. Therefore, theology is doctrine (Isa. 51:4; 2:3; Ps. 19:7). For this reason, it is everywhere called "teaching"[192] and "instruction";[193] likewise a "pattern
of doctrine"[194] (Rom. 6:17), a "teaching according to godliness"[195] (1 Tim. 6:3;
cf. John 7:16–17; 1 Tim. 4:6). Moreover, we call it doctrine, not because we reject
the names of the philosophical habits of understanding, knowledge, wisdom,
prudence, and art. For we see that in the Scriptures theology is commonly designated, sometimes as understanding (Prov. 2:6; Col. 2:2), sometimes knowledge
(Mal. 2:7; Isa. 53:11; 2 Cor. 8:7), sometimes wisdom (1 Cor. 1:21; 2:6; James
3:17), sometimes prudence (Prov. 1:2–3; Eph. 1:8), and it is mentioned, instead
of as an art, in equivalent terms[196] as senses that have been exercised for the
discernment of good and evil (Heb. 5:14). Theology is not so bound to any of
these habits that the rest are excluded, but rather it contains the perfection of
all of them par excellence,[197] for which reason we prefer the broader term "doctrine" so that all the habits can be included in it. There is yet another underlying
reason for this appellation: sacred theology originates preeminently[198] through
doctrine, or revelation (Isa. 51:4; Matt. 16:17; John 1:18; Gal. 1:11–12). By
contrast, any other kinds of sciences owe their origin to nature and human investigation—since their *principia* are innate in us—and are developed and moved
forward to their own completion by sense, observation, experience, comparison,
and induction. Yet, at the same time, the genuine *principia* of saving theology as
such are not present in us by nature and cannot be developed or moved forward
to any completion by study or industry alone (Matt. 16:17). I add as a third reason, that not only systematic theology, or theological precepts, but also habitual
theology, or the skill of living for God, which arises from the precepts, depends
upon divine faith, and so therefore must also be taught or revealed by God.

How doctrine is taught

Moreover, this doctrine is taught partly by God—externally by revelation
(Gal. 1:11–12) and inwardly by illumination (Eph. 1:17–18), concerning which

---

192. διδαχή
193. διδασκαλία
194. τύπος διδαχῆς
195. διδασκαλία κατ᾽ εὐσέβειαν
196. ἰσοδυναμῶς
197. κατ᾽ ἐξοχήν
198. ἐξόχως

see above[199]—and partly by men, who accordingly are designated as teachers (Eph. 4:11).

The object of theology is "living."
XXXIX. Again, theology is the doctrine of living, and of living for God, and for God through Christ. I say "living" because we will now develop with reasons what we a little while ago proved from the Scriptures (Rom. 6:11; John 6:68; Acts 5:20). These reasons are as follows: (1) No discipline exists that morally or spiritually shapes the whole of life, and so accordingly this task falls to theology. (2) The Word of God, and the Holy Spirit with the Word, by theological precepts, not only forms this or that action of our life, but forms all of our actions as a whole (1 Thess. 5:23; 2 Tim. 3:16–17). (3) The noblest discipline ought necessarily to be occupied with the noblest object, but there is no object nobler than life (Job 2:4), since that is the most universal act, which is laid as a foundation for all the rest such that no action can exist without life.

Living for God
XL. Indeed, we do not call theology the doctrine of living only, but rather the doctrine of living for God, in accord with those things that we noted from Scripture in §XXXVI. For since our life ought necessarily to be directed toward God as the supreme and ultimate end (1 Cor. 10:31; Phil. 1:21), without whom all life's actions will fly off track, and, moreover, since our life is not directed to him by any other discipline, it is altogether necessary that it be directed by theology.

Different kinds of life
XLI. Moreover, there are three kinds of life directed toward God: (1) that of nature (Gen. 2:7), arising from a union of the body and soul, by which a person can naturally move himself; (2) that of grace (Gal. 2:20), flowing from the union of original righteousness with the soul, by which it can move itself spiritually or morally; and (3) that of glory (John 17:3), resulting from the union and communion of the whole person with God, out of which one acts blessedly.

The life of nature
The life of nature, although not properly subject to theological precepts by reason of its first act, yet, on account of its second acts, it is, according to circumstances, either destroyed, afflicted, or prolonged as a reward or punishment for having done good or evil (1 Tim. 4:8; Ex. 20:12). And these second acts,

---

199. §XXX.

moreover—vegetative, sensitive, and rational—are directed and turned toward God by theological precepts.

The life of grace
The life of grace, both with respect to its first act and its second acts, is subject more directly to the laws of theology since spiritual life and death are destroyed and restored by sin and faith, respectively (Eph. 4:18; 2:5–6). Likewise, good works (1) flow from the life of grace, or from faith, conveyed by regeneration (John 3:5–6; Rom. 14:25;[200] Heb. 11:6); (2) are directed toward the glory of God (Gal. 2:19–20; 1 Cor. 10:31; Phil. 1:20–21); and (3) are ordered to the precept of the will of God (1 Peter 4:2, 6).

The life of glory
The entire life of glory depends upon the directing of theology (John 17:3; 1 Peter 1:9) that it may start here by the life of grace and be consummated hereafter in heaven (John 3:36; 5:24; 1 John 3:15); and it is not different from the life of grace except by degrees.

Living for God through Christ
XLII. But it is not sufficient for Christian theology that we live for God, unless this life is lived through Christ (Rom. 6:11). For in this our theology differs from the theology of our first parents[201] when they were first created. Likewise, it differs from natural theology, and also from any so-called[202] theology which does not have the "sound words of Christ."[203] Without Christ, however, we cannot live for God (Gal. 2:20; John 15:5). And even if we could live for God without Christ, it would not be acceptable to God apart from Christ (Eph. 1:6).

The many ways this life is lived
We live for God through Christ, then, insofar as (1) only in Christ can our life please God (Eph. 1:6), that is, in him with whom the Father is well pleased (Matt. 3:17). (2) Christ by his own merit procured the Spirit for us (John 16:7), by whose work we are made alive (Rom. 8:2, 11) and are led (Rom. 8:14). Otherwise we would be dead in sins, that is, unfit for every good work—in fact, prone to every evil work. (3) Christ, united with us by faith, makes us, who were

---

200. In some Bibles, Romans 16:26. Mastricht is citing a manuscript tradition of Romans 14 that places Romans 16:25–27 after Romans 14:23.

201. *Protoplastorum*

202. ψευδονύμῳ

203. ὑγιαίνοντας λόγους Χριστοῦ

dead, alive (Eph. 2:4–7); communicates the strength for living for God, as the root communicates strength to the trunk, and the head to the members (John 15:4); brings forth the strength conveyed, moves it toward an action, and makes it fruitful (John 15:5); prescribes the laws for living for God (Matt. 5:2); and goes before us by his example (Matt. 11:29; Phil. 2:5). Finally, he himself lives in us (Gal. 2:20) and takes possession of all our faculties in such a way that in all things, at all times, and everywhere, Christ's humility, obedience, holiness, and righteousness flourish and shine forth, and that Christ's life, in all these ways, is made manifest in us (2 Cor. 4:11).

The first deduction, concerning the end of theology
XLIII. From what has been said it is evident, first, that since living for God embraces two things, living well and living blessedly[204] (the former of which considers the glory of God, and the latter, our salvation), it must be established with regard to the ends of theology that the highest end is indeed the glory of God (1 Cor. 10:31; Prov. 16:4; Rom. 11:36), and second to that, our salvation (1 Peter 1:9). However, these two ends do not differ so much in their substance as in our reason, since our salvation does not consist in anything but the glorification of God, when, by our union and communion with God and our enjoyment of him (in which our salvation consists) God is by that very fact recognized and celebrated as our highest good and our ultimate end.

Several cases
From what has been said we can easily respond to several questions: (1) May someone act for the sake of his own salvation as if that were his highest end? I respond that it is entirely permitted because it is undoubtedly permitted to act for the sake of God, since by the very fact of acting for his salvation he has God as his highest end. Likewise, (2) must we pursue the glory of God rather than our life? Rather than our own salvation? I respond that while we pursue our own salvation, in that same work we pursue the glory of God; nevertheless, to the extent that those two things differ in concept, we should regard God's cause as altogether prior to our own advantage. But (3) will it not seem quite mercenary to live for God for the sake of a reward? I respond, certainly so, if it is for the sake of a reward properly so called, whether congruent or condign, and still more is it mercenary if it is for the sake of a reward separated from God. However, it is by no means mercenary, when by this very fact of seeking a reward, we show that God is our highest end and prize (Gen. 15:1).

---

204. εὐζωίαν *et* εὐδαιμονίαν

Its object

XLIV. Also evident, second, is the object with which theological precepts should be occupied, namely, first, the forming of the intellect, so that worship becomes "reasonable"[205] (Rom. 12:1), and second, the forming of the will, or heart (Matt. 15:19; Prov. 4:4, 23; 23:26), and finally, the forming of the whole life, in each and every one of its human acts, that they be directed to God as much as possible. For skill in theology is the habit of the whole person, by which he is brought to possess God and to act according to his will and for his glory. For this reason the whole person and all his parts are said to be sanctified (1 Thess. 5:23), but especially the will, which is the *principium* that commands all spiritual actions.

Its excellence

XLV. Third, it is evident how great the preeminence[206] of Christian theology is. For, although by the order of doctrine, according to our method of proceeding, it comes last in our curriculum, yet by the order of nature and of dignity it easily occupies the first rank, and, with respect to the highest end, it is the director and architect of all, advanced in an eminent manner by God, occupied with God and divine things, striving toward God, and guiding men to him. For these reasons it is no less rightly designated as "the life of God,"[207] or "the work of God,"[208] than "the science of God"[209] to which one can add what we have already mentioned on this matter in §XXIX.

The Elenctic Part

Problems

XLVI. Indeed, I suppose there is no Christian who would deny that theology is the doctrine of living for God through Christ. Granted, they may define it in one way or another, differing more in words than in substance, for which we will not criticize them. For this reason, with respect to controversies, we will only mention rather than examine closely one or two problems customarily debated among the orthodox at the beginning of works of this sort.

1. Is theology wisdom or prudence?

First, then, it is asked, can any of Aristotle's intellectual habits, discussed in book 6 of his *Nicomachean Ethics*, be employed in theology, that is to say, is

---

205. λογικός
206. ὑπεροχή
207. θεοζωία
208. θεουργία
209. θεολογία

theology best called wisdom, or prudence, or one of the other habits? There are those who define it as wisdom, that is, they define the most perfect discipline by the most perfect habit. Thus, this definition pleases those who maintain that theology is a theoretical discipline. There are those who prefer to define theology as prudence, namely, those who maintain that theology is practical. There are those who admit neither, inasmuch as theology is not a natural habit, but a supernatural one. There are those who think that all the habits of Aristotle are suited to it; thus they suppose that theology is: understanding, since it is conveyed in its first principles by a simple apprehension; knowledge, since it draws conclusions by reasoning from first principles; wisdom, since it builds upon first principles with conclusions in a most perfect way; prudence, since it directs its first principles toward their inherent action; and art, since it directs them toward their applied action.[210] It would be most secure to take the middle position: theology is not, according to its form (so to speak), one habit to the exclusion of the others, but rather, according to its eminence, theology is all of the habits, since it possesses the perfections of them all. For this reason we have most carefully defined it as "doctrine," which implies all of these habits and does not restrict theology to any one habit.

2. *What is its object?*

XLVII. Second, what object belongs to theology? There are those who say that its object is contemplating God, which is why it is named *theology.* There are those who prefer to say that its object is God and his works. There are those who think his worship needs to be included. The debate could be ended by distinguishing between theology's primary object, which would be God, and its adequate object, which would by no means be God. They appear to speak most fittingly who with us prefer to say that its adequate object is living for God through Christ, because, on the one hand, it contains nothing except what most properly applies to theology and, on the other hand, it does not neglect anything that concerns theology. For in order to live for God, we need to know God and his works. But it is insufficient for theology that we know God and his works, if we also do not worship God, that is, if we do not live for God through Christ.

---

210. Latin: *et ars, quatenus ad transeuntem.* Dutch: *en ene konst, voorzoverre zy dezelve richt tot ene overgaande doening.* Cf. Thomas Aquinas who distinguishes between prudence and art in *Summa Theologiae* IaIIae, q57 arts. 3–5 in approximately the same terms.

3. Is it a theoretical or a practical habit?

XLVIII. Third, is theology a theoretical, practical, or theoretical-practical habit?
On the one hand, that which we call theoretical here is not something that simply
does not act, for all disciplines have their own sort of best practices,[211] but something that by its own nature does not proceed to action, such as metaphysics. On
the other hand, what we call practical is not something that absolutely does not
contemplate, but something that by its own nature does not stop at contemplation, such as logic or ethics. Furthermore, here we distinguish the practical[212]
from the productive,[213] because the productive produces its own object, while
the practical only requires an action with respect to its object. Thus, although
God could not be produced by our own productive work,[214] yet an action of
love and veneration, in which action is praxis, can be elicited with respect to
him. Here there are those who want theology to be a merely theoretical habit,
such as Aquinas and his followers, because our salvation is directed toward our
most perfect contemplation of God (John 17:3; 1 Cor. 13:12). But they do so
incorrectly because our salvation does not consist in knowledge alone, but in a
knowledge that comes from love (John 17:3; 1 Cor. 13:13). Nor do we find in
the Scriptures only a knowledge that consists in bare speculation and cognition,
but also a kind that includes love (Ps. 1:6; Matt. 7:23). On the other side, there
are those who prefer that theology be merely practical, such as Scotus and his
followers, which, in a healthy sense, we will also accept. Furthermore, there are
those who say that theology is neither speculative nor practical, but rather refer
to it as loving and affective. They are the rarest type because, without a doubt,
loving something and moving the affections are practical matters. Finally, there
are those who define theology as both theoretical and practical, since on its one
side, that is, with reference to things that must be believed concerning God, the
Trinity, the personal union of the two natures in Christ, it is theoretical only, but
on the other side, concerning things that must be done, it is merely practical. But
they do not make this designation carefully enough, because for theology, by its
nature, to consist in contemplation and in addition, by its nature, to require practice, implies a contradiction. We certainly do not deny that there are things in
theology that cannot be produced (e.g., God, the Trinity, the union of the natures
in Christ, and others), and which therefore are certainly not productive.[215] But
there is nonetheless nothing with respect to which an action cannot be elicited;

---

211. εὐπραγία
212. πρακτικόν
213. ποιητικῷ
214. ποιήσει
215. ποιητικά

from which it can be called practical.[216] We therefore, just as we deny that theology is entirely productive, also deny that it is merely theoretical,[217] because all its contents, by their own nature, demand activity with respect to the object known. Moreover, we also deny that theology is theoretical-practical, properly speaking and in itself, although from our method of treatment we have characterized it in this way. Rather, we call it practical, and even preeminently[218] practical, for the following reasons: (1) It is called the doctrine according to godliness. (2) Knowledge without practice is everywhere called vain (1 Cor. 8:1–3; 13:1–2), and even dead (James 2:17). (3) Everything in theology is concerned with either the end or the means, and all such things are practical. (4) In the sacred page, each and every head of theology is assigned its own practice. For example, there is a practice assigned to Scripture (2 Tim. 3:16–17), the proclamation of the gospel (1 Tim. 1:5), the hearing of the Word (Matt. 13:23; James 1:22–23), faith (1 Peter 1:9; Rom. 1:5), the sacraments—the Supper ("do this,"[219] 1 Cor. 11:24) and baptism ("teach them to observe everything," Matt. 28:19–20). And also, (5) because the practice we have proposed, living for God, is by far the most complete practice of all.

The Practical Part

The first use, reproof. Who should be reproved

XLIX. So then, first, it is not true theology, and a person is not a true theologian—and thus not a genuine Christian—(1) who either in speech or in deed, makes theology and the Christian religion the art of knowing and disputing, while at the same time he ignores and neglects the practical knowledge of living and is one who has merely the words of the saints, but not their life, as Bernard of Clairvaux said somewhere.[220] Even Seneca calls this a fatal itch of clever men, that they prefer disputing rather than living;[221] (2) who passes himself off

---

216. πρακτική

217. θεωρετικήν

218. εξόχως

219. τοῦτο ποιεῖτε

220. This is most probably not from Bernard of Clairvaux but from Isidore of Seville's *Sententiarum Libri Tres*, cap. XXIV.1, see *PL* 83:0699A. "Hypocrita verba sanctorum habet, vitam non habet: et quos per sermonem doctrinae genuerit, non fovet exemplis, sed deserit, quia quos verbo aedificat, vita et moribus destruit."

221. Mastricht states: "fatalem Seneca vocat, ingeniorum scabiem, ut disputare malint, quam vivere." Cf. Seneca, *Ad Lucilium Epistulae Morales*, trans. R. M. Gummere, vols. 1–3 (Cambridge, Mass.: Harvard University Press, 1917–1925), 108.23 "sed aliquid praecipientium vitio peccatur, qui nos docent disputare, non vivere, aliquid discentium, qui propositum adferunt ad praeceptores suos non animum excolendi, sed ingenium. Itaque quae philosophia fuit, facta philologia est."

as a theologian and a Christian, but in the meantime does not live for God through Christ, but rather lives—be it for the world, or the flesh, or leisure— fundamentally, for himself; or (3) who though perhaps he even strives to live for God, does not live for God so much through Christ as through his own strength.

The grounds of reproof

However, (1) although this person is reputed the sharpest professor and the keenest defender of the Christian cause, yet he is no more a theologian and a Christian than an orator who cannot speak or a physician who cannot heal. Such a person deserves in the highest degree that most disgraceful stigma which the apostle applied to Jewish hypocrisy (Rom. 2:17ff.). What is more, (2) such a person is rather a liar who says and does not do (Matt. 7:21; 23:3); what he speaks with his mouth he denies with his deeds (Titus 1:16). And moreover (3) he is vain (James 1:26), and a hypocrite, "having a form of religion but denying its power"[222] (2 Tim. 3:5). In fact, (4) he is spiritually dead, since he is unacquainted with living (Eph. 2:1; Matt. 8:22). And thus (5) by all this theology of his he produces nothing for himself but his own destruction (Matt. 7:21). For whoever does not desire to live for God in the present life will not live in the one hereafter. For godliness[223] holds promise for this life and also for the life to come (1 Tim. 4:8).

The second use, examination. Of theology

L. Therefore, the second use is that we should seriously examine here both our theology and our theologians. We should examine our theology, indeed, or our religion, as to whether it (1) is the doctrine that originates from and is revealed by God (Isa. 51:4); (2) makes for Christian practice; (3) directs our life in no other way than toward God, that is, to the accomplishment of the glory of God in our eternal salvation; (4) whether it lays the foundation of our whole life in Christ alone (John 15:4). These are the principal marks of genuine theology, together with those that we enumerated above in §XXXIII.

Of theologians

But let us also examine theologians, and Christians, and let every person examine himself, to determine whether he is, (1) taught, not by men only, or by books, but rather by God (Gal. 1:1); (2) taught, not for disputing or discoursing, but for living; (3) for living not for himself, the world, or anything else, but for God;

---

222. μόρφωσιν ἔχων εὐσεβείας, τὴν δὲ δύναμιν ἀπαρνούμενος
223. εὐσέβεια

(4) and that through Christ, that is, by the power of Christ alone. These are the chief evidences, springing from our definition of theology, of an authentic theologian or Christian. For the nature of a matter and its innate character are not more perfectly perceived from any other source than from its careful definition.

The third use, exhortation, that we live for God
LI. But, third, this is the principal thing. Since we are theologians and Christians, then surely we who have professed ourselves to be devoted to theology should, in keeping with our profession, strive for this: that we live for God alone through Christ. And because of this, it is incumbent upon us to speak somewhat more distinctly of the following four things.

What does living for God require? In general
First, what exactly does living for God require? Although the answer in fact extends through the whole syntagma of theology that we will expound in each of the theological heads, with God's help, nevertheless, presented in summary form[224] it contains, first in general, the following: (1) We should establish God as the sole object of this spiritual life (Ps. 16:8), that is, in every part of our life and with a singular focus we should endeavor to serve and to please God (Gal. 1:10; 2 Cor. 5:9) which is what it means, according to the Scriptures, to live for God. (2) We should make the will of God the sole norm of our life (1 Peter 4:2, 6), for this is what it means to live according to God. (3) We should set God before us as the goal of our whole life (Phil. 1:20–21; 2 Cor. 5:9). Finally, (4) we should endeavor and do all of this by the power of God. So then, as we taught above, living for God, at least generally, is nothing other than directing every act of our natural, civil, and spiritual life according to the precept of the divine Word, for the glory of God, by the power of God that is in us while we act.

Living for God demands specifically: 1. The threefold aim
LII. Specifically, living for God demands three things. First, it demands that we set before us the proper goal of our life, that is, so that we may not run aimlessly and beat the air (1 Cor. 9:26), as an archer without a target. For the end directs the use of the means. It removes our aversion to them, or at least mitigates it, when we forget what is behind us, and are carried toward the goal that is in front of us (Phil. 3:14). Moreover, the proper goal of life has in all three parts: (1) The highest goal is the glory of God, and naturally so, because for this we were made

---

224. ὡς ἐν ἐπιτομῇ

(Isa. 43:7), for this we were remade and born again (1 Cor. 6:20), and for this we are called by the gospel (Matt. 5:16). Therefore, let us be carried toward this point in all our actions (1 Cor. 10:31), and willingly expend ourselves and our goods (Phil. 1:10, 21). (2) The intermediate goal is the salvation of our own soul (1 Peter 1:9) in which God is especially glorified, and which accordingly we are most of all constrained, after the glory of God, to pursue. (3) The last goal is the advantage of our neighbor, for we are not born only for ourselves, but also for our neighbor. To this end Paul directed himself and everything he had (1 Cor. 9:19, 21). To this end our Savior directed himself (Matt 18:11). To this end we should direct ourselves: that we promote the salvation of our neighbors. Let us light their way to it by the holy example of our life, and let us avoid scandals most earnestly (1 Cor. 10:32).

2. The threefold norm
LIII. Moreover, second, to that goal let us entirely direct our actions, according to the right norm, which is likewise threefold: (1) The Word of God (Ps. 119:17; Gal. 6:16). (2) The life of Christ, because of whom we are called Christians. Christ personally commends his life to us as an example (Matt. 11:29), and Paul professes that he is pursuing it (1 Cor. 11:1). By this Christ lives in us (Gal. 2:20) and shines in us (2 Cor. 4:10), and also, his life presents the most accurate exemplar for our own. (3) Our own conscience rightly conformed to the Word of God (Acts. 24:16) also presents us both with a norm and with a judge subordinate to God.

3. The order
LIV. Not only this, but third, in all our striving, we should pursue that fitting order in which (generally speaking at least) we prefer spiritual things to corporeal things. We should prefer, I say, the former, though we should not totally neglect the latter (Matt. 6:33; John 6:27). We follow this proper order: (1) if, when corporeal matters arise at the same time as spiritual matters in such a way that we are unable to provide for both at the same time, in accord with the grace of God we rather disregard and neglect corporeal matters (that is, other things being equal) than spiritual matters (Heb. 10:34; 11:26); (2) if, in accord with the grace of God, we care for these earthly things with a spiritual mind, with regard for God, that is, according to the precept of God, for his glory, for the advantage of the divine kingdom, and for the advancement of our spiritual life; (3) if we set aside not only the recurring seventh day of our life to God, but also some small parts of every day, in which we fully and wholly set ourselves apart

to God and to divine things. David designated these kinds of canonical hours for himself (Ps. 55:17), and Daniel did as well (Dan. 6:11).

Nine motives to live for God

LV. The following reasons persuade us to live for God in this way: (1) Because we are the children of the living God, should we not live also, and live for him, and for his glory, and by his precepts, since he is our Father (Mal. 1:6)? (2) We are members of Christ, united with him who lives in his people (Gal. 2:20). Will we not live in him? How can we be dead men in union with the living one? (3) We have in Christ the Spirit of life (Rom. 8:14). Should we therefore lie down like the dead? (4) We are, if true Christians, living members, living stones (1 Peter 2:4–5), trained in a living faith (James 2:17, 26). By this faith, then, should we not live? Especially since there is no life where there is no power to operate by oneself, and to what end does that operative power exist except to act? (5) We have God, who lives and gives life (Rom. 9:26; 1 Thess. 1:9). We have the Father, who grants life to us (Gen. 2:7), and that spiritual and immortal; the Son, who by his death acquired and restored life to us (Eph. 2:5); the Holy Spirit, who by regeneration confers the seeds of spiritual life (John 3:5–6), and that by a living seed (1 Peter 1:23). And why did the triune God do all these things, except that we might live for him, that we might render our life to him? (6) Our Savior Jesus devoted himself and everything that was his—his life, death, resurrection, and all things—"so that those who live should no longer live for themselves, but for him who died for them and rose again" (2 Cor. 5:15). For this reason, "none of us lives for himself, and none of us dies for himself. For if we live, we live for the Lord.... For to this end he both died and rose again" (Rom. 14:7–9). In fact, (7) to this end he created us, preserves us, and fills us with every kind of spiritual and temporal benefit, that we might live for him. To this he daily calls us out and calls us forward by the precepts of his Word. Should he have done these things to no purpose (2 Cor. 6:1)? Certainly he would have, if we do not render our life to God. However, we say only "to no purpose," for he would not have communicated life and all things for the purpose of eternal death. And (8) for whom rather should we live than for our most excellent Creator,[225] our most faithful Redeemer, our most delightful guide[226] and Paraclete? In addition, (9) if we have not begun to live for God in time, we will not continue in eternity. For the life that endures eternally began here first (John 3:36; 1 John 3:15).

---

225. *Conditor*
226. ὁδηγῷ

The manner of living for God, in three things

LVI. Nevertheless, we must consider how we should conduct this work of living for God: (1) with integrity, that we make every act of our life conform to every tenet of God's good pleasure (Jer. 42:3, 5) and restrain ourselves from every evil (Ps. 119:101), which according to the apostle is "to abound in the work of the Lord at all times"[227] (1 Cor. 15:58); (2) with diligence, with fervor, "making every effort"[228] (2 Peter 1:5), that we devote our first and chief concern to it (Matt. 6:33; Luke 10:40); (3) with constancy, "steadfast and immovable"[229] (1 Cor. 15:58), not haphazardly, not now and then, but rather always and continually (1 Chron. 16:11; Matt. 24:13), whether in hope or fear, wholly unwavering (Dan. 3:17–18). We could easily find more arguments of this kind if more were needed.

Finally, six means

LVII. And finally, so that we might be able to live for God, we must also attend to the means. Among these regeneration holds the first place (John 3:5), by which the first principle of spiritual life is restored to those dead in sin, and by this we are made alive (Eph. 2:1, 5–6). Prior to this it is completely impossible to elicit any spiritually living action. For whatever is of the flesh is flesh and whatever is of the Spirit is spirit (John 3:6; Rom. 8:7). The second is a true and living faith, for by this the righteous live (Rom. 1:17; Gal. 2:20). The third is union with Christ, accomplished by faith and the Spirit, so that through Christ we may live for God (Rom. 6:11), and Christ may live in us (Gal. 2:20). For without Christ we can do nothing (John 15:5), just as also in Christ we can do all things (John 15:5; Phil. 4:13). The fourth is a fixed and unmoved intention of living for and serving God (Ps. 119:44; Heb. 13:18). The fifth is a steadfast striving to obtain what we earnestly seek, with all our strength directed to that end (2 Cor. 5:9; Acts 24:16). The sixth is ardent prayers, with which we would weary God so that he would enliven us and create a new heart in us. We should also pray that he would by his grace preserve the good work he began in us and make it fruitful, until it attain to eternal life (1 Cor. 15:10; 1 Thess. 5:23–24). "And as many as walk according to this rule, may peace and mercy be upon them"[230] (Gal. 6:16). Many more things of this kind will occur in their own place in the Ascetic part.[231]

---

227. περισσεύειν ἐν τῷ ἔργῳ τοῦ κυρίου πάντοτε
228. σπουδὴν πᾶσαν παρεισενέγκαντες
229. ἑδραῖοι καὶ ἀμετακίνητοι
230. καὶ ὅσοι τῷ κανόνι τούτῳ συστοιχήσουσι, εἰρήνη ἐπ᾽ αὐτοὺς καὶ ἔλεος
231. TPT 4.1–3

CHAPTER TWO

Holy Scripture

All Scripture is divinely inspired and useful for teaching, rebuke, correction, and instruction in righteousness, so that the man of God may be complete, thoroughly equipped for every good work.

— 2 Timothy 3:16–17

The second of the prolegomena of theology, its principium
I. The skill of living for God is not a natural power, one to which we are not taught but made; it is instead an acquired faculty, and therefore it certainly demands a rule to direct it, and in fact one that has been prescribed by God, as we taught just above. Over and above the life of Christ and one's own conscience, we previously established that this rule is the Word of God, or Scripture. And as it is the norm for living, it is thus also a common complex of precepts and rules that apply to living. For this reason it is called the *principium* of theology. We will build our reflection on this point on the words from 2 Timothy 3:16–17 above.

The Exegetical Part
It is built upon an analysis of the text.
II. With these words as the motivating argument, the apostle, who intends to stir Timothy up to a serious study of the sacred letters, presents to him the most splendid commendation of Scripture. In this commendation two things are prominent:

    A. The subject commended: "all Scripture."[1] Here "all"[2] is used to mean "the whole of,"[3] and "Scripture"[4] must be limited by the description *holy*,[5] so

---

1. πᾶσα γραφή
2. πᾶσα
3. ὅλη
4. γραφή
5. ἁγία

that the phrase consequently means *the whole of holy Scripture*, that is, not only the canon of Scripture in its entirety, but also its individual parts.

B. The predicate, or the basis of the commendation, which displays three things about Scripture:

1. Its origin, from which its authority results: "God-breathed,"[6] which adjective is not part of the subject, but of the predicate. And also, the substantive verb *is*, left out by Hebraic ellipsis, should be added, so the phrase is rendered, *all Scripture is divinely inspired*. Scripture is "God-breathed,"[7] because holy men of God wrote it down, not by some sort of visible manifestation[8] (Rom. 1:19), but by the immediate and infallible inspiration of God (2 Peter 1:20–21).

2. Its utility: "and profitable."[9] This denotes not only (as the Romanists prefer to say) its utility and its applicability of every kind, but also its sufficiency, necessity, and perfection, and thus it is equivalent to the adjective "self-sufficient."[10] Moreover, its utility is noted distinctly in four ways:

   a. "For teaching."[11] This expresses its use for instruction,[12] since Scripture is not only noetic, but also dianoetic, and thus teaching, when it makes one statement, sometimes excludes many others, or confirms others different from itself.

   b. "For rebuke,"[13] which can be understood with respect to the rebuking either of errors or of vices. I prefer the former, because the latter concerns the use that follows it. Therefore, this phrase signifies the polemical[14] use of Scripture, by which a teacher is able "to rebuke gainsayers"[15] (Titus 1:9), that is, to refute them plainly and fully, and also to "stop their mouths"[16] (Titus 1:11).

---

6. θεόπνευστος
7. θεόπνευστος
8. φανερώσει
9. καὶ ὠφέλιμος
10. τῷ αὔταρκες
11. πρὸς διδασκαλίαν
12. Latin: *informatio*; Dutch: *onderwyzing*
13. πρὸς ἔλεγχον
14. πολεμικόν
15. τοὺς ἀντιλέγοντας ἐλέγχειν
16. ἐπιστομίζειν

c. "For correction."[17] A correction presupposes an evil and, accordingly, because there are two sorts of evil, sorrowful evil and shameful evil, there are also two sorts of correction.[18] By one we are freed from sorrowful evil, and it is called consolation; by the other we are freed from shameful evil, and this is rebuke. The word *correction*[19] includes both.

d. "For direction in righteousness."[20] "Direction"[21] denotes instruction as well as direction. "Righteousness"[22] designates here, by synecdoche,[23] any sort of moral good, whether a virtue or deed. The article τὴν seems to be added diacritically,[24] for the sake of distinction, so that instruction in righteousness may be distinguished from instruction in teaching,[25] which he expressed first when he said that Scripture is useful "for teaching." So then, by these words a paraenetic, or hortatory, use is expressed. And so, in these four uses, the whole practical application of Scripture is described.

3. Its end and goal: "that the man of God may be complete, thoroughly equipped for every good work."[26] In these words is expressed the twofold end of Scripture:

a. The end of the recipient, that is, the person to whom the aforementioned usefulness of Scripture is aimed: "the man of God."[27] Indeed, it especially applies to Timothy and other ministers of the divine Word, since throughout Scripture they preeminently[28] are called "men of God" (1 Sam. 2:27; 1 Kings 17:18; 2 Kings 4:7; 1 Tim. 6:11), yet it also includes any Christians, to whom the aforementioned fourfold usefulness of Scripture applies.

---

17. πρὸς ἐπανόρθωσιν
18. ἐπανόρθωσις
19. ἐπανόρθωσις
20. πρός παιδείαν τὴν ἐν δικαιοσύνῃ
21. παιδεία
22. δικαιοσύνη
23. *synecdochikῶς*
24. διακριτικῶς
25. παιδείᾳ τῇ ἐν διδασκαλίᾳ
26. ἵνα ἄρτιος ᾖ ὁ τοῦ θεοῦ ἄνθρωπος, πρὸς πᾶν ἔργον ἀγαθὸν ἐξηρτισμένος
27. ὁ τοῦ θεοῦ ἄνθρωπος
28. ἐξόχως

b. The end of the content, that is, the good that is aimed at the person: "that he may be complete,"[29] namely, formed according to godliness. This includes:

   i. The godliness that Scripture forms: "for every good work."[30] Namely, godliness gains for us the ability to work, to work what is good: not just this good or that good, but every good, that is, every sort of good—natural, moral, and spiritual.

   ii. The formation in that godliness, by which not only does the man of God become ἄρτιος, that is, complete or whole, particularly in terms of arithmetic perfection (for this word is used for even numbers, which are called ἄρτιοι, that is, "those that are equal when divided"[31] in such a way that nothing is lacking in them and likewise nothing is left over), but he also becomes ἐξηρτισμένος, that is, fully and entirely, absolutely and in all aspects complete, by a perfection not only of parts but also of degrees, that is to be obtained, not here, but hereafter. Thus Alphonso Salmeron wrongly deduces from this phrase the perfection of good works in this life.[32] For the text does not express the perfection of man so much as the perfection of Scripture. And even if it does express the perfection of the man of God,

---

29. ἵνα ἄρτιος ᾖ

30. πρός πᾶν ἔργον ἀγαθόν

31. τοῖς ἑαυτῶν μέρεσιν ἴσοι εἰσί

32. See Alphonsus Salmeron (1515–1585), *Alphonsi Salmeronis Doctoris Toletani e Societate Jesu theologiae praeclarissimi, Commentarii in evangelicam historiam, et in Acta Apostolorum: nunc primum in lucem editi*, 16 vols. (Cologne, 1612), see 15:607, *Disputatio* 4 on 2 Timothy: "Furthermore the end of Scripture is 'so that the man of God may be perfect in righteousness,' that is, complete and constant with respect to all the requirements for perfecting the man of God, that is, a bishop or Christian doctor. For here is the man of God, as we have said previously, and that he is to be equipped for every good work. For the end of the Holy Scriptures is faith, but the end of faith is good works, by which eternal life is achieved. Therefore, one must also be equipped for understanding, but also for working: because faith without works is dead: which the heretics will not willingly hear inasmuch as they contend for an empty faith. Weigh carefully also from this passage that a person can arrive at some measure of perfection in this life, even if it may not be equal to what is expected for the reward by all in the heavenly homeland, or what would have been demanded once in the state of innocence where there was an amazing tranquility of the flesh and spirit, of the body and soul, and of man and all the animals subject to him: which, except in Christ, does not occur in those who are living. Yet we can attain such a perfection that does not allow any lethal sin. For the lesser and venial sins do not deprive one of righteousness, grace or love." For further information on Salmeron, see Augustin de Backer, D'Alois de Backer and Charles Sommervogel, eds., *Bibliotheque de la Compagnie de Jesus* (Louvain: Chez L'Auteur A. de Backer, 1876), 3:502–505.

it does not express an actual and absolute perfection that he could possess in this life, but rather the potential and conditional perfection that Scripture could confer, and that he also could achieve, if he would follow Scripture perfectly. But even if you prefer to take this as an actual and absolute sort of perfection, then it must not be understood as one that is obtained here in this life, but one that will be obtained hereafter in the life to come.

The Dogmatic Part

Scripture is the perfect rule of living for God.

III. Thus it is apparent that Holy Scripture is the perfect rule of living for God. Yet the fourfold use alone, which the text attributes to Scripture, does not exhaust the entire method of living for God, but one should also add that by Scripture's aid a person can be rendered complete for every good work, and even absolutely complete.

It is proven by Scripture

Accordingly, Scripture is in many places pointed out as a light and a lamp to our feet (Ps. 119:105; 2 Peter 1:19), and expressly as a "measuring line"[33] (Ps. 19:4)—unless you prefer to understand that passage differently—and a "rule"[34] (Gal. 6:16; Phil. 3:16). It is in addition called "perfect" (Ps. 19:7), since it is able to "make us wise for salvation"[35] (2 Tim. 3:15). This is exactly what is intended also by those passages that bind us to the Scriptures (Isa. 8:20) in such a way that they make the blameless depart from it neither to the right hand nor to the left (Deut. 4:1–2; 12:28, 32; Rev. 22:18–19).

It is confirmed by reasons: The first reason, derived from hypotheses

IV. For nature itself presupposes the following: (1) There is a God, or some first being, by whom all things exist, who is the ultimate end to whom all things aim, and who consequently is above all things. (2) He must be worshiped, or, what is the same thing, life must be lived for him. For if we have all things from him, and we have them so that we may give them back to him, and if likewise he is over all things and more perfect than all things, certainly it is evident that all these truths must be acknowledged with due reverence, and in doing so the

---

33. קו. cf. Heb. Ps. 19:5
34. κανών
35. σοφίσαι εἰς σωτηρίαν

worship of God is performed. (3) This worship of God is not a work of nature, such as seeing, hearing, and walking, which accordingly do not require a rule to direct them. Rather, the worship of God is a certain art that must be directed by certain rules. (4) The rule is not reason, because it is corrupted, as anyone who is rich in reason acknowledges, and something that is corrupt cannot be the measure of right. Neither is the rule the statutes of the wise, for they depend upon reason alone (which we have already excluded from this axiom), and from it they borrow their authority. Neither is it the sayings of the church fathers, for all of them were men just as we are and, to that extent, not only were they bound to a certain rule in the same way that we are, but they were also fallible and, what is more, often wrong. So they cannot compose any rule except a pliable one,[36] which is not one at all, since the rule ought to be infallible. Neither is the rule the Jewish Talmud, since, due to the unwritten[37] tradition through which it has been handed down from Moses to the Jews, not only is its truth uncertain, but also, on account of the fables with which it overflows, its falsity is certain. Neither is it the Qur'an of the Muslims, since it too readily reveals its own ineptitude by its superstitious and scurrilous nonsense. So then, there is no rule that remains standing except our Holy Scripture, and thus we declare it to be our axiom.

The second reason, from the five requirements of a rule
V. In this we are even more justified, because the nature and requirements of a rule fit as exactly as possible with Scripture alone. First, the rule of living for God, without doubt, ought to be prescribed by God alone (Deut. 12:32; Matt. 15:9). For a rule cannot be prescribed by any other than by the one whom the rule concerns. Now, Scripture alone has been prescribed by God as the rule for us (2 Tim. 3:16; 2 Peter 1:21), and due to the sublimity of the matter it could not be revealed and prescribed by anyone but God. Then second, the rule ought to be known, clear, and perspicuous, for otherwise how could it lead us into a knowledge of what is incumbent upon us to do? Scripture is such a rule, as will be apparent in its own place. Third, the rule ought to be constant and immovable, always and everywhere consistent. If it were not, how could it supply a certain measure for ruling? Indeed, Scripture is such a rule, namely, the "surer

---

36. *regula lesbia*, a flexible tool used by masons to measure gaps and to scribe irregular shapes to build a piece to accommodate or fill a gap in the masonry. In Aristotle's usage it describes accommodating laws of equity to the circumstances, rather than judging inflexibly. See *Nicomachean Ethics*, 5.10.

37. ἄγραφον

prophetic word" (2 Peter 1:19).[38] Fourth, the rule ought to be adequate for ruling and ought to stand in an indivisible way, so that it may not be augmented or diminished even the least bit. For unless it were so, it would be incompetent to measure its own object. Now, Scripture is such a rule. For nothing is incumbent upon us, either to believe or to do, that Scripture itself does not prescribe. And in turn Scripture does not prescribe anything that is not incumbent on us to receive or that does not concern living for God (2 Tim. 3:16; Rom. 15:4). Finally, the rule must be received and be public, for otherwise how will it solve controversies that arise among brothers? Likewise, Scripture is also such a rule, namely, one prescribed by the public authority of God (Ps. 147:19–20; Rom. 3:2), and received by common consent, at least of the Christian church, which is perhaps why the church is called the "pillar and buttress of the truth" (1 Tim. 3:15).[39] If perhaps there are additional general requirements for rules, for the sake of brevity we will pass these by at this point. They could easily be applied to the Scriptures, so that from them it would be made more completely known to us that Scripture is the perfect rule of living for God. Compare this with what we will set forth below for asserting the authority of the Scriptures against the pagans.

Holy Scripture is explained in four points: 1. The term Scripture
VI. Now, by *Holy Scripture* we understand nothing other than "the doctrine of living for God insofar as that the doctrine, once written down, is preserved in books."[40] For although God had preserved and propagated this doctrine in an unwritten way[41] by a living tradition through the patriarchs for several ages until Moses, at last it pleased him to commit it to writing, for the following reasons: (1) the shortness of human life, which was gradually decreasing from the time of Moses and before him (Gen. 5:5ff.; cf. 47:9; Ps. 90:10); (2) both the number of human beings and of members of the church, which was increasing gradually (Gen. 15:18); (3) the danger and unfaithfulness of the protection that can be expected from tradition alone, for many corruptions had crept in formerly during the time of tradition (Josh. 24:2; Ezek. 20:7; Gen. 35:2); (4) the weakness of human memory (2 Peter 1:15); (5) the stability of the heavenly teaching (Luke 1:3–4; Phil. 3:1); and (6) the perversity of heretics, who easily abuse unwritten[42]

---

38. βεβαιότερος προφητικὸς λόγος
39. στύλος καὶ ἑδραίωμα τῆς ἀληθείας
40. Latin: …*quatenus illa literis continetur descripta;* Dutch: …*voorzoverre die in geschrifte beschreven begrepen en vervat wordt.*
41. ἀγράφως
42. ἀγράφοις

traditions for the sake of their own errors. And for these reasons, the doctrine of living for God is called "Scripture." But why is it called "holy"? Consider the following reasons: (1) it derives its origin from the Most Holy Spirit (2 Peter 1:21); (2) it bears the holiest subject, that is, the art of living for God through Christ (John 6:68; Acts 5:30); (3) it holds before itself the holiest ends—the glory of God, the edification of men, and eternal salvation; and finally (4) it produces the holiest fruits (1 Thess. 2:8–9; Heb. 4:12).

Synonyms of Scripture

VII. Holy Scripture is sometimes indicated simply by the term *Scripture*, which means *writing*. This is speaking, of course, by way of eminence,[43] since it is by far the most excellent of all writings. It is also frequently referred to as the "Word of God" (1 Thess. 2:13; Ps. 119:9, 11, 16), the "oracles of God" (Rom. 3:2; 1 Peter 4:11; Heb. 5:12),[44] and the "word of God" (Heb. 4:12),[45] inasmuch as it evidently is from God, is about God, and leads to God. It is also referred to as God's "law"[46] (Ps. 19:7), "judgments,"[47] "commanded precepts,"[48] "statutes,"[49] and "commandments"[50] (although these expressions are employed on many occasions to distinguish ceremonial, political, and moral laws). Finally, it is referred to as "the Law and the Prophets" (Matt. 22:40; Luke 16:16), "Moses and the Prophets" (Luke 16:29, 31), or simply "the Prophets"; as "the sacred thing"[51] by the Hebrews; and as "the books"[52] by the Greeks; and by any other synonyms there are for Holy Scripture.

2. *The canonical parts of Scripture*

VIII. We divide Scripture into its two Testaments, the Old and the New. Of the Old Testament, which has the covenant of grace under a testator who was yet to die, we, together with the ancient church of the Jews, to whom the "oracles of God"[53] during this period are said to have been entrusted (Rom. 3:2), receive only thirty-nine books. These the Jews reference as twenty-two books, according to the number of the letters of their alphabet, and divide into three classes,

---

43. ἐξόχως
44. λόγια τοῦ θεοῦ
45. λόγος τοῦ θεοῦ
46. תורה, Heb. Ps. 19:8
47. משפטים
48. פקדים
49. חקים
50. מצות
51. מקדש
52. βιβλία
53. λόγια τοῦ θεοῦ

namely, the Law,[54] the Prophets[55]—both the former[56] and the latter[57]—and the Writings.[58] In Luke 24:44, the Savior seems to allude to this distribution. Christians separate them into the Law and the Prophets (Acts 28:23), into Moses and the Prophets (Luke 16:23, 29, 31; 24:27), and they distribute the prophetic books again into historical, dogmatic, and prophetic books. Of the New Testament, which has the covenant of grace under a testator who has already died, we number twenty-seven books, arranged into historical and dogmatic books, as well as one prophetic book.

The apocryphal books are rejected

IX. In addition to these, in the ancient church there were apocryphal books of two sorts. First, there were the spurious, extraneous—or even heretical, prohibited—ones, concerning which see Baronio's *Annales Ecclesiastici*, at the year AD 44.[59] This sort included five supposed books of Peter (concerning which see Jerome's account of Peter),[60] of John[61] and of the rest of the apostles separately, of all of the apostles conjointly, the Gospel of Judas the traitor, and of Jesus, the *Magia Jesu Christi*, supposedly written by Christ himself to Peter and Paul.[62] Pope Gelasius condemned these and others by a specific decree in a Roman council around AD 393, which is on record in the *Corpus Iuris Canonici*, distinction 15, chapter 3, where these are called "apocryphal."[63] Of the

---

54. תורה

55. נביאים

56. ראשנים

57. אחרונים

58. כתובים, *Hagiographa*

59. Cesare Baronio, *Annales Ecclesiastici auctore Cesare Baronio Sorano…tomus primus incipiens ab adventu D. N. J. C. perducitur usque ad Trajani Imperatoris exordium*, 6 vols. (Prague: Paul Lochner, 1736), 1:54–58.

60. For a Latin and Greek text of Jerome's account, see Jerome (Eusebius Hieronymus), *De Viribus Illustribus*, 827–30 in *PL* 23:637–40.

61. Jerome, *De Viribus Illustribus*, 844–46, *PL* 23:653–58.

62. Augustine of Hippo mentions an apocryphal work, *Magia Jesu Christi*, in *De Consensu Evangelistarum*, 1.9.14. For an English translation of Augustine's comments, see *Nicene and Post-Nicene Fathers*, Series I (*NPNF1*), ed. Philip Schaff (New York: Christian Literature Co., 1887–1900; reprint Peabody, Mass.: Hendrickson, 1994), 6:83–84. For an eighteenth-century discussion of this particular work, see J. A. Fabricius, *Codex apocryphus novi testamenti collectus, castigatus testimoniisque, censuris & animadversionibus illustratus*, 2nd edition, 3 vols. (Hamburg: Benjamin Schiller & J. C. Kisner, 1719), 1:303–307. For a nineteenth-century edition of texts and commentary with an English translation, see "Fragmenta scriptorum apocryphorum quae Jesu Christi auctoris nomen prae se ferunt" in J. A. Fabricius, *Codex apocryphus novi testamenti: The uncanonical gospels and other writings*, 2 vols., trans. J. A. Giles (London: D. Nutt, 1852), 2:xxxv–xxxvii.

63. See *Decretum Gratiani emendatum et notationibus illustratum una cum glossis Gregorii XIII Pont. Max. iussu editum* (Rome, 1582), coll. 72–74.

same kind are *The Letter of Christ to Agbarus, Toparch of Edessa* (concerning which see Eusebius, *History*, bk. 1, ch. 14),[64] *The Canons of the Apostles, The Letters of Paul to Seneca, The Shepherd of Hermas,* and others. Second, there are those that are surely useful for private reading, yet not produced by divine inspiration. And again these are either the kind that are recognized as such by the unanimous consensus of Christians, such as the third and fourth book of Esdras, the third book of the Maccabees, Psalm 151, the appendix of the book of Job, or the little preface to the Lamentations of Jeremiah; or they are the kind that the Romanists hold as canonical, which include the books of Tobit, Judith, Wisdom, Sirach, Baruch, the Epistle of Jeremiah, the appendices to Esther and Daniel, the Prayer of Azariah, the History of Susannah, Bel and the Dragon, the Prayer of Manasseh, and the two books of the Maccabees. The Reformed excluded all these from the canon by this one general argument: whatever books were not inspired by God (2 Tim. 3:16; 2 Peter 1:20–21), nor handed down to the church to be its canon (Ps. 147:19–20; Rom. 3:2; 9:4), nor received by the Jewish church, nor approved by Christ and the apostles (John 5:39; Luke 24:27), are not canonical. All four are true of these books: (1) They were not inspired by God, since they contain many things that are contrary to the Spirit of truth, who leads us into all truth, things that are false, improper,[65] fabulous, magical, and repugnant to history, just as, regarding each book, the following writers have shown: John Rainold, *On the Apocryphal Books*;[66] William Whitaker, *A Disputation on Holy Scripture*;[67] and our Dutch translators, more briefly, in the preface to the Apocryphal books,[68] together with others. (2) They were not

---

64. *Euseb. Hist. lib. 1. Cap. XIV.*: see instead Eusebius Pamphilius, *Eusebius: The Ecclesiastical History*, trans. K. Lake, 2 vols. (Cambridge, Mass., 1926–1932), 1.13.1–20, 1:84–97; cf. *NPNF2*, 1:100–102.

65. ἄτοπα

66. Mastricht could have two of Rainold's works in view, in order of likelihood: John Rainold (Johannes Rainoldus), *Censura librorum apocryphorum veteris testament adversum inprimis Robertum Bellarminum: qua tum divina et canonica sacrae scripturae autoritas asseritur solidissime, tum variae quaestiones & controversiae*, 2 vols. (Oppenheim: Hieronymus Gallerus, 1611); idem, *Johannis Rainoldi Angli sex theses de sacra scriptura & ecclesia…et Apologia contra pontificios Elymas, Stapletonum, Martinum, Bellarminum, Baronium, Iustum Calvinum vetera* (Hanover: Guilelmus Antonius, 1603).

67. William Whitaker, *Disputatio de sacra scriptura contra huius temporis papistas, inprimis Robertum Bellarminum Jesuitam… & Thomam Stapletonum…sex quaestionibus proposita & tractata a Guilelmo Whitakero* ([Cambridge]: Christopher Corvinus, 1588). For an English translation, see idem, *A Disputation on Holy Scripture against the Papists, especially Bellarmine and Stapleton* (Cambridge: Cambridge University Press, 1849).

68. The *Statenvertaling*, or States Translation, published by order of the Protestant Dutch Republic in 1637, contained a translation of the Apocrypha with a prefatory warning to the reader. See "waerschouwinge aen de lesers vande Apocryphe Boecken" in *Biblia, dat is, de gantsche*

handed down to the church as canonical, for they were written in a tongue foreign to the Jewish church. (3) Nor were they received and acknowledged by the Jewish church, as Josephus witnesses in *Against Apion*,[69] together with all the Jews throughout every age, which even papists acknowledge. (4) Nor were they approved by Christ and the apostles, inasmuch as they did not approve any books except those in which the Jews believed that they had eternal life, and which Christ says testify concerning himself (John 5:39). If you are anxious to know the contents, parts, arrangement, and method of the entire holy canon, consult Alsted in his *Praecognita Theologica*,[70] or Johann Himmel in his *Memoriale Biblicum*,[71] or Moses Pflacher[72] and Jacob Brandmüller in their respective analytical tables,[73] Eder in his *Oeconomia Bibliorum*,[74] and other matters.

The authentic edition of Scripture

X. Now, those books of both Testaments are not considered canonical and authentic unless they are in their original and authentic languages, because: (1) They are public testaments that are valid only in those languages in which they were composed. When controversies arise, only the original exemplar is acknowledged as authentic, as is apparent in diplomatic letters of kings, testaments, and others matters. (2) Only prophets and apostles could publish

---

H. Schrifture vervattende alle de canonijcke boecken des Ouden en des Nieuwen Testaments (Leiden: Paul Aerts, 1637), foll. †2r–†4v.

69. See *Against Apion*, 1.38–42 in Flavius Josephus, *Josephus in eight volumes, The Life | Against Apion*, trans. H. Thackeray (New York: G. P. Putnam's Sons, 1926), 1:179–81.

70. J. H. Alsted, *Praecognitorum theologicorum libri duo: naturam theologiae explicantes & rationem studii illius plenissime monstrantes* (Frankfurt: Antonius Hummius, 1614).

71. For Himmel's overview of the canonical and apocryphal books, mnemonic devices and chart of the canonical books, see J. Himmel, *Memoriale Biblicum Generale hoc est: analytica disposition singulorum librorum totius codicis sacri* (Iena: Johann Beithmann, 1623), 2–12.

72. Moses Pflacher (Pflacherus), *Analysis typica omnium cum veteris tum novi testamenti librorum historicorum ad intelligendam rerum seriem et memoriam iuvandam accommodata* (Tübingen: Georg Gruppenbach, 1587, 1595). The same publisher of Brandmüller's set in Basel, Ludovicus König, published a fifth edition of Pflacher in 1621. Since Mastricht refers to these two authors as "Mos. Phlacherus cum Brandmullero in Tabulis Analyticis" it is quite possible he was utilizing the Basel editions of both authors' works, see n440.

73. Jacob Brandmüller (also Jacob Brandmyller), *Analysis methodica typica evangeliorum dominicalium et festalium, cum observationibus...locorum item communium theologicorum* (Basel: Ludovicus König [Rex], 1620); idem, *Analysis Typica Librorum Veteris Testamenti Poeticorum... propheticorum...veluti pars altera ad analysin typicam librorum V. T. historicorum per D. Mosen Pflacherum olim institutam pertinens* (Basel: Ludovicus König [Rex], 1621); idem, *Analysis typica omnium N. T. epistolarum apostolicorum* (Basel: Ludovicus König [Rex], 1622).

74. Georg Eder, *Oeconomia bibliorum sive partitionum theologicarum libri quinque: quibus sacrae scripturae disposition seu artificium et vis atque ratio in tabulis velut ad vivum exprimitur* (Koln: Gervinus Calenius & haeres Ioannis Quentelii, 1582).

Scripture that is "God-breathed"[75] (2 Tim. 3:16) and authentic, since they were instructed by the immediate and infallible leading of the Holy Spirit (2 Peter 1:21). But what then are those authentic languages? I respond: All acknowledge that the Old Testament, given specifically to the Jewish church, was composed in the Hebrew language, except for certain small parts of Ezra, Daniel, Esther, and Jeremiah that are set forth in the Aramaic language. The New Testament, written to the universal Christian church, is acknowledged to have been written in the Greek language only. For this reason, we only receive Scripture as canonical and authentic that is in those languages. And that applies not only to the autographs, which for many reasons, according to his most wise counsel, God in his providence has allowed to pass away, but also to the apographs as well. And thus formerly the Israelite church held no edition to be authentic except the Hebrew Old Testament, and the Christian church held no edition to be authentic except the Greek New Testament.

Editions in the vernacular

XI. And yet Holy Scripture is not so tied to those languages that it cannot, and also ought not, be translated into other languages for the common use of the church. Likewise, all versions in those languages are considered authentic to the extent that they express the sources, according to which they must always be measured. For this reason, the providence of God was always so illustrious and praiseworthy in preserving the sources, not only that they might not completely pass away but also that they might not be mutilated by the loss of any of the books, or that they might not be deformed by any grave defect, while in the meantime not even one of the more ancient translations has come down to us whole and intact. For this reason also, "in human translations," as Ames says,

> all those things that are necessary for salvation can be perceived, if only they agree with the sources in their essential parts, as all the translations received by the churches usually do, although they may differ from the sources and be deficient in many rather insignificant things. Yet we must not therefore rest in any one version, but rather take care with all reverence that the purest and most correct interpretation is set forth to the church.[76]

---

75. θεόπνευστον

76. William Ames, *Guielmi Amesii Medulla Theologica* (Amsterdam: Joannes Janssonius, 1641), 1.34.32–33. For an English translation, see idem, *The Marrow of Sacred Divinity drawne out of the Holy Scriptures and the interpreters thereof, and brought into method* (London, 1639), ibidem; idem, *The Marrow of Theology*, ed. J. D. Eusden, 3rd edition (Grand Rapids: Baker Books, 1997), ibidem.

3. The origin of Scripture

XII. Its origin, upon which its authority is built, first may be considered with respect to its amanuenses (whom Gregory in this regard calls "the hands of the Holy Spirit" in his *Preface on Job*).[77] These were holy men of God (2 Peter 1:21), the prophets and apostles. For this reason, we are said to be built upon the foundation of the prophets and the apostles (Eph. 2:20). Some of those evangelists inspired by God,[78] Mark and Luke, for example, are accordingly in a broader sense called prophets (1 Cor. 14:29, 32), and apostles (Rom. 16:7; Phil. 2:25). "The Holy Spirit employed the work of these men with some variety," says Ames,

> for some of the things they would write were altogether unknown to the writer beforehand, as is sufficiently shown in the history of creation past and in the predictions of future things. But some things were known to the writer beforehand, as is evident in the history of Christ written by the apostles. And some of these matters were grasped by a natural knowledge, and others by a supernatural one. In secret and unknown matters, divine inspiration supplied all things by itself. In those matters that were known to the writer or were able to be discovered by ordinary means, the writers also added their devout study, with God assisting in such a way that they did not err in writing. In addition, the Holy Spirit aided them with his sweet accommodation so that each and every writer made use of the modes of speaking that were most fitting to his person and condition.[79]

Second, the origin of Scripture may be considered with respect to its author, who is indeed God, speaking of the Godhead in general. For this reason Scripture is everywhere called the Word of God, and God is said to speak in it. As to the individual persons, the author of Scripture is God the Father, who in the Scriptures "spoke at many times and in many ways"[80] (Heb. 1:1); the Son, who not only sent the apostles to teach, undoubtedly, as the occasion arose, but also ordered them to write (Rev. 1:19); and the Holy Spirit, who inspired the Scriptures (2 Tim. 3:16; 2 Peter 1:21), and who for this reason is said to testify and to speak in them (Heb. 10:15). This occurred to such an extent that in the inscriptions of the holy books, or in matters regarding the amanuenses themselves, there is often a deep silence, doubtless so that the books' authority would be less impaired, and be preserved for the principal cause alone.

---

77. For Gregory's comments on the Holy Spirit, in Latin see Gregorius Magnus, *Moralium libri sive expositio in librum B. Job* in PL 75:515–18; in English, see Gregory the Great, *Morals on the book of Job*, 3 vols. (Eugene, Ore.: Wipf & Stock, 2013), 1:14–16.

78. θεόπνευστοι

79. Ames, *Medulla*, 1.34.5.

80. πολυμερῶς καὶ πολυτρόπως ἐλάλησε

The method of composing Holy Scripture

XIII. Moreover, God composed Scripture partly through revelation and partly through canonization. God accomplished revelation (1) by writing it down, as is clearly seen in the Decalogue; (2) by commissioning that it be written (Deut. 31:19; Rev. 1:19); and (3) by inspiring it (2 Tim. 3:16), that is, by bringing to mind the things to be written and infallibly directing the writing. Therefore we can say that in all things, whether they were *de facto* or *de jure* matters, God not only inspired the matters themselves, but he also dictated the individual words. Canonization, moreover, is the process whereby the things written by inspiration were delivered to the church (Deut. 31:9; Ps. 147:19; Rom. 3:2) and sealed (Rev. 22:18–19). Ames writes, "For if any book is written by some extraordinary servant of God or by the certain direction of the Spirit, this is still insufficient to constitute it part of Scripture unless it is also given by divine authority to the church, and sanctified for this purpose: so that it might be its canon or rule."[81] This is the end and use of this God-breathed inspiration[82] and canonization, that is, that it might supply the rule of living for God—the rule of believing (John 20:31) and also of doing (Rom. 15:3–4)—for the universal church and for each of its members.

4. The properties of Scripture

(1) Its authority

XIV. Therefore, after what has been said, we still need to distinguish the chief properties of Scripture. Most of these properties are disputed with the papists, and so in opposition to them, they will be vindicated in their own place, in the elenctic section below. The first property is its supreme and independent authority, by which, whether in itself or in regard to us, it does not depend upon any source other than God. For this reason it is called the foundation (Eph. 2:20), since it sustains the entire weight of the Christian faith and life. Moreover, it is called the first article of faith (2 Peter 1:20). And all this because it is from the Holy Spirit (2 Peter 1:20–21), who judges all things and is judged by no one (1 Cor. 2:15). From this authority, it obtains its power (1) to decide all theological controversies (Isa. 8:20; Matt. 22:29), (2) to direct one's life and morals (Deut. 4:1–2; 12:28, 32; Neh. 8:2, 14–15ff.), and (3) to judge every one of us (Heb. 4:12), just as if God himself was speaking (Heb. 10:15). Nevertheless, here we must properly distinguish between historical authority,[83] which

---

81. Cf. Ames, *Medulla*, 1.34.9.
82. θεοπνευγίας
83. αὐθεντίαν *historiae*

expresses the bare truth of history or fact (and thus to that extent applies to all the holy narrations), and a norming authority,[84] which in addition directs our faith and life.

(2) Its truth

XV. Second is its truth, certitude, and universal stability[85] by which it is incapable either of deceiving or being deceived (2 Peter 1:19; Ps. 19:7; Dan. 10:21; John 17:17). This general truth implies certain specifics: its doctrinal and historical statements are most accurately consistent with the matter and the facts (Isa. 34:16); its practical statements with the will of God (Ps. 19:7); its prophecies, promises, and threats with the future event—no differently and no less than if they had been eyewitness testimonies (Matt. 5:18; Isa. 34:16). And that is the case because it has the God of truth as its author; Christ as the very truth it contains, and as its faithful witness; and the Holy Spirit, truth's infallible inspirer, as its guide.[86] Because of these things, its stability[87] is so great that it should be preferred far more than the revelation of any other (2 Peter 1:19), even if that revelation should come from a dead man (Luke 16:31), in fact, even if it should come from the very angels themselves (Gal. 1:8)!

(3) Its integrity

XVI. Third is its integrity, wherein through the singular providence of God it exists free from all corruption and thus not only would the whole or any of its books never cease to exist, but also, it could not, especially in those matters that regard living, be marred by any serious flaw (Matt. 5:18; Ps. 19:7; 1 Peter 1:23, 25).

(4) Its sanctity

XVII. The fourth property of Scripture is its sanctity and purity (Ps. 12:6; 18:30; 119:40; Prov. 30:5; Rom. 1:2; 2 Tim. 3:15), by which not only is it far removed from all impurity and indecency itself and in its narrations, but also it shows itself to be the source of all our holiness and purity, in our thoughts, words, and deeds (John 15:3). And this is the case by reason of (1) its principal cause, God, who is most holy (Isa. 6:3; Dan. 9:24); (2) its amanuenses, who are called holy men of God (2 Peter 1:21); (3) its matter, that is, the holy will of God (Rom. 12:2); and (4) its end, which is our sanctification (John 17:17) and the sanctification of all things that exist for our use (1 Tim. 4:5).

---

84. αὐθεντίαν *normae*
85. ἀσφάλεια
86. ὁδηγόν
87. ἀσφάλεια

(5) Its perspicuity

XVIII. Fifth is its perspicuity, or the clear and evident manifestation of the truth that is contained in it. For this reason, it is frequently called light (Ps. 119:105; 2 Peter 1:19; 2 Cor. 4:3–4, 6) and clear (Deut. 30:11), that is, luminous and illuminating. For otherwise it could not be the rule of believing and living. It is, moreover, clear and perspicuous in this sense: although the subjects of Scripture are often difficult to understand, nevertheless, its mode of teaching and explaining them, especially in those things that are necessary, is clear and perspicuous, at least for those who have the power of spiritual sight. So then, if some obscurity is perceived in the Scriptures, it is surely not due so much to Scripture as to the feebleness of our intellect. Nor is it due so much to the obscurity of its explanation as to the majesty of its subjects. Or, if some ambiguity inheres in the words themselves, it certainly does not appear in such things that are absolutely necessary, unless they are clearly taught in another place in Scripture.

(6) Its perfection

XIX. Sixth is its perfection, in which it lacks nothing at all that would produce living for God, that is, nothing necessary to believe or do for salvation. Moreover, this perfection is twofold. It is either an integral and systematic perfection of the books, in which it gradually grew by adding books until finally at the sealing of the canon (which is shown in Rev. 22:18–19), it obtained entire perfection (on this see §XVI, just above). Or, it is an essential perfection of the doctrine itself, which is contained in the books, and this kind of perfection is the substance of this locus. Scripture claims this perfection for itself both expressly (2 Tim. 3:14–17; Ps. 19:7–8), and by implication,[88] when it most rigidly prohibits every addition or subtraction (Deut. 4:2; 5:32; 12:32; Gal. 1:8; Rev. 22:18–19), when in matters of faith and obedience it sends us back to Scripture alone (Deut. 17:18–19; Isa. 8:20; Luke 16:29; Acts 24:14; 1 Cor. 4:6), and when it pronounces that we will be judged on the appointed day according to its dictates (John 12:48; 2 Thess. 1:8). Also, reason chimes in: (1) For it would not be the rule of faith and morals (as we demonstrated above) unless it was perfect. (2) Since it is the very first *principium* and the last resort of our faith (2 Peter 1:20–21), it is therefore perfect. For true and perfect conclusions and demonstrations cannot be deduced except from perfect *principia*, because a cause is never in any case inferior to its own effect. (3) Since it is perfect in its essential parts, that is, in its matter and form, as well as in its integral parts (in the law and the gospel), therefore it is also perfect in the whole. (4) Since every part or book of Scripture has its own integral

---

88. κατ᾽ ἰσοδυναμίαν

perfection by which it is abundantly sufficient for its own purpose as well as for its own time, therefore, the essential and entire perfection of Scripture cannot but follow. Moreover, by that perfection Scripture contains first, speaking in general, all that is necessary for salvation (John 5:39), and second, specifically, (1) that which must be believed (John 20:31; Rom. 15:4–5; 2 Tim. 3:15), (2) that which must be done (2 Tim. 3:17), and (3) whatever is necessary for the establishment and edification of the church, such that there is nothing necessary to observe in the church of God at all times and in all places that depends upon either some tradition or any sort of unwritten authority. For we read that by Scripture the "man of God,"[89] that is, the minister of the Word, is "thoroughly equipped"[90] "for every good work,"[91] namely, every good work that concerns the establishment and edification of the church. Although at the same time the *ecclesiasticalia* (rites and ceremonies), that is, those that are changeable and particular to circumstances, depend upon the prudent determination of each church (1 Cor. 14:40). Now Scripture is not perfect because all these things are set forth in it expressly[92] and literally[93] (although this is so in most instances, and especially in those necessary things), for it is sufficient that everything else is taught in Scripture by necessary consequence,[94] by an equivalent meaning,[95] or by implication[96] (Matt. 22:31–33; Rom. 4:5, 11).

(7) Its necessity

XX. The seventh property is its necessity, by which now the church and its members ought not, and cannot, exist without Scripture. Now this is not so by absolute necessity, but by a consequent necessity of the divine will[97] that willed Scripture to be the means to salvation (John 5:39; 2 Tim. 3:17). This necessity is evident (1) explicitly[98] (Jude 3); (2) from the commands, not only the general commands to teach (Matt. 28:19), which undoubtedly included writing, so that the teaching might endure until the consummation of the age (Matt. 28:20; cf. 2 Peter 1:21), but also the specific commands to write (Ex. 17:14; 34:27; Deut. 31:19; Jer. 30:2; 36:2; Rev. 1:11), together with the ones to copy, to read,

---

89. ὁ τοῦ θεοῦ ἄνθρωπος
90. ἐξηρτισμένος
91. πρὸς πᾶν ἔργον ἀγαθόν
92. αὐτολεξεί
93. κατὰ τὸ ῥητόν
94. κατὰ διάνοιαν
95. κατ᾽ ἰσοδυναμίαν
96. *per* συνακολούθησιν
97. *ex hypothesi voluntatis divinae*
98. ῥητῶς

to meditate upon Scripture (Deut. 17:18–19; 31:9–13; John 5:39; Ps. 1:2; 19:8, 12; 1 Tim. 4:13); (3) from its manifold and absolutely necessary use (2 Tim. 3:15–17; Rom. 15:4; John 20:31; 1 John 1:4); (4) from the motives which led God to require his amanuenses, the prophets and apostles, to write, which we mentioned previously in §VI.

(8) Its efficacy

XXI. The eighth property is its efficacy, on account of which "power"[99] is attributed to it (Rom. 1:16), by which it is called "able"[100] (James 1:21) and "active"[101] (Heb. 4:12) and is said to "work effectually"[102] (1 Thess. 2:13). For this reason it is compared to various things that excel in efficacy, for example, water (Isa. 55:10; Deut. 32:2; Heb. 6:7), fire (Jer. 5:14; Luke 24:32), a hammer (Jer. 23:29), a "two-edged sword"[103] (Heb 4:12), a "sharp double-edged sword"[104] (Rev. 1:16), and thunder (Ps. 68:33). Nevertheless, this efficacy, with regard to spiritual things, is not so much physical and principal, as the Lutherans would have it, as it is moral and instrumental, flowing as it does from the Holy Spirit, who is like the arm of God (Isa. 53:1). For this reason the Word and Spirit are united, or rather subordinated, one to the other (Isa. 59:21), and the gospel is said to be the "ministry of the Spirit"[105] (2 Cor. 3:8) and its efficacy is not in word alone, but also in power and in the Holy Spirit (1 Thess. 1:5), since the Spirit acts through the Word. This efficacy (1) penetrates into the inmost heart (Heb. 4:12–13); (2) uncovers its secrets and hidden recesses (1 Cor. 14:23–25), which the Samaritan woman experienced (John 4:29); (3) amazingly afflicts, pierces, and crushes a person's spirit (Acts 2:37; Isa. 66:2); (4) illumines the mind (Ps. 19:7–8; Acts 26:17–18); (5) regenerates and converts the heart (James 1:21); (6) kindles faith (Rom. 10:17; Gal. 3:5); (7) sanctifies the whole person (John 17:17); (8) strengthens, so that one might overcome the world (1 John 2:14); (9) consoles (Rom. 15:4; Ps. 119:50, 92); (10) saves eternally (Rom. 1:16) since it is "able to save souls"[106] (James 1:21). The amazing efficacy of the divine Word was experienced by Justin Martyr, who had been deluded for quite a long time by philosophers of every sort, when, upon being advised by an eminent man, he undertook the reading of the prophets and apostles and sensed, "this

---

99. δύναμις
100. δυναμένη
101. ἐνεργής
102. ἐνεργεῖσθαι
103. *gladio* διστόμῳ
104. ῥομφαίᾳ διστόμῳ ὀξείᾳ
105. διακονία τοῦ πνεύματος
106. δυνάμενος σῶσαι τὰς ψυχάς

alone is the philosophy that is both trustworthy and profitable";[107] by Cyprian, when he was converted through the reading of Jonah, which was explained to him by Caecilius the presbyter of Carthage;[108] by Augustine, when he read the passage Romans 13:13–14, after a voice (whether heavenly or earthly) sang to him, "pick up, pick up, and read";[109] by Luther, when he discovered and read the Bible in the monastery at Erfurt, as Melchior Adam testifies in his biography of Luther;[110] and by Franciscus Junius, when he read the first chapter of John;[111] and by a thousand others. Indeed, people the world over sense the efficacy of the Word when they are converted by the mere preaching of the gospel (cf. Ps. 2:8–9; 2 Cor. 10:4–5). Moreover, even reprobates themselves experience it when they lose their speech (Matt. 22:46), when they yield (Mark 6:20), when they fear (Mark 6:20; Acts 24:25), when they are converted, at least outwardly (Ps. 18:45; 1 Kings 21:27; Acts 26:28), and when they are hardened and blinded (Isa. 6:9–10). Furthermore, what should be said about the interpretation of Scripture, first elenctic, then practical, we will reserve, each for its own place.

The Elenctic Part

It is asked: 1. Is there any written Word of God?

XXII. Up to this point we have dealt with friends in a constructive way;[112] from here on we deal with enemies of this locus in a deconstructive way.[113] We divide these enemies into two classes: unbelievers and pseudo-Christians. In the former class, the first place goes to the pagans, the second to Muslims, and the last to Jews. The first place, I say, deservedly belongs to the pagans. We dispute

---

107. See Justin Martyr, *Dialogue with Trypho*, ch. 8, in English, *ANF* 1:198, in Greek and Latin, *Patrologia Graeca (PG)*, ed. Jacques-Paul Migne (Paris, 1857–1866), 6:491–92. This is Mastricht's partial quotation: ταύτην μόνην φιλοσοφίαν, ἀσφαλῆ τε καὶ συμφέρον.

108. Mastricht cites Jerome's commentary on Jonah, ch. 3:6–9, where Jerome mentions that Cyprian was converted after reading Jonah's message to Nineveh; *PL* 25:1143. See also Cyprian, *Epistola Ad Donatum*, 3–4 in Latin, *PL* 4:198–202; in English, Cyprian, Epistle 1.3–4, *ANF* 5:275–76.

109. Augustine, *Confessiones*, 8.12.28–30 in Latin, *PL* 32:761–63; in English, Augustine, *Confessions* in *NPNF1* 1:127–28.

110. According to Adam, this incident occurred in 1501 in the library at Erfurt. See in Latin, Melchior Adam, *Vitae Germanorum theologorum qui superiori seculo Ecclesiam Christi voce scriptisque propagarunt et propugnarunt* (Heidelberg: J. G. Geyder, 1620), 103; in English, *The Life and Death of Dr. Martin Luther* (London, 1641), 5.

111. Franciscus Junius, *A Treatise on True Theology with the Life of Franciscus Junius*, trans. David Noe (Grand Rapids: Reformation Heritage Books, 2014), 34. For the Latin text, see Franciscus Junius, *Opera theologica* (Geneva: Peter and Jacob Chouët: 1613), 1:11.

112. κατασκευαστικῶς

113. ἀνασκευαστικῶς

with them regarding whether there is any written Word of God at all. Because the pagans refer the whole of humanity's guidance to reason, and because they teach that this reason, in itself at least, is uncorrupted, they spurn any necessity for divine revelation, or if they allow any at all, they substitute their own oracles, such as those of Jupiter Ammon, the Delphic oracle, and so forth, or another revelation in the place of the truly divine one. Conversely, because all Christians affirm that divine faith and obedience are necessary in religion—although they do so in different ways or degrees—they assert that divine revelation in a written word is necessary. Therefore, that we may, if possible, refute the heathen, we must bring forward at this point what we have already taught in §IV, and then, additionally, we must strive not only to have unconquerable lines of argument at hand, but also to arrange them in a suitable order. To do so, we must demonstrate step by step, first the omnimodal truth of Scripture, and then its divine authority.

Answer: The universal truth of Scripture in six arguments.
And we will certainly maintain Scripture's truth as we desire if we use the following helps. First, we should carefully inquire into whether these pagans with whom we have dealings have some writings they acknowledge as true. Then we should seek out the reasons why they believe these writings are true. If they should provide reasons that are true, you will easily be able to adapt those reasons to our Scriptures.

Second, you should especially study the marks and evidences of any written truth, then bring them into contact with our Scriptures. The marks in general are: (1) the writers were honest and frank men; (2) they were not promoting their own cause, from which they could have received some sort of worldly advantage, but rather the cause of another; (3) they were, in fact, promoting a cause from which they could not obtain for themselves anything except dangers, losses, and destruction; (4) many such writers agree in the same things so exactly; (5) even their enemies do not deny the matters of fact, but only attribute them to other causes; and (6) they narrate matters contemporaneous with themselves. If you should show these marks, and similar ones, in our Scriptures, as can be done without difficulty, then undoubtedly you will maintain that our Scripture is the most true.

Third, you should add an argument from the contents of Scripture, that they (at least to the extent that they are subject to reason) so exactly accord with right reason. For if they deal with moral matters, Scripture has nothing that is contrary to right reason; or if the ethical manuals of the philosophers are the judge, right reason also does not demand in them anything that Scripture does not demand more perfectly. And if they deal with historical matters, you will discover that our Scripture conforms at every point to the actual events, as both induction and a response to objections will easily show. From this it remains that there is nothing in the Scriptures that is repugnant to the truth.

Fourth, you should take up natural theology, both in its theoretical and in its practical heads of doctrine—or, if you are eager to save time, take only those heads that your adversary agrees with—and show that the very same things are taught, and in fact taught much more perfectly, by our Scripture. And in this way you will more easily succeed in defending the trustworthiness of the Scriptures regarding the rest, that is, the more supernatural matters. For there is no reason to suspect that what you discover to be most true always and everywhere in natural and known things will be false in supernatural and less known things.

Moreover, fifth, the truth of supernatural dogmas (at least as far as its possibility and plausibility) should be added to the furthest extent possible from the principles of nature before you undertake to prove the divinity of Scripture.

Sixth and finally, after these things, a response should follow to whatever objections there are against the truth of Scripture.

The divine authority of Scripture is demonstrated by testimonies and seven reasons. XXIII. If by these helps you are able to maintain the universal truth of Scripture, it will be easier next to demonstrate its divinity, first by using testimonies adduced from Scripture itself in support of its own divinity, which, since Scripture's universal truth has already been asserted and maintained, will most powerfully bind an adversary; and second, by using reasons.

The first reason can be drawn from the necessity of some sort of infallible rule that directs us to live for God, which we have asserted by several hypotheses above in §IV.

The second reason is from the necessity for some divine word, from which we gather either that our Scripture is that Word of God or that there is absolutely no word of God in the nature of things. But since the latter is absurd it remains that the former must be asserted. The argument depends on confirming a twofold hypothesis, namely: (1) It is necessary that some written word of God is given. This is proven first from the nature of God, who requires worship and obedience, which can in no way be offered unless both the manner of worshiping and the will to which obedience is due are revealed by God himself. It is also proven from the nature of man, which, since it consists in an immortal soul capable of either eternal felicity or eternal misery, needs to be directed by certain means to avoid the latter and obtain the former. But since these things are hidden from us, they must be revealed by some word of God. (2) Nothing else is or is able to be the Word of God besides our Scripture. On the one hand, this is evident partly from induction, which we mentioned in §IV, and will confirm each in its own place, namely, that neither reason, nor the fathers, nor enthusiasms, nor the Talmud, nor the Qur'an, is the word of God. On the other hand, this is evident partly from reason, because mysteries that are necessary to know for the worship of God and the blessedness of the soul—of which sort are the Holy Trinity, the incarnation, the union of the two natures in the Mediator, regeneration, and so forth—are revealed, and can be revealed, in no other writings.

The third reason is from the nature of the things taught in the Scriptures. These things are such that they could not be delivered by the devil or impious persons because the Scripture's precepts are deadly to them. And these things could not be delivered by angels or honest persons because it does not belong to these to lie and to claim divinity for their own precepts; and therefore, since Scripture everywhere attributes divinity to itself, this indicates that it did not proceed from angels or honest persons. For this reason, there is no conclusion left except that Scripture has its origin from God, and thus it is of divine authority.

The fourth reason is from the nature of the amanuenses, compared with the majesty and sublimity of the truths taught in the Scriptures. For the mysteries of the Scriptures are so great that they exceed the capacity of even the most acute reason, which is evident in the articles concerning the Holy Trinity, original sin, the hypostatic union of the two natures, the redemption of men through the blood of the Son of God, and so forth. They exceed even the induction of the most sagacious philosophers, who, all joined into one with the powers of their talents combined, and aided by so many books as reinforcements, were by no means able to investigate such great mysteries. Nevertheless, these mysteries are seen traced out in Scripture, not just by men, but by men of the lowest sort, that is, shepherds, herdsmen, fishermen, uneducated men having no tinge of erudition, dialectic art, or practical skill in speaking. For all these reasons, it is perfectly certain to conclude that those mysteries were inspired in them by God.

The fifth reason is from divine providence, which offered, as it were, so many plainly extraordinary events as evidence of his approval for the Scriptures, for their writers, and for the doctrine written in them. For whether you consider the miracles that were done in support of Scripture, which we will soon treat expressly, or the manner in which the doctrine contained in the Scriptures was to be disseminated, preserved, and defended by the apostles, you will everywhere encounter the singular and extraordinary watchfulness of divine providence. Consider, namely, (1) the sending of the apostles, whether it argues for the extraordinary providence of God that Christ chose men of the lowest sort, not equipped with any gifts by nature or by learning, and sent them off into the whole wide world to proclaim a certain Jesus crucified in Judea, promising the reward of eternal life for those who received him and the penalty of eternal destruction for those who rejected him, and that what was founded through such means made, in such a short time, so many and such great advancements throughout the whole world. Consider also (2) the preservation of the apostles, whether it argues for an extraordinary providence that though these peaceful and unarmed men were sent out in the midst of rapacious wolves, and likewise though the churches built by them were small and weak, Christ has so powerfully protected them, even to this day, against the attack of nearly the entire world. Additionally, (3) if you observe the quite dreadful judgments that were executed against the persecutors of the doctrine delivered by the apostles, such as Herod, Pilate, Julian the Apostate, and others, would you not recognize the extraordinary providence of God? If, finally, (4) you consider the punishments carried out against the profaners of the teaching of the scriptural commands, will you speak against the extraordinary providence of God? So then, since God has offered, as it were, all these things combined as evidence of his approval of Scripture, and since he does not, and cannot, approve of anything but the truth, will you not then conclude that Scripture is of divine origin and authority, since it everywhere attributes this fact to itself?

The sixth reason is from miracles, by which God has so often proved the truth and divinity of the Scripture. This is so because (1) miracles can be performed, properly speaking, only by God; and (2) God cannot do miracles in support of lies; and yet (3) it is certain that the most marvelous and the greatest number of miracles have been performed in support of Scripture, as is evident from the testimonies both of others concerning Scripture and of Scripture concerning itself. Yet these testimonies to Scripture must not be presented here as divine, so that we might not argue in a circular way, but rather as human, although they are altogether true, based on what we presuppose from the preceding paragraphs. (See also John Cameron, "On the Word of God," *Opera*, vol. 3, pp. 327ff. in the Saumur edition).[114]

---

114. See *Ioh. Cameronis S. Theologiae in academia Salmvriensis nvper professoris, praelectionum*

Finally, the seventh reason is from Scripture's innate marks and characteristics of divinity, for example, its antiquity, perpetuity, authority, the harmony of its parts, the majesty of its humble style, which comes with such great efficacy, the method of its preservation, its prophecies, and other points that are explained in many places by the writers of *Loci Communes*. See, for example, William Perkins's *Cases of Conscience* (II.3),[115] John Cameron's *On the Word of God*,[116] as well as Hugo Grotius's *On the Truth of the Christian Religion*,[117] Juan Luis Vives's *The Truth of the Christian Faith*,[118] Marsilio Ficino's *On the Christian Religion*,[119] and recently, Pierre-Daniel Huet's *An Evangelical Demonstration*.[120] See also, finally, the writings against the pagans by the fathers: Justin,[121] Athenagoras,[122] Tatian,[123]

---

in selectiora quaedam N. T. loca Salmurij habitarum tomus primus-[tertius] (Salmuri: Typis L. Guyoni, sumptibus C. Girardi & D. Lerpinerii, 1626–28), 3:327ff. For the reference in the more ubiquitous volume of his collected works, see *Ioannis Cameronis, Scoto-Britianni Theologi Eximij* ΤΑ ΣΩΖΟΜΕΝΑ *Opera…* (Genevae: Petri Chouët, 1659), 417–94.

115. William Perkins, *Cases of Conscience* (Hanover, 1609), II.3, pp208–36; in English, idem, *The whole treatise of the cases of conscience distinguished into three books* ([Cambridge]: John Legat, 1606), II.3, pp223–50.

116. Cf. n114.

117. For one of several editions perhaps used by van Mastricht, see Hugo Grotius, *De Veritate Religionis Christianae* (Amstelaedami: apud Henricum Wetstenium, 1684). For an English edition see *The Truth of the Christian Religion in Six Books*, 4th ed. by Jean Le Clerc, trans. John Clarke (London: for John and Paul Knapton, 1743). Specifically, note: Book II.viii— "That the Christian Religion exceeds all others" (p. 130); Book II.xviii "The excellency of the Christian Religion proved…from the wonderful propagation of this religion" (pp. 160–63) and "…from the weakness and simplicity of those who taught it in the first Ages" (pp. 165–167); and Book III.i–xvi, which is generally on the authority of the books of the Old and New Testament (pp. 172–208).

118. See the work of Juan Luis Vives (Ioannes Ludovicus Vivus), *Ioannis Lodouici Viues Valentini De veritate fidei christianae libri 5: in quibus de religionis nostrae fundamentis, …exactissime disputantur* (Basileae, 1544).

119. See Marsilio Ficino, *De Religione Christiana & fidei pietate opusculum Xenocrates de morte eodem interprete* (n. p.: Bertholdus Rembolt, 1510) specifically the following chapters: chapter 26, "the authority of the prophets, the nobility of the Old Testament and the excellence of the New Testament," foll. XIV recto – XXIV recto; chapter 27, "the testimony of the prophets concerning Christ," foll. XXV verso – XXXVIII recto; chapter 28, "solutions to doubts about the prophets," foll. XXXVIII recto – XLI verso ; and chapter 35, "the authority of Christian doctrine," foll. XXXV recto – LVIII recto.

120. For an edition contemporary with Mastricht, see Pierre Daniel Huet's work *Demonstratio Evangelica* (Amstelodami: apud Jonsson Waesbergios et Henricum Boom, 1680). The first edition was published in Paris in 1679 after Huet received holy orders in 1676 but before he became the bishop of Soissons (1685–1689).

121. For Justin Martyr's works in Greek and Latin, *PG* 6; in English, *ANF* 1.

122. For Athenagoras's works in Greek and Latin, *PG* 6; in English, *ANF* 2.

123. For Tatian's works in Greek and Latin, *PG* 6; in English *ANF* 2.

Lactantius,[124] Tertullian,[125] Cyprian,[126] Athanasius,[127] Clement of Alexandria,[128] Origen's *Against Celsus*,[129] and also Eusebius's *Proof of the Gospel* and *Preparation for the Gospel*.[130]

Opponents' contrary arguments

Moreover, the arguments that can be produced by the pagans against the truth and divinity of Scripture, from its supposed absurdities, contradictions, and falsehoods, are frequently repeated. Learned men have collected and struck down these arguments in dense volumes—men such as Franciscus Junius in *Sacred Parallels*,[131] Maimonides in *The Guide for the Perplexed*,[132] Manasseh ben Israel in his *Conciliator*,[133] Frédéric Spanheim Jr. in his *Dubia Evangelica*,[134] Michael Walther Jr. in his *Harmony of Scripture*,[135] as well as others, to whom we, for the sake of brevity, refer the reader.

2. Has our Scripture been so corrupted that it was necessary to substitute the Qur'an for it?

XXIV. We have been rather prolix against the pagans, because fewer systematicians are used to arguing with them. The Muslims will be dealt with next.

---

124. For Lactantius's works in Latin, *PL* 6–7; in English, *ANF* 7.

125. For Cyprian's works in Latin, *PL* 4; in English, *ANF* 5.

126. For Tertullian's works in Latin, *PL* 1–2; in English, *ANF* 3–4.

127. For Athanasius's works in Greek and Latin, *PG* 25–28; in English, *NPNF2* 4.

128. For Clement of Alexandria's work in Greek and Latin, *PG* 8–9.

129. For Origen's works in Greek and Latin, *PG* 11–17; in English, *ANF* 9.

130. For an edition contemporary with van Mastricht, see Eusebius, *De demonstratione evangelica libri decem…Quibus accessere nondum hactenus editi…contra Marcellum Ancyrae episcopum libri duo; de ecclesiastica theologia tres : omnia studio R[icardi] M[ontacutii]* (Coloniae, 1688). For more recent editions of Eusebius's works in Greek and Latin, *PG* 19–24; in English, *NPNF2* 1.

131. Franciscus Junius, *Sacrorum Parallelorum libri tres: id est, Comparatio locorum Scripturae Sacrae, qui ex Testamento Vetere in Novo adducuntur…* (Heidelbergae: Hieronymus Commelinus, 1588). Mastricht is more than likely referring to the prefatory letter of this work in which Junius treats of the hostility of Satan and the lies that are often levied against Scripture through atheistic philosophers, see A2v–A5r.

132. See *Rabbi Mosis Majemonidis Liber Moreh Nevukhim Doctor Perplexorum* (Basilae: Ludwig I. König & Johann Jakob Genath [the older], 1629). For a critical English translation of the Arabic, see *The Guide of the Perplexed*, trans. Michael Friedlander (London: George Routledge & Sons, 1956). Mastricht is probably referring to Part II, chs. 32–48.

133. For the Latin edition of the first part (the Pentateuch), see *Menasseh Ben Israel Conciliator, sive De convenientia locorum S. Scripturae, quae pugnare inter se videntur. Opus ex vetustis, & recentioribus omnibus Rabbinis, magna industria, ac fide congestum* (Francofurti, 1633).

134. Frédéric Spanheim Jr., *Dubia Evangelica CCLXXXV in tres partes distributa*, 3 vols. (Geneva: J. A. Chouët & David Ritter, 1700).

135. Michael Walther, Jr. *Harmonia Biblica sive brevis et plana conciliatio locorum veteris et novi testamenti apparenter sibi contradicentium*, 7th ed. (Nürnberg: J. A. Endter, 1665).

Therefore, it is asked whether our Scripture has been corrupted to such an extent that the Qur'an ought to have been either added to it or substituted for it. Muhammad (*Desiderius*, from חמד), an Arab of Mecca, a merchant turned prophet, was about to found his new religion and sect and observed that the foundation of the prophets and apostles would not be suitable to sustain it; indeed, they would cause it to collapse. He did in fact recognize the Scripture of both the Old and the New Testaments, but he increased the number of the books more than was just, counting in total 104, of which ten were attributed to Adam, fifty to Seth, thirty to Enoch, ten to Abraham, the law to Moses, the Psalter to David, the Gospel to Jesus, and the Qur'an to Muhammad. But he added that our Scripture had been egregiously corrupted, either by the Jews or by the Christians, and to such a degree that he considered it necessary to substitute his Qur'an for it, or to add it to it.

Three things we must do at this point
Our entire contention with the Muslims will be wholly concerned with these three things: (1) maintaining that our Scripture is not corrupted, and, with that granted, the rest of their errors will be dispelled without any trouble; (2) teaching that Muhammad should not by any means be considered a true prophet, by which rationale his Qur'an will topple to the ground; and finally, (3) holding that the Qur'an is not divinely inspired writing, but worthless. To accomplish all of these things, we say the following:

1. Scripture has not been corrupted
To begin with the first point, our Scripture has not been corrupted. It will stand firm for as long as they allege the contrary. And we have no need of additional siege engines, beyond what you will add out of the law, the Psalter, and the Gospel, which are the writings that the Muslims prefer to all the rest, to show that our Scripture was untouched: the law forbids anyone from adding or subtracting anything (Deut. 4:2; 12:32), the Psalter states that the law of God is perfect (Ps. 19:7 and elsewhere), and the Gospel condemns every addition as the doctrines of men (Matt. 15:9). If they would insist, on the contrary, that it has not remained so, it is sufficient to reply that it is their burden to prove it, for every man remains innocent until the contrary has been proved. Moreover, if it had been corrupted, it could not have been by the Jews—for how could they, with the Christians resisting them?—or by the Christians—for how could they, with copies disseminated almost boundlessly throughout the entire world? Nor would it by any means have been possible by sects, who were mutually resisting one another. Even our adversaries would be able to produce copies of Scripture

that are purer than ours. I will add, if it were the Christians' intention to corrupt their own Scripture, why would they not have sprinkled in those things that would expressly[136] condemn the Muslim heresy? The Muslims raise two objections above all: (1) They say that the Jews removed from the law the name of Muhammad, the apostle of God, and they say that the Christians erased these words of Christ from the Gospel: "I announce to you the good news that after me will come the apostle and prophet whose name is Muhammad." I respond: Let them say when, where, and by whom—whether Jew or Christian—this was done. Let them note the corrupted book and passage in either the law or the gospel. Let them produce an ancient manuscript that has it in the way they allege. (2) They say that our Scripture has many contradictory, false, and insoluble things, which Ahmad ibn Zayn al-Ābidīn Alawi the Persian enumerates in a book that he calls *The Polisher of the Mirror*. But Filippo Guadagnoli solves all those things in chapter four of his apology, *A Defense of the Christian Religion*.[137]

2. Muhammad is not a true prophet

XXV. Second, that Muhammad was not a true prophet—much less that he should be preferred to Moses and Jesus—is evident from the following: (1) It cannot be proved by those who affirm it. (2) He presented nothing that would argue that he was a prophet, or indeed such an exceptional one. For what mystery did he reveal? What prophecies did he utter? What miracles did he perform? (3) He taught things diametrically contrary to Moses and the undisputed prophets, as is evident from a comparison of Scripture with the Qur'an, and even things diametrically contrary to himself, since the Qur'an says in one place that it was delivered to him by God in heaven, but in another that it was sent to him by the angel Gabriel; in one place that it was composed by God, and in another place that it was composed by men. (4) He was a monster of lust, keeping eleven, or as others say, seventeen wives, in addition to his concubines, and also the most shameful sort of adulterer (cf. Juan Andrés the Moor, *The Confusion of*

---

136. ῥητῶς

137. See Filippo Guadagnoli's work, *Apologia pro Christiana religione, qua respondetur ad objectiones Ahmed filii Zin Alabedin, in libro inscr. Politor Speculi* (Romae: Typis Sacra Congregatio de Propaganda Fide, 1632). The 1637 edition is entitled *R. P. Philippi Guadagnoli, Clericorum Reg. Minorum pro Christiana religione responsio ad objectiones Ahmed filii Zin Alabedin, Persae Asphahanensis…* (Romae: Typis Sacra Congregatio de Propaganda Fide, 1637). For another response to Ahmad ibn Zayn al-Ābidīn [Alawi], see Bonaventura Malvasia's *Dilucidatio speculi verum monstrantis, in qua instruitur in Fide Christiana Hamet, filius Zin Elabedin in regno Persarum princeps; et refellitur Liber a Doctoribus Persis editus sub titulo, Politor speculi verum monstrantis* (Romae: Typis Sacra Congregatio de Propaganda Fide, 1628).

Muhammad's Sect, ch. 7),[138] and likewise the cruelest sort of plunderer and, what is more, a perpetrator of plunderings against his own people (Qur'an 19; 71ff.). While he lived he was frequently considered, even by his own people, an idiot, a fanatic, and a demoniac, which he often complained about (Qur'an 31; 35; 38; etc.). He was the most shameful imposter, contriving visions of angels, conversations with them, and so forth. Now, what if his own should plead for him that nevertheless he had communion with God, as Moses did, and with the blessed angels, such as Gabriel, and therefore he was blessed with revelations, which is especially fitting and proper for prophets? I respond: (1) Thus it falls back on them to prove their claim. (2) What if his very own wife Khadija chided him on this account (which, we heard recently, she did more than once), that these revelations were nothing except diabolical promptings and delusions, frenzies, and deadly bile? What if the common people testified to the same things, a fact that he often complains about (Qur'an 21; 35; 38; 51; etc.)? What if Christians also testified to them? How will his followers effectively blunt these accusations, especially when his teaching on the majority of the evangelical mysteries diametrically opposes Moses and Christ, who were without a doubt true prophets (as we will hear more fully in its own place)? And finally, who will grant to such a man as we have described the ability to have dealings with the most holy Deity, with the blessed angels, and with divine revelations?

3. The Qur'an is not a divine writing

XXVI. But also, third, we should proceed to the Qur'an itself. At this point it is asked whether that writing is divine, and whether it surpasses the law of Moses and the gospel of Christ in authority? *Al-Qur'ān* (אלקוראן), where אל is the article ὁ or τὸ, for which reason some call it *Qur'an*, which means "a reading," or "a collection," that is, of precepts; or, as others prefer, "a correction," that is, of the Old and New Testaments. Among the Muslims it is called *Al-Furqan*,[139] (from פרק, "he divided"), what you might call "a volume of distinctions." It

---

138. For a recent facsimile edition with critical notes on the 1543 Italian edition (first edition 1537) of Juan Andrés's work in multiple languages, see *Confusión o confutación de la secta Mahomética y del Alcorán. Opera Chiamata. Confusione della setta*, 2 vols., ed. Elisa Ruiz Garcia (Merida: Regional de Extremadura, 2003). For the Utrecht edition of the Latin translation, with an endorsement by the Utrecht theologian G. Voetius, see *Confusio sectae Mohametanae: Liber a Iohanne Andrea…nunc autem interpretatione latine expositus a Iohanne Lauterbach…* (Trajecti ad Rhenum, 1646). For an English translation, see Johannes Andreas, *The Confusion of Muhamed's Sect, or a Confutation of the Turkish Alcoran. Being a discovery of many secret policies and practices in that religion, not till now revealed*, trans. Joshua Notstock (London: for H. Blunden at the Castle in Cornhill, 1652).

139. Cf. J. Andreas, *Confusio*, 28.

consists of 114 chapters, and in Latin translations, 124, which the Muslims call "suras." In these suras it contains, as it were, good things mixed in with the bad. Muhammad acknowledges God, his worship, his creation, his providence, condemns idolatry, and so forth. He added circumcision, a fast in the month of Ramadan, five prayers, and pilgrimages to the temple at Mecca. He prohibits eating blood, animals that are found dead, and pork. He declares himself to be a prophet and apostle, greater than Moses and the son of Mary (see Hottinger, *History of the Orient*, II.3).[140] He disagrees with Christians about most things: about Scripture, the Trinity, and Christ the Son of God, about various created things, the world, angels, heaven, and so forth; washings, oaths, polygamy and divorce, the prohibition of wine, and on and on. Now concerning this Qur'an, it is disputed whether it is a writing of divine origin and authority. Christians deny this; Muslims affirm it. So then (1) they are compelled to prove it; (2) it has for its author the greatest rogue that ever walked on two feet; (3) it does not show the characteristics of divine origin that we designated in §XXIII; and (4) it is everywhere repugnant to the law, the Psalter, and the Gospel. Nor is there anything that Muslims can say in favor of the Qur'an, except that it originates from God, through the ministry of Gabriel, but they only say it, they do not prove it. If anyone is eager to see more regarding Islam, let him go to Johannes Hoornbeeck in his *Summa Controversiarum* (in the chapter on Islam),[141] Juan Andrés the Moor in his *Confusion of Muhammad's Sect*,[142] Filippo Guadagnoli in his *Defense of the Christian Religion against the Polisher of the Mirror of Achmed Alabedin*, and in various others.[143]

With the Jews it is asked: 1. Has the oral law been given
in addition to the written law?
XXVII. From here we proceed to the Jews, with whom we have four points of controversy. The first concerns the oral law, or שבעל פה.[144] At this point it is asked whether Moses on Mount Sinai, in addition to the law that was written

---

140. See Johann Heinrich Hottinger, *Historia Orientalis quae ex variis orientalium monumentis collecta, agit de muhammedanismo…de saracenismo…de chaldaismo…de statu christianorum & judaeorum tempore orti & nati Muhammedismi* (Zürich: J. J. Bodmerus, 1651). Cf. "De Muhammedismo" in J. H. Hottinger, *Historiae ecclesiasticae novi testamenti seculum X, pars II* (Zürich: J. H. Hamberg, 1651), 2:89–119.

141. J. Hoornbeeck, *Summa controversiarum Religionis cum infidelibus, haereticis, schismaticis, id est, Gentilibus, Iudaeis, Muhammedanis, Papistis, Anabaptistis, Enthusiastis, et Libertinis* (Colberg: Joannes Kwicel, 1676), 2:62–70.

142. See n137.

143. For Guadagnoli, see n141.

144. Lit., *that is upon the mouth*, i.e., oral.

or that was to be written, also received a law that was to be propagated only by a living voice. Among the Jews, the Pharisees sought an oral law of this kind since they did not find any defense for their limitless superstitions in the written law. The Sadducees did oppose them, rejecting those traditions, as did the Essenes and Samaritans, but by that opposition they rejected the entirety of Scripture, except perhaps for the law of Moses. Moreover, the Karaites or Scripturalists among them flatly denied an oral law.

Arguments

At least on this head, the Reformed join with the Karaites principally for the following reasons: (1) It is incumbent upon the Pharisees who affirm the oral law to prove it. (2) On the sacred page nothing is seen regarding such a second law being received, or regarding an oral tradition, propagated by tradition up to the time of the Talmudists. (3) If the written law was once lost (2 Kings 22–23), how much more should that oral law have passed away? Or, if the oral law is preserved, how could the written law have been lost? And if there was an oral law, Moses both wrote it and was ordered to write it (Ex. 24:3–4; 34:27; Deut. 31:9, 24). Joshua follows Moses in writing: "and he wrote there upon the stones a copy of the law[145] that Moses had written in the presence of the children of Israel" (Josh. 8:32), undoubtedly the same law that God commended to him (Josh. 1:7–8; cf. 2 Kings 17:13, with v. 37; 2 Chron. 17:9). (4) The written law of Moses is perfect in all its parts (Ps. 19:7; Deut. 4:1–2; 12:32; Prov. 30:5–6), to such an extent that there is nothing necessary to believe for salvation that is not contained in the written law. Therefore, the oral law is superfluous. (5) God demands from us an observance of the written law only, never of an unwritten law (cf. Deut. 11:32; 10:12–13 with 28:1; Josh. 1:7–8; 2 Kings 14:6; 2 Chron. 25:4). (6) Add here also that this oral law, as it was subsequently written down (as they hold) in the Talmud, is in many places contrary to the law of Scripture, as we shall observe shortly in §XXVIII.

Objections

They do not, however, labor any less to promote their oral law, even with arguments from the written law, which in other respects they force beneath the oral law since they judge it to be more obscure and to need the help of the oral law for its interpretation.

---

145. משנה תורה, δευτέρωσιν legis

1. They allege, first, the text of Exodus 34:27: "Write for yourselves these words, for על פי, according to, these words I have fixed my covenant with Israel." They say that here you see the twofold law: written (כתב) and oral, that is, "according to the mouth" (על פי). From these words they argue in this way in the Gemara, Gittin 5 and Temura 11 (see also Mannaseh Ben Israel in *Conciliator* on Exodus, question 50).[146] I respond: (1) Let them prove that על פי is the same as פה תורה שבעל[147] and also that על פי denotes anything other than "according to," as in Leviticus 27:8, 18; Proverbs 22:6; and other places. (2) "According to these words" should be referred to the words to be written, not to some kind of different or oral law. (3) Their argument presupposes that the divine covenant was entered into not according to the written law, but according to an oral law, which Scripture speaks against everywhere.

2. Second, they allege the text of Exodus 24:12: "And so I will give you stone tablets, and this law, and the commandment which I have written, for teaching them," which in b. Berakot 5a, they interpret in this way: "and I will give you stone tablets," that is, the ten commandments, that is, Holy Scripture; "and the commandment," that is, the Mishnah; "which I have written," namely, the Prophets and the Writings; "for teaching them these things," that is, the Gemara. By this we are taught that all these things were given to Moses on Mount Sinai. Rabbis Solomon ben Isaac (Yarchi), Aben Ezra, and Maimonides say the same. I respond: (1) All these things must not be asserted as if from on high, but they must be demonstrated with care. For where in the entire holy Instrument is the term *commandment* understood to mean the Mishnah, and also the Gemara? That term generally denotes whatever God commands. (2) Moreover, it must be proven that here "commandment"[148] and "law"[149] express two different things, even though the copulative "and"[150] is able to be explanatory,[151] as it frequently is in Scripture. But (3) it expressly says in the text, "the precept which I *have written*." How therefore can it denote the *oral* law? Compare the previous passage with 2 Kings 17:34–35.

---

146. Menasseh ben Israel, *Conciliator sive de convenientia locorum S. Scripturae, quae pugnare inter se videntur* (Amsterdam, 1633), 168–78.

147. The Oral Law

148. מצוה

149. תורה

150. ו

151. ἐξηγητική

3. Moreover, third, Manasseh ben Israel, in his *Conciliator* on Exodus, question 50, alleges that Exodus 18:16 must be compared with Deuteronomy 17:8–11, and from these gathers that all passages in the written law are not always exactly clear, and thus an interpretation must be established, and this is to be done from the oral law.[152] I respond, the claim that the passages in the written law are not equally clear, and also that an interpretation of the law is sometimes necessary, are not the issues we are debating.[153] But that the interpretation of more obscure passages must be made from some kind of oral law, the texts do not say, nor does Manasseh prove, since a more obscure passage is able to be clarified from other clearer passages in the written law.

4. And with this one principle carefully observed, the fourth objection also falls to the ground. The same Manasseh in the same chapter makes this objection from reason, that in many written laws there is frequently something lacking or excessive, and therefore the oral law is necessary to supplement them. Of course, these things do not evince that the oral law is necessary, but only that interpretation is necessary, which can be made sufficiently from the other written laws compared among themselves.

2. Does the Talmud have divine authority?

XXVIII. They separate the oral law into the Talmud and the kabbalah, which we will treat individually. Concerning the Talmud, it is asked whether the Jewish Talmud has a divine origin and authority. *Talmud*, from למד ("to teach"), denotes teaching or a book for teaching, or the sum of Jewish teaching revealed by God to Moses on Mount Sinai in order to be propagated only by a living voice. But on account of the harshness of the times, because the Jews were dispersing, it was rendered into written books. Now, they have a twofold Talmud, the Jerusalem Talmud and the Babylonian Talmud. The Jerusalem Talmud, also known as the Mishnah,[154] originated around AD 140 with Rabbi Judah HaKadosh ("The Holy One") as its author,[155] and this they separate into six *sedarim*, that is, orders and chief heads. After several years, Rabbi Yochanan augmented these *mishnayot*[156] to a remarkable degree, and from this, the Jerusalem Talmud was

---

152. Manasseh ben Israel, *Conciliator, sive de convenientia locorum S. Scripturae, quae pugnatur inter se videntur*, 177.

153. *non sunt* κρινόμενα *probanda*

154. משנה

155. Rabbi Yehuda HaKadosh (b. circa 135 A.D.) is also commonly known as Rabbeinu HaKadosh (our Holy Rabbi) or as Rabbi Yehuda haNasi (Judah the prince).

156. משניות, "teachings," plural of Mishna

born. Now, because it was rather obscure and difficult, Rabbi Ashi supplemented it with several books and expositions around AD 427. Finally, in 500 it was brought to its conclusion, and now the Jews are not permitted to add or subtract anything. And this at last is the whole Babylonian Talmud, in two parts, namely, the *mishnayot*,[157] in which is the text, as it were, and the Gemara, in which there are disputations, commentaries, and a supplement. It is divided into six orders, each order into different books, and each book into its own chapters. Concerning this Talmud, we were just now asking whether it has a divine origin and authority. The Pharisees with their followers affirm that it does. The Sadducees, Samaritans, and Essenes, whom the Christians join, cry out against it. They usually do so for these reasons: (1) It is incumbent upon the Jews who affirm it to prove it. (2) There is no oral law that differs from the written law delivered by God to Moses (see the preceding section). (3) It bears no form of law, much less of a divine law. For it presents the various and disagreeing opinions of the schools and their masters, Hillel and Shammai, and their disputations over them. Laws, especially divine laws, do not customarily present themselves in this way. (4) The Jew cannot present anything in favor of the authority of the Talmud that likewise the Muslim could not present for his own Qur'an. If a Jew should say that the Talmud was delivered to Moses by God, likewise the Muslim may assert that the Qur'an was delivered to its own prophet through the agency of Gabriel. (5) Since, as the Jews admit, it originated by a private impulse, and not by any specific divine commandment or prompting, accordingly it is not a God-breathed[158] writing. (6) It is evident by induction that neither Rabbi Yehuda Hannasi (Judah HaKadosh), the author of the *mishnayot*, nor Rabbi Yochanan, the author of the Jerusalem Talmud, nor Rabbi Ashi, the author of the Babylonian Talmud, were divinely inspired,[159] as even the Jews themselves testify. (7) It was not only by a private impulse, but also a depraved and perverse one, that they committed the oral law to writing, since it is contrary to the prohibition of Moses and the prophets, which even the Jews themselves assert. (8) It contains many absurdities, falsehoods, and wicked things, injurious to God, men, and the truth. Likewise, it contains a great many things fabulous, unbecoming, and unspeakable, just as Christians have pointed out in reliable commentaries, such as Pietro Galatino, *On the Secret Things of Catholic Truth* (bk. 1);[160] Sixtus

---

157. משניות

158. θεόπνευστον

159. θεόπνευστοι

160. See book 1, "The Talmud and matters pertaining to it" in Pietro Galatino, *Petri Galatini de arcanis catholicae veritatis libri XII* (Frankfurt: J. G. Seyler, 1672), coll. 1–38.

of Siena, *Bibliotheca Sancta* (bk. 2);[161] Theodoricus Hackspan, in his work against that of Rabbi Yom Tov Lipmann Muelhausen (ch. 1, p. 260ff.);[162] Viktor von Karben, a Jewish convert, *Judenbüchlein* (bk. 1, ch. 9–10);[163] and Marquardus de Susannis, *Treatise on Jews and Other Infidels* (pt. 3, ch. 1).[164] (9) Together with us, the Karaites, the Sadducees, and others reject the Talmud. The arguments in favor of the Talmud coincide with those concerning the oral law, which we vanquished above.

3. Does the kabbalah have divine authority?

XXIX. Our third controversy with the Jews concerns the kabbalah. *Kabbalah*, according to the Jews, sometimes denotes the whole oral law, at other times, the mystical sense of Scripture. Ordinarily, however, it denotes that doctrine which consists principally in the permutation of the letters by temurah, as they call it, or in the arithmetic computation of the same by gematria, and in the forma-tion of different words from individual letters through notariqon. In addition, the Jews include in total thirteen remaining methods or rules beyond those we just mentioned. For a specific treatment of them all, see Hoornbeeck's work against the Jews (bk. 1, ch. 2).[165] As to its origin, as Reuchlin testifies, there are many among the Jews who state that Adam learned kabbalah from Raziel, Abraham from Zadkiel, Isaac from Raphael, Jacob from Peliel, that is, from spirits who were the teachers of these patriarchs. It is commonly believed that Moses received it from God on Mount Sinai in the oral law. They divide it into contemplative and practical kabbalah. They principally place the former in the permutation and arithmetic power of letters. For example, from the fact that in the first verse of Genesis the letter א appears six times, they conclude that the world will endure for six thousand years. The latter they set in magical productions, which magic they say is now forbidden to them. Now it is asked

---

161. See Sixtus of Sienna, *Bibliotheca Sancta*, 2nd ed. (Köln: Maternus Cholinus: 1576).

162. Hackman's work begins at page 215 in Yom Tov Lipman Muelhausen, Theodoricus Hackspan, *Liber Nizachon Rabbi Lipmanni conscriptus…oppositus Christianis, Sadducaeis, atque aliis…Theodorico Hackspan…tractatus de usu librorum Rabbinicorum prodromus apologiae pro Christianis adversus Lipmannum triumphantem* (Nürnberg: Wolfgang Endter, 1644), 260–92.

163. *Contra Jud. Lib. 1 capp.* 9–10: see Viktor von Karben, *Hyerinne würt gelesen, Wie Herr Victor von Carben, welcher ein Rabi der Juden gewesst ist, zů Christlichem glaubem kommen. Weiter findet man darinnen ein köstliche disputatz eines gelerten Christen, und eines gelerten Juden* (1550), fol. Biiii recto – Bv verso.

164. Marquardus de Susannis, *Tractatus de Judaeis & aliis infidelibus* ([Venice], 1558), 85v–130r.

165. *apud Hoornbekium contr. Jud. lib. 1, c. 2.* However, there are no works with precisely this title. The most probable candidate is Johannes Hoornbeeck, *Tesuvah Jehuda: sive, pro convincendis et convertendis judaeis libro octo* (Leiden: Petrus Leffen, 1655), 1.2.89–111. Book 1 in *Tesuvah Iehuda* addresses questions of Scripture and bk. 1, ch. 2 specifically addresses the kabbalah.

whether this doctrine has divine origin and authority. The Jews affirm that it does, the Christians deny it, usually with these arguments: (1) The Jews cannot by any means prove that it belongs to the law delivered to Moses. (2) Its rules can be used just as well to produce and confirm things that are improper, false, and impious. (3) It ought to be examined by Scripture, which the Jews concede, and for this reason it is not credible in itself.[166] (4) An *ad hominem*: Christians have proved most of the heads of the Christian faith using kabbalah, and to such an extent that Count Giovanni Pico della Mirandola asserted that there was no knowledge that makes us more certain about the divinity of Christ than kabbalah.[167] So argues Johann Capnion (or Reuchlin); Archangelo da Burgonuovo, in his new commentary on the dogmas of the kabbalists;[168] and Jacques Gaffarel, *The Secret Mysteries of Occult Kabbalah*,[169] and in a peculiar book, Elchanan Paulus of Prague, a Jewish convert, which he entitled *Mysterium Kabbalae*.[170] And so most, if not all, the heads of Christianity are able to be demonstrated by kabbalah.[171] The Jewish objections on this point plainly coincide with those by which they contend for their oral law.

4. Does the New Testament have divine authority?

XXX. Therefore, the last and chief controversy between us and the Jews is concerning the gospel, or the New Testament, and whether it is God-breathed[172] and has infallible truth and divine authority in the same way as the Old Testament. Here indeed the Anabaptists strike violently at the Old Testament since they suppose it to be abrogated because now we are no longer under the law. The Socinians do the same since they depreciate the Old Testament and think that it is nearly useless to read because the religion of the Old Testament in its very essence differs from the religion of the New Testament. However, all who

---

166. αὐτόπιστος

167. Giovanni Pico della Mirandola, *Omnia Opera* (Basel, 1557); idem, *Conclusiones nongentae: Le novecento tesi dell' anno 1486*, ed. Albano Biondi (Florence: Olschki, 1995). Cf. idem, *Cabalistarum selectiora obscurioraque dogmata...et ab Archangelo Burgonovensi...nunc...interpretationibus illustrata* (1569).

168. See n162.

169. Jacques Gaffarel, *Abdita divinae Cabalae mysteria, contra Sophistarum logomachiam defensio* (Paris: Jerome Blageart, 1625).

170. Elchanan Paulus, *Mysterium Novum Ein new herrlich vnd gründtlich beweisz aus den Prophetischen Schrifften/ nach der Hebreer Cabala daß...Jesus Christus warhafftig sey der verheissene Messias* (Vienna: Micheael Apffel, 1582).

171. See Johann Reuchlin, *De arte cabalistica libri tres* (N.p.: Thomas Anshelmus, 1517); idem, *On the Art of Kabbalah*, trans. M. & S. Goodman (Lincoln, Neb.: University of Nebraska Press, 1973).

172. θεόπνευστον

profess Christ admit that the Old and New Testament have the same truth. On the other hand, the Jews rise up against the New Testament with pure hatred for the Messiah, our Jesus, and the gospel, by not receiving its truth or divine authority. The Reformed state that the New Testament has the same truth and authority as the Old Testament. In this disagreement stands the hinge of all the other controversies with the Jews, and also the pillar and buttress[173] of the whole of Christianity. For this reason, using a reliable method, we must here contend to force the Jews to admit the universal truth of the New Testament, and then its divine authority. And so first we demonstrate its truth in five ways. First, we use the same arguments that the Jews used to demonstrate the truth of the Old Testament. Second, we appeal to the trustworthiness[174] of the writers, inasmuch as: (1) They were eyewitnesses[175] in regard to the matters narrated concerning Christ (John 19:35; 1 John 1:1–4; Acts 4:20), just like the writers of the Old Testament. (2) There was not one witness, not two or three (Deut. 17:6), but twelve, in fact more than five hundred believers (1 Cor. 15:6–8), while in the event of Elijah ascending into heaven the Jews believe (and rightly so) the one witness of Elisha. (3) There was no sufficient reason for them to lie—whether for honors or for wealth and other benefits—as is evident through the many dangers, losses, hostile pursuits, false accusations, poverty, and any other things to which they were liable. (4) They did not refrain from narrating their own faults (Luke 18:34; 22:24; Matt. 16:22). (5) While they were narrating the events, a great many people were still alive who were present for the events narrated, who had seen and heard Jesus, and who knew most of the things about Christ very well. (6) They add to their accounts the circumstances of the places, times, and feasts in which things were done, and in these circumstances they do not disagree, although they often lived at quite a distance from one another. (7) They do not recount things that occurred here or there in some secret corner, but rather what was done in full view of all people, in the presence of their very enemies. (8) They sealed their accounts with unbearable torments and cruel death (2 Cor. 4:8–9; 11:24–26; 1 Cor. 4:9–12). And given all these things, how could writers such as these not be truthful and trustworthy?[176] Third, we demonstrate the truth of the New Testament by the truth of the matters written in it. This truth is proven on the one hand by their universal and most accurate agreement with the writings of the Old Testament, which are undoubtedly

---

173. στύλος καὶ ἑδραίωμα, 1 Tim. 3:15
174. ἀξιοπιστία
175. αὐτόπται
176. ἀξιόπιστοι

God-breathed,[177] and on the other hand by their very makeup: all their contents agree and are in harmony (1) with each other, with such accuracy, although they are so different with respect to both their places and their times; (2) with the nature of the things they describe; (3) with any other true history, whether Jewish or Gentile, as commentators will show particularly on each matter; and in fact (4) with the Jews themselves, inasmuch as some have proven that the great majority of Old Testament passages cited in the New Testament had been expounded in the very same sense by the ancient Jews. Recently Joseph de Voisin has shown this in his *Proemium* to *Martin Raymund's Dagger of Faith*.[178] Fourth, moreover, that the more principal heads of the New Testament are clearly prominent in the Old Testament, can be demonstrated, and in fact has been demonstrated from the Old Testament. Fifth, I add also that enemies of the New Testament— both present and past—have not by solid arguments ever convicted it of any falsity. But surely any document remains true as long as it is not solidly convicted of falsity.

Our eleven arguments for the divine authority of the New Testament
XXXI. With truth of the New Testament presupposed from these arguments, it is time to continue on to its divine origin and authority, and we will wrench admission of this out of the Jews by these and other devices:[179] (1) The testimony of the New Testament itself concerning its own divinity (1 Thess. 2:13; 2 Peter 1:19; 2 Tim. 3:16). And so that you do not say that 2 Timothy 3:16 only has regard to the writings of the Old Testament, consider 2 Peter 3:16: "just as also the rest of the Scriptures." This testimony, with the New Testament's universal truth presupposed from the preceding demonstrations, is most powerfully binding. (2) All those arguments that a Jew would use to demonstrate the divinity of the Old Testament. (3) In the New Testament God speaks, just as he did in the Old (Heb. 1:1)—the Father (Matt. 3:17; 17:5), the Son (John 14:24; Rev. 1:8), and the Holy Spirit (Rev. 2:29). For this reason Paul says that he had been called not by men, but by Jesus Christ (Gal. 1:1; 1 Thess. 2:13). Also, (4) the doctrine of the New Testament, which not only exactly agrees with, but also, as to its chief point, is the same as the Old Testament. For this reason Paul, though he had proclaimed the whole counsel of God (Acts 20:27),

---

177. θεοπνεύστοις

178. See Voisin's substantial "Proemium" in Martin Raymund and Joseph de Voisin, *Raymundi Martini ordinis praedicatorum pugio fidei adversus Mauros et Judaeos cum observationibus Josephi de Voisin* (Frankfurt: Johann Wittigau, 1687), 6–190.

179. *quam Judaeis extorquebimus, his aliisque fidiculis. A fidiculum* is an ancient instrument of torture, similar to a rack. E.g. Suetonius, *Lives*, Tib. 62.2, Cal. 33.1.

says that he had said nothing beyond the Old Testament (Acts 26:22); and Christ and the apostles eagerly invoke the Old Testament (Luke 4:20–21; John 1:23; 5:39; Matt. 22:32, 44; Rom. 9:10–11; Heb. 1:5–6; etc.). For this reason, (5) the teaching of the New Testament, which is perfectly true and just as holy as that of the Old Testament, inculcates the observance of all the precepts of the Decalogue, and of spiritual duties, the denial of the self, the endurance of the cross, the mortification of sins, the crucifixion of the flesh and of depraved affections, heavenly behavior, the knowledge, love, and worship of God, and so forth. A writing of this sort, by the judgment of all, even of the Jews, must be divine. (6) The miracles, by which God shows his approval of the New Testament, are plainly divine (Matt. 10:8; Mark 16:17–18; Heb. 2:4), and are the type of miracles that were to be done by the Messiah (Isa. 35:4–6), which were never done under the Old Testament (John 9:32), which in regard to every kind of creature in heaven and on earth, and for the entire human race, were never harmful and always advantageous, miracles such as feeding, healing, raising the dead, and so forth. (7) Prophecies (Matt. 21:45; Luke 19:43; 21:25; Matt. 24:8; 2 Thess. 2:4; and the entire book of Revelation), for true prophecies are indubitable signs of divinity (Isa. 46:9–10; 41:22–23; Deut. 13). (8) The martyrdoms of the apostles and of all kinds of other men, by which the truth of the doctrine of the New Testament has been sealed (2 Cor. 4:8–9; 11:24–26; 1 Cor. 4:9–13; Acts 7), especially during the first three centuries of Christianity, when myriads of Christians of every kind sealed the teaching of the New Testament with their own blood. And why did these things happen, except because the Holy Spirit desired to give, with particular power, testimony to the doctrine of the New Testament? And if such testimonies do not persuade the Jews when it comes to the martyrdoms of the Christians, then neither should they persuade them when it comes to the martyrdoms of the Jews under Antiochus Ephiphanes. (9) The effectiveness with which, through the apostles and evangelists, who were uneducated, the doctrine of the New Testament was disseminated into nearly the entire world. Compare what we have observed concerning this matter in §XXIII. Additionally, (10) the divine providence, by which God so powerfully protected the doctrine of the New Testament and those who professed it against the attack of the most powerful persons throughout nearly the whole world. The Jews argue in defense of the Old Testament that the same thing happened under the Babylonian devastation and under the negligence of the Israelites (2 Kings 22–23). Why should we not argue the same point even more? Especially if we consider that the New Testament was preserved through three hundred years of the direst persecution, persecution of a kind that the Jews never endured, especially under Emperor Diocletian, who worked in every way to hunt down and burn the books of the Christians. And if we also consider that it has been translated into nearly every language, and that it has not been corrupted despite so many frauds of heretics. Finally, (11) because the style of the New Testament has such great simplicity, such great effectiveness, that it can so powerfully penetrate into human hearts and gently draw them to faith and godliness (1 Cor. 1:17; 2:4; 4:19–20). Gerson offers an outstanding example of this from his own experience as a Christian converted from being a Jew, in the preface of his book on the Talmud.[180]

Objections of the Jews

If they would object, first, that almost all our arguments rest on nothing but the credibility[181] and the authority of the New Testament, which is the very point we are trying to prove,[182] then we will respond: (1) By all means we rest on the credibility of the New Testament, but we proved that true just moments ago by many arguments. (2) The Jews, moreover, could not prove the teaching and miracles of the Old Testament in any way other than by the credibility of the Old Testament. (3) Neither can we, or do we usually, proceed in any other way in these sorts of questions of fact. They object, second, against the miracles of the New Testament, that Simon Magus also, and Apollonius of Tyana, and the papal monks, boast of many miracles. I respond: (1) Do the apostles, therefore, also boast? Surely not the prophets of the Old Testament as well? (2) They boast, but in a way and manner as different as earth and heaven. The former do so with a tenuous credibility, as many have shown; the latter do so with proper credibility, as truthful authors, as we have demonstrated at length. The former performed their miracles almost as far away as in India, or in other far-off places, or at the least with no witnesses, somewhere in a corner; the latter performed theirs in the sight of all the people, and even the most hostile enemies, who contradicted not one part. If they allege, third, against the martyrdoms of Christians who died for the teaching of the New Testament, that many went to their death on account of their evildoing, due to weariness of this life, or for some other cause, men, for example, like Erastrotes, Cajanus, and others,[183] I respond: (1) They

---

180. Christian Gerson, *Juden Thalmud Fürnembster inhalt und Widerlegung in zwey Bücher verfasset im ersten wird die ganze Jüdische Religion und falsche Gottsdienste beschrieben im andern werden dieselbe bendes durch die Schrift des Alten Testaments und des Thalmuds selbst gründlich widerlege* (N.p.: Goslar bey Johann Vogt, 1607), foll. aii recto – cv recto.

181. *fides*

182. *ipsum hujus loci* κρινόμενον

183. Cf. Johannes Müller, *Jüdaismus oder Jüdenthumb, das ist ausführlicher Bericht, von des Jüdischen Volcks Unglauben Blindheit und Verstockung* (Hamburg: Zacharias Hartels, 1707), 1045.

were imposters, the worst sort of persons. Were the apostles, who were truthful and godly men, therefore also imposters? Were the prophets therefore also imposters—Jeremiah, Isaiah, Daniel, and others, whoever has endured his own hardships? (2) Whatever those imposters endured, they nevertheless did not endure it for a doctrine, and certainly not for a doctrine of the kind that agrees with the writings of the prophets, as did the apostles and so many Christians. Finally, fourth, they raise many objections against individual passages of the New Testament to convict it of error and untruth. For us to prove the truth of these individually would be a nearly infinite task and is altogether disconnected from our present business. Those who write against the Jews and those who interpret the Scriptures have performed this task in many places. Yet generally we say: (1) No difficulty can be advanced by any Jew against the apostles and the Scripture of the New Testament, against which we could not show something similar that is an equal, or even a greater difficulty, for the prophets and Scripture of the Old Testament. Thus the Jews are not able to brandish against us any apparent contradiction[184] without us being able to retort against them the same, and indeed much more strongly. (2) They will not bring up any difficulty against the New Testament that has not already been previously brought up by others and that has not also been more than sufficiently solved by Christians. See, for example, Spanheim in *Dubia Evanglica*, Johannes Müller in *Judenthumb* (bk. 2, ch. 28; bk. 3, ch. 2), Nicholas of Lyra in his *Response to the Objections of the Jews*, and in his other works.[185]

Other objections

XXXII. In addition, various objections are raised by various Jews. Notable among them is Rabbi Isaac ben Abraham, who published a whole book in which he is totally absorbed with surveying the untruth and ungodliness of the New Testament, and most of all with proving, from the New Testament itself, the falsehood of the deity of Christ, the virginity of Mary, the genealogy of Christ from the family of David, likewise Christ's teaching, miracles, prophecies, holiness of life, and likewise the New Testament's citations of the Old. Against

---

184. ἐναντιοφανές

185. Frédéric Spanheim Jr., *Dubia Evanglica CCLXXXV in tres partes distributa*, 3 vols. (Geneva: J. A. Chouët & David Ritter, 1700); Johannes Müller, *Judaismus oder Judenthumb, das ist: ausführlicher Bericht von des jüdischen Volckes Unglauben, Blindheit und Verstockung, darinne sie wider die prophetischen Weissagungen...straiten* (Hamburg: Hertel, 1644); regarding what Mastricht calls *Responsione ad object. Judaeorum*, Nicholas of Lyra had several quodlibetals on Judaism which were compiled and circulated under various names in manuscript and printed form, for example, Nicholas of Lyra, *Quaestiones disputatae contra Judaeos* (Paris: Michel Le Noir, 1496).

these things, those who write against the Jews have solidly responded in their own places. The Portuguese Rabbi, in his *Colloquium Middelburgense*, adds a great amount of this stuff, which Johannes Müller most solidly quashed in his own *Judenthumb*.[186] This rabbi in particular personally attacks the authors of the New Testament, saying that (1) they were insane persons and drunkards (Acts 2); (2) they were sluggards who advocated for having all goods in common so that they might sustain their life from the goods of others; (3) they lied about the miracles; (4) they did not prohibit lying; (5) they had their own errors in their doctrine and life; and so forth. I respond: (1) All these and similar things are utterly false, never to be proven. (2) Similar things were also hurled against the prophets (Jer. 5:13; 2 Kings 9:11; 1 Kings 18:17; 22:24; Dan. 6:12). And (3) though they have been accused, they have never been convicted. (4) They have strenuously and solidly cleared themselves from blame. We have opened up this controversy a little more fully than the previous one, because it shows not only the basis of our conflicts with the Jews, but also the basis of all Christian faith and godliness.

Do believers possess inspirations from the Holy Spirit?
XXXIII. Now let us admit the army of pseudo-Christians into the arena. First the enthusiasts present themselves, with whom we dispute whether believers now, after the canon has been sealed, possess enthusiasms,[187] or inspirations, of the Holy Spirit. These inspirations are to them the most certain word of God, to which one must submit just as much, if not in fact more, than to the Scriptures. The Pelagians and Socinians, to the exent that they give more consideration to nature, reason, and free will, attribute less than what is right to the Holy Spirit and think that his illumination is not necessary for understanding the Scriptures. At the other extreme, the enthusiasts such as Valentin Weigelius, Caspar Schwenckfeld, and David Joris attribute more than what is right to the operations of the Holy Spirit. Indeed, they acknowledge that Scripture is the Word of God, but it is not to be understood except according to the breathings or the inspirations of their Spirit, a certain sort of internal word, as it were. The Reformed acknowledge that in the patriarchs, prophets, and apostles, there were true enthusiasms,[188] and that in ordinary believers there are indeed operations of the Holy Spirit that illuminate, convert, and sanctify, but there are

---

186. Cf. Müller, *Jüdenthum*, 42. The *Colloquium Middelburgense*, attributed to R. Jacob Judah Aryeh Leon Templo, is a manuscript work that may no longer be extant.

187. ἐνθουσιασμοῖς

188. ἐνθουσιασμούς

no enthusiasms, no inspirations, in the sense of the infallible direction of the Holy Spirit, which has now been removed from all men. This heresy is refuted by a destruction of this twofold false hypothesis: First, they claim that Scripture is not a complete and sufficient rule of faith and morals in itself. For if Scripture's sufficiency[189] stands, enthusiasm falls on its own. Now, its sufficiency stands by those things that we have said in favor of the perfection of Scripture in §XIX above, and by the things we will say below in favor of the same against the papists. Second, they claim that even now enthusiasms or infallible revelations of the Spirit are given, which are different from the scriptural enthusiasms, and with the help of which the Scriptures must be interpreted. However, the sacred page does not know of such revelations; indeed, it even rejects them, since it is perfect, and sufficient of itself in every respect; and it pronounces that they are joined with the most pressing danger of seduction (2 Cor. 11:14; 2 Thess. 2:2; 1 John 4:1–2). Those things that could be produced in favor of these sorts of enthusiasms are mainly (1) that Scripture is called a dead letter (2 Cor. 3:6), that is, it is dead without the interpretation of their own private Spirit. I respond that this is not spoken about Scripture, but about the covenant of works, in contradistinction to the covenant of grace. (2) There are passages that speak of revelation and of the illumination of the Holy Spirit. I respond that those passages are not speaking about the kind of enthusiasms that direct infallibly and that reveal other objects to us, different from those things—indeed, even contrary to those things—that Scripture holds, but rather, those that bring light to the intellect, so that we might be able to discern and distinguish the things revealed in the Scriptures (Eph. 1:17–18). Consider also Frédéric Spanheim Jr.'s *Syntagma of Theological Disputations* (pt. 2, disps. 16–20),[190] Philips of Marnix of St. Aldegonde's *Against the Enthusiasts*,[191] and Calvin against the same.[192]

---

189. αὐταρκείᾳ

190. *Disp. Miscell. Part. 1 Disp. XVI – XX.*: The correct citation is Frédéric Spanheim, Jr, *Friderici Spanhemii disputationum theologicarum syntagma | Disputationum theologicarum miscellenearum pars secundae quae celebres aliquot anti-anabaptisticas controversias complectitur* (Geneva: Chouët, 1652), 2:281–317.

191. *Contra Enthusiast.*: Mastricht broadly references a wide-ranging, multifaceted work. For example, for Marnix's primary controversies with the enthusiasts (*geestdrijvers*) on how they test doctrine by private spirits (pt. 1, ch. 1); on means and the power of God's Word (pt. 2, chs. 6–8); see Philips of Marnix of St. Aldegonde, *Ondersoeckinge ende grondelijcke wederlegginge der geestdrijuische leere* (The Hague: Aelbrecht Heyndrickszoon, 1595), 10 verso – 13 recto, 39 verso – 55 recto.

192. See John Calvin, *Institutes of the Christian Religion*, ed. J. T. McNeill, trans. F. L. Battles (Louisville, Ky.: Westminster John Knox Press, 1960), 1.9.1–3; for the Latin, *Ioannis Calvini opera quae supersunt omnia*, ed. Edouard Cunitz et al. (Brunsvigae: C.A. Schwetschke, 1863–1900), 2:69–72; for the 1560 French edition, *Calvini opera*, 3:110–13.

Is human reason the infallible norm of interpreting Scripture?

XXXIV. Let the Socinians come next after the enthusiasts in the army of pseudo-Christians. It is asked whether human reason is the infallible norm of expounding the Scriptures. Here the papists sin in defect when, in order to raise the authority of the pope, they axiomatically refer the infallible norm partly to the church, that is, the pope, and partly to the fathers, the counsels, and so forth. We will examine the papists elsewhere. The Lutherans of the past also sinned in defect. When it came to the matters of the communication of attributes and of the omnipresence of Christ's flesh, in order more boldly to oppose our arguments made from reason, they proceeded to postulate that reason should not be listened to in the mysteries of religion, and then, furthermore, that in the same mysteries, reason is contrary to the Scriptures. We will examine the Lutherans elsewhere. The Socinians sin in excess, who, since they have hardly anything from Scripture that they might oppose to the mysteries of the Christian faith—such as the Trinity, the deity of Christ, the personal union of the natures in Christ—strive against them more boldly with reasons. Thus, they effectively set up reason as the infallible norm of expounding the Scriptures. Moreover, a certain *Exercitator Paradoxus* also sins in excess.[193] In order to adapt the principles and hypotheses of Cartesian philosophy to theology and the Scriptures, he says that we have innate ideas of all things, which in accordance with this assertion are like oracles, and likewise that clear and distinct perception is the supreme rule of all truth. For this reason, in his dense *Exercitatio* he maintains that philosophy is the infallible interpreter of Scripture. On entirely the same hypotheses, the rationalist theologians who have recently arisen among us suppose that the divine authority of Scripture itself cannot be demonstrated from any other source than from reason, and if a conflict seems to exist between Scripture and reason, then reason must be listened to rather than Scripture. The Reformed think about reason as an instrument, as an argument, and as a norm and principle.[194] As an instrument, they state that its use is necessary in every inquiry of truth, even of

---

193. Lodewijk Meyer (1638–1681) is credited as the author of an anonymous work entitled *Philosophia S. Scripturae Interpres; Exercitatio Paradoxa in qua veram philosophiam infallibilem S. Literas interpretandi normam esse, apodictice demonstratur, & discrepantes ab hac sententiae expenduntur ac refelluntur* (Eleutheropolis [Amsterdam], 1666). In English, *Philosophy as the Interpreter of Holy Scripture*, trans. Samuel Shirley (Milwaukee: Marquette University Press, 2005). In this context, an *exercitatio* is a written form of a disputation that was not orally defended before an academic body, but went straight to print. Mastricht refers to the author as the *Exercitator Paradoxus* from the subtitle of this work, and takes issue with him throughout his own responses to various strands of Cartesianism in Petrus van Mastricht, *Novitatum cartesianarum Gangraena* (Amsterdam: Jansson, 1677).

194. *principium*

that which is occupied with Scripture. As an argument, they state that its use is helpful, namely, so that the truth derived from Scripture, as from its own first and unique principle, we may also confirm with natural reasons. But as a norm and principle of truth on account of which something is believed, they by no means admit it. And thus, if there seems to be a fight between Scripture and nature, they choose to yield, not to the latter, but to the former. The Reformed present their case mainly with these eight reasons: (1) Reason is blind (1 Cor. 2:14–15), darkened (John 1:5), deceptive and inconstant (Rom. 1:21ff.), and finally, imperfect (cf. Rom. 1:19 with 1 Cor. 2:12)—and the nature of a norm or principle rejects such things. (2) The heads of religion transcend reason because they are mysteries (1 Tim. 3:16; Matt. 13:11; 1 Cor. 2:7; 4:1), paradoxes (Luke 5:26), and spiritual things (1 Cor. 2:14). (3) If reason were a norm or principle, then Scripture and the Holy Spirit would be subject to reason and to man, which is contrary to the dignity of Scripture and the Holy Spirit, as well as to Christ's way of thinking (John 5:30, 34). (4) Christ, the prophets, and the apostles never refer us back to reason but always to Scripture (Isa. 8:20; 2 Peter 1:19; 2 Tim. 3:14). (5) Scripture speaks against reason in many places (2 Cor. 10:5; 1 Cor. 1:17, 19–22; 2:1, 4–6). (6) If reason were a norm, then the final arbiter of our faith would be, not so much Scripture, but rather reason, all of which is contrary to Scripture (2 Peter 1:20). (7) Thus reason would be prior, more esteemed, and more certain than Scripture (2 Peter 1:20). (8) Finally, in this way the Christian religion would depend on reason, and that state of affairs is contrary to Scripture (Matt. 16:17; 1 Cor. 2:7–8; John 1:18). From the things the Reformed have already conceded, one will be able to satisfy the objections to the contrary without difficulty. For if they allege (1) that without reason Scripture could not be understood, we will answer that, without reason as an instrument, we admit this to be the case. For brutes and senseless people cannot understand the Scriptures. From this, however, it is not also then concluded that reason is a norm or principle. If they allege (2) that the truth of nature is not contrary to the truth that is in Scripture, I respond that, at the same time, it does not follow from this that reason is the norm of Scripture. And if at any time there seems to be a conflict between reason and Scripture, Scripture ought not to yield to reason, but rather reason to Scripture. If they allege (3) that the marks of divinity, from which the divinity of Scripture is demonstrated, belong to the province of reason, I respond that those marks belong to Scripture itself, so that Scripture is recognized as divine of itself, not from reason, just as the sun is recognized by its very own light, and not from another source (see Johannes Hoornbeeck, *Socinianism Refuted*, bk. 1, ch. 6;[195] compare also Nicolaus Vedel, *Rationale Theologicum*[196] and those who have written against the *Exercitatio Paradoxa*).

*Is the Old Testament now abrogated or less necessary to read
than the New Testament?*

XXXV. It is asked whether the Old Testament is now abrogated, or at least less necessary and useful to read than the New Testament. On this point, the Jews sin in defect by completely repudiating the New Testament. We have already vanquished them. The Manichees sin in excess by rejecting the Old Testament as if it had originated from an evil principle. And the Anabaptists suppose that the Old Testament has now been abrogated, inasmuch as we are said not to be under the law but under grace, by which they confuse the law with the Old Testament. The Socinians state that the religion of the Old Testament is different in its entire essence from the religion of the New Testament in that men were saved during the Old Testament by the observance of the law, while we are saved by the observance of the gospel. And so they hold the opinion that it is not necessary to read the Old Testament, or at least it is less useful. On the contrary, we Reformed state that the divine authority of both Testaments is the same even under the New Testament, and so we also state that the Old Testament is as necessary and useful to read as the New Testament. Our reasons are as follows: (1) The books of the Old Testament are divinely inspired[197] to the same degree as the New Testament ("all Scripture,"[198] 2 Tim. 3:16; 2 Peter 1:20–21) and thus also infallible in their truth and authority. (2) The Old Testament is given to the church as the rule of faith and morals, just as the New Testament is (Ps. 147:19–20; Rom. 3:2; 9:4). (3) There is no place in the New Testament where we read that the Old Testament has been abrogated. We read instead that it was (4) confirmed by Christ, both by precept (John 5:39; Matt. 5:17–18) and by practice (Luke 24:27) whenever he refers us back to the Old Testament (Luke 16:29). In addition, he is constantly refuting his adversaries from the Old Testament (Matt. 4:7; 19:3–5; 12:3–4; 22:29–43).

---

195. See "An ratio humana sit judex controversiarum theologicarum?" in Johannes Hoornbeeck, *Socinianismus Confutatus*, 3 vols. in 2 tomes (Amsterdam; Utrecht: Johannes a Waesberg, 1650–1662), 1:86–130.

196. Nicolas Vedelius, *Rationale theologicum seu de necessitate et vero usu principiorum rationis ac Philosophiae in controversiis theologiae...oppositi sophisticae ultimorum temporum* (Geneva: Jacob Chouët, 1628).

197. θεόπνευστοι

198. πᾶσα γραφή

The same is done by the apostles, by Peter (Acts 3:20–22), by Paul (Acts 18:28), and so forth. (5) The whole teaching of the New Testament is contained in the Old. In Acts 26:22, Paul declares that he has said nothing beyond the Old Testament. This is the case to such a degree that the Bereans examined the teaching of the New Testament from the Old Testament (Acts 17:11). Indeed, all the prophets are said to bear witness to Jesus (Acts 10:43; Luke 24:27). (6) Even more, certain heads of our faith are shown more clearly and copiously in the Old Testament than in the New Testament, for example, the creation of the world, the fall of humanity, and so forth. (7) The Old Testament is called the foundation of the faith, and of the Christian church (Eph. 2:20; Acts 24:14). (8) The Old Testament has a diverse and powerful usefulness even now under the New Testament (2 Tim. 3:15–17; Rom. 15:4).

Objections

XXXVI. Whatever objections the Anabaptists have they borrow from the Socinians. (1) If they allege that the Old Testament has been abrogated, then that is what they should prove, and not construct their argument from passages that say that the law has been abrogated, unless they demonstrate that the terms *law* and *Old Testament* have equivalent force. Furthermore, we readily grant that the ceremonial law was abrogated by the death of Christ, while at the same time we deny that the Old Testament books have been abrogated, until they prove it. (2) If they say that whatever comprises religion and salvation is sufficiently contained in the New Testament, let them prove the consequent—namely, that the Old Testament is therefore abrogated—seeing that God wanted us to see whatever comprises religion and salvation not only sufficiently, but also abundantly. For he could have displayed all such things in a single book, but he did not. (3) If they say that the New Testament is contrary to the Old Testament on the points in Matthew 5 concerning the sword, murder, retaliation, and oath-taking, and on divorce in Matthew 19, we respond that according to Christ's judgment the Pharisaical corruptions are contrary to the Old Testament, just as they are to the New, but that neither the Old Testament nor the law of Moses is contrary to the New Testament and to Christ. (4) If the Socinians should say that the religion of the Old Testament in its entire essence is different from the religion of the New Testament, we will deny it from what has been said, and above all, from Acts 15:11 (cf. Hoornbeeck, *Socinianism Refuted*, bk. 1, ch. 4;[199]

---

199. *contr. Soc.*: see "An sub Novo Testamento, Veteris Testamenti lectio non sit necessaria, magnique adeo momenti?" in Hoornbeeck, *Socinianismi Confutati*, 1:56–65.

Abraham à Doreslaer, *A Clear Demonstration*, ch. 8;[200] and Spanheim, *Syntagma of Theological Disputations*, pt. 1, disps. 2–5).[201]

With the papists it is disputed: Does the authority of Scripture depend on the church?

XXXVII. Bringing up the rear are the papists, with whom we have various controversies concerning the Scriptures. In all of these controversies, or at least most of them, the source of their primary error[202] is either in the absolute rule of the pope, or in the doctrine of transubstantiation. Therefore, it is first asked whether the divine authority of Scripture depends on the testimony of the church. The enthusiasts, whom we have already repulsed, make Scripture's authority depend on the dictates of one's private Spirit. The Socinians and rationalists, whom we have likewise just now examined, make it depend on reason. The papists, in order to elevate the authority of the pope above the Scripture, acknowledge that the authority of Scripture considered in itself depends on the fact that it is inspired by God, but that the authority of Scripture considered in respect to us depends on the testimony of the church, that is, the pope. The Reformed, however, make the authority of Scripture in every way depend on Scripture itself, and on the divine brilliance that is clearly seen in it. Our arguments against the papists are mainly these: (1) The authority of Scripture depends on its author alone, for it is a testimony, the authority of which customarily depends on the veracity of the one testifying. (2) The authority of Scripture is credible in itself[203] and trustworthy,[204] and it is also the first article of faith[205] (2 Peter 1:20, "knowing this first of all, that no prophecy of Scripture comes from someone's own interpretation").[206] For this reason David, from those very testimonies, says that he acknowledged that God had established them forever (Ps. 119:152). (3) The authority of Scripture is sufficiently grasped from the marks of divinity innate in it, as we taught against the pagans above. (4) The very authority of the church, even in respect to us, depends on the testimony of Scripture. For

---

200. *Advers. Anabapt.*: see "van 't geschreven Woordt Gods" in Abraham à Doreslaer, *Grondige ende klare vertooninghe van het onderscheydt in de voornaemste hooftstucken der Christelijcker religie: tusschen de Gereformeerde ende de Weder-dooperen...uyt ordre ende last des Noordt-Hollandtschen synodi ghemaeckt ende uyt-geghevhen*, 2nd ed. (Enchuysen: Albert Wesselsz Kluppel, 1649), 113–29.

201. Spanheim, *Disputationum theologicarum syntagma*, 1:5–30.

202. πρῶτον ψεῦδος: for errors in reasoning built on a previously accepted false premise or "first falsehood," see Aristotle, *Prior Analytics* 2.18.

203. αὐτόπιστος

204. ἀξιόπιστος

205. *primum credibile*

206. τοῦτο πρῶτον γινόσκοντες etc.

this reason our adversaries customarily demonstrate the authority of the church from the Scriptures. Thus it would be the most absurd sort of circular reasoning if the authority of Scripture in some way is made to depend on the church. (5) It would follow from their argument that our faith would not so much rest on the foundation of the prophets and apostles (Eph. 2:20), as on the testimony of the church. (6) Experience cries out in protest, since there are myriads of people who recognize the authority of Scripture, who meanwhile do not recognize the authority of the Roman church.

Objections

XXXVIII. They object: (1) The church is called the "pillar and buttress of the truth" (1 Tim. 3:15). I respond that the church has been built upon the foundation of the prophets and the apostles (Eph. 2:20), unless you prefer to say with John Cameron that the apostle indicates that it is not so much the "church" (1 Tim. 3:15) as the "mystery of godliness" (v. 16) that is the foundation and pillar of the truth. (2) Without the tradition of the church, the Scriptures would not have come down to us, nor would we know that the Scriptures had been written by those whose names they bear, and so forth, except by the testimony of the church. I respond that from this we by no means deduce that Scripture borrows its own authority from the church, just as the official letter of a king by no means receives its authority from the clerk who presents it. (3) The church was prior to Scripture. I respond that priority of time does not imply a priority of dignity, and even much less a dependency of authority. Compare especially William Whitaker, *A Disputation on Holy Scripture;*[207] William Ames, *On the Circular Argument of the Papists;*[208] and Gisbertus Voetius, *Disputation on the skepticism of Loyola's followers concerning the principles of the faith.*[209]

---

207. William Whitaker, *Disputatio de sacra scriptura contra huius temporis papistas, inprimis Robertum Bellarminum Jesuitam… & Thomam Stapletonum… sex quaestionibus proposita & tractata a Guilelmo Whitakero* ([Cambridge]: Christopher Corvinus, 1588). For an English translation, see idem, *A Disputation on Holy Scripture against the Papists, especially Bellarmine and Stapleton* (Cambridge: Cambridge University Press, 1849).

208. This work is a posthumous collection of orations, disputations, and minor works written and perhaps delivered on various occasions in Ames's life. The part of this work that Mastricht probably has in view is the "Fides vera et conscientia bona non nisi in Scriptura acquiescent" in William Ames, *Guil. Amesii disceptatio scholastica de circulo pontificio* (Amsterdam: Johannes Jansson, 1644), 6–23.

209. See "Novus scepticismus Lojolisticus circa principia fidei Christianae" in Gijsbert Voet (Voetius), *Gisbertii Voetii… selectarum disputationum theologicarum,* 5 vols. (1648–1669), 1:108–114.

Should the books that we call the Apocrypha be numbered
with the canonical books?

XXXIX. Our second controversy with the papists concerns the number of books to which this divine authority applies, that is, whether those that we call the Apocrypha, such as Tobit, Judith, and so forth, are to be added to the canonical books. This we deny by the reasons set forth above in §IX. The papists would invest supreme authority in the church on the basis of the power of canonizing books, which they attribute to their own Pope Innocent I (who lived at the beginning of the fifth century), inasmuch as he was the first to put the holy canon into this order. They affirm that those apocryphal books are canonical, for generally no other reasons than the following: (1) They are frequently cited by the fathers. I respond that this also happens with books undoubtedly apocryphal. (2) They are also quite frequently called canonical by the fathers. I respond that it is in an improper, more general, and broader sense that these books, which are read in the church for edification, are called canonical (see Augustine, *City of God*, bk. 15, ch. 23; bk. 18, ch. 35; *Against Gaudentius*, bk. 1, ch. 31; *On Christian Doctrine*, bk. 2, ch. 8;[210] cf. William Whitaker;[211] Daniel Chamier;[212] William Ames, *Bellarmine Enervated*;[213] etc.). (3) They were delivered into the catalogue of canonical books by Pope Innocent I, and that catalogue was then handed down to the Council of Trent. I respond: (1) Our canon was sealed by the apostle John (Rev. 22:18–19), and (2) the Jewish church, to whom the Old Testament canon was given, never received those books as canonical. (3) Pope Innocent did not have the power to change the canon sealed by the apostle.

---

210. *August. de Civitate Dei lib. xv. cap. 23 & xviii cap. 35 Lib. 2 Contr. Epist. Gaudent. cap. xxiii de Doct. Christ. cap. viii.*: Mastricht's original referent, *Contra Gaud.*, is non-existent and the reference in *On Christian Doctrine* is incomplete; instead see the plausible correction for the former and the expansion of the latter: Augustine, *City of God* 15.23 PL 41:468–71, NPNF1 2:305; *Contra Gaudentium* 1.31.38 PL 43:729–30; *On Christian Doctrine* 2.8.12–13 PL 34:40–41, NPNF1 2:538–39.

211. See Question 1, chapter 4, "Wherein the argument of the adversaries is proposed and confuted" and chapter 5 "Wherein reasons are alleged against the books of the second kind," in William Whitaker, *A Disputation on Holy Scripture*, 39–49, 49–54.

212. See "de canone...de differentia canonorum & apocryphorum" in Daniel Chamier, *Danielis Chamieri Delphinatis Panstratiae catholicae sive controversiarum de religione adversus pontificios corpus*, 4 vols. (Geneva: Roveriani, 1626), 1:91–105. Also, there was a subsequent *supplementum tomi quarti* and volume 5, Daniel Chamier, *Danielis Chamieri panstratia catholica completa sive controversiarum de religione adversus pontificios corpus supplementum tomi quarti et tomus quintus de ecclesia* (Geneva: 1626).

213. William Ames, *Bellarminus Enervatus sive disputationes anti-Bellarminae*, 4 vols. (Amsterdam: Johannes Jansson, 1630), 1.1.2 (pp. 6–17).

Are any non-original editions authentic?

XL. It is asked whether the editions of the Scriptures not written in Hebrew (in the case of the Old Testament) and not written in Greek (in the case of the New Testament) are authentic. Isaac Vossius, either due to an itch to innovate, or because he has wrongly persuaded himself that the chronologies of the patriarchs according to the seventy Greek translators[214] more closely correspond with the truth than those in the Hebrew edition, has stated that the Hebrew edition, as it flowed forth from its authors, altogether perished during the Babylonian captivity, or during the time of Antiochus Epiphanes, with the exception that genuine copies of it were still available to the seventy translators. Whatever the case, it has since that time completely passed away. For these reasons, he holds the opinion that the Greek edition, translated by the seventy from the untouched and pure sources, must be preferred to the corrupt sources.[215] Jean Morin stated the same in his *Exercitationes Biblicae*.[216] The papists separate into factions. For among them are those who prefer the original edition to the Latin Vulgate, such as Benito Arias Montano,[217] Santes Pagnino,[218] Siméon

---

214. I.e., of the Septuagint edition.

215. Mastricht is summarizing the preface and chapters one and two in Vossius, *Isaaci Vossii de septuaginta interpretibus eorumque tralatione & chronologia dissertationes* (The Hague: Adrian Vlacq, 1661, 1689), 1–240.

216. This reference could intend several different chapters, but *exercitatio III* is devoted to the questions of the Hebrew codex and the integrity of the Septuagint, see Jean Morin (Johannes Morinus) C.O., *Exercitationes biblicae de hebraei graecique textus sinceritate, germana LXXII…pars prior* (Paris: Anton Vitray, 1633), 121–55. Posthumously, a compilation of Morin's various topical *exercitationes* combined several previously separated works into two books. Thus the relevant disputations cited by Mastricht are included in the first part of the second book: the *alter de hebraei gracique textus sinceritate*. NB: there is an independent pagination of the two works; first on the origin of the patriarchs and papal primacy, and second, the two-part work on the Greek and Hebrew texts. See item, *Ioannis Morini…exercitationes ecclesiasticae et biblicae, primae quae est de patriarcharum et primatum origine…alterius de hebraei graecique textus sinceritate similiter libri duo* (Paris: Gaspar Meturas, 1669), bk. 2, part 1, exerc. 3, pp. 61–79.

217. For the 1571 Antwerp Polyglot, which is also known as *Biblia Regia* or the Plantin Polyglot, see Benito Arias Montano (Benedictus Arias Montanus), *Biblia Sacra Hebraice, Chaldaice, Graece & Latine…Pietate et studio ad sacrosanctae ecclesiae usum*, 8 vols. (Antwerp: Christopher Plantin, 1568–1573). In a single volume interlinear Hebrew and Latin bible, Montanus also has a prefatory letter, "In Latinam ex Hebraica veritate veritatis testamenti interpretationem," in *Hebraicorum Bibliorum veteris testamenti Latina interpretatio, opera olim Xantis Pagnini Lucensis, nunc vero Benedicti Ariae Montani…* (Antwerp: Christopher Plantin, 1572), fol. †2 recto – †4 recto.

218. See the preface to the reader, which also begins with an allusion to 2 Tim. 3:16–17, in Santes Pagnino (Xantes Pagninus), *Biblia… & librum de interpretamentis hebraicorum, arameorum, graecorumque nominum, sacris in literis contentorum* ([Lyons]: Antonius du Ry, 1528), foll. d iiii recto – [d vi] verso.

Marotte de Muis,[219] François Vatable,[220] and others, whom their fellow papists call Hebraizers. Others maintain that the Vulgate is of equal authority with the originals. Generally, after the decree of the Council of Trent canonizing the Vulgate, the Vulgate is preferred to the sources, not only so that they might more conveniently claim that the sources are corrupted, but even more, so that by the use of one, common Latin language, the members of the church might be more conveniently unified, both among themselves, and with their head, and that by this means, the pope may more effectively exercise his dominion. The Reformed recognize that the Scriptures are authentic only in the original languages. We have asserted the reasons for our opinion in §X above. For the opinion of the papists, Bellarmine enumerates these five reasons in the first general controversy on Scripture (bk. 2, ch. 10),[221] namely: (1) The Vulgate is approved by its long use through the ages. I respond that from this its usefulness is indeed proved, but not its authenticity. (2) It has the testimony of the ancients. I respond that the ancients do not testify that it is authentic in the same way as the Greek and Hebrew sources. (3) The Hebrews had authentic Scripture in their own language, and the Greeks, in Greek, and so also the Latins, in Latin. I respond that for this same reason the Germans should have it in German, and the English, in English, and so forth. Moreover, this is a question about translations. And in that regard, the Hebrews did not have an authentic translation, nor the Greeks, and so then neither did the Latins. (4) If this were so, the church would have been poorly provided for, since in its councils there were either very few, or sometimes none, who knew Hebrew. I respond: Let them impute this to themselves, and to their own ignorance, not to the providence of God.

---

219. See the posthumous compilation of Muis's works in a controversy between Muis and Morinus on the role of the Hebrew text, entitled *Triplex Assertio veritatis hebraica adversus exercitationes Ioannis Morini* in Siméon Marotte de Muis, *Opera Omnia in duos tomos distributa* (Paris: Mathurinus & Joannes Henault, 1650), 2:129–258. In their original form, the works by Muis on this point are: item, *Assertio veritatis Hebraicae adversus exercitationes ecclesiasticas* (Paris: Joannes Libert, 1631); item, *Assertio Hebraicae veritatis altera* (Paris: Joannes Libert, 1634); *Castigatio animadversionum M. Ioannis Morini…sive, Hebraicae veritatis assertio tertia* (Paris: Guillelmus Pelé, 1639).

220. Besides François Vatable's many commentaries on various books of Scripture, select annotations were included in editions of Robert Estienne's (Stephanus) Bible, for example, *Biblia sacra, cum…annotationibus* (Paris: Robert Estienne, 1545).

221. *de S. Script. lib. 2 cap. 10.*: See "de auctoritate Latinae editionis vulgatae" in Robert Bellarmine, *Ven. Cardinalis Roberti Bellarmini politiani S. J., Opera Omnia ex editione veneta, pluribus tum additis tum correctis iterum*, 12 vols. (Paris: L. Vivès, 1870–1891), 1:138–41; idem, *Disputationes de controversiis Christianae fidei* (Ingolstadt: Adam Sartorius, 1601), 1:114–19. For an English translation, see the relevant section in Robert Cardinal Bellarmine, *Controversies of the Christian Faith*, trans. K. Baker (Saddle River, N.J.: Keep the Faith, 2016).

Furthermore, such councils are incapable of recognizing the authentic editions. (5) The heretics forge translations that are so diverse, and that differ so much among themselves, that nothing certain can be found in them. I respond: Is the Vulgate translation therefore authentic? Augustine tells us that prior to Jerome there were innumerable Latin editions (*On Christian Doctrine*, bk. 2, ch. 11).

Are the Hebrew and Greek sources corrupted? Arguments

XLI. From that point, it is asked whether the Hebrew and Greek sources are corrupted. The Muslims assert that the Scriptures are corrupted so that they might conveniently add their own Qur'an to the Scriptures, or substitute it for them. The papists state that the sources are corrupted so that they might not only more conveniently substitute the Vulgate in the place of the sources, but also so that they might maintain that Scripture is not a complete canon, and thus that traditions are necessary in addition to it, and that moreover, the supreme authority in the church rests in the hands of the pope, who is able to judge infallibly concerning the sense of Scripture and current controversies. We deny this for the following reasons: (1) It seems to be contrary to the providence of God. When he watches over everything for us, even down to the hairs on our head, would he not have watched over the ground of our faith and salvation (Eph. 2:20)? (2) This is contrary to the testimony of Scripture (Matt. 5:18; Luke 16:29). (3) The authority of Scripture would, by this very reason, fall to the ground, since it rests upon the sources, according to those things we have said above in §X. (4) Neither the Hebrew of the Old Testament, nor the Greek of the New Testament has been corrupted. Therefore, none of it has been corrupted. The former has not been corrupted, since, on the one hand, the Jews were far too superstitious about it to do so, as is evident from the Masorah, from the testimonies of Philo (*Concerning the departure of the Children of Israel from Egypt*),[222] of Josephus (*Against Apion*, bk. 1), and of Eusebius (*History*, bk. 3, ch. 10 and *Preparation for the Gospel*, ch. 2), from the integrity of the prophecies about Christ, and from the fact that Christ and the apostles never charge the Jews with this fault. On the other hand, much less would the Christians have desired to corrupt the Old Testament, since they were too scrupulous to do so. Nor, even if they had especially desired to do so, could they have, because of the abundance of copies that were scattered about, because of the different sects, and because of the great population of Jews around them. Thus the text

---

222. This currently non-extant work of Philo was commonly cited in the early modern period, generally indirectly through what was known as Eusebius of Caesarea's *Praeparatio Evangelica* | Προπαρασκευὴ Εὐαγγελική, 8.2, see PG 21:600–602.

was corrupted by no one, and therefore it stands uncorrupted. Neither has the Greek of the New Testament been corrupted, for as with the Old Testament, such corruption is against the wisdom and goodness of God. It is also against the vigilance that the pious doctors of the church had against corruptions. In that vigilance they most carefully corrected the distortions introduced by their adversaries.

Objections

XLII. First, certain objections distinctly fight, first, against the integrity of the Hebrew of the Old Testament. Here Bellarmine, in his first general controversy on Scripture (bk. 2, ch. 10), amasses many passages that he considered corrupted, but those who write against him refute this and vindicate the individual passages he cites (cf. Ames's *Bellarminus Enervatus*).[223] Second, they fight against the purity of the Greek of the New Testament, which they say has been corrupted, either by heretics or by copyists, which they strive to prove by several claims: (1) They say the codices are distorted. I respond that certain ones are distorted, but not all of them. Hence for this reason not the New Testament, but this or that edition of it, is rightly called corrupted. (2) They point to the variety of textual readings. I respond that no corruption can be inferred from this either, except the corruption of certain codices, which can be removed with help from the most ancient and accepted codices (see François Luc de Bruges in the preface to *A Pamphlet of Notes on the Various Readings that Occur in the Gospels*).[224] (3) They point to the eagerness of heretics to pervert the Scriptures. I respond that the attempt to corrupt does not always imply success, since of course this is opposed by the godliness of the doctors of the church and their diligence in protecting the sources. (4) They also present examples of the corrupted Greek text, from Bellarmine in his first general controversy on Scripture (bk. 2, ch. 7).[225] I respond that against him his opponents take their stand as the most careful defenders of these passages.

---

223. Cf. *Opera Omnia*, 1:188–93; item, *Disputationes de controversiis*, 1:114–19; William Ames, *Bellarminus Enervatus*, 1:17–38.

224. Mastricht's reference could indicate at least two different, but similar works: first, there is the more widely disseminated: "Notarum ad varias lectiones in quatuor Evangeliis occurrentes, Libellus duplex, quorum uno Graecae, altero Latinae varietates explicantur" in François Luc de Bruges, *In sacrosancta IV Iesu Christi evangelia Francisci Lucae Brugensis…Commentarius*, 4 vols. (Antwerp: 1606–1616), 2:1019–119, especially 2:1024. Second there is the "prefatio" in François Luc de Bruges, *Notationes in Biblia Sacra quibus variantia discrepantibus exemplaribus loca, summo studio discutiuntur* (Antwerp: Christopher Plantin, 1580), 16–20.

225. Bellarmine, *Opera Omnia*, 1:132–133; idem, *Disputationes de controversiis*, 1:105–107.

Should Scripture be translated into the vernacular languages?

XLIII. It is asked whether Scripture ought to be translated into the vernacular languages. Protestants affirm this, chiefly for these reasons: (1) God himself composed the Scriptures in the vernacular languages of the church: Hebrew, Aramaic, and Greek. (2) The reading of the Scriptures is required of all believers without exception (John 5:39), as we will soon prove; therefore, they should be translated. (3) The use and enjoyment of Scripture—for example, edification, consolation, exhortation, the glorification of God, and so forth (2 Tim. 3:16–17)—is for everyone; therefore, it ought to be translated. (4) Divine worship ought to be conducted in ordinary languages (1 Cor. 14); therefore Scripture ought to be translated, since divine worship cannot be conducted without it. (5) The Scripture of the Old Testament church was translated into common languages, as the Aramaic paraphrase, Origen's *Hexapla* and *Octapla*, and others show.

The reasons of the papists

XLIV. The papists deny that the Scriptures are to be translated into the vernacular languages. They do this, on the one hand, more effectively to prevent the common people from reading the Scriptures, so that their own errors, idolatries, and superstitions should not offend the eyes of the common people too powerfully, and, on the other hand, so that by the use of only the Latin Vulgate the Romanists might cleave more closely to their head, and that head might rule his members more effectively. They generally give these petty little reasons: (1) It is sufficient that the Scriptures are extant in those three languages in which the placard[226] on the cross of Christ was written (John 19:20). I respond that this connection is trifling. (2) From the time of Ezra up to the time of Christ, the Old Testament was not extant in the vernacular language because the use of Hebrew at that time had already fallen from memory. I respond that both claims are false, for even to this very day among the Jews the Hebrew language is most familiar. (3) The apostles preached throughout the whole world, and yet they did not translate the Scriptures into the languages of those nations. I respond: it is doubtful this was so afterward; they never prohibited it beforehand. Moreover, they could not translate them for lack of time; and perhaps they did not desire to do so, so that multiple authentic editions would not exist and so that quarrels would not be sown in the church due to questions over the authority of the editions. (4) It is conducive for the unity of the church and the communication of the churches, that the Scriptures are published in the most common language, namely, Latin. I respond: agreed, but not in Latin only, and not as the only

---

226. ἐπιγραφή

authentic translation. Furthermore, this unity and communion of the churches can be sufficiently preserved by a single authentic Hebrew and Greek edition. (5) Scripture in the common languages would be to no purpose because it would still not be understood. I respond that we deny both claims with Deuteronomy 31:11. Moreover, (6) in every age the vernacular languages change. I respond, not so much that they cannot be understood, especially those whose use continues unbroken. Moreover, why not also change the translations themselves in such a small way? (7) It is contrary to the majesty of Scripture that it would be extant in the common languages. I respond, not so.

Should Scripture be read by the common people?

XLV. It is asked whether the Scripture, translated into the common languages, ought to be read by the common people. The orthodox affirm that it should for these reasons: (1) God commands it (Deut. 6:6–8; 30:11–12; Isa. 34:16; John 5:39; Luke 16:29; Col. 3:16; 4:16; 1 Thess. 5:27). (2) The reading of Scripture was familiar to the Israelite church (Acts 15:21; 8:30; 17:2). (3) God especially approves of such reading (Ps. 1:2; 119:2; Acts 17:2; 2 Peter 1:19; Rev. 1:3). (4) The use and enjoyment of the Scriptures is for all people without distinction (Rom. 15:4; John 20:31; 2 Tim. 3:16–17).

Objections

The papists deny this so that the common people would not notice that their doctrine is of the lowest quality and so that they would more willingly depend on the dominion of the pope. Their reasons are: (1) Certain people pervert Scripture to their own destruction (2 Peter 3:16). I respond that this is not due to a fault in reading, but a fault in themselves. (2) The Scriptures everywhere narrate sins that could easily present a stumbling block to the more ignorant sorts of people. I respond that this happens only incidentally, by a fault in the readers, not in Scripture or in its reading.

Is Scripture obscure?

XLVI. It is asked whether Scripture is obscure. Protestants deny this, in the sense, and for the reasons, already presented in §XVIII. The papists affirm this, not only more effectively to drive away the common people from reading the Scriptures, but also to maintain the necessity of some sort of interpreter—and indeed an infallible one—and to confer that dignity upon the pope,[227]

---

227. Latin: *eamque Spartam Papae conferant*; Dutch: *en om die waardigheit toetebrengen aan den Paus.*

that at the same time he might sit secure from all the assaults of Scripture, being the judge of his own case. The papists affirm this with these arguments: (1) What is said in Scripture. For example, David prays for understanding and the uncovering of his eyes, and so forth. I respond that David is praying for light for his own intellect, not for the greater perspicuity of Scripture—that is, light for himself, not for Scripture. Moreover, Christ interprets the Scripture (Luke 24:27). I respond, this means that he recites and applies the Scripture, from which its obscurity is wrongly inferred. Also, the eunuch says that he cannot interpret Scripture without an interpreter (Acts 8:30–31). I respond that indeed he did not understand that passage, but the universal obscurity of Scripture is most wrongly concluded from this. Further, they note that Peter says that certain things in the writings of Paul are difficult to understand[228] (2 Peter 3:16). I respond: Peter says, "certain things." Is Scripture therefore as a whole obscure? If that were the case, there would not be any author that is not obscure. (2) They argue from the difficulty and obscurity of the things that are contained in Scripture. I respond that even the most difficult things are explained clearly in the Scriptures, especially those things that concern salvation. (3) They argue that there are many things in the Scriptures that on the face of things seem to be contradictory. For instance, there are some ambiguities, there are also incomplete sentences, there are sentences out of order, there are phrases proper only to the Hebrews, and moreover, there are a great many figures of speech. I respond that nowhere do such things occur in passages that concern what is necessary to know and understand for salvation, unless they are explained elsewhere. Thus, in sum, not the Scriptures, but these particular passages of Scripture, consequently may be called obscure. On this question, compare Bellarmine, first general controversy on Scripture (vol. 1, bk. 3, ch. 1–2)[229] with his opponent Ames, *Bellarmine Enervated* (vol. 1, bk. 1, ch. 4).[230] On that particular topic observe especially Ames's most careful formation of the state of the controversy, from which point all the objections topple over with little effort.

Does Scripture allow more than one sense?
XLVII. It is asked whether Scripture allows more than one sense. Many of the fathers, among whom Origen leads the chorus, slipped from the literal sense of Scripture into the allegorical and mystical senses, inasmuch as they supposed

---

228. δυσνόητα
229. See Bellarmine, *Opera Omnia*, 1:170–73; idem, *Disputationes de controversiis*, 1:159–169.
230. *Bellarmin. Enervat. Tom.* 1 pag. 39: See "de Scripturae perspicuitate" in Ames, *Bellarminus Enervatus*, 1:39–43.

that the literal sense was too simple and not of such a kind that it could commend the wisdom of the Christian religion to the pagans. The Jews do the same thing in their midrashim, but all the enthusiasts especially do so. And certain innovators are no different when, in order to construct anything out of anything, and to be able to apply prophecies according to their own pleasure with any appearance of plausibility, they teach this universal rule: the words of Scripture signify whatever they can signify, from which also a manifold sense usually results. Since the papists hold that Scripture is obscure, that the common people ought not read it, that it requires an infallible interpreter, and that this interpreter is not, nor can be, anyone other than the Roman pontiff—therefore, they do the following: (1) They enumerate a fourfold sense of Scripture, namely, the literal, which the letters themselves provide; the allegorical, by which something in the New Testament is signified that concerns Christ and the church; the tropological, when something is signified that pertains to morals; and finally, the anagogical, when eternal life is signified. (2) Next, they say that it is not improbable that sometimes several literal senses are found in the same sentence. (3) At the same time, they claim that efficacious arguments against adversaries must be sought from the literal sense alone (see Bellarmine on the Word of God, vol. 1, bk. 3, ch. 3).[231] The orthodox allow only one sense, and that the literal, namely, that which the writer himself intends by his words. At the same time, they confess that this sense is sometimes composite, as occurs in figurative and typical phrases, where part of the sense is the proper signification of the words and part of it is figurative of the things signified. Indeed, they even call the mystical senses literal when it is certainly evident that they are intended by the Holy Spirit. The arguments of the orthodox are: (1) The true sense of Scripture is certain and firm (2 Peter 1:19); moreover, it is pure and altogether free from impurities, that is, it is entirely without any mixture (Ps. 12:6; 119:140; Prov. 30:5). Certainly, whatever is equivocal or ambiguous, or whatever allows for several senses, is not pure, certain, and firm. (2) That which does not signify one thing surely signifies nothing. (3) The sense is like the form of the words. Therefore, since the words have but one form, they also have but one sense.

Objections
XLVIII. The arguments of the papists are: (1) The apostle makes mention of a certain typical sense in 1 Corinthians 10:11, such that what happened to the Jews literally, he applies to Christians spiritually. I respond that the sense of Scripture must not be confused with its varied application. The application of

---

231. See Bellarmine, *Opera Omnia*, 1:174–76; idem, *Disputationes de controversiis*, 1:169–74.

each passage can be manifold (2 Tim. 3:16), while at the same time one sense remains. (2) They amass various passages of Scripture that have an allegorical sense (Gal. 4:24, among others), an anagogical sense (Heb. 3 and 4, concerning the Israelites' rest), or a tropological sense (1 Cor. 9:9). I respond that the sense of Scripture is singular, whether it is simple, in histories, dogmatic texts, and those prophecies that are related in a straightforward manner, or the sense is composite, expressed in types or in figurative words. At the same time the application can be manifold (Rom. 15:4), and when the literal sense is applied in the Scriptures by allegory, it is for teaching[232] (Gal. 4; Heb. 3 and 4), and by tropology, for correction[233] (1 Cor. 10:11) or for training[234] (1 Cor. 9:9). So then, this certainly does produce a varied use of Scripture, but that is not the same thing as a varied sense.

Is there, besides and beyond Scripture, any infallible norm for interpreting it?
XLIX. From the obscurity and difficulty of something written arises the necessity of interpreting it. Regarding this, there is a dispute, first, concerning the norm according to which one ought to speak when interpreting Scripture; and second, concerning the judge whose responsibility it is to pronounce on a controversy that arises regarding the sense of Scripture. In the first controversy it is asked whether there is, besides and beyond Scripture, any infallible norm for interpreting it. The orthodox, although they grant that there are various means of interpreting Scripture, and likewise various rules, such as the analogy of faith and of context, careful comparison of passages, and parallelism of sentences, nevertheless do not acknowledge any infallible norm different from Scripture as it explains itself. The reasons of the orthodox are that: (1) We do not read that God bestowed this sort of dignity and power over his word upon anyone. (2) There is nothing besides Scripture that has infallible truth (Ps. 116:11), as will be readily evident by induction: not the fathers, not councils, and so forth. (3) It is absurd to think that the Holy Spirit and his thoughts should be examined by another norm (1 Cor. 2:11, 16). Finally, (4) Scripture is the norm of all other things (Isa. 8:20; Gal. 6:16). For this reason, nothing can be its norm without introducing the most vicious circularity.

---

232. διδασκαλίαν
233. ἐπανόρθωσιν
234. παιδείαν

The affirmative position

L. The enthusiasts say that this infallible axiom is their own inspiration. The Socinians and rationalists, as we taught, say that this axiom is their own reason. The papists, so that they may more securely turn away from Scripture as the supreme and infallible norm of interpreting itself, ascribe that axiom, first, to the fathers. On the contrary, (1) they do not produce any written proof of this matter. (2) The fathers, to a man, could err, and in fact have erred, as our opponents themselves testify (see Bellarmine, the first general controversy on the Word of God, bk. 3, ch. 10).[235] (3) Those same fathers reject this dignified position. (4) Those same opponents sometimes treat the fathers' position as of no importance, even when the fathers agree with them, as André Rivet shows in chapter 7 of his prefatory "Treatise on the authority of the fathers" in his *Critici Sacri Libri IV*.[236] (5) Their writings have not always been extant. (6) Of those that are extant, many are not genuine. (7) Those who have the task of interpreting the sense of Scripture cannot consult everything written by every father (cf. Rivet, *Critici Sacri Libri IV*,[237] and also Jean Daillé, *A Treatise on the Right Use of the Fathers*,[238] Johann Gerhard, *Loci Theologici*, locus 1, ch. 22, para. 463).[239] Second, the papists ascribe that axiom to the decrees of the Roman pontiffs. Thomas Stapleton says, "One must not believe God as he speaks in his written word unless the authoritative judgment of the pope stands in between ("The authority of the church formally considered," *A Demonstration of the Doctrinal Principia of the Faith*, controversy 4, q. 1, art. 3).[240] I respond, let our adversaries

---

235. Bellarmine, *Opera Omnia*, 1:188–93; idem, *Disputationes de controversiis*, 1:192–200.

236. *Riveti Critic. Sacr. cap. 7*: This chapter reference must belong to the prefatory treatise in André Rivet, *Andreae Riveti…Critici Sacri Libri IV…praefixus est Tractatus de patrum authoritate, errorum causis, & nothorum notis*, 5th ed. (Francfurt: G. H. Fromann, 1690), 40–48.

237. This may be at least a reference to chapter 2 of *Tractatus de patrum authoritate* entitled "in the opinion of the orthodox what sort and how much authority do the fathers have in matters of faith and morals," see Rivet, *Critici Sacri*, 12–19.

238. *Dalleum, de usu et abusu patrum*: See Jean Daillé, *Traicté de l'employ des saincts Pères pour le jugement des differends qui sont aujourd'hui en la religion* (Geneva: Pierre Auber, 1632); for a Latin translation from French, see idem, *Joannis Dallaei de usu patrum ad ea definienda religionis capita quae sunt hodie controversa libri duo*, trans. I. Mettayerus (Geneva: J. A. Chouët, 1686); for English, item, *A Treatise Concerning the Right Use of the Fathers in the Decision of the Controversies that are this Day in Religion* (London: John Martin, 1675); also, idem, *A Treatise on the Right Use of the Fathers in the Decision of Controversies Existing at this Day in Religion*, trans. T. Smith, 2nd ed. (London: H. G. Bohn, 1843).

239. *Joh. Gerard. Loc. 1. cap. v.*: The correct reference is locus 1, ch. 22, para. 463, where the margin reads "5. Patres." See Johann Gerhard, *Ioannis Gerhardis Loci Theologici*, 9 vols. (Berlin: G. Schlawitz, 1863–1875), 1.22.463, 1:205–206.

240. *Deo inquit loquenti in verbo suo scripto, non est credendum nisi interposito judicio auctoritativo pontificis*. This exact statement has not been found in any of Stapleton's twenty-three chapters of

prove it. We will demonstrate the contrary in the following question. Third, they ascribe that axiom to the decisions of councils. See Bellarmine, the fourth general controversy on councils and the church, book 2;[241] the Council of Trent, session 4.[242] However, (1) councils often contradict themselves, (2) they can err and they have erred, and (3) they repeatedly stray from the truth because of precedents. The papists ascribe that axiom, fourth, to traditions, which we will speak openly about below. For the arguments—both for and against—compare Bellarmine, in the cited passage, and his opponents Ames, *Bellarmine Enervated* (vol. 2, bk. 1, ch. 5),[243] and Whitaker, *Praelectiones* (third controversy, "On councils," q. 2).[244]

Is there some infallible judge of controversies on earth?
LI. In reference to the second disputed matter,[245] two questions are asked. First, among men, is there a visible judge of those controversies concerning the sense of Scripture and religion, to whose opinion the consciences of all must submit? The orthodox deny this for the following reasons: (1) The power of judging does not belong to men, as if it were the power of a king or magistrate over God

---

the fourth controversy. This remark seems to be a summary of Stapleton's general argument that the formal object of faith is the voice of God. But the voice of God is not the Scriptures (i.e. the material object of faith); the voice of God through the Church, that is, the voice of the Church as it teaches (*vox Ecclesiae docens*), is the only infallible *norma et regula fidei*. Thus, the judgment and decision of controversies belongs "under no condition but simply and absolutely" to the *persona Ecclesiae Catholicae et Apostolicae Romanae*, which is not in the body of the church as a whole (*in toto suo Corpore*) or in any member of the body, but "in the pastors and bishops," and "especially and chiefly in the head of that body, the successor of St. Peter, the Roman pontiff." Thomas Stapleton, *Thomae Stapletoni Angli, Sacrae Theologiae Doctoris, Opera Omnia*, 4 vols. (Paris: M. Sonnius, 1620), 1:308; idem, *Principiorum fidei doctrinalium demonstratio methodica per controversias septem in libris duodecim tradita in quibus ad omnes de religione controversias diiudicandas sola & certissma norma, & ad easdem semel finiendas sola & suprema in terris authoritas, via, & ratio demonstrantur* (Paris: M. Sonnius, 1582), 323.

241. Book 2 is entitled "De potestate conciliorum" and is comprised of nineteen chapters and three appendices in Bellarmine, *Opera Omnia*, 2:237–313; idem, *Disputationes de controversiis*, 2:67–132.

242. See Philip Schaff (ed.), *Bibliotheca Symbolica Ecclesiae Universalis: The Creeds of Christendom, with a history and critical notes* (New York: Harper and Brothers, 1877), 2:79–83. For the debates at the Council of Trent leadimg up to the canons of session 4, see Augustinus Theiner (ed.), *Acta Genuina SS. Oecumenici Concilii Tridentini sub Paulo III. Julio III. et Pio IV. PP. MM. ab Angelo Massarello Episcopo Thelesino ejusdem Consilii secretario conscripta*, 2 vols. (Zagreb: Breithopf et Härtel, 1874), 1:48–87.

243. See "De certitudine sententiae a concilio pronunciatae" in Ames, *Bellarminus Enervatus*, 2:24–35.

244. See "A quo & cuijus authoritate cogenda sunt Concilia" in William Whitaker, *Praelectiones...in quibus tractatur Controversia de Consiliis* (Herborn: Christophor Corvinus, 1601), 30–77.

245. See §XLIX for the enumeration of the two disputed issues.

and divine matters. (2) The judgment of anyone, except that of the Scripture itself, is liable to errors. (3) So then it must be examined by the touchstone of Scripture (1 John 4:1; 1 Thess. 5:21; cf. Isa. 8:20; Acts 17:11), and to this extent no one can be established as a judge without introducing a vicious circularity. (4) God alone is the author of Scripture (2 Tim. 3:16), the highest and only lawgiver in the church (James 4:12), the one infallible teacher (Matt. 23:8, 10). (5) In both Testaments, God attributes to the Scripture alone this axiomatic status, since he continually sends us back to the Scriptures whenever controversies arise (Isa. 8:20; Luke 16:29; 2 Peter 1:19; Deut. 17:20).

What the papists claim

LII. The Jews formerly had their own high priests, bound by a divine constitution to the family of Aaron alone, to whom belonged the oversight[246] of sacred things, but who nonetheless are nowhere called judges of controversies concerning the Scriptures. And the Roman pagans used to have their own supreme pontiffs, descending from Numa Pompilius, as Livy testifies in *History of Rome*, book 1.[247] Festus says that this man was "the judge and arbiter of divine and human affairs."[248] Likewise the Muslims have their own mufti, who is their highest overseer of sacred things, "from whom," says Busbecq in his *Turkish Letters*, letter 3, "in doubtful matters, they seek an answer as from the Dodonaean oak."[249] The papists, so that their pope might sit secure in his own case as the supreme judge, agree at least in this, that, beyond the Scriptures, there is given on earth some visible and infallible judge of controversies, but they separate into factions to argue over whether it is the pope, an ecumenical council, or the pope together with the council. Next there is a recurring question whether the root of infallibility is located in the pontiff or in the council. And furthermore, it is asked whether the power of the pope is spiritual only, or temporal as well, and whether this power is of himself, or only on account of the church. All of them at least make the pope the judge of controversies and the interpreter of the Scriptures, for these petty reasons: (1) This prerogative once belonged to

---

246. ἐπισκοπή

247. Livy, *History of Rome*, 1.20.

248. Rufus Festus, *The Breviarum of Festus: a critical edition with historical commentary*, trans. J. W. Eadie (London: Athlone Press, 1967), 5.3.5c.

249. Ogier Ghiselin de Busbecq, *Avgerii Gislenii Bvsbecquii D. legationis Turcicae Epistolae quatuor* (Paris: Officina Plantiniana, 1595), 96 verso; idem, *The Life and letters of Ogier Ghiselin de Busbecq*, trans. C. T. Foster and F. H. B. Daniel (London: C. Kegan Paul & Co., 1881; Cambridge: Cambridge University Press, 2012), 1:272. Dodona was an ancient site dedicated to the worship of Zeus. A religious cult arose that claimed to interpret the rustling leaves of a sacred tree as messages from the gods. See Sophocles, *Trachinae*, 173.

Moses and Aaron (Ex. 18:26; Deut. 17:8ff.; Eccl. 12:11; Hag. 2:12; Mal. 2:7; 2 Chron. 19:11), and the pontiff is their successor. I respond that we deny both claims, and the passages adduced do not prove such a thing, as an inspection[250] will show. (2) Peter was once the supreme judge of controversies (Matt. 16:19; John 21:16; Luke 22:32; Acts 15:7; Gal. 2:9), and the pontiff is Peter by succession. I respond that again we deny both claims, and the adduced passages do not prove this—as is clear if you only examine them. (3) Final judgment in controversies belongs to the representative church (Matt. 18:17; 23:2). I respond that this is begging the question, and that this argument is not present in these passages. Indeed, we acknowledge that a certain kind of judgment is attributed to the church (Matt. 18:17), but it is neither a final nor an infallible judgment, since it must be examined from the Scripture (Acts 17:11; 1 Thess. 5:21). Christ does not want the scribes and Pharisees, as those who are sitting in the seat of Moses (Matt. 23:2), to be listened to except when, and to the extent that, they teach from Moses (cf. the opponents of Bellarmine: Ames and others).

Should the judgment of controversies be relinquished to some
sort of private judgment?
LIII. The second question, therefore, is this: should the interpretation of Scripture and the judgment of controversies be relinquished to someone's private judgment? When the Reformed censure the papists because they set up the Roman pontiff for themselves as the supreme judge of controversies, the latter will fling the criticism back and strike at the Reformed, saying that they make every private person, down to the common girl, a judge of controversies. But they are wrong. For the Reformed answer the question expressly in the negative, just as the papists do. So then, the papists fling such an objection at the orthodox, but only by mere slander. Meanwhile the Reformed (1) divide judgment into public and private. (2) Again, they make public judgment twofold. It is either simply and absolutely authentic and also definitive, binding people's consciences to faith. The Reformed deny that any such judgment exists on earth, beyond the Scriptures. Or it is limited, pertaining to the ministerial vocation, a judgment of discernment, declaring what, by a due inquiry, it has found to be set down in the Scriptures, and binding to faith no further than it is able to show that what it sets forth is the Word of God. (3) Finally, they say that private judgment belongs to individual people, discerning and proving for themselves alone what is set forth to them, but not, on the basis of some special calling, declaring anything for others. How, therefore, will quarrels about religion be decided?

---

250. ἐποψία

I respond: We deny that in order to settle theological controversies some sort of visible power has been set up in the church, as if it were a royal and magisterial power. Thus we are convinced that God has imposed the duty of inquiry upon men, that likewise, he has communicated to them the gift of discernment (both public and private), that additionally, he has appointed them, each in proportion to his calling, eagerly to promote the knowledge and practice of known truth, and that finally, he has joined to these things his promise of guidance and bless-ing. And all these things together we judge to suffice for deciding controversies.

Is Scripture the perfect norm of faith and life?[251]
LV. We move then to the next controversy[252] with the papists, concerning the perfection of Scripture. Here it is asked, first, whether Scripture is so perfect that it embraces all dogmas necessary for faith and life. The orthodox affirm this, generally by these arguments: (1) Nothing is to be added or subtracted from Scripture (Deut. 4:2; Gal. 1:8). (2) It sets forth the whole counsel of God concerning our salvation (cf. Acts 20:27 with 26:22). (3) It renders us complete for salvation (2 Tim. 3:15–17). Compare what we said previously in §XIX.

Objections
The Jews, Muslims, and papists deny that Scripture is the perfect norm of faith and life. The Jews do so in order to keep their oral law intact, and the Muslims, their Qur'an. The papists do so in order that they might somehow support their infinite superstitions from another source, since they are not able to sustain them by the Scriptures. And they do so also in order to establish the absolute rule of the pope, since the pope would not be able thus to exercise this rule in instructing, prohibiting, and counseling, if all things necessary to be believed and to be done for salvation were in the Scriptures. The papists generally dispute using these weak reasons: First, Scripture does not contain many things that are necessary to know, such as (1) what the remedy was for original sin for little girls in the Old Testament, and likewise what it was for little boys dying prior to circumcision in the Old Testament; (2) how some Gentiles were saved in the Old Testament; moreover, it teaches nothing (3) about the perpetual virginity of Mary; (4) about celebrating Easter or the Lord's Day; and (5) about paedobaptism, and so forth. I respond that either those things are not necessary

---

251. The 1689/1699 Latin text skips §LIV, as do the subsequent Latin editions in 1715 and 1724, and the 1749–1753 Dutch translation. The original numbering is retained here for ease of reference.

252. Mastricht calls this the fifth controversy.

to know for salvation, of which sort are (3) and (4); or Scripture does contain them. For example, with respect to (1), Scripture sets forth the universal remedy for original sin, the blood or grace of Christ, under both Testaments (1 John 1:7; cf. Acts 15:11), which was sealed, rather than produced, by circumcision (Rom. 4:11). We can likewise answer and apply the same to (2). To (5) we say that paedobaptism is shown in the New Testament. For it expressly says that baptism is applicable to all who receive a share in the blood and Spirit of Christ (Acts 10:47), and that infants are fit to receive the blood and Spirit of Christ (Luke 1:15; Jer. 1:5). We will present the other arguments on this matter in its own place. Second, the papists say that many books of Scripture that were truly canonical have truly been lost. From the Old Testament, they point to the books of Nathan and Gad (1 Chron. 29:29), of Ahijah and Iddo (2 Chron. 9:29), and of Solomon (1 Kings 4:32). From the New Testament, they point to the epistle to the Laodiceans (Col. 4:16) and one to the Corinthians (1 Cor. 5:9). I respond that either they were not canonical or they were not lost, according to the argument of Matthew 5:18. The books of Nathan and Gad are perhaps included in the histories of Samuel and Kings, given that their names were omitted there but mentioned by Ezra in his Chronicles. The writings of Solomon that have ceased to exist, we deny to have been canonical. We do not acknowledge the epistle to the Laodiceans, for the apostle in Colossians 4:16 calls to mind an epistle, not "to the Laodiceans,"[253] but "from Laodicea."[254] If that epistle to the Corinthians was lost it was not canonical. In 1 Corinthians 5:9 the prepositive τῇ seems to indicate that it refers to 1 Corinthians itself. And suppose certain canonical books were lost (which we completely deny): even so, we will not properly infer the essential imperfection of Scripture from this unless it first should be demonstrated that those lost books contained some dogma necessary for salvation that the extant books do not contain. Third, they say that either individual books of Scripture are perfect individually, and contain all things necessary for salvation, or all together. It cannot be that each are perfect individually, for why are there so many books? Nor are they perfect all together, because many have perished. I respond both that the individual books are essentially perfect, since they are perfectly sufficient for their own end and time, and that the entire canon is integrally perfect, if not insofar as it grew gradually by the addition of books, at least insofar as it now stands perfect. And besides this, we have already for good reason denied that any canonical book has been lost. Fourth, their final argument is from traditions, which we will openly address right now.

---

253. πρὸς Λαοδικεῖς
254. ἐκ Λαοδικείας

Are sacred traditions besides Scripture necessary?

LVI. It is asked whether besides and beyond Scripture there are certain traditions of Christ and the apostles that are also the Word of God and obtain equal authority with the written Word. The Reformed, although they allow as necessary the tradition by means of which the Scripture itself comes to us, nevertheless do not allow any traditions to become dogmas or commands that are necessary in addition to the Scriptures. They deny these because: (1) Scripture is in every way perfect, per §XIX. (2) Traditions are the doctrines of men, which are forbidden in Matthew 15:9 and Colossians 2:22–23. (3) Our adversaries cannot produce any examples of such traditions that we cannot easily dispel. For example, see those things that we noted in the preceding section, concerning the remedy for original sin and so forth. (4) The traditions of the papists are uncertain, since some affirm, while others deny, that the one and the same tradition of the ancients is apostolic; the traditions are contrary to the written Word of God; certain ones are fabulous as well as ridiculous; and they are mutable, for we read that they have been changed in various ways according to circumstances of times, places, and persons.

What the papists claim

LVII. The Pharisees, in the spirit that we depicted in the preceding controversy, deny that traditions are unnecessary. The papists, according to the Council of Trent, session 4, make the same denial, using these weak arguments: (1) The apostle calls us to these things (1 Cor. 15:3). I respond that the term "tradition" does sometimes denote doctrine that has been handed down in some way, though it is expressly included in Scripture (1 Cor. 11:23; 2 Thess. 2:15). This applies to 1 Corinthians 15:3, as the doctrine expressed there irrefutably demonstrates. (2) The apostles handed down certain things and therefore they were unwritten (1 Cor. 11:34). I respond: It is incoherent to say they handed them down, therefore they did not write them down, since such handing down (per the previous response) can take place as much by the written word as by the living voice. Nor does it follow to say that the apostle handed down certain things, which in that epistle are not displayed in a written form, and therefore, Scripture does not hand them down anywhere; or that, if Paul personally does not hand it down in writing, then no apostle or prophet does so. Suppose that he has handed down things that he did not write. By this rationale will it be evinced that those things are necessary to be known for salvation? (3) Christ had many things to say to the apostles that they could not bear (John 16:12). I respond: Traditions do not follow from this. Also, Christ made known to his own all things that he heard from the Father (John 15:15), in such a way that the Holy Spirit would have to do nothing but recall to mind all that he said[255] (John 14:26). Therefore, the Savior is not speaking about certain new points of dogma yet to be received, but about such things that he himself in fact frequently taught, but that the disciples, because of their weakness, had not perceived, things that they would perceive under the guidance of the coming Spirit. (4) Paul often makes mention of the "deposit"[256] (1 Tim. 6:20; 2 Tim. 1:14). In a similar manner he entrusts to his disciples the things they heard from him (2 Tim. 1:13; 2:2). I respond that he certainly does not entrust to his Timothy the papists' traditions, but the whole body of sound doctrine, which is plain to see (1 Tim. 6:20; 2 Tim. 1:13–14). (5) Paul does not wish to write about all things, but to set forth many things face to face ("the remaining things,"[257] and so forth; 1 Cor. 11:34). I respond that he is speaking not about the necessary articles of faith, but about preserving order in the churches, of which they could have remained ignorant without losing salvation. (6) John did not want to put down all things in ink (2 John 12; 3 John 13). I respond: Are there, then, certain things necessary for salvation that are not set forth in the entire Bible? (7) The apostle undoubtedly had the names of the two magicians by means of tradition (2 Tim. 3:8). I respond that it must be proved that the apostle did not have them at that time either in extant, written records, or by the inspiration of the Holy Spirit. And, they were not dogmas of the faith necessary for salvation. (8) We would not have the Scripture of the Old and New Testaments, and we would not know that the biblical books were written by those whose names they bear, except by the tradition of the church—first the Jewish church, and then the Christian one. I respond that we have distinguished the handing down of Scripture from the handing down of things apart from Scripture; we embrace the former and reject the latter.

Is Scripture necessary now for the church?

LVIII. It is asked whether Scripture is necessary now for the church. The enthusiasts deny the necessity of the written Word, because private inspirations of the Spirit are sufficient for them. The papists, in order to hold tradition as more necessary, the reading of Scripture as less necessary, and the infallibility of the pope as most necessary, deny the necessity of the written Word. Additionally, they do this so that they might all the more extol the necessity of the Roman pontiff, on whose word we should all hang. And they hold this for these reasons: First, for two thousand years from Adam to Moses, religion was preserved by

---

255. ἀναμιμνήσκειν ὅσα εἶπε
256. παραθήκην
257. τὰ λοιπά

tradition alone; therefore the Scripture is not necessary *simpliciter*, that is, absolutely. I respond that (1) we do not say that it is necessary *simpliciter*, but rather *ex hypothesi*, that is, by a decision of the will of God who prescribes to us his Word, as we have seen above.[258] (2) At that time Scripture was not necessary, since the living voice of God was providing what was still needed. Therefore, to say that it is not now necessary, when the living voice of God has ceased, does not follow. (3) Religion was not preserved so much by tradition as by the living voice of God through the patriarchs. Second, they say that the Scriptures, when they were extant afterward, were only for the Jews, while in the meantime others, who did not belong to the church, made use of tradition only, just as Job and his friends did. Indeed even the Jews themselves made use of tradition more than Scripture. I respond that (1) Job and his friends lived before the law of God had been written, and they had the living voice of God, as is evident from the book of Job. (2) With the pious who lived outside the visible church of the Jews, God acted extraordinarily; but to therefore deny the ordinary necessity of Scripture is just the same as if, from the extraordinary sustaining of Moses and Christ without bread, you chose to deny the necessity of food and drink. (3) We confess that the Jewish church attributed just as much to the Talmudic traditions of the fathers as to the Scripture, though only in the time of Christ and a little before, and through the worst sort of corruption, which was most frequently reprehended by Christ. But because of this, the necessity of Scripture will not be more correctly abrogated, than if because of the most corrupt practice of the papists to prefer their own traditions to the Scriptures, we conclude that we are allowed to abrogate the necessity of the divine Word. Third, they claim that after the advent of Christ, for many years the church was without Scripture. I respond that (1) the church has never been without Scripture, at least from the time of Moses, for it has always had the Old Testament, (2) although, however, it was without the apostolic writings for some time. This occurred because the apostles were to preach the gospel first with a living voice, and then to write it. (3) The living voice of the apostles, and to that extent also the voice of the Holy Spirit, was supplying what was necessary. Then, after this voice ceased, the teaching of the apostles emerged as recorded in writing. For this reason the necessity of Scripture is most powerfully reinforced. Against these objections, the orthodox assert the necessity of Scripture by many arguments, some of which we set forth in §XX above.

---

258. §XX.

Did Scripture arise only by fortuitous circumstances, and not by divine command?
LIX. It is asked whether Scripture arose only by fortuitous circumstances, and not by divine command. The Reformed, with the apostle, hold that holy men of God spoke, not at their own pleasure, but as they were moved by the Holy Spirit (2 Peter 1:21). They bring forward as arguments, (1) the command to teach all nations, even those that would exist in the future, throughout the whole earth, until the consummation of the age (Matt. 28:19–20), which could hardly be accomplished without any writing. (2) God, by an express command, declared to certain men the necessity of writing—for example, Moses (Ex. 17:14; 34:27; and other places), Isaiah (Isa. 8:1), Jeremiah (Jer. 30:2), Habakkuk (Hab. 2:2), and John (Rev. 1:11). To all these men, inspiration (2 Tim. 3:16) and the impulse of the Holy Spirit (2 Peter 1:21) were according to a command. (3) These writers were faithful ambassadors of Christ (1 Cor. 4:1–2), and it does not belong to ambassadors to act without a command. This is why certain men found it necessary to write (Jude 3); in fact, such is true of all who wrote Scripture.

Objections
The papists, in order to diminish the necessity of Scripture, to elevate the necessity of the pope, to drag the common people away from the Scriptures, and to draw them to the pope, deny the necessity of Scripture generally by these reasons: (1) If it were the intention of the prophets and the apostles to consign the teaching of religion to books overtly, then undoubtedly they would have prepared a catechism or a similar book, but they did not do this; therefore Scripture is not necessary. I respond that it is not a logical consequence of this argument that Scripture is not necessary. Also, the assumption is false, for are not the epistles to the Romans, Ephesians, and so on, catechisms and systems of theology? And also, are there not sayings of Scripture that designate catechetical heads, such as Mark 1:15; 2 Timothy 1:13; Titus 3:8; and especially Hebrews 6:1–2? (2) They say that the apostles were not commanded to write. I respond that we just now abundantly demonstrated the contrary, and also in §XX. (3) They say that the apostles wrote from the necessity of the opportunities before them, but not from the necessity of a divine command; therefore Scripture is not necessary. I respond that subordinate things are not contradictory. They wrote by the command of Christ as the principal impelling cause, and with the opportunity before them as the less principal impelling cause.

Is Scripture not so much the perfect rule of believing and living
as it is a useful kind of reminder?

LX. From this question, another arises: should Scripture not rather be called a useful kind of reminder than a perfect rule of faith and morals? The papists, in order to seek a perfect rule of believing and living, not in Scripture, but in the pope, and then to lure those who have turned aside from Scripture to the pope, choose the former option, for these weak reasons:

Objections

(1) It is the proper and chief end of Scripture to present a certain kind of reminder in order to preserve faith (Rom. 15:4; 2 Peter 1:13; 3:1), and its style is clearly exhortatory or suitable for reminding. I respond that subordinate and coordinate things are not contradictory. To say that it is a reminder, and therefore it is not a canon, does not follow. In fact, it is also called a canon (Gal. 6:16; Phil. 3:16). (2) By necessity a rule ought to be adequate for what it regulates, that is, it ought to contain all things, and only those things, that pertain to faith. But this is by no means applicable to Scripture, because traditions are required in addition to it; therefore it is only a useful reminder. I respond that we have shown that the minor premise is false in §V above, and also that traditions are vain in §LVI. (3) A rule is a work of one piece. Scripture is not such a work, for it contains histories, sermons, prophecies, songs, and letters. I respond that the antecedent is true concerning what we call a rule properly speaking, that is, a builder's rule. Scripture, however, is called a rule only metaphorically speaking, just as the church is often called a house, an edifice, a foundation, and so forth. The Reformed affirm that Scripture is indeed a perfect rule for faith and morals, for the reasons furnished a little earlier in §§IV–V. And we will not add anything here, except that if it were otherwise, we would not have a divine rule of living for God, and therefore neither would we have divine faith or divine obedience. For where God does not speak, there we also are not able to believe; and where he does not command, there also we cannot obey. But he does not speak except in the Scriptures. If you should say that what he says by way of reminder, he still says, then I will respond: but then what must be believed or done that is beyond this "reminder" of yours. God did not say, if the reminder were not the perfect rule of believing and doing. For this reason the papists are to be pitied, and especially the common people among them, for whom the reading of Scripture is prohibited, because they have no rule, indeed no divine rule, of believing and obeying God, since the pope is not God.

The Practical Part

The practice concerning Scripture is summed up in eight uses. The first use,
impressing the authority of Scripture upon its hearers. Five motives

LXI. Therefore it stands firm against all opponents that Scripture is the most perfect norm of living for God. And so, for the first practice, it is altogether incumbent upon doctors and ministers frequently and seriously to inculcate and urge Scripture's divine authority upon their hearers, equally from the doctor's chair as from the minister's pulpit, and not, as is done, to presuppose it as an indemonstrable principle—with the goal that their hearers receive it, not as the word of men, but (as it actually is) as the Word of God (1 Thess. 2:13). Let doctors and ministers consider the following: (1) This is the first basic principle of Christianity, the first thing to know ("knowing this first, that...,"[259] 2 Peter 1:20–21). Accordingly, it generally obtains the first place in most prophecies: "the word of the LORD that came"[260] (Hos. 1:1; Joel 1:1; Jonah 1:1; Mic. 1:1); likewise also "thus says the LORD"[261] (Obad. 1; and so forth). (2) Not only is it the basic principle of religion, but also its only fulcrum and foundation (Eph. 2:20), which must be rightly and solidly laid by the spiritual master builder before all else ("like a wise master builder I have laid a foundation...,"[262] 1 Cor. 3:10). (3) In fact it is such a foundation that without it no faith or obedience can subsist in the hearers. For what is faith other than to assent because God speaks? Therefore, unless you are persuaded that God has spoken those things that are set forth in Scripture, where will your faith rest? In turn, what is obedience other than to do what God commands? Therefore, unless you are certain that God has spoken those things which are commanded in Scripture, how will you obey? For this reason Paul in 1 Thessalonians 2:13 says, "you received it, not as the word of men but rather (as it truly is) the Word of God that also works in you who believe."[263] (4) The more the conviction of this principle thrives in its hearers, the more their entire Christianity will thrive—their zeal for good works, their avoidance of sins, and so forth—and thus a more ample harvest of all of our labors will result. (5) How great is the number of those who either are ignorant of, or even deny, this authority of the Scriptures, not only beyond the walls of the Christian church, but also in its innermost parts! How great likewise is the number of those who carp at it! How great, finally, is the number of those who

---

259. τοῦτο πρῶτον γινώσκοντες, ὃτι...

260. דבר יהוה אשר

261. כה אמר יהוה

262. ὡς σοφὸς ἀρχιτέκτων θεμέλιον τέθεικα

263. ἐδέξασθε, οὐ λογον ἀνθρώπων, ἀλλὰ (καθώς ἐστιν ἀληθῶς) λόγον θεοῦ, ὅς καὶ ἐνεργεῖται ἐν ὑμῖν, τοῖς πιστεύουσιν

doubt it!—not to mention that hardly anyone is found who is so Christian that small doubts about this matter do not constantly arise.

The way to assert and urge the divine authority of Scripture
LXII. Now, the way to assert and urge the divine authority of the Scriptures embraces three things. First, teachers and ministers should instruct their people in those supports by which the divine authority of Scripture can be made known to us, namely: (1) The marks of divinity impressed upon Scripture by God, that is, the sublime divinity of the things written, the most accurate harmony of the parts and the whole, and the humble majesty of the writing itself, which breathes divinity in every part (cf. §§IV, XXII, XXIII, XXX, XXXI). (2) The internal persuasion of the Holy Spirit (1 Cor. 2:12), which is not in the least an enthusiastic persuasion, as if it proffered and instilled that truth in our mind, but rather an illuminative persuasion, by which the very power of our understanding is elevated so that it can perceive those marks of divinity that God impressed upon Scripture. (3) The testimony of the church, as a kind of secondary means. Second, they should build and demonstrate by unconquerable arguments the origin and authority of the Scriptures against the pagans and the paganizing pseudo-Christians, by which arguments the whole assembly of their hearers will be admirably strengthened on this principle of Christianity. We presented these very arguments in part above in §§XXII–XXIII. Third, they should carefully remove all scruples from those who doubt and who are uncertain, scruples such as: (1) Those that concern the divinity of Scripture itself, whether Scripture is most certainly the Word of God. And indeed, we observe that the leading[264] cause of this doubt is to indulge in known sins, that is, sins against conscience. For it readily and generally happens that, in order to avoid the sentence of Scripture against our sins, we call its competency into doubt. The inciting cause[265] of this doubt is the apparent contradictions,[266] that is, the impossible things, that meet us in Scripture, for which reason their universal truth and divine authority seems to us to start to falter. We will remove such causes if we carefully keep ourselves from every known sin, but also then if, first, we consult the help afforded by commentators who solve Scripture's apparent contradictions,[267] inconsistencies,[268] and so forth; commentators such as Junius, Spanheim, Walther, Maimonides, and the like; furthermore, if we consider that at that time

---

264. προηγουμένη
265. προκαταρκτική
266. ἐναντιοφανῆ
267. ἐναντιοφανῶν
268. ἀτόπων

people's customs, proverbs, dialects, and such, were different from ours, and thus, that it is not strange if the perception of these things does not so readily occur to us; and if, finally, we find fault with the slowness and sluggishness of our intellect rather than the precision[269] of Scripture (2 Cor. 10:5). (2) There are those scruples that concern the testimony of the Holy Spirit, since (according to the theologians) short of that testimony, no one is persuaded, or can be persuaded, of the divinity of Scripture. "But I," someone might say, for example, "have never felt this testimony, and even now I do not feel it; how will I rightly believe in the divinity of Scripture?" We reply in one word: This testimony of the Holy Spirit does not consist in some kind of enthusiasm, which, as it were, instills and insinuates this axiom into our mind that the Scripture is from God, but rather, it consists in the illumination and elevation of our intellect, that we may acknowledge and discern the marks of divinity divinely impressed upon Scripture. And in this way the Spirit, as it were, "witnesses with our spirit"[270] (Rom. 8:16). So then, if we admit the marks of divinity, and through them the divine authority of the Scriptures, we are likewise certain, due to these effects, of the testimony of the Holy Spirit, just as we rightly deduce the faculty of sight from the recognition and differentiation of objects. (3) There are also those scruples that concern the agreement of the versions with their sources. For however certain I may be concerning the truth and divinity of the sources, how will I be certain concerning the integrity of their translations,[271] if the original languages are inaccessible to me? I respond that although all translations may differ and be deficient in quite a few rather insignificant things, nevertheless in the essential things, which more closely concern our salvation, they agree with their sources. Moreover, this agreement can become evident to those ignorant of the original languages on the testimony of those who are skilled in those languages, however alien those people might be to the Christian faith. The testimony of Jews, Turks, heretics, and others like them, although it may not be divine, is nevertheless morally certain and infallible. And furthermore, the Holy Spirit, as with his own signet ring,[272] inwardly seals this external testimony as he guides his people into all truth (John 16:13). For if anyone wills to do what God wills, he will know whether the teaching is from God (John 7:17). For this reason, lastly, although those unskilled in the original languages may not have, regarding this agreement of the translations with the sources, a grammatical

---

269. ἀκρίβειαν
270. συμμαρτυρεῖ τῷ πνεύματι ἡμῶν
271. μεταφράσεων
272. σφραγίδι

certitude, and the certitude of knowledge, nevertheless they have a spiritual certitude, and the certitude of faith.

The second use concerns the love of the divine Word.
1. The parts of this love
LXIII. The second practice, then, concerns everyone in general whose heart is to live for God, and it is that they love and magnify the unique rule that he has given us (Ps. 119:127; 2 Thess. 2:10). This love of the divine Word consists in (1) An affection toward the Scripture, an affection so inclined that we honor Scripture as we would God speaking to us with his own mouth. That is, we should honor its commandments with such great submission, its prohibitions with such great pains and aversion, its promises with such great delight and desire, and finally its threats with such great fear and concern—all as if we had God speaking such things in our presence (1 Thess. 2:13). (2) A vigorous appetite and desire for it, just as a famished person has for sustenance (for it is the sustenance of the soul), and that constant and new every day, just as for eating and drinking (1 Peter 2:2; Job 23:12; Ps. 119 passim). (3) An earnest and indefatigable effort to procure for ourselves an abundant supply of the divine Word, and to use it and enjoy it, as a thing on which the life and salvation of our soul hinges (Col. 3:16; Amos 8:12; Ps. 42:1–2; John 6:27). (4) A delight and sweetness from the use of the sacred books (Ps. 1:1–2; 19:10; 2 Cor. 2:4, 15). (5) A hatred, avoidance, and detestation of all things that are in any way inimical to Scripture or that attempt to take away and diminish its use and enjoyment (Ps. 119:104, 113, 128, 163; 31:6). Finally, (6) a godly concern and careful fear, lest at any time the lampstand of the divine Word be removed from us and ours (Rev. 2:5; Amos 8:12).

2. Seven motives for loving Scripture
LXIV. The following supply us the reasons why we ought to be moved to love the Word of God. (1) Its origin and author, who is not some common person, wise man, or great man, some prince and secular monarch, but rather, the King of kings, the Lord of lords, Father, Son, and Holy Spirit, the great and mighty God (2 Tim. 3:16), for which reason Scripture is called the oracle of God (Rom. 3:2), of Christ (Col. 3:16), and of the Holy Spirit (Acts 28:25; 2 Peter 1:21). But if, therefore, we love the writings of pious, wise men, why would we not love the writings of the wisest and best God—especially when all human writings are spattered with falsities, ignorance, vanities, and so forth, while on the contrary the divine oracles are in every respect perfect and satisfactory, far from any vanity (Ps. 19:7–8); most wise (Ps. 19:7, 9); and most pure and refined (Num. 12:3;

Ps. 12:6)? (2) We ought to be moved by its amanuenses and instruments, men who were by all standards the best. For example, Moses was the meekest among mortals (Num. 12:3), and God for this reason dealt with him face to face (Ex. 33:11); Solomon was the wisest of kings (1 Kings 3:12); David was a man after the very heart of God (Acts 13:22); and Paul was God's chosen instrument to the Gentiles (Acts 9:15). In a word, down to each one, they were all holy men of God, moved by the Holy Spirit (2 Peter 1:21). (3) We ought to be moved by its dogmas or contents, matters most excellent, and equally profound, concerning, for example, God, his attributes, his persons, his works, the divine counsels and decrees; concerning the fall, redemption, calling, regeneration, justification, adoption, sanctification, and glorification of man; concerning the covenant of God with men and its most wise dispensation through so many ages; and concerning the duties of man toward God, his neighbor, and himself, both in his estate of grace, and in his estate of sin, in life and in death, and so on, all which are certainly matters most worthy and necessary to know. (4) We ought to be moved by its form and structure, most elegantly variegated by precepts and examples, by commands and prohibitions, by promises and threats, all of which are most advantageous for practice and salvation. (5) We ought to be moved by its end or uses, equally most excellent and most ample, and for which reason it is called "profitable"[273] not only for some things, but for all things—that is, so that by it the man of God may be complete and completely equipped for every good work; and (6) by its efficacy, for which reason power[274] is attributed to it (Rom. 1:16; James 1:21), and energy[275] (Heb. 4:12; 1 Thess. 2:13). This is not common efficacy, but efficacy to grace, to the life and salvation of the soul, for which it is called the word of grace (Acts 14:3; 20:32), and likewise, the word of reconciliation (2 Cor. 5:19), the word of life (John 6:68; Phil. 2:16), and the word of salvation (Acts 13:26; Heb. 2:3). Indeed, neither is this a slight and vain efficacy, but by far the greatest sort of efficacy, for which reason it is likened to things that are most powerful in their efficacy—for example, fire (Jer. 5:14; Luke 24:32), water (Isa. 55:10; Deut. 32:2), a hammer (Jer. 23:29), and a double-edged sword (Heb. 4:12), and so forth. What is more, its efficacy is also manifold and varied: it illuminates the mind (Ps. 19:8–9; Acts 8:31; 26:17–18); it sanctifies the heart (John 17:17); it converts (Ps. 19:7); it regenerates (James 1:18); it kindles faith (Rom. 10:17; Gal. 3:5); it penetrates and lays bare the secret things of the heart (Heb. 4:12–13; 1 Cor. 14:23–25); it strengthens (1 John 2:14) so that

---

273. ὠφέλιμος
274. δύναμις
275. ἐνέργεια

we might be able to conquer all things, the world, the devil, and so forth; it comforts (Rom 15:4); and it guides[276] (Acts 8:31). (7) We ought to be moved by its absolute necessity for living for God, concerning which see §XX above.

3. The manner of loving Scripture, consisting in two things
(1) Four affections

LXV. Now we turn to the manner of loving the Word of God. For it is not sufficient to love it, but it must be loved rightly. Even hypocrites sometimes love the Word, so that they hear it with much affection, they receive it, and indeed in many ways they render themselves compliant to it (Matt. 13:20–21; Mark 6:20; Isa. 58:2; Heb. 6:5). Therefore this affection must be: (1) sincere, deep, and intimate (Matt. 13:5, 21), not remaining only on the lips, that we say it, nor in external things or outward performances, that we attend its hearing, reading, and similar things; but rooted in the heart, the kind of affection shown by Psalm 119 and the men on the road to Emmaus (Luke 24:32); (2) constant and perpetual, new every day, just as with hunger and thirst (Ps. 1:2); (3) superlative, surpassing any other love, that is, the Word of God should be sweeter to us than any honey, and likewise more endearing and more dear than the purest gold (Ps. 19:10; 2 Cor. 2:14–15; Ps. 119:14, 72, 111); (4) universal, extending itself to all parts of the Word (Ps. 12:6), not only to the gospel and its promises, but also to the law and its threats; not only to those things that are favorable and pleasing to us, but also to those things that are unfavorable and burdensome (Jer. 42:5–6), and especially to those things that are especially inimical to our sins.

(2) Three effects

Our love of the Word should be such that it (1) propels us to gratitude toward God on account of the abundant supply of his Word that he has conferred to us, a gratitude in which we recognize from our heart the mercy of our benefactor and the excellence of his benefits (Ps. 147:19–20), we praise both with our mouth (Ps. 147:19–20; all of Ps. 119), and we repay them with our work, that is, with faith and observance of things revealed in the Word (Heb. 4:2; Jer. 42:5–6). (2) Next, such a love urges us to study the divine Word (Ps. 1:2), which consists in its religious reading, hearing, meditation, and observance (we will treat each of these individually in what follows). (3) Then, it kindles in us a love, honor, and support for those who deliver and explain the Word of God to us (1 Thess. 5:12; 1 Tim. 5:17; Gal. 6:6).

---

276. ὁδηγεῖ

4. The means to kindle love for Scripture
LXVI. The efficacious means for kindling this love are: (1) frequent and devoted consideration of the divine Word, that its excellence, usefulness, and necessity may be more and more made known to you. For you will not love what you do not know. Added to this should be (2) prayers that God would illumine our intellect that we may behold wondrous things out of the law (Ps. 119:18), and that he would kindle in our will an appetite for the Word, which the psalmist so frequently asks God to give him in Psalm 119. (3) Zeal for profiting from the Word of God. For just as the harvest will stir up the farmer's love for the field, so also fruit will stir up our love for the divine Word. (4) Finally, a living and effective ministry of the Word does much for kindling a love of the Word. So then let that kind of ministry be sought after and pursued.

The third use, concerning contempt or hatred of the divine Word
LXVII. The following are repugnant to this love of the Word: a contempt and despising of the divine Word (Jer. 6:10; 8:9; Amos 2:1; Matt. 23:27; 2 Chron. 36:16); a hatred (Job 21:14), by which we plug our ears to it (Ps. 58:4–5); a loathing and avoidance (Job. 21:14; Num. 21:5; Prov. 3:11); neglect (Jer. 18:18; 19:15; Zeph. 3:2); resistance (Acts 13:45) and criticism (Isa. 5:24). For these sins God pronounces the most grievous judgments (Jer. 6:19; 7:13; Prov. 1:12ff.; Matt. 23:37–38; Amos 8:11–12), and also inflicts them (Acts 13:46; Rev. 2:5).

The fourth use, the study of the divine Word, in four parts
LXVIII. The fourth practice follows the love of the divine Word—its study.

What this study is
This study includes hearing (Neh. 8:1–7; Luke 10:38; Rom. 10:17), reading (Deut. 17:18; Josh. 1:8), scrutinizing (John 5:39) and ruminating (Ps. 23:2; cf. Lev. 11:3; Ps. 119:97, 148), examining and investigating (Acts 17:2; 1 John 4:1), consulting, on more obscure things, with those who are more experienced (Deut. 17:8ff.; Acts 8:30–31; Matt. 13:36), and conversing or making joint inquiry[277] with others (Luke 18:31; 24:27; Deut. 6:7).

That it should be done
Study of this sort is urged by (1) the divine command, in both the Old and New Testaments. Indeed the former provides the greatest number of passages on this point, for example, Deuteronomy 6:6–9; Joshua 1:8–9; Isaiah 8:20; and Psalm

---

277. συζήτησις

1:2. But in the latter, see John 5:39; Colossians 3:16; and Jude 17. It is urged by (2) examples, both from the Bible, such as David (Ps. 119), Job (Job 23:12), the eunuch (Acts 8:28), the Bereans (Acts 17:11), and Timothy (2 Tim. 3:14–15), and also by examples from the church, such as Hilarion the Anchorite (Flacius, *Ecclesiastical History*, 4th century, vol. 2, ch. 10),[278] John of Egypt (Baronio, *Annales*, at AD 309),[279] and the Waldensians, who were always memorizing most exactly, and reciting, whole books of Scripture, such as Job, the Psalms, and Proverbs. Indeed, it is certain from the writings of the historians that the reading of Scripture was also a favorite practice of rulers, for example, Queen Elizabeth of England; her cousin Jane Grey; György Rákóczi the elder, Prince of Transylvania;[280] and others.

Why

It is commended by the characteristics of the study itself: (1) its dignity and excellence, which we have summarized in chapter 1 §XXIX, and this chapter §LXIV; (2) its pleasantness and sweetness (Ps. 119:14–16, 70, 72, 103; Jer. 15:16; Rev. 10:9–10); (3) its usefulness above all other studies, which we have noted in the passages just cited compared with 1 Timothy 4:8. For this reason, in the Talmud, *Sanhedrin*, it is said that man was created "for the work of the law."[281] (4) Its necessity, because without this study we could not live for God, neither here in grace, nor hereafter in glory. For Scripture is, as our theorem holds, the sole rule of living for God. So then, without Scripture, we will be dead to God. (5) The promises made by God to those who study it (Ps. 1:2–3; Prov. 8:34ff.). (6) Finally, the disgrace, dangers, and evils, so many and so great, that rest upon neglect of the divine Word (Prov. 13:13ff.; cf. §LXV).

---

278. Matthew Flacius Illyrius (Matthias Vlacich), *Decima centuria ecclesiasticae historiae…in urbe Magdeburgica*, 2 vols. (Basel: Joannes Oporinus, 1562), 2:1295–97.

279. Baronio, *Annales*, 1.313.

280. The lesser known of these figures to the English-speaking world is György Rákóczi the elder, or George I Rákóczi (1591–1648), who was a prominent Hungarian Protestant prince and general who militarily secured toleration for Protestants in Transylvania against the Hapsburgs through the Treaty of Linz (1645) in conjunction with a line of several other Protestant Hungarian princes, such as István Bocskai (1557–1606) and Gabriel Bethlen de Iktár (1580–1629), among others. For a good introduction on his role in the rise of Reformed Protestantism in Hungary, see David P. Daniel's "Calvinism in Hungary: the theological and ecclesiastical transition to the Reformed faith," in *Calvinism in Europe (1540–1620)*, eds. A. Pettegree, A. Duke, and G. Lewis (New York: Cambridge University Press, 1996), 205–30.

281. לעמל התורה.

How

Meanwhile, we must attend also to the manner of this study, that it proceed from a sincere love and desire for the Word (Ps. 119:143; 1:2); with whatever sort of other cares and business removed (Luke 8:7); with the legitimate goal of learning and doing set before us (James 1:22–26); applying, in addition, diligence, by which we examine (John 5:39) and pay constant attention day and night (Ps. 1:2); simplicity of heart (2 Cor. 1:12); prayers (Ps. 119:18; 25:4); and practice (Ps. 25:4). See Hoornbeeck, *Practical Theology*, part 1, book 1, chapter 3, on the study of the divine Word.[282]

The fifth use, the reading of the divine Word, in three parts:
(1) That we should read it
LXIX. Because that study especially expends itself in reading, hearing, interpretation, meditation, comparison, and practice, we will treat each of these individually, but briefly. Therefore, let the fifth practice be the reading of the divine Word, as much public (Deut. 31:11–12; Col. 4:16; Luke 4:16; Neh. 8:6) as private (Col. 3:16), which, in the first place, is urged by commandments (Deut. 17:18; Josh. 1:8; Rev. 1:3; James 1:23–24; Acts 8:30; 17:11) and, second, is set forth by examples (2 Kings 22:8; Acts 8:30; 17:11).

(2) Why

And third, it is commended by motives, both general ones, which, with the necessary changes made, are found in the preceding section, and special ones, from those things that reading can supply more particularly. For example, (1) It provides acquaintance with divine things (2 Tim. 3:15). (2) It confirms the word that has been heard. Accordingly, the Bereans, after hearing Paul, directed themselves to the reading of Scripture (Acts 17:11). (3) It confirms the soul in Christian virtue, for which reason it was prescribed for the Israelite king (Deut. 17:19). (4) It aids against temptations, as the sword of the Word (Eph. 6:17). (5) It provides perpetual material for meditating (Ps. 1:2). (6) Likewise, the fashion of our times could stand as a motive, since in our times the use of the divine Word is so free, so abundant for us, beyond that of our predecessors under the papacy, when it was almost a sin to look at Scripture.

---

282. "De studio verbi divini" in Hoornbeeck, *Theologia practica*, 2nd ed., 2 vols. (Utrecht: Johannes & Guilelmus van de Water, 1689), 1:45–84.

(3) How

Meanwhile, let us read attentively, with reverent stillness,[283] so that the words might be, as it were, in our heart (Deut. 6:6); with understanding (Matt. 13:19; Acts 8:30); eagerly, so that our delight is in the law of God (Ps. 1:2) and also that the Word is received with all willingness[284] (Acts 17:11); with faith (Heb. 4:2); with suitable affections—joy concerning the promises, sadness concerning the judgments, fear concerning its threats, and so forth (Isa. 66:2; 2 Kings 22:11, 19); with diligent frequency (Ps. 1:2; Josh. 1:8; Ps. 119:44, 55, 60); and with a pure soul, for holy things are for the holy[285] (Matt. 7:6; Ex. 19:10–11). Compare these with the general principles of study from the preceding section.

The sixth use, the hearing of the Word, likewise in three parts:
(1) That we should hear it (2) Why

LXX. The sixth practice concerns the hearing of the Word, which again, in the first place, is urged by commandment (Deut. 5:1; 6:4; Prov. 1:8; 4:1; Isa. 55:3; Luke 16:29; Matt. 17:5). It is recommended by examples such as David (Ps. 85:8) and many others. Second, it is commended by motives, first general ones (see §LXIV), then specific ones. The specific motives are supplied partly by the Word that has been heard, and its excellence, as gold that is most pure (Ps. 19:10); its sweetness, like honey (Ps. 19:10); its efficacy, as it recalls fire and other things, as we have shown above in §XXI. These motives also are supplied partly from the use and necessity of hearing for conversion (Ps. 19:7; 1 Peter 1:23), and for faith (Rom. 10:17). And they are supplied partly from its hearers, for whom it offers evidence of regeneration (John 8:47), of sincerity (John 10:27), and of the fear of God (Acts 13:16).

(3) How

But third, the chief point is in the manner of hearing (Luke 8:18), which itself consists in three things. To begin, it consists in the due preparation of the soul (Eccl. 5:1, 2; Ex. 19:14–15), for the fruitfulness and fruit of hearing greatly depends on this (Ps. 81:11). Five things principally accompany this preparation: (1) That we ready our soul in a timely manner for reverence, humility, and devotion, by meditation on the divine presence (Eccl. 5:2). (2) That we remove from our mind the prejudices and other vices by which the harvest of the Word is impeded (1 Peter 2:1; James 1:21), likewise also anxieties and vain,

---

283. μετὰ μυστικῆς ἡσυχίας, lit. "with mystical stillness."
284. μετὰ πάσης προθυμίας
285. τὰ ἄγια, τοῖς ἁγίοις

carnal, and worldly thoughts, and so on. (3) That we stir up our appetite and desire to hear the Word—"long for it,"[286] Peter commands us (1 Peter 2:2; cf. Ps. 119:40)—just as the Bereans "received the word with all eagerness"[287] (Acts 17:11), and just as Sergius Paulus "desired"[288] to hear the Word (Acts 13:7). Moreover, that appetite is stirred up by a consideration of the dignity and excellence of the Word (John 6:68; Acts 5:20), its efficacy (Rom. 1:16; Heb. 4:12; Isa. 55:11; 2 Cor. 2:15–16), and its utility (Ps. 19:7–8). (4) That we fortify our soul in advance with the resolution that we, simply and absolutely, without exception and discrimination, are going to receive whatever will be revealed to us, whether it will be threats or promises (Jer. 42:5–6; Ps. 119:6; Acts 10:33; Ex. 24:7). (5) That we pray earnestly before God, that, in his grace, he would breathe upon our hearing, so that it might prove to be saving for us (Ps. 25:4–5; 119:4–5). Second, the proper manner of hearing consists in a suitable disposition of the soul during that hearing. This includes that we hear (1) with an attentive mind (Prov. 2:2), following the example of Lydia (Acts 16:14), Mary (Luke 10:39), and the crowd (Acts 8:6). This attention certainly requires inquiry (Isa. 58:2) and examination (Rom. 12:2). (2) With the intention of the will to observe the things that are said (Ps. 119:6, 106). (3) With faith (John 5:24; Heb. 4:2; Isa. 53:1). For by that we cling to the Word (Ps. 119:31), and the Word itself clings to us and is sown in us as the engrafted Word (James 1:21). (4) With hope, expecting the things promised, and life (John 5:39; Ps. 130:5). (5) With love (2 Thess. 2:13). (6) With reverence, fear, and trembling (Isa. 66:2). (7) With humility (Acts 10:33; James 1:21). (8) With observance (Deut. 5:1; James 1:22). Third, the proper manner of hearing consists in the duties that ought to follow the hearing of the Word, such as (1) holding in our memory the things we have heard (James 1:23–25), (2) ruminating on them and turning them over in our mind (Luke 2:51; Ps. 119:15–16), (3) repeating them and discussing them with others (Deut. 11:18–19), and (4) persisting in the things we have heard throughout our entire life (Ps. 119:60). See Hoornbeeck, *Practical Theology* (pt. 1, bk. 1, ch. 3);[289] and Ames, *Marrow* (bk. 2, ch. 8); *Cases of Conscience* (bk. 4, ch. 2).[290]

---

286. ἐπιποθήσατε
287. μετὰ πολλῆς προθυμίας ἐδέξαντο λόγον
288. ἐπεζήτησε
289. Hoornbeeck, *Theologia practica*, 1:45–84.
290. Ames, *Medulla*, 2.8.1–43; item, *Guilielmi Amesii de conscientia, et eius iure vel casibus libri quinque* (Amsterdam: Joannes Jansson, 1635), 4.2.1–23.

The seventh use, the interpretation of Scripture
LXXI. Now, because without the genuine sense of Scripture, all the study of it that we spend in reading, hearing, and so forth, is entirely vain, it is altogether necessary that the interpretation of the Scriptures should follow as the seventh practice, whether that interpretation is scholastic, seeking the genuine sense, or ecclesiastical, principally seeking practical efficacy, or private, including both in its own way.

Motives
Moreover, the interpretation of Scripture is necessary for many reasons, inasmuch as, first, many things occur in the sacred page that at first glance seem obscure and "hard to understand"[291] (2 Peter 3:16). Second, the life-giving words of the omnipotent God are set forth in it (John 6:68), which words require a person's most careful consideration. Third, in Scripture is transacted the business of eternal salvation, which depends on Scripture's genuine sense (2 Tim. 3:15). Fourth, human nature possesses the most profound sleepiness, congestion, and sluggishness in divine things (1 Cor. 2:14). Fifth, the maliciousness and astuteness of Satan and the followers of heretics in perverting the divine records is astounding (2 Cor. 11:3). For this reason, we poor souls must labor, by religious interpretation of the Scriptures, that we may certainly grasp their genuine sense.

The means of interpreting Scripture: For those educated in letters[292]
LXXII. Now, the means for this endeavor are of two kinds. The first kind is for those educated in letters. These means are: (1) sufficient expertise in the original languages of Hebrew, Aramaic, and Greek, and (2) prudent use of logic for a methodical analysis of the sacred text. Ambrose, in epistle 8, says, "For although the sacred authors did not write according to art, but according to grace, which is above every art; nevertheless, those who have written about art have discovered art in their writings."[293] These means also include: (3) the use of rhetoric for examining the tropes and figures of the text; (4) the aid of philosophy, since, besides the mysteries, the majority of things in Scripture are encountered in philosophy also; (5) the comparison of sacred history with human history; and not least, (6) the parallel comparison[294] of the translations with their sources, of

---

291. δυσνόητα
292. Note that the Latin editions mistakenly label the following section LXXI, and so section numbers from here to the end of the chapter will be one higher than the original.
293. *PL* 16:912.
294. παραλληλουχία

translations both ancient and modern, in their various languages, and especially of the ancient Septuagint translation and of the Syriac New Testament; (7) prudent use of orthodox commentaries. Yet we should use all these means in such a way that (8) we leave all the languages, arts, histories, translations, and commentaries in their own proper place, namely, that those things might be servants to the Scriptures and not masters of them.

The means of interpreting for everyone

LXXIII. The former means concerned principally those educated in letters. Other means concern everyone indiscriminately. These are: (1) Prayers for spiritual wisdom (James 1:5), by which we may behold wondrous things in the law (Ps. 119:18), and by which we may reach the bottom of the well (John 4:11). (2) That we approach the interpretation of the Scriptures imbued with the same spirit of grace by which they were composed, that is, with pure eyes (Matt. 5:8) and an illuminated and cleansed mind (Eph. 1:18). This is that anointing that teaches us all things (1 John 2:27). (3) That we turn over the Scripture continually with a submissive mind, denying ourselves. For "if anyone seems to himself to know something, he does not yet know anything as he ought" (1 Cor. 8:2). For how shall men who are proud, swollen with prejudices, and expecting all things from their own wisdom follow the mind of Scripture? (cf. Prov 11:2; Ps. 25:9; Matt. 11:25). (4) That we be accustomed to a reading and studying of the Scriptures that is both constant and methodical. I say constant (Ps. 1:2; Col. 3:16; Josh. 1:7; Deut. 6:6–9), namely, so that the sense of Scripture may become familiar, as well as easy, to us; and also methodical (Ps. 50:23), for just as method is the fulcrum of the memory, so also is it the light of the intellect. (5) That we approach Scripture equipped with the analogy of faith, which the apostle designates as "the pattern of sound words"[295] (2 Tim. 1:13), and which he commends (Rom. 12:3, 6). Nothing contrary to this must be admitted as the sense of Scripture. To put this another way, we must cautiously and prudently observe the universal agreement and harmony of the Scriptures. For although they were written by different people, in different times and places, nevertheless they were inspired by one Spirit, for which reason they are always consistent with themselves, and if there is any discord, it is not in the Scriptures, but in our mind. Moreover, whatever apparent contradiction[296] occurs in the Scriptures, we see that it arises from one of these five sources: a phrase or a certain word is employed in a different sense in different

---

295. ὑποτύπωσιν ὑγιαινόντων λόγων
296. ἐναντιοφανές

places; or the same words are uttered in diverse places, but not about the same fact or subject; or when they do speak about the same thing, they do not speak about the same part of it; or they speak about the same thing, but in a different respect; or finally, they speak about a different time. To demonstrate them individually by examples would be easy, if the pursuit of brevity would bear it. (6) That we interpret Scripture by the Scriptures, as in the example of Peter (Acts 2:25–32). Augustine says in *On Christian Doctrine* (bk. 3, ch. 25), "where the thoughts are set down more openly, there we should learn how to understand them in the obscure places." For Scripture does not present any difficulty without at the same time revealing its remedy. It is helpful (7) that we keep in our minds and at hand the whole plan of Scripture, that is, the order of the books, the inscriptions[297] of each one, the time in which they were written, the author, the occasion of writing, the purpose, and the principal parts. In this way, we will have an idea as well as a skeleton of each book, and, at the same time, a key and compass, as it were, to show the writer's purpose and the means by which he pursues that purpose. And that in addition to all these, (8) we add practice, by which we use the things we have learned. "For if anyone wills to do God's will, he will recognize whether the teaching is from God" (John 7:16–17; cf. Ps. 119:98–100). For as Bernard of Clairvaux says, "Whoever rightly reads the divine Scriptures turns its words into deeds" (*Treatise on the Right Order of Life*).[298] There are other grammatical, rhetorical, logical, and historical tools for interpreting. Concerning these see Salomon Glass's *Sacred Philology* (bk. 2, pt. 2);[299] and Michael Walther Sr.'s *Biblical Workshop* (thesis 2, art. 5).[300]

The eighth use, meditation, in four parts (1) What is meditation?
LXXIV. The eighth use under this heading is about meditation on the divine Word. We will be more copious on this topic since our countrymen who teach ascetics write on this topic either less often, or with more restraint. We will cover the whole business with these four little questions that we are about to mention. First, what is meditation? Scripture customarily indicates it, sometimes by metaphorical names, as when, for example, Scripture calls it ruminating, which

---

297. ἐπιγραφάς

298. *Tractatus de ordine vitae*, PL 184:566.

299. Salomon Glass, *Philologiae Sacrae qua totius sacrosanctae veteris & novi testamenti Scripturae tum stylus et litteratura, tum sensus et genuinae interpretationis ratio expenditur libri quinque*, 5th ed. (Frankfurt: J. T. Fleischer, 1686), 2.2, pp. 351–60.

300. Michael Walther Sr., *Michaelis Waltheri…officina biblica adperta…de s. s. scriptura in genere et in specie*, 3rd ed. (Wittenberg: J. W. Meyzer & G. Zimmermann, 1703), thes. 2, art. 5, §§263–72, pp. 95–103.

was proper to clean animals (Deut. 14:6), and likewise eating the received Word (Jer. 15:16; Ezek. 3:1–3; Rev. 10:9); sometimes by more proper names, such as studying (Ps. 1:2), examining (John 5:39; Ps. 78:7), pondering it in the heart (Luke 2:19), and "seeking to understand"[301] (Luke 1:29; cf. Ps. 19:14; 49:3; 119:97, 99). Now, under this heading we take the word *meditation* not altogether strictly, such that it is distinguished from thinking, considering, contemplating, and so forth, but broadly, so that it may connote all those things. Thus indeed, for us, meditation is nothing other than a fixed and firmly standing actuation of all the faculties of the soul for this purpose: that we may not only grasp the genuine sense of the divine Word in our mind, but also experience the force of it in our heart. It is called an actuation of the faculties of the soul, that is, the intellect, the will, and the affections, just as though it were an act of bringing them together and applying them to this or that theme—and that not superficial and perfunctory, but fixed and composed, by which the Word, as it were, dwells in us[302] (Col. 3:16). Its end is twofold: (1) That we grasp the genuine sense of the Word with our mind. This sort of meditation generally is the customary practice of the studious, a meditation which aims only at this, that they might understand. (2) That we experience in our heart the force and efficacy of the Word we have received, "and bear fruit"[303] (Luke 8:15). This is a general description of this sort of meditation. Now, in particular it embraces: (1) Remembering the Word we have heard and read (Luke 2:19; Prov. 2:1; Ps. 119:11; Eccl. 9:1) and recollecting it (Deut. 4:39; Mal. 4:4). (2) Examining it, pondering on it, either on our own, by talking to ourselves (Luke 2:19), or with other people (Deut. 6:6–7; 11:18–19; Luke 24:14–15, 17). (3) Distinctly observing, weighing, and applying each particular thing until from every little part of the divine Word, as from its fibers and veins, we suck out and extract for ourselves, as it were, its quintessence, just as spices are customarily rubbed well, that they might give off their fragrances.

(2) That we should meditate
LXXV. Second, that we should meditate is demanded, first by commands (Josh. 1:8; Hag. 1:3, cf. v. 5; John 5:39; Col. 3:16; Luke 9:44; Prov. 2:1) and then by examples: David (Ps. 77:6; 19:14; 119:97, 99, 103, 140), Solomon (Prov. 24:32), and Mary (Luke 2:19).

---

301. διαλογίζεσθαι
302. ἐνοικεῖ ἡμῖν
303. καὶ καρποφοροῦμεν

(3) Why should we meditate?

LXXVI. Third, why should we meditate? Namely, because (1) the Word of God is a particular kind of food for the soul, for which reason it is compared to bread (Amos 7:12), milk (1 Peter 2:2; 1 Cor. 3:2), honey (Ps. 119:103), and with these ministers are said to feed us (Jer. 3:15). Now, to what does food refer if not to eating? And what is eating the Word if it is not meditating upon it (Jer. 15:16)? (2) So then, the Word will not profit us unless it is properly meditated on, just as food does not profit us unless it is chewed up and descends into the stomach, and there, by continual agitation, is heated up and digested. Accordingly, without meditation the Word is, as it were, without root (Matt. 13:21), and it is not the "implanted word"[304] (James 1:21). (3) Meditation is greatly profitable for illuminating the intellect, correcting the will, stirring up the affections, and leading us both in truth and in goodness (Prov. 6:22–23), to such an extent that it makes those things our supreme happiness (Ps. 1:2). (4) If some sort of bitterness, difficulty, or ambiguity appears to be mixed with the Word of God, or some sort of pestilence is smeared on it by the heretics, it is easily discovered by serious and constant meditation, just as by chewing we easily discover a foreign object in bread. See the other reasons in Hoornbeeck, *Practical Theology* (bk. 1, ch. 3).[305]

(4) How must we meditate? Four things must be observed

LXXVII. Fourth and finally, how should we meditate? Here the following four things must be noted. First, note the qualification of one who intends to meditate, namely (1) that he be regenerate, and illuminated by regeneration, for by nature we are blind (Eph. 4:17–18), and the natural[306] person does not perceive those things that are of the Spirit (1 Cor. 2:14; Isa. 6:9); (2) that he be pure in heart, and purged from sins, for such are those who see God and the things of God (Matt. 5:8); (3) free from temporal cares (Matt. 13:22); (4) constant and fixed in his purpose of meditating, undistracted by any scheme of any person (Neh. 6:2–3). Second, note the selection of the circumstances, that is: (1) The place. It should be solitary and secret, whether at home (Matt. 6:4, 6, 8) or outdoors (Song 6:11–12), following the example of Isaac (Gen. 24:63), the Savior (Mark 1:35; Matt. 14:23), John in the desert (Luke 1:80), and David on his bed (Ps. 16:7; 6:6). (2) The time, whether in the morning (Ps. 5:3), in the evening (Gen. 24:63), or at night (Ps. 16:7), provided that, in general, it is stated and fixed, so that we put aside time for it daily (Ps. 55:17), and most solemnly so

---

304. ἔμφυτος λόγος
305. Hoornbeeck, *Theologia practica*, 1:45–84.
306. ψυχικός

on the Lord's Day, following the example of John (Rev. 1:10), since we see that
God set that day apart for meditating on the works of the other six days[307]
(Ex. 20:11); and in an extraordinary way, whenever God, by either blessings or
afflictions, as it were, summons us to it, namely, on days, either of fasting (Lam.
3:19–20, 40) or of cheerful solemnity (Ps. 103:1, 2, 4). (3) The posture. For it
is performed either by standing (Luke 18:11, 13), by prostrating oneself (Dan.
9:18), by walking around (Gen. 24:63), or with bent knees and uplifted eyes (Acts
7:55) and hands (Ps. 28:2) and so forth, provided that, in general, we use such
postures that especially rouse the soul to devotion and attention. (4) The subject
or theme that one ought to have here: not vain, or worldly, or natural, or political,
or historical, but spiritual and divine (Ps. 119:37, 54); for example, God and
his attributes, his works, creation, providence, redemption, and so forth. Third,
note here the impediments that must be removed, which include: (1) depraved
fellowship (Acts 2:37, cf. v. 40; Ps. 104:35); (2) the multitude of worldly cares
(Luke 10:41); (3) ignorance (Ps. 119:99); (4) the natural aversion of our soul to
this exercise (Luke 24:25); and (5) the roving diversion of our thoughts (Matt.
15:8), which must be restrained (Ps. 42:5, 11; 43:5). Fourth and finally, there is
an order to be pursued in meditating, and that (1) pertaining to our entrance
into meditating, where preparation must be employed, such as we described
with respect to the hearing of the Word in §LXX above. With the necessary
changes being made, that same preparation can be employed here. (2) Pertaining
to our process of meditating, where we must work by a certain method so that
the mind might be properly drawn from one thing to another. Different methods
are pursued by different people. We are quite happy to make the method a
matter of discretion, provided it is not inconsistent and disordered.[308] These
two things, at least, should be asked of every subject and text: first, what truths
it contains to form our judgment; second, what good things it contains to stir
up our affections and likewise to correct our morals. And for every one of these
things, we should first set it forth, and then confirm it by Scripture's statements,
examples, and reasons, then explain it in all its parts, and finally, apply it, as is
customarily done in the meditation that sermons offer. (3) Lastly, there is an
order that concerns our departure from meditating, where we must be watchful
that we do not cease from meditating before we have gained the genuine sense
of Scripture in our intellect, and likewise its force and efficacy in our will, as
well as in our affections. What we treated above in §LXVIII, on the study of
the divine Word, applies to this point and can be considered together with it.

---

307. ἐξαημέρου
308. ἄτακτος

The ninth use, conversations about the Scriptures

LXXVIII. Following meditation and talking to ourselves about the Word of God are conversations,[309] joint inquiries,[310] talking to others (Isa. 50:4), in which we pour out to them with our mouth the things meditated on in our heart, and we have discussions[311] about those things for mutual edification (Rom. 1:11–12). Holy conversations of this sort are urged by the commandments of God (Deut. 6:7; Eph. 4:29; Col. 3:16; 1 Thess. 5:11; 1 Peter 4:11; Josh. 1:8; Prov. 5:2); and they are commended by examples, such as David (Ps. 119:97, cf. v. 172; 71:15), Job (Job 4:3–4), Abraham (Gen. 18:19), and those on the road to Emmaus (Luke 24:15, 17, "What are these words that you discuss together?"[312]).

Motives

LXXIX. A great many things commend conversations about the Scriptures. First, they are indicators of a spiritual and heavenly soul. For whatever the heart is full of, the mouth overflows with the same (Matt. 12:34; Ps. 119:11, 13, 15), just as a Gileadite was recognized from his "shibboleth"[313] (Judg. 12:6). Second, they sharpen the intellect, rouse the will to the good, and strengthen the memory. Third, they propagate the knowledge of God, together with all Christian virtues—faith, hope, and love—just as depraved conversations corrupt (1 Cor. 15:33; Luke 24:17, cf. v. 23). Fourth, they prevent vain, useless, and harmful discussions (1 Cor. 15:33).

Those obliged to this duty

LXXX. Godly conversations of this sort ought to flourish, first, among everyone indiscriminately, both the learned and the unlearned (Col. 3:16; Eph. 4:29; 1 Thess. 5:14–15), and then, according to each particular estate. Indeed, these conversations should occur in the domestic estate, between spouses (1 Cor. 14:35) and between parents and their children (Deut. 4:9; 6:7, 20; Ps. 78:5–6; Eph. 6:4; Gen. 18:19; Prov. 4:3–4; 31:1–3; 2 Tim. 1:5; 3:15). They should occur in the political estate, among all sorts of citizens—men and women, the elderly and youths—who have some measure of experience in the Scriptures (Titus 2:3–4). In this way, Aquila and Priscilla spoke with Apollos (Acts 18:26), and Abigail spoke with David (1 Sam. 25:25). In particular, they should take place among kings and princes (Deut. 27:11, 19; Ps. 119:172). These conversations

---

309. ὁμιλίαι
310. συζητήσεις
311. ἀντιβάλλομεν
312. Τίνες οἱ λόγοι οὗτοι οὓς ἀντιβάλλετε πρὸς ἀλλήλους
313. שבלת

should especially occur in the ecclesiastical estate, between pastors and their hearers (Mal. 2:7; 1 Tim. 4:6; Matt. 3:7ff.). And this sort of conversation[314] must not only thrive among any persons whatsoever, but also in any time and place whatsoever (Ps. 1:2; 119:97; Deut. 6:7)—and not only once in your life, as the Jews are only circumcised once, nor only once a year, as they celebrated the Passover, nor even three times a year, as they used to ascend to Jerusalem three times a year, nor only on the Sabbath day, but every day, day and night, that is, morning and evening, always and everywhere (Ps. 1:2).

Impediments
LXXXI. The following things hinder these kinds of conversational[315] exercises: ignorance of the Scriptures, and of divine matters (Luke 24:25); weariness, boredom, and contempt of spiritual things (Jer. 6:10); a fleshly and worldly soul (Matt. 7:18; 12:34–35); the "cares of life"[316] that swarm in the heart to such a degree that it cannot but spew out the same kinds of things[317] (Luke 21:34; 10:11); corrupt fellowship (1 Cor. 15:33); a distorted upbringing of one's offspring (cf. Prov. 22:6); a rotten heart (Gen. 6:5; Matt. 12:34); and a perverted sense of shame (cf. Ps. 119:46; Rom. 1:16).

Aids
LXXXII. On the other hand, the following things promote this sort of conversation: that we abstain from the vices designated above, and become accustomed to their opposing virtues; that we saturate our soul in the knowledge of the Scriptures and divine things, so we might have material for our discussions (Matt. 12:35); that we learn the language of Canaan (Isa. 19:18), and seek to obtain it from God (Ps. 119:43; 141:3; 51:15).

The manner
LXXXIII. Having pursued these things, let us also be careful: (1) That we not express anything about God and divine things rashly, imprudently, or jokingly, as did the Jews (Isa. 28:10), either by abuse (Acts 19:13), contempt (2 Peter 3:3–4), "contending about words"[318] (2 Tim. 2:14; 3:13), or also by haughtiness, being proud (1 Cor. 4:6). (2) That, while conversing, we have right before our eyes as our target the glory of God (James 3:9) and the edification of our neighbor

---

314. ὁμιλίαι
315. ὁμιλιτικά
316. μέριμναὶ βιωτικαί
317. ὁμογένεα
318. λογομαχίαν

(1 Thess. 5:11). (3) That we strive to have or to pursue an accurate knowledge of those things that we plan to speak about (Rom. 15:14; Ps. 39:1). (4) Before we converse, we should consider where, when, and to whom we will speak, that we may speak suitably (Prov. 25:11) and not undertake a topic that exceeds our capacity (Ps. 131:1).

The tenth use, the observance or practice of the Word, in three parts:
(1) That it should be done (2) Why
LXXXIV. There is yet one use of this topic left, namely, the practice and observance of the divine Word. In the first place, God requires this in Scripture in so many commands (Deut. 17:9–10; Josh. 1:16–18; Ps. 119:33–34; Prov. 7:1; Isa. 2:3; 55:3; Matt. 7:24; 5:19; Luke 8:15; 11:28; John 13:17; James 1:22; Rev. 1:3). Second, it is commended by the most powerful reasons, by which the following are evident: (1) This is the goal of all the study that we devote to the Word of God (Deut. 5:1). (2) It is not the one who merely reads and hears it who will be blessed, but the one who also does it (James 1:25; John 13:17). (3) The Word of God is harmful when unobserved (2 Cor. 2:16; Luke 12:47; Heb. 6:7–8). (4) On the other hand, it is profitable in every way when studiously observed. Now first, we will observe the Word generally if we are not content with reading, hearing, and meditating on it, but in addition, (1) we universally believe everything in it (Acts 24:14–16); (2) we apply it to ourselves (Ps. 27:8), since the Word of God is supplied to us for this purpose (Rom. 15:4), just as the apostles apply the words of Christ to themselves (Matt. 26:22; 19:25–27); (3) we bind ourselves by vows and oaths to a universal observance of it (Jer. 42:5–6; Ps. 119:106). And second, we will observe the Word specifically if (1) we pursue the things it commands and prohibits, in submissive obedience, by doing the former and shunning the latter; (2) we lean on its promises with a fixed and firm confidence in our soul (Ps. 130:5); (3) we receive its threats with fear (Isa. 66:2); and (4) we believe the things narrated in it. Compare the things that we considered on this matter above in chapter 1, §§XXXII–XXXV, and what we will consider in its own place in the chapter on observance.[319]

---

319. *TPT* 2.1.1.

CHAPTER THREE

The Distribution of Theology

Hold the pattern of sound words that you have heard from me, in faith and love.
—2 Timothy 1:13

The third of the prolegomena of theology, the distribution of theology.
I. It is proper to represent the art of living for God, whose norm is Scripture, in its distinct parts in relation to both our judgment and our memory. And this is what the apostle commends and teaches in the words above.

The Exegetical Part

The text is resolved and explained.
II. In these words he expresses an exhortation concerning the sacred theology that Timothy must protect and observe according to its essential parts, namely, faith and love. Three things must be considered here:

    A. The thing distributed, which is "the pattern of sound words."[1] By this we understand what is commonly indicated by the term *theology*. In the phrase itself it is called:

        1. A "pattern,"[2] that is, a "sketch,"[3] model, form, system, syntagma, complex of theological truths, "plan,"[4] or "summary."[5] It is, according to Beza, a figure taken from painters.[6] The apostle here hints that a methodical structure for theological matters is entirely necessary for theologians.

---

1. ὑποτύπωσις ὑγιαινόντων λόγων
2. ὑποτύπωσις
3. σκιαγραφία
4. *een ontwerp*
5. *een kort begrijp*
6. Cf. Theodore Beza, *Annotationes Majores in Novum Jesu Christi Testamentum* (Geneva: [Jérémie Des Plaches], 1594), 466.

2. "Of sound words."[7] This is the subject matter of the system of theology, which we saw above, in chapter 1.

3. "Which you have heard from me."[8] This is the organic cause of the theological subject matter. For it must rest on the foundation of the prophets and the apostles (Eph. 2:20). We saw these things above in chapters 1 and 2.

B. The distribution, or the parts of the thing distributed: "in faith and love."[9] It matters little whether you refer these words back to "hold,"[10] so that they express the parts of habitual theology, or to "the pattern of sound words,"[11] so that they designate the parts of systematic and doctrinal theology, since the first option is nothing but a derivative[12] of the second, unless perhaps (and I am not opposed to this) you prefer to refer the words to both, because subordinate things are not contradictory. It is sufficient to conclude that faith and love are the parts of theology, either of habitual theology or of doctrinal theology, or, what is best, of both. It should be noted that "faith" especially pertains to what must be believed, and "love" pertains to what must be done, or observance.

C. The practice or duty to observe concerning this distribution: "Hold it" or "have it."[13] That is: (1) Preserve it, or keep it ready for yourself, that you may carry it with you everywhere. (2) Observe it, that you may conform your teaching[14] to it; likewise (3) so that you may establish your arguments against those who contradict it;[15] and finally, (4) so that you may direct your whole practice, together with that of your people. These are the chief ends, both of the "pattern"[16] and of its parts, that is, faith and love.

The Dogmatic Part

The parts of theology are faith and love.

III. In the interest of our aim, we will now construct from the text nothing other

---

7. ὑγιαινόντων λόγων
8. ὧν παρ' ἐμοῦ ἤκουσας
9. ἐν πίστῃ καὶ ἀγάπῃ
10. ἔχε
11. ὑποτύπωσιν ὑγιαινόντων λόγων
12. ἀποσκιμάτιον
13. ἔχε
14. διδασκαλίας
15. ἀντιλέγουσι
16. ὑποτυπώσεως

than this, that the best way to distribute sacred theology or the Christian religion is into faith and love.

It is proved by the Scriptures.

We see clearly that not only do the testimonies of Scripture applaud this distribution (Ps. 37:3; 1 Tim. 1:19; John 13:17) but also the examples of Scripture, since the theology of Paul is made up of these parts, both his habitual theology (Acts 24:14–16; Titus 3:8) and his doctrinal theology, as is evident in most of his epistles, which generally divide into these two parts, as we see in his epistles to the Romans, Ephesians, Colossians, and others. Also, the consensus of the orthodox writers of antiquity applauds this distribution. In the fourth lecture of his *Catechetical Lectures*, Cyril of Jerusalem speaks in the following way: "The method of godliness consists in these two things: the precision of godly doctrines and of virtuous practices."[17] Likewise Anastasius of Nicaea in *Bibliotheca Patrum* asks, "What is the sign of the complete Christian?" and he answers, "faith and good works."[18] See more testimonies from both the ancients and those who are more recent, in Amandus Polanus's *Syntagma* (bk. 2, ch. 1).[19]

---

17. Τῆς εὐσεβείας τρόπος ἐκ δύω τούτων, συνήστηκε· δογμάτων εὐσεβῶν ἀκριβείας, καὶ πράξεων ἀγαθῶν. Cf. Cyril of Jerusalem, *Catechetical Lectures*, 4.2 in *NPNF2* 7:19.

18. There is a substantial lack of clarity as to which patristic-era Anastasius this quote belongs. Mastricht cites the response as *fides & bona opera* from Anastasius of Nicea, which is correlated by Jodocus Coccius, *Thesaurus Catholicus, in quo controversiae fidei jam olim nostraque memoria excitatae* (Köln: Arnoldus Quentelius, 1601), 2:232, but Coccius sources this to Anastasius Nicaenus and it is quoted as *recta fides & pia opera*. Mastricht cites a short title of *Bibliothec. Patr.*, which most likely is the massive and revised edition of a 27-volume set: Marguerin de La Bigne, *Maxima Bibliotheca Patrum* (1677). However, in La Bigne, *Maxima Bibliotheca Patrum* (1677), 9:957, Mastricht's exact citation of the question (*Quodnam sit signum veri Christiani?*) is (1) answered with *recta fides & pia opera* and (2) reproduced in a selection from an obscure seventh century Greek monk, Anastasius Sinaitus, a work that is commonly known simply in Latin as *Quaestiones et Responsiones*. For the Greek textual basis for this citation, see J. C. A. M. von Aretin, *Beyträge zur Geschichte und Literatur vorzüglich aus den Schätzen der pfalzbaierischen Centralbibliothek zu Münich* (Münich: Kommision der Schererschen Kunst und Buchhandlung, 1805), 5:229, τί ἐστὶ τὸ σημεῖον τοῦ τελείου χριστιανοῦ. Α. πίστις ὀρθὴ καὶ ἔργα εὐσεβῆ. However, von Aretin references the question and response to a Greek manuscript of yet another Anastasius, the Coptic archbishop of Alexandria, Anastasius, whose reign was from 605–616 (or in the Coptic tradition Pope Anastasisus of Alexandria), rather than Anastasius of Nicea as Mastricht does or Anastasius of Sinai as La Bigne does. Cf. "Anastasius" in Aziz S. Etya ed., *The Coptic Encyclopedia*, 8 vols. (New York: Macmillan, 1991), CE:125b–126b.

19. Amandus Polanus, *Syntagma Theologiae Christianae ab Amando Polansdorf iuxta leges ordinis Methodici conformatum* (Hanover: Wechel, 1610), 1:843–56.

It is confirmed by four reasons. First
IV. Nor do we lack good reasons for this distribution. First, if you consider
the object of theology, you will discover that this distribution corresponds as
accurately as possible to its parts. This is vigorously stated by William Ames: "A
property of this partition (which is required in a genuine distribution of any art)
is that it flows from the nature of its object. For since the principle or first act
of spiritual life (which is the proper object of theology) is faith, and the second
act, as the operation emanating from that principle, is observance, it necessarily
follows that these two are the genuine parts of theology, and no others must be
sought" (*Marrow of Theology*, I.ii.2).[20]

Second
Next, if you compare this division with the thing divided, you will see that the
parts are most exactly adequate to the whole, which is required in every legitimate division. For there is nothing contained in theology that does not come
under one of these parts, and there is nothing contained under these parts that
does not pertain to theology.

Third
In fact, third, the parts are not only adequate to the thing divided but are also
contradistinguished without overlap, which also is required in a genuine distribution. For just as we observe in natural life that those two acts—its first and
second act—are mutually contradistinguished from each other, so also in spiritual life, faith and love, which correspond to those two parts of natural life, are
mutually set apart from each other.

Fourth
Fourth, I do not need to speak about the fact that natural theology, which has
bits and pieces of revealed theology, applauds this distribution. For surely even
philosophy, to the extent that it represents natural theology, exhibits the faith of
the philosophers in its metaphysics or pneumatics, and in its ethics and the like,
it exhibits their observance and love, as Ames has said in the place previously
cited from him. Polanus has given, in the passage already cited, other reasons
that we choose not to describe here.

It is explained in three parts. First
V. Thus it remains briefly to ascertain in what sense we understand faith and love
as the parts of theology. Here, first, by the word *faith* we understand not only

---

20. Ames, *Medulla Theologiae*, I.ii.2.

that faith which is believed, that is, the things that must be believed; nor only the faith by which we believe, that is, the habit of believing; but both conjointly: *faith* signifies the faith by which we believe, just as it signifies the faith that we believe, just as in the word *love*, or observance, all the practical duties of theology are universally included.

Second
Furthermore, second, when we acknowledge that these are the parts of Christian theology, we mean not only that they are its essential parts, dissecting the whole body of theology, but also that they are its integral parts, corresponding properly to each individual element of theology. For every article of theology has its own theory (or faith) and practice (or observance) as we have shown in chapter 1.

Third
Finally, third, we certainly recognize that these parts differ from each other as much by their nature as by their precepts, but yet we do not tear them apart. For in their use and exercise they always walk in step. But we do make this distinction, that the first place is appointed to faith and the second to observance. For no vital actions can be be elicited from anything unless there is a preexisting principle of life.

The Elenctic Part
Theologians' contrary or different distributions are examined.
VI. Furthermore, because what is straight is its own norm as well as the norm for what is crooked, it is easy to perceive, from what we have already said, what we must think about discordant distributions of theology. Certainly, we do not wish to reject simply and absolutely[21] all other divisions that differ, whether in words or even substance, in any way from ours, since they often are perfectly suitable for the particular goal of each author. Yet, if you would seek an accurate and adequate distribution, you will scarcely find one more preferable than this one.

It is asked whether the Socinian and Arminian distributions are genuine.
VII. The Socinians, so that they might abrogate the eternal deity of Christ and might contradistinguish Christ from God, separate theology into two parts, one concerning God and the other concerning Christ. And because their gospel, since it agrees with their theology, is summed up in two parts, precepts and Christ's

---

21. ἀποτόμως

promises, they therefore think that all theological topics[22] are comprehended in those two things, precepts and promises. The Remonstrant apologists are not far removed from them. Though they really are Socinians in almost all the heads of theology, they would not like to be counted in their number (for Socinians have been removed by our civil laws from the fellowship of our republic),[23] and so they recommend adding another part, and thus distribute theology into three parts: faith in the divine promises, obedience to the divine precepts, and the reverence due to the Scriptures. These parts, in words at least, seem to differ from those of the Socinians, but in fact they agree with them. They reduce all these things to this, that they eliminate from Christianity the consubstantial[24] deity of Christ, his equivalent satisfaction for our sins, faith in Christ, insofar as it receives him as our only Redeemer, and other essentials of the Christian faith. So then, these distributions are not only, first, narrower than the matter that must be distributed, but also, second, diametrically opposed to our text and to those Scripture passages, as well as to those arguments, which we used just above to reinforce the practice of observance.[25] I do not need to add, third, that they would utterly overturn the foundation of Christianity, laid by a thousand testimonies of Scripture—that we are saved by a practical knowledge of God and Christ (John 17:3) and by faith alone in both. Nor do our adversaries dispute properly in favor of their own distributions, but rather, they carelessly commit them only to their own hypotheses.

The Practical Part
The first use is for rebuke. In it we find 1. The rebuking of sins
VIII. It remains then for us, in a word or two, to touch upon this chapter's practice. I say in a word or two because practice belongs not so much to the distribution itself as to the distributing parts, which will be expressly examined later. The first practice, then, of this passage rebukes those, whether theologians or ordinary Christians, who most wickedly tear apart those essential parts of religion that are so tightly intertwined and in so doing, as it were, slay religion. This sin is usually committed in two ways. First, in regard to theory, by theologians who (1) pursue faith in such a way that they neglect love. These the apostle

---

22. θεολογούμενα
23. For a brief history of censorship and suppression of Socinianism and Socinian writings in the Dutch Republic from the late sixteenth century through the seventeenth century, see "Socinian Authors and Books" in *Bibliographia Sociniana: A bibliographical reference tool for the study of Dutch Socinianism and Antitrinitarianism*, ed. Piet Visser (Hilversum: Uitgeverij Verloren, 2004), 19–26.
24. ὁμοούσιος
25. 1.1.2 §LXXXIV

denounces (1 Cor. 13:1–2). Such men (2) are more intent on speculations and debates about faith than on faith itself (1 Tim. 6:3–5). And thus (3) in their teaching they press for the faith *that* we believe rather than the faith *by which* we believe. Second, in regard to practice, this sin is committed practically either by those who (1) put effort into faith only in order to know it for themselves alone (1 Cor. 8:1–3), or only to explain it to others (Titus 1:16), or only to defend it against those that speak against it (Rom. 2:18–20); or by those who (2) profess both faith and obedience or love, but only in word, while neglecting them in deed, and thus they argue indeed for the faith that belongs to the pattern[26] of theology, and even for love, but they do not do so in faith and love (James 2:18).

2. Arguments for rebuking

All of these sorts of people are worthy of rebuke, based especially on these arguments: (1) They rejoice in a faith that is dead (James 2:17), and thus in a faith that is not faith. For a dead faith is not faith, just as a dead man is not really a man. (2) In addition, they are not theologians or Christians (Rom. 2:19ff.) except in name[27] only. Indeed, these mutilated men are missing the second essential part of theology and Christianity, which is by far the chief part (2 Tim. 3:5). And thus (3) by this theology of theirs, and by its profession, though it be true, they show themselves to be liars (Titus 1:16; Rev. 2:2; 3:1). Furthermore, (4) they publicly dishonor God and also themselves (Rom. 2:17–25). And for this reason (5) they, together with all this theology of theirs, and their profession of it, however splendid, will most certainly one day be rejected by Christ (Matt. 7:22–23). Consider also, in this *Theology*, ch. 1, §§XXXII–XXXV.

The second use, for exhortation concerning connecting the parts of theology

IX. The second practice of this distribution calls all people to attention, that they hold together, both in their teaching and in their living, these things that are naturally interconnected, and that are so tightly connected by the Holy Spirit in this text and in other places, namely faith and observance, or love. That is, not only should they seriously pursue both parts of the theology of the Christian religion, faith and observance, but they should also pursue them *in* faith and observance. Or, what amounts to the same thing, not only should they learn both parts for themselves and teach them to others theoretically, but in both parts, in faith and in observance, they should also walk practically. Moreover, since this practice is basically the same as the one we considered above in the place just cited, so that

---

26. ὑποτυπώσεως
27. ὁμονύμως

we do not tread the same ground again, it is sufficient here simply to refer you back to it. Furthermore, we are reserving the distinct consideration, as much theoretical as practical, first of faith, then of love, each for its own proper[28] place.

The delineation of this whole theology text

X. As a corollary, we will append the arrangement[29] of this whole theology text. It consists in faith, which we have already published in eight books, and observance, which will include: First, moral theology, concerning simple virtues and vices, in three books, which will contain: (1) general matters of obedience—its nature, its norms, namely the law and conscience, its affections, and its parts; (2) religion, or duties toward God; and (3) righteousness, or duties toward our neighbor. Then second, ascetic theology, or composite virtues in their use and exercise, likewise in three books, which will concern both (1) more general matters of the Christian life and its establishment, its development, and its contraries—profanity and hypocrisy—then (2) more specific duties, namely, (a) those that concern knowing, loving, and worshiping God, both publicly (the reading and hearing of the divine Word, prayers, the sacraments) and privately (our domestic duties); and (b) those that concern our neighbor, where we will consider solitude and conversation, and the latter generally (in gatherings, in business), then specifically, with individuals of a certain kind (the afflicted, the lapsed, the good, the evil), of a certain condition (friends, enemies, by reconciliation, or by judicial litigation), and of a certain rank (domestic, political, or ecclesiastical); (c) those that concern ourselves, both in life and in death. In life, we will encounter general things concerning vocation, food and drink, clothing, recreations, the ordination of holy persons, together with holy times, namely, the Lord's Day, a fast day, a day of thanksgiving, and any ordinary day. As for specific things, in a second book we will treat, first, favorable things. In the first place we will consider, generally, prosperity and the world, namely, its abuse, use, and vanity. In the second place we will consider, specifically, the vanity of good things, namely, of the soul, wisdom, etc.; of the body, good health, etc.; of fortune, wealth, etc. Next, we will consider adverse things, again generally and specifically: generally, concerning misery and its origin, namely, various trials of the devil; specifically, concerning misery as it comes from evils: of the body, from disease, etc.; of fortune, from poverty, etc.; of the soul, from evils—partly irrational[30] evils, that is, perplexing terrors, and

---

28. οἰκεῖον
29. σύνταξιν
30. ἀλόγοις

partly rational evils,[31] such as, various spiritual desertions, doubts concerning the love of God, election, etc. So far concerning duties for life. Those that are occupied with death will bring up the rear: namely, how we meditate on it, show contempt for it, and prepare for it.

---

31. λογικοῖς

Scripture Index

Subject Index